Costa Rica

Dellplain Latin American Studies

Costa Rica: A Geographical Interpretation in Historical Perspective
Carolyn Hall

Costa Rica has long attracted the attention of natural scientists, because of its extraordinary ecological diversity, and of social scientists, because of its stable parliamentary democracy and welfare state, unparalleled in Central America, if not in most of the Third World. This is the first book in English, however, to present an overall geographical analysis of the country. It draws on the author's research and first-hand knowledge of the country, as well as on recent research of others in geography and related disciplines, much of which has circulated little outside Costa Rica. This book, not a historical geography in the strict sense, interprets contemporary Costa Rica in a historical perspective that looks both back to the past and forward to the future, assessing the prospects for the continuation of Costa Rica's democracy and socioeconomic reforms in the face of political revolutions currently taking place in neighboring countries in Central America.

Carolyn Hall is professor of geography at the University of Costa Rica.

DELLPLAIN LATIN AMERICAN STUDIES

PUBLISHED IN COOPERATION
WITH THE DEPARTMENT OF GEOGRAPHY
SYRACUSE UNIVERSITY

EDITOR

David J. Robinson
Syracuse University

EDITORIAL ADVISORY COMMITTEE

David A. Brading
University of Cambridge

William M. Denevan
University of Wisconsin

John H. Galloway
University of Toronto

John Lynch
University of London

Linda Newson
University of London

EDITORIAL ASSISTANT

Pam Walker

Costa Rica
A Geographical Interpretation
in Historical Perspective
Carolyn Hall

Dellplain Latin American Studies, No. 17

Westview Press / Boulder and London

(∞) The paper used in this publication meets the requirements of the American National
Standard for Permanence of Paper for Printed Library Materials Z39.48-1984.

Dellplain Latin American Studies

Copyright © 1985 by the Department of Geography, Syracuse University

Published in 1985 in the United States of America by Westview
Press, Inc.; Frederick A. Praeger, Publisher; 5500 Central Avenue,
Boulder, Colorado 80301

Library of Congress Cataloging in Publication Data
Hall, Carolyn
    Costa Rica, a geographical interpretation in
historical perspective.
    Bibliography: p.
    Includes index.
    1. Costa Rica--Description and travel--1981-
I. Title.
F1544.H35 1985   972.86'053   85-17887
ISBN 0-8133-7128-7

Composition for this book was provided by the author

Printed and bound in the United States of America

10 9 8 7 6 5 4 3 2

to Rodrigo

Contents

List of Tables xi
List of Figures xiii
Preface xvii
Acknowledgments xxi

Chapter 1   THE PHYSICAL ENVIRONMENT AND THE INDIGE-
             NOUS ECOSYSTEM 1

  Landforms 3
  Climate and Natural Vegetation 12
  Life Zones 23
  Soils 30
  Pre-Columbian Occupation of the Land 32
  Surviving Indian Communities 40

Chapter 2   THE LEGACY OF EUROPEAN COLONIZATION . . . 51

  The Nation-State of Costa Rica 51
  Hispanic American Society 60
  Economic Underdevelopment 72
  Ecological Changes 81

Chapter 3   THE EXPANSION OF THE HISPANIC AMERICAN
             OECUMENE 91

  Colonial Settlement 91
  Population Growth and Centrifugal Migration . . . 99
  Agricultural Colonization 108
  The Development of Transport 122
  The Foundation of Villages and Towns 131

Chapter 4   THE RURAL AREAS 139

  Farming Systems 140
  Agricultural Land Use 154
  Agrarian Problems and Reforms 190

Chapter 5   THE URBAN AREAS 205

  Centripetal Migration and the Growth of Urban
    Population 205
  Urban Morphology 210
  Tertiary Urbanization 223
  Manufacturing Industry 227

Chapter 6   REGIONAL STRUCTURES 243

    The Distribution and Density of Population . . . 245
    The Hierarchy of Central Places 249
    The Transport Network 256
    Spatial Disparities in Wealth and Welfare 269
    Administrative Areas 278
    Planning Regions 286

Conclusion 305
References 311
Index 339
List of Dellplain Latin American Studies 349

Tables

1.1 Area of life zones 26

1.2 Indian population, c. 1500-1978 43

1.3 Regional distribution of Indian population,
     1801 43

1.4 Area sown in crops native to America, 1973 . . . 49

2.1 Racial composition of the population during
     the colonial period 62

2.2 Foreigners in the population, 1864-1973 69

2.3 Racial composition of the population, 1927
     and 1950 70

2.4 Structure of the economy, 1950, 1963, and 1973 . 79

2.5 Area sown in Old World crops, 1973 86

3.1 Farm area, 1950, 1963, and 1973 122

3.2 Length of road network, 1924-1977 129

4.1 Tenure of farmland, 1973 141

4.2 Farms classified by farming systems, 1973 . . . 143

4.3 Land use, 1973 145

4.4 Subsistence production, 1973 146

4.5 Farms administered by managers, 1973 150

4.6 Yields of major crops, 1973 153

4.7 Major categories of agricultural land use,
     1950, 1963, and 1973 155

4.8 Cultivation of major export crops, 1973 160

4.9 Cultivation of major food crops, 1973 174

4.10 Expansion of cattle rearing, 1950-1973 183

4.11 Major categories of land capability 193

4.12 Use of energy and machinery on farms, 1973 . . . 198

5.1 Growth of urban and rural population, 1927-1973 . 206

5.2 Urban employment, 1963 and 1973 224

5.3 Composition of urban employment, 1973 224

5.4 Origins of industrial raw materials, 1975 234

6.1 Road network, 1977 258

6.2 Railway network, 1977 265

6.3 Freight carried by FECOSA, 1978 265

6.4 Distribution of family income, 1971 270

6.5 Variables used in the factor analyses of wealth
     and welfare 273

6.6 Structure of F_1 and F_2 in the analysis of
     wealth and welfare (varimax rotation) 275

6.7 Population and area of wealth and welfare re-
     gions 276

Figures

1.1 Position of Costa Rica 2

1.2 Physical structure of Central America 4

1.3 Structural subdivisions of Costa Rica and adjoining areas 5

1.4 Morphological regions 8

1.5 Atmospheric circulation: a) northern hemisphere winter, b) northern hemisphere summer . . 13

1.6 Precipitation: a) seasonal distribution, b) annual average total 16

1.7 Annual average temperatures 20

1.8 Chart of life zones in Costa Rica 24

1.9 Life zones 25

1.10 Archaeological regions 36

1.11 Present-day Indian communities and reserves . . 47

2.1 Geopolitical structure of Central America . . . 53

2.2 The Spanish province of Costa Rica 55

2.3 Territorial evolution of the republic of Costa Rica 57

2.4 Racial composition of the population in the principal colonial settlements: a) 1601, b) 1801 64

2.5 Exports of coffee and bananas, 1890-1977 76

2.6 Composition of foreign trade, 1976 80

2.7 Trading partners, 1976 82

3.1 Colonial settlement 93

3.2 Regional distribution of population during the colonial period 94

3.3 Population growth, 1824-1979 100

3.4 Birth, death, and natural population growth
     rates, 1885-1977 100

3.5 Expansion of the Hispanic American oecumene,
     c. 1840-1980 104

3.6 Changes in the regional distribution of popu-
     lation, 1836-1973 106

3.7 Internal migration, 1950, 1963, and 1973 107

3.8 Agricultural colonization, nineteenth and
     twentieth centuries 109

3.9 Model of transport expansion 124

3.10 Evolution of the transport network: a) 1870
     and 1925, b) 1950 and 1980 126

3.11 Foundation of villages and towns, sixteenth
     to twentieth centuries 133

4.1 Regional distribution of farming systems:
     a) number of farms, b) area 147

4.2 Generalized land use, 1971 157

4.3 Distribution of coffee, 1973 159

4.4 Production of major export crops, 1973 162

4.5 Distribution of sugar cane, 1973 165

4.6 Distribution of bananas, 1973 168

4.7 Distribution of cocoa, 1973 171

4.8 Distribution of rice, 1973 173

4.9 Production of basic food crops, 1973 175

4.10 Distribution of maize, 1973 177

4.11 Distribution of beans, 1973 179

4.12 Distribution of pasture, 1973 184

4.13 Distribution of cattle, 1973 186

4.14 Production of beef and dairy cows, 1973 188

4.15 Land capability 192

4.16 Lorenz curves of land tenure, 1950, 1963, and
     1973 200

4.17 Agrarian reform projects 203

5.1 Distribution of urban population, 1973 209

5.2 Internal migration, metropolitan region of
     San José, 1950, 1963, and 1973 211

5.3 Land use in San Isidro de El General 213

5.4 Land use in the center of the metropolitan
     area of San José 215

5.5 The metropolitan region of San José 216

5.6   Bus routes in the metropolitan area of San
      José 221

5.7   Distribution of urban employment, 1973 225

5.8   Growth of manufacturing industry, 1952-1975 . . 228

5.9   Production and distribution of electric power . 233

5.10 Composition of manufacturing industry, 1975 . . 235

5.11 Distribution of employment in manufacturing
      industry, 1975 238

5.12 Industrial zones in the metropolitan region
      of San José 240

6.1   Model of central and peripheral regions 244

6.2   Lorenz curve of population distribution, 1973 . 246

6.3   Population density, 1973 247

6.4   Central place hierarchy: rank-size relation-
      ships 250

6.5   Central places and their areas of influence . . 252

6.6   Distribution of central places in population
      space 255

6.7   The transport network, 1980 257

6.8   Road networks as topological graphs: a) na-
      tional network of trunk roads, b) regional
      network in the Valle Central 259

6.9   Traffic flows on main roads 262

6.10 Bus routes, 1980 264

6.11 Wealth and welfare, 1973 277

6.12 Administrative areas 279

6.13 Problem regions for which plans have been
      prepared 287

6.14 Planning regions: a) Nuhn, 1973, b) OFIPLAN,
      1975, c) OFIPLAN, 1978 293

6.15 New roads, projected and under construction . . 300

Preface

The recent sociopolitical upheavals in several of the small republics of Central America have focused attention on a region previously little known to the outside world. Even general geographical surveys of Central or Middle America have been few and far between (Lasserre 1976; Sorre 1928; West and Augelli 1966), and scarcely any geographical analyses of the individual republics have been published in languages other than Spanish or widely circulated beyond their country of origin. Yet, the diversity within this region cannot be understood without detailed studies of each country to complement the general surveys.

Costa Rica, located in the southern part of the isthmus between Nicaragua to the north and Panama to the south, is particularly interesting both because of its extraordinary ecological diversity, paralleled in Central America only by that of Guatemala, and its welfare state and parliamentary democracy, which have no equal in the isthmus nor, indeed, in most countries of the third world. It remains to be seen whether Costa Rica, which has achieved a considerable degree of socioeconomic development via progressive reforms, will remain immune to the revolutionary movements that have taken hold in neighboring republics.

The existing geographies of Costa Rica are limited to a series of books published more than a quarter of a century ago (León 1943a; Monge 1942; Quiros Amador 1954), the didactic text prepared by Lic. Eusebio Flores Silva (1979) for the country's Open University, and to the regional planning studies of Dr. Helmut Nuhn (1973a, 1978a). The present book has been written with two basic objectives in mind. First, it attempts an interpretation of the geography of Costa Rica that, I hope, may be useful to university students, to teachers, and to laymen wishing to know more about this fascinating region. The second, more ambitious, aim of any synthesis is to stimulate further research. The limitations of our current knowledge are apparent throughout the book. In every branch of geography, further original research in Costa Rica could contribute to our understanding not only of that country, but of the tropical, developing world in general.

The content and structure of the book reflect three fundamental notions about the nature of geography. The first is that geography is anthropocentric. It is a social science concerned with spatial variations in culture, in social, economic, and political organization, and in man's occupation of the land. The book deals with Costa Rica's physical environment as the habitat of man, stressing the interactions between the two and the ways in which man has transformed the environment. The second concept is that geography is holistic. It analyzes the complex interrelations of a wide range of spatially varying phenomena. Each chapter is devoted to a broad aspect of Costa Rica's geography, rather than to a particular topic or region. The chapters are subdivided into sections concerned with interrelated themes, some of which, in different ways, come up more than once in the course of the exposition. Also implicit in a holistic approach is the need to place the geography of a particular country in a wider context. Costa Rica is studied not only as part of Central and Latin America, but also as one of the many tropical countries of the third world. The final premise is that geography is dynamic. Some present patterns reflect the persistence of spatial structures over many centuries; others are but cross-sections through processes of change. Thus, while the book is not, strictu sensu, an historical geography, it interprets contemporary Costa Rica in an historical perspective that looks both back to the past and forward to the future.

Chapter 1 is concerned with the physical environment and the indigenous ecosystem. It looks at the diversity of landforms, climate, life zones, and soils, at man's occupation of the land during the long pre-Columbian era, and at the surviving Indian communities in modern times. From the sixteenth century onwards, the native cultures were disrupted by European settlement. Chapter 2 considers the legacy of Spanish colonization: the geopolitical reorganization that culminated in the consolidation of the nation-state of Costa Rica; the racial and cultural transformation of the population that produced a new, Hispanic American society; the perpetuation, long after political independence, of a typically colonial economy and the concomitant problems of underdevelopment; and the introduction of alien ideas about the relationship between man and the land, which led to profound ecological changes. Hispanic American settlement during the colonial period, from 1502 to 1821, was restricted to quite small areas. It accelerated rapidly after independence until, today, most of the republic of Costa Rica has been occupied by Hispanic American society. Chapter 3 examines the nature of colonial settlement and the processes that transformed the cultural landscape during the nineteenth and twentieth centuries: population growth and centrifugal migration; agricultural colonization; the development of transport;

and the foundation of villages and towns. Chapter 4 deals
with the contemporary occupation of rural areas now that
the prolonged process of primary colonization is finally
drawing to a close. It discusses farming systems, land
use, and agrarian problems and reforms. During the past
50 years, the processes of centrifugal migration and agricultural colonization have been accompanied, and partially
replaced, by those of centripetal migration and urbanization. Chapter 5 looks at the growth of urban population,
the morphology of the urban areas, the predominance of
tertiary economic activities in the towns and cities, and
the development of manufacturing industry within the framework of the Central American Common Market. The concentration of urbanization and industrialization in the core
area of the state exacerbated the dichotomy between a more-
developed center and a less-developed periphery inherent
in the geography of Costa Rica since the colonial period.
Chapter 6 analyzes the regional imbalance in the distribution of population, the central place hierarchy, the transport network, and the distribution of wealth and welfare,
and the incipient replacement of the anachronistic administrative areas by a system of planning regions that, hopefully, will spread socioeconomic development more evenly
over the country.

A book of this nature necessarily draws heavily on
the work of other researchers, as the lengthy list of
sources indicates. Indeed, one of its aims has been to
bring together the results of recent research in many disciplines, mostly little known outside Costa Rica. Substantial gaps, however, were encountered in the existing
bibliography, so every chapter also contains original
analysis, both of census and yearbook statistics and of
unpublished material. I am most grateful to the following
people who generously gave of their time and knowledge to
provide me with data specifically for the preparation of
this book: Ing. Eduardo Bravo Pérez, Lic. Jorge Brenes
Cedeño, Ing. Manuel Antonio Brenes Monge, Ing. José Chacón,
Arq. Garrett Cotter, Lic. Nydia Fórmiga, Sr. Victor
Labarca, Lic. Eduardo López Pizarro, Srta. María Oliva
López, Ing. John Mannix, Sr. Luis Guillermo Marín Rojas,
Ing. Alvaro Morera, Ing. Fernando Ocampo Córdoba, Ing.
Rafael Ocampo, Ing. Guillermo Porras Sandoval, Lic. Eduardo
Protti Martinelli, Lic. Francisco Ribera, Ing. Agustín
Rodríguez, Arq. Zuleyka Salóm, Lic. Elena Terán de Beck,
Ing. Franz Ulloa Chaverrí, Sr. Juan Vargas Soto, and Ing.
Eladio Zárate Hernández.

Partly because of the need to investigate many topics
from primary sources, the research for and writing of this
book spanned four years, from 1978 to 1982. From March
1980 onwards, the University of Costa Rica reduced my
teaching load to allow more time for research and contributed towards cartographic costs. The construction of the
maps and graphs, mainly from primary data, constituted a
major portion of the research effort. I am greatly indebted

xx

to Sr. Eduardo Bedoya Benítez, assistant of the Department
of Geography of the University of Costa Rica, who worked
with me for more than a year drawing the fair copies of
the figures.

Dr. John P. Augelli, Dr. Jean-Pierre Bergoeing Guida,
Dr. Luis Guillermo Brenes Quesada, Dr. Carlos Meléndez
Chaverri, Dr. James J. Parsons, and Dr. Héctor Pérez Brignoli very kindly read the whole of the penultimate draft
of the manuscript. Their constructive criticisms helped
me make a more thorough final revision than would otherwise have been possible, though they are not, of course,
in any way responsible for the end result.

Carolyn Hall

Acknowledgments

The author and publisher would like to thank the following for permission to reproduce copyright material: Dr. Gabriel Dengo and the Geological Society of America for Figure 1.3; Dr. L. R. Holdridge and the Tropical Science Center for Figure 1.8; Dr. Bruce Malfait and the Geological Society of America for Figure 1.2; Dr. Helmut Nuhn and the Instituto Geográfico Nacional for Figures 1.6, 1.9, 4.2, 4.15, 6.3, 6.5, and 6.15; and Dr. Richard Weyl and the Instituto Geográfico Nacional for Figure 1.4. They would also like to thank the following for permission to reproduce unpublished material: Lic. Luis Carlos Alfaro for Figure 5.4; and Ing. Eladio Zárate Hernández for Figure 1.5.

                                                    C. H.

1
The Physical Environment and the Indigenous Ecosystem

Costa Rica occupies part of the isthmus of Central America, the only region in the world both interoceanic and intercontinental. The country lies entirely within the tropics, between 8 and 11° north of the equator (Figure 1.1). Given this isthmian location and small latitudinal range, its physical environment would be relatively homogeneous were it not for the great complexity of surface landforms. Geologically young, Costa Rica is traversed by high, rugged cordilleras. These mountains modify climate and vegetation to produce an ecological diversity peculiar to the world's tropical, mountainous regions, where elevation and aspect are responsible for much more rapid, and qualitatively different, environmental changes than those associated with variation in latitude. Less than one hundred kilometers separate hot, humid, coastal lowlands, once covered with dense selva, from cold, bleak, mountain summits that support only a thin, scrubby vegetation. In spite of her small area, 51,100 square kilometers, Costa Rica therefore contains a complex ecological mosaic and a wide range of natural resources.

During the many millenia of the pre-Columbian era, the country formed part of an American culture realm having no regular contacts with other continents. The land was occupied by Amerindians, descended from Asian migrants. They created a niche in the tropical forest ecosystem, living by hunting, fishing, gathering, and primitive cultivation. The native economy was unable to support dense populations, urban centers, or complex political systems, but it was an ideal system for exploiting the natural environment while simultaneously conserving its potential resources. European settlers and their descendents, for whom the tropics were an unknown and, to a certain extent, hostile world, disrupted the indigenous way of life by incorporating Costa Rica into the colonial system and by introducing alien patterns of land use. The modern cultural landscape, evolved in the wake of permanent forest clearance, dates back no more than 450 years in the oldest areas of Spanish settlement and less than a century in many

2

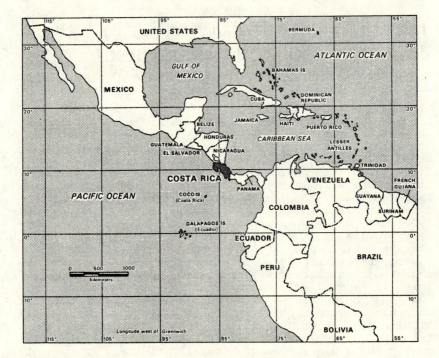

Figure 1.1 Position of Costa Rica

peripheral regions. Yet, the transformation of the physical environment and the destruction of native cultures have been such that only a modified indigenous ecosystem survives precariously in small parts of the country.

LANDFORMS

Geologically, the isthmus of Central America stretches more than 2,000 kilometers from the Tehuantepec isthmus of Mexico in the north to the Atrato basin of Colombia in the south, linking the North and South American continents (Figure 1.2). It is subdivided into two sections by the low-lying Nicaragua Depression. In northern Central America, the basement rocks are of Paleozoic age and the predominantly east-west structural trend continues into the Greater Antilles. Costa Rica lies entirely within southern Central America, geologically much younger, with a predominantly northwest-southeast structural trend. Until the early Tertiary era, the North and South American continental blocks were separated by a sea, beneath which the Middle American Trench divided the Caribbean Plate to the northeast from the Cocos Plate to the southwest. The territorial formation of the southern section of Central America during the Tertiary and Quaternary eras resulted from the subduction of the Cocos Plate beneath the less dense Caribbean Plate. Plate tectonics provoked volcanic activity, orogenesis, and seismic movements.

The basic structure of southern Central America consists of a series of arcs, similar to those found at the junction of tectonic plates in other parts of the world, for example, the Sunda arcs in Southeast Asia. Three principal components can be distinguished: an Outer Pacific Arc, containing the oldest rocks formed in a prototectonic phase; an Inner Arc, including the highest mountains that emerged during the main phase of the Laramide orogeny; and a series of basins, including the Limón Basin in Costa Rica, formed by sedimentation on the concave, northeastern side of the Inner Arc (Figure 1.3). Superimposed on the older structures in both northern and southern Central America is a zone of Quaternary volcanism along the Pacific margin of the isthmus, parallel to the Middle American Trench. This volcanic axis stretches approximately 1,500 kilometers from southern Mexico to western Panama.

The oldest rocks of Costa Rica, the Nicoya complex, were formed beneath the sea during the Upper Cretaceous. They were probably associated with the development of an arc of volcanic islands located close to the present Pacific coast. Pillow lavas, marine sediments, and igneous intrusions are now exposed in the western peninsulas of Nicoya, Herradura, Osa, and Burica. In the Santa Elena peninsula, the Nicoya complex is partially overlain by peridotite and serpentine. Sedimentation took place in basins to the northeast, forming rocks now exposed in the

4

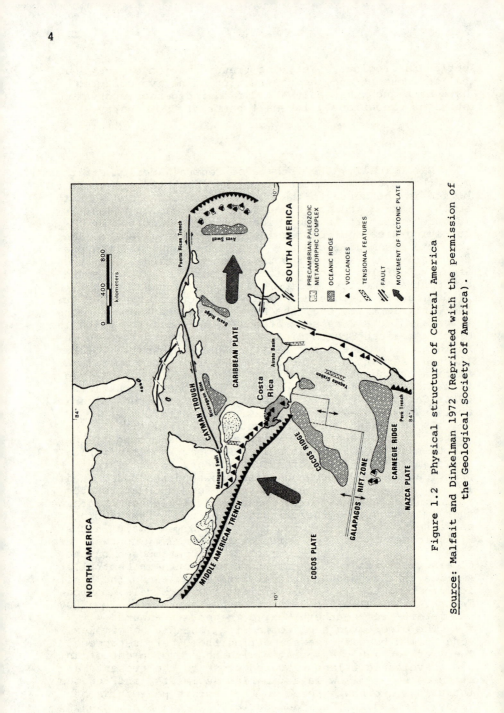

Figure 1.2 Physical structure of Central America

<u>Source:</u> Malfait and Dinkelman 1972 (Reprinted with the permission of the Geological Society of America).

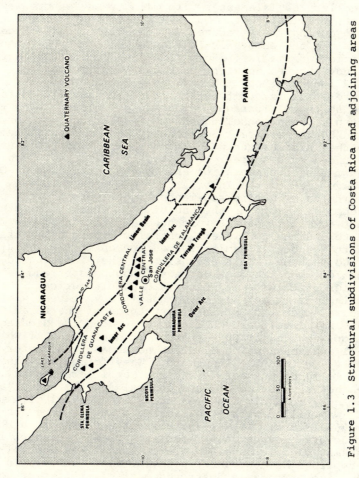
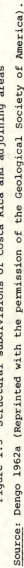

Figure 1.3 Structural subdivisions of Costa Rica and adjoining areas

Source: Dengo 1962a (Reprinted with the permission of the Geological Society of America).

Pacific coastal lowlands.

After a quiescent phase between the Middle Oligocene and Lower Miocene, the tectonic activity of the Laramide orogeny was concentrated in the Inner Arc, separated by faults from the Outer Arc to the southwest. Mountain building reached a climax during the Middle and Upper Miocene, with the emergence of the battholith that now forms the Cordillera de Talamanca. Its main trend is northwest-southeast, parallel to the Outer Arc. Volcanic activity continued during the Pliocene, forming the Cordillera de Tilarán along the same axis as the Cordillera de Talamanca, and a series of smaller ranges with a predominantly east-west trend, located between these two cordilleras.

In Pliocene times, the Caribbean Sea and Pacific Ocean were still intermittently linked in northern Costa Rica and southern Nicaragua. Subsequent uplift during the posttectonic phase consolidated the land bridge between North and South America. Sedimentary basins were filled in on either side of the main mountain arc. To the southwest, bounded by a series of faults, the Terraba Trough received marine sedimentation and igneous intrusions. On the concave side of the Inner Arc, the Limón Basin was filled with thick marine sediments, interspersed with volcanic deposits. Towards the end of the Tertiary era, the incipient formation of the volcanoes of the Cordillera de Guanacaste and the Cordillera Central provoked sedimentation in the graben or fault-bounded trough in the northeast of Costa Rica. This extension of the Nicaragua Depression followed the same northwest-southeast trend as the earlier structures of southern Central America.

During the Quaternary era, andesitic volcanoes were superimposed upon the Tertiary structures of the Laramide orogeny. Small volcanic outliers penetrated the Nicaragua Depression. The major Quaternary volcanoes, many of which are still active, developed in the northwest and center of the country, within the Inner Arc. They formed two ranges: the Cordillera de Guanacaste and the Cordillera Central. The area between the Cordillera Central and the Cordillera de Talamanca, commonly known as the Valle Central or Meseta Central, was filled with volcanic and alluvial deposits (Dengo 1962a, 1968; Lloyd 1963; Malfait and Dinkelman 1972).

Structural change associated with plate tectonics is still taking place. Several severe earthquakes and volcanic eruptions have occurred within living memory. In 1910, a large earthquake destroyed most of the former colonial capital, Cartago, in the eastern Valle Central, leaving several hundred dead. A series of strong tremors in 1924 caused serious structural damage in and around the towns of San Ramón, Naranjo, and Orotina, in the western Valle Central. Other earthquakes, like those of 1904 and 1941 near the modern town of Neily in the southwest, or that of 1973 close to Tilarán in the northwest, although of catastrophic proportions, occurred in sparsely populated regions and therefore caused little loss of life

(Miyamura 1976; Sauter 1980). Irazú volcano in the Cordillera Central was active for nearly two years between 1963 and 1965. Thick deposition of ash and rock fragments was accompanied by earth tremors, mud flows, and floods (Murata et al. 1966; OFIPLAN 1964). In 1968, eruptions of Arenal volcano in the Cordillera de Guanacaste were also accompanied by seismic movements. Gases at temperatures of 600-800°C formed <u>nuées ardentes</u> that spread ash and fragmented lava over an area of 1,850 square kilometers (Chaves and Sáenz 1970). Historical documents provide evidence for intermittent seismic and volcanic activity since the sixteenth century (González Víquez 1910). Indigenous settlement must also have been subject to these environmental hazards, although, as yet, little archaeological evidence of the effects of earthquakes and volcanic eruptions in pre-Columbian times has been found.

Scientific study of seismic and volcanic activity in Costa Rica is very recent. In the past, little practical precaution was taken to minimize loss of life and destruction of property. Few buildings had an adequate antiseismic structure. Agricultural colonization took place on the slopes of active volcanoes. Both seismic risk and volcanic activity are concentrated in the center and western sections of the country. A zone of intense, shallow seismic activity occurs beneath the landward margin of the Middle American Trench. The foci of several major earthquakes have been located close to the northwest-southeast trending fault that extends along the entire Pacific coastal lowlands and probably coincides with the subduction zone of the Cocos Plate (Dr. Jean-Pierre Bergoeing, personal communication). The depth of earthquake foci increases to the northeast, along a Benioff zone of friction (Mortgat et al. 1977, 5-7). The particularly high seismic risk in the extreme southwest of the country is attributed by Malfait and Dinkelman (1972) to the "zippering shut" of the subduction zone along the Middle American Trench by segments displaced from the Cocos Ridge. There are at least six active volcanoes in the Cordillera de Guanacaste and Cordillera Central, located between 100 and 200 kilometers to the northeast of the Middle American Trench. Of Costa Rica's present population, 70 percent lives in areas affected by both seismic movements and Quaternary volcanism, attractive sections because of their fertile soils and relatively dry climate. In the future, the large number of dormant volcanoes may pose as great a threat as those that have recently erupted (Raccichini 1977-1978).

Because of her recent formation, Costa Rica's landforms still reflect underlying geological structure (Weyl 1971). A mountain zone traverses the entire country, bounded to the southwest by faults along the subduction zone, and to the northeast by the edge of the Nicaragua Depression (Figure 1.4). The mountains become higher and broader towards the southeast, where they constitute the greatest barrier to settlement and transportation. Most

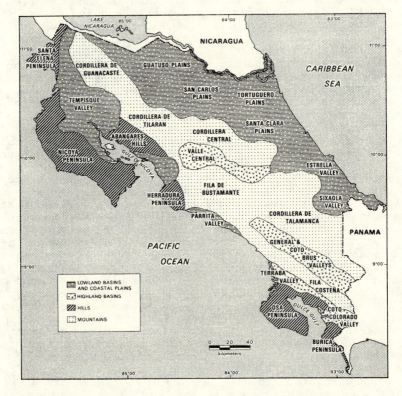

Figure 1.4 Morphological regions

<u>Source</u>: Weyl 1971 (Reprinted with the permission of the
Instituto Geográfico Nacional).

slopes have an inclination of 30-45 percent, and mountain crests rise more than 600 meters above the level of adjacent valley floors. The alternation of Quaternary volcanic ranges with cordilleras dating from the Laramide orogeny subdivides the mountain zone into four morphological units.

In the northwest, the Cordillera de Guanacaste rises from the adjacent plains to a maximum height of just over 2,000 meters above sea level. It is composed of a single chain of Quaternary volcanoes, several having a compound structure (Healy 1969). Arenal, on the southern margin of the cordillera, is the only volcano in Costa Rica that produces intermittent Pélean eruptions characterized by nuées ardentes (Dr. Jean-Pierre Bergoeing, personal communication). The volcanoes of the Cordillera de Guanacaste are separated by passes of less than 1,000 meters above sea level, the lowest, and potentially the easiest, routes across the entire mountain chain.

The Cordillera de Guanacaste is bounded to the southeast by a small rift valley occupied by Lake Arenal. This lake marks the beginning of the Cordillera de Tilarán, part of the older structure of the Inner Arc, composed mainly of Pliocene rocks of the Aguacate formation. Volcanic edifices can still be distinguished, but none are active. The highest summits rise to more than 1,500 meters above sea level. The remnant of an old erosion surface at approximately 1,000 meters has been dissected by rejuvenated rivers, producing extremely rugged topography (Dengo 1962b, 83-106). In contrast to the Cordillera de Guanacaste, the Cordillera de Tilarán contains no easy passes across the mountains, in spite of its generally lower elevation.

To the east, the Cordillera de Tilarán merges with the Cordillera Central, formed of four, large, potentially active volcanic edifices. Like many of the volcanoes of the Cordillera de Guanacaste, these edifices are compound Quaternary structures, superimposed on the Tertiary basement of the Inner Arc. The volcanoes in the Cordillera Central are the highest in Costa Rica; the summit of Irazú is 3,432 meters above sea level. The northern slopes of the entire range are extremely steep, rising 2,000-3,000 meters over distances as small as 25 kilometers. They have been deeply eroded by heavy orographic rainfall, and a series of alluvial cones has been deposited at the foot of the mountains (Bergoeing and Brenes 1978). The southern slopes, by contrast, receive more moderate rainfall and are less dissected. Located in the lee of the prevailing northeast trade winds, they have been partially buried beneath volcanic sediments; the elevational range between the foot of the mountains and the summits is only 1,000-1,500 meters. Irazú and Turrialba, the two most easterly volcanoes, are not separated by a pronounced gap. The passes between the remainder rise to barely half the elevation of the summits.

The largest and most massive mountain chain is the Cordillera de Talamanca in the south of the country. Its complex geological structure includes marine sediments, lava flows, and igneous intrusions. It is the major component of the Inner Arc and the highest range in southern Central America, rising to 3,819 meters above sea level. Above 3,400 meters on the summits of Chirripó and Kamuk, a glaciated landscape of cirques, horns, arretes, U-shaped valleys, and moraine-dammed lakes was formed during the last cold period of the Wisconsin or Würm glaciation (Bergoeing 1977; Weyl 1955). Several ancient peneplain surfaces are visible in small areas of relatively flat terrain at high elevations, but the range's northeastern and southwestern slopes contain deep, rejuvenated river valleys. Access into the mountains is therefore difficult, particularly from the steep, faulted, southwestern slope where a series of alluvial cones has formed (Bergoeing and Brenes 1978).

Two depressions with more gentle relief lie within the mountain zone. The Valle Central, ranging in elevation from 600 to 1,500 meters above sea level, contains undulating terrain and several areas of virtually flat land, interrupted only by the incised meanders of narrow river gorges 100-150 meters below the general surface level. The bottoms of these valleys expose the marine sediments of the Tertiary base rocks of the Inner Arc; elsewhere, the surface of the Valle Central is largely covered with recent volcanic and alluvial deposits (Crosby 1942; Malavassi and Madrigal 1967). The continental divide is located at 1,550 meters above sea level in the Cerros de la Carpintera, formed by Plio-Quaternary volcanism. These hills bisect the Valle Central into an eastern section on the Caribbean slope, drained by the River Reventazón and its tributaries, and a western section on the Pacific slope, drained by the Virilla and Grande, tributaries of the River Tárcoles.

A second intermontane depression, derived from the Térraba Trough, is drained by two tributaries of the River Térraba, the General and Coto Brus. It follows a northwest-southeast trend and is separated from the Pacific coastal lowlands by the Fila Costeña, through which the antecedent River Térraba has cut a spectacular gorge to the sea. The General-Coto Brus depression is lower than the Valle Central, ranging from 100-1,000 meters above sea level. Flat land is limited to the valley floors and small river terraces. The majority of the depression is undulating, with slopes of 10-30 percent.

Costa Rica's mountainous backbone separates her two zones of coastal lowlands. The Pacific lowlands, occupying the Outer Arc, are composed of complex landforms. Hilly peninsulas, formed from Upper Cretaceous and Teriary rocks, alternate with Quaternary alluvial and volcanic deposits in the valleys. The Santa Elena, Nicoya, Herradura, Osa, and Burica peninsulas rise to scarcely 1,000 meters above sea level, but they are highly dissected as a result of folding, faulting, and erosion. The largest area of flat land in the Pacific lowlands is the tectonic depression of the River Tempisque in the northwest, which contains deep alluvial sediments. The northeastern section of the Tempisque basin, in the lee of the volcanic Cordillera de Guanacaste, is covered with ignimbrites deposited by nuées ardentes, forming an uncommonly large meseta some 100 kilometers long and 20-30 kilometers wide (Dr. Jean-Pierre Bergoeing, personal communication). Along the central and southern Pacific coast, there are only small areas of flat land in the Parrita, Térraba, and Coto Colorado valleys. Behind the narrow coastal plain, the rugged Fila Costeña, composed of folded Tertiary sedimentary rocks, rises to more than 1,500 meters above sea level (Bergoeing and Brenes 1978). The Pacific rivers are navigable for only short distances, but the coast, composed of 1,016 kilometers of peninsulas, islands, and bays, is ideal for local shipping. It affords many natural harbors, particularly in the two largest gulfs, Nicoya and Dulce.

The Caribbean lowlands contrast markedly with those of the Pacific slope. The straight east coast, only 212 kilometers long, contains few natural harbors. To the north of Limón, it is fringed by swamps and lagoons. Its only promontories are the outcrops of Tertiary sedimentary rocks at Limón and Punta Mona and the tombolo connecting a former coral island to the mainland at Cahuita (Dr. Jean-Pierre Bergoeing, personal communication). Behind the coast extends the largest region of low-lying plains in the whole of Costa Rica, a triangular area that occupies about one-fifth of the country. Small volcanic outliers, aligned along the fracture of the Nicaragua Depression, protrude 200-300 meters above the general surface. Elsewhere, at an average elevation of less than 100 meters above sea level, the surface geology is composed mainly of recent alluvial deposits and lahares. Many areas are subject to periodic flooding. The Caribbean lowlands are traversed by the only rivers in Costa Rica navigable for any distance; the San Carlos and Sarapiquí can be plied by small vessels for about 50 kilometers upstream of their confluences with the San Juan.

Little work has been carried out on the weathering and erosion of the land surface. The combination of high temperatures and heavy rainfall during much of the year produces rapid chemical weathering and deep soils. Water is the major agent of erosion. The dense drainage network receives abundant surface run-off and large volumes of sediment during and after heavy rains (Bergoeing 1978). In the indigenous ecosystem, the tropical forest protected the soil. Deforestation in the expanding Hispanic American oecumene, particularly during the nineteenth and twentieth centuries, has accelerated the natural processes of erosion, producing soil slumping over wide areas of the country (Brenes Quesada 1976). Overgrazing and the burning of pastures and stubble leave the ground unprotected by vegetation and vulnerable to eolian erosion by the strong trade winds during the dry season.

CLIMATE AND NATURAL VEGETATION

Although Costa Rica lies entirely within the tropics, the basic climatic patterns attributable to seasonal variations in atmospheric circulation are modified by elevation, slope, and aspect. As in other tropical, mountainous areas, there is a complex succession of microclimates that vary over very short distances. Temperature decreases with elevation to produce cool, montane climates that contrast with the hotter climates near sea level. The whole country receives heavy rainfall, but seasonal regimes range from alternating wet and dry seasons to year-round precipitation. Because of her varied climates, Costa Rica contains a diversity of natural vegetation and land use uncommon for a country of such limited territorial extent.

Atmospheric circulation is dominated by the trade wind system located between the subtropical high pressure zone and the intertropical convergence zone or ITCZ, a belt of low pressure lying close to the thermal equator. In winter, there is a continuous belt of high pressure over the subtropical latitudes of both the North American continent and the adjacent oceans (Figure 1.5a). The ITCZ lies to the south of Costa Rica and the whole country comes under the influence of strong, northeast trade winds. Between November and January, cold fronts of polar air, funneled southwards between the major mountain ranges of North America, penetrate into tropical latitudes. Although considerably weakened by the time they reach Costa Rica, they bring cool winds, known locally as nortes. In few other parts of the world does polar air penetrate so close to the equator (Portig 1959). In summer, the atmospheric circulation system shifts northwards (Figure 1.5b). Pressure weakens over the heated continents and the ITCZ lies over or close to Central America. Weak, equatorial westerly winds predominate on the Pacific slope of the isthmus. The subtropical high pressure belt persists over the cooler Atlantic Ocean, and weakened northeast trade winds continue to reach the Caribbean slope of Costa Rica (Barrett 1970; Zárate 1977, 5-11).

These zonal patterns of atmospheric circulation are complicated by the development of local land and sea breezes, and mountain and valley winds. On the Pacific slope, the diurnal sea breeze blows in the opposite direction from the prevailing northeast trades, reinforcing the equatorial westerlies. Strong trade winds in winter often impede its formation. In summer, the Pacific sea breeze may develop either as an independent feature, forming a

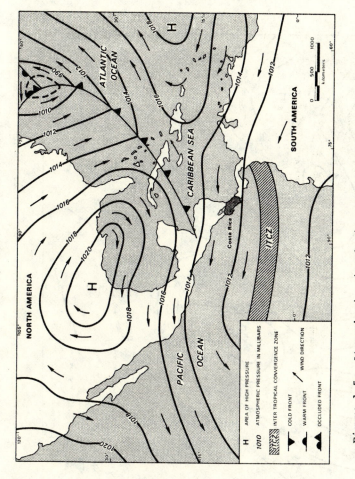

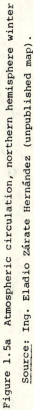

Figure 1.5a Atmospheric circulation, northern hemisphere winter

Source: Ing. Eladio Zárate Hernández (unpublished map).

14

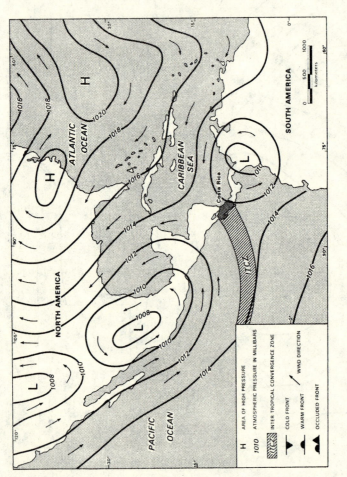

Figure 1.5b Atmospheric circulation, northern hemisphere summer
Source: Ing. Eladio Zárate Hernández (unpublished map).

local breeze front as it meets the northeast trades, or, united with the equatorial westerlies, it may produce a true ITCZ along the line of contact with the trade winds. The nocturnal land breeze on the Pacific slope flows in approximately the same direction as the predominant trade winds. The land and sea breezes on the Caribbean slope blow in opposite directions than those on the Pacific slope. The diurnal sea breeze reinforces the trade winds, whereas the nocturnal land breeze, blowing from the west, produces breeze fronts as it meets the northeast trades. Mountain and valley breezes are still more localized than land and sea breezes and have been little studied outside the Valle Central, where they reinforce the land and sea breezes.

Because the mountain zone lies perpendicular to the principal winds, the Caribbean and Pacific slopes have different rainfall regimes (Figure 1.6). On the Caribbean slope, heavy rains occur when cyclonic disturbances develop within the trade wind system or when the trade winds converge with other airflows. Between November and January, the arrival of polar air produces cold fronts on the Caribbean slope. During the rest of the year, high temperatures over the Caribbean Sea produce troughs of low pressure, known as easterly waves, and deeper, circular zones of low pressure that may develop into hurricanes in the Antilles, although not over Costa Rica. These cyclonic disturbances become embedded in the trade wind flow; as they move westwards or southwestwards, they bring rain to eastern Costa Rica. A third source of precipitation on the Caribbean slope is the development at night of local fronts between the westerly land breeze and the northeast trades (Zárate 1977, 56-60).

The entire Caribbean slope receives heavy precipitation. The mean annual total everywhere exceeds 2,000 millimeters. There is no pronounced dry season. Plants grow throughout the year, and farmers must adapt to an excess rather than to a shortage of water. The heaviest rainfall occurs not along the coast, but inland, on the windward northern and northeastern slopes of the cordilleras, where some areas receive more than 9,000 millimeters a year. The orographic effect persists to about 2,500 meters above sea level. Above that elevation, the air masses have lost much of their moisture. Precipitation decreases but, because of the low temperatures, humidity is high and there is frequent cloud and fog (Holdridge et al. 1971, 45).

For precipitation to occur on the Pacific slope--including the western Valle Central and the General-Coto Brus depression--the northeast trades must be temporally displaced by westerly airflows. These air patterns are of three principal types. When tropical cyclones develop over the Caribbean Sea, synoptic westerly winds blowing around the low pressure zone may affect the Pacific slope. Whether these winds produce wet or dry weather is apparently related to humidity conditions and the vertical

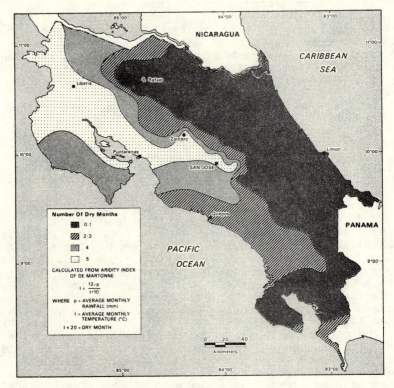

Figure 1.6a   Seasonal distribution of precipitation

<u>Source</u>: Nuhn 1978b (Reprinted with the permission of the
Instituto Geográfico Nacional).

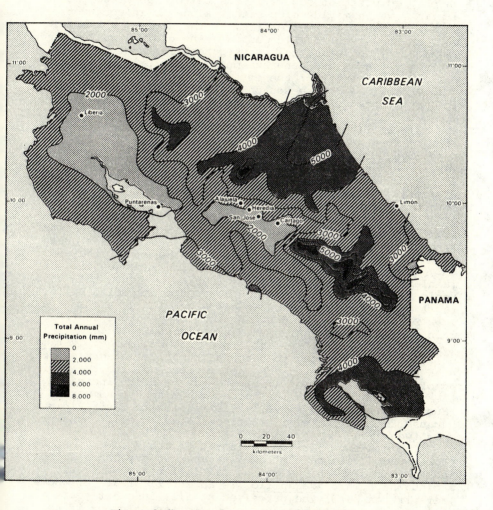

Figure 1.6b Annual average precipitation
Source: IPGH 1976.

extent of the westerly airflow. In summer, equatorial westerlies reach the Pacific slope, and the ITCZ that develops at the junction of these westerlies and the northeast trades is an unstable zone of low pressure, along which precipitation occurs. This third type of westerly airflow, which may develop either alone or in conjunction with the equatorial westerlies, is the diurnal sea breeze and, in the western Valle Central, the diurnal valley wind. These airflows form local convergence fronts with the northeast trades and generate much of the precipitation in the west and center of the country (Zárate 1977, 7-12).

There is a dry season on the Pacific slope. It is most pronounced in the northwest and center of the country, where the northeast trade winds inhibit the development of westerly airflows and convergence fronts for five to six months, from November to May. In the northwest, high temperatures during the cloudless days of the dry season cause heavy evaporation, and many crops require irrigation. In the Valle Central, where higher elevation reduces temperatures, there is less surface evaporation, but even here crop growth is restricted by draught towards the end of the dry season. On the southern part of the Pacific slope the dry season is shorter. This region is the first to experience westerly flows in April, and the last area from which they retreat southwards at the end of the year. Only three months, from January to March, are generally rainless. Agriculture is less affected by draught in this region, and in the extreme south, around the Golfo Dulce, there may be no dry season at all.

Since precipitation rather than temperature is the main source of seasonal climatic variation, the terms "winter" and "summer" are reversed in local usage: "verano" or "summer" being used to describe the pleasant dry season, even though this period does not correspond with the period of overhead sun; and "invierno" or "winter" indicating the wet season, really the northern hemisphere summer. "Spring" and "autumn" have little meaning to Costa Ricans because their climate, if differentiated at all, contains only two seasons.

The country lies too far north of the equator for the pronounced development of two wet and two dry seasons, but the Pacific slope has a second rainfall minimum in July and August. This "veranillo" is an erratic feature. Some years it can hardly be perceived at all, in other years a prolonged dry spell leads to heavy losses of crops if no irrigation is available. The veranillo seems to be associated with a temporary extension southwards of the North Atlantic anticyclone and a consequent increase in pressure and strengthening of the trade winds (Trewartha 1961, 64-70; Zárate 1977, 11).

Because of the dry season, rainfall totals are generally lower on the Pacific than on the Caribbean slope. On the coastal lowlands, they range from less than 1,500 millimeters in the northwest and center of the country to

5,000 millimeters in the extreme south. As on the Caribbean slope, precipitation is heavier on exposed slopes where there is orographic uplift and lower in sheltered depressions such as the Tempisque, General, and Coto Brus valleys.

In Costa Rica, as in most tropical areas, the diurnal distribution of rainfall is more regular than in middle latitudes and has important practical implications. Transport is treacherous under heavy downpours; outdoor activities, such as farming and building, are timed to take advantage of the dry hours of the day. During the rainy season on the Pacific slope, dry, sunny mornings are followed by overcast, wet afternoons when the sea and valley breezes attain their maximum development, forming convergence fronts with the northeast trades. Only the synoptic westerlies associated with tropical cyclones in the Caribbean Sea bring continuous rains during day and night on the Pacific slope. On the Caribbean slope, the breeze front that develops with the convergence of the land breeze with the northeast trades produces a nocturnal rainfall maximum. Precipitation associated with other types of disturbances may occur at any time.

Throughout the country, rainfall is of two basic types. Torrential downpours, the result of convection and the development of cumulo-nimbus clouds along convergence fronts, are known locally as aguaceros. They are often spatially concentrated: heavy rainstorms accompanied by thunder and lightning may affect areas only a few kilometers in diameter, while surrounding regions remain quite dry. This typically tropical rainfall--much more intense than that of the temperate zone--has great erosive force, particularly on soils unprotected by vegetation. On the Pacific slope, rainfall concentration during the hottest hours of the day reduces its effectiveness for agriculture, since there is heavy loss through evaporation. Continuous rains associated with cold fronts, easterly waves, or cyclonic disturbances are known in Costa Rica as temporales. Stratus clouds produce much larger amounts of rain than what falls during aguaceros, but precipitation is less intense. Temporales often cause flooding on low-lying ground, a phenomenon exacerbated in recent years by widespread deforestation in the hills and mountains.

Costa Rica's latitudinal range of 3° is insufficient to produce marked differences in temperature between the north and south of the country. Temperature varies mainly with elevation and, to a lesser extent, slope and cloud cover (Figure 1.7). At sea level, on both the Pacific and Caribbean slopes, mean annual temperatures everywhere exceed 24°C and reach 27°C in the dry northwestern region. Temperature falls more rapidly on the Caribbean slope, where there is heavy cloud cover throughout the year, than on the Pacific slope, where there is a higher incidence of sunshine. In the intermontane depressions and on the lower mountain slopes, mean annual temperatures range from

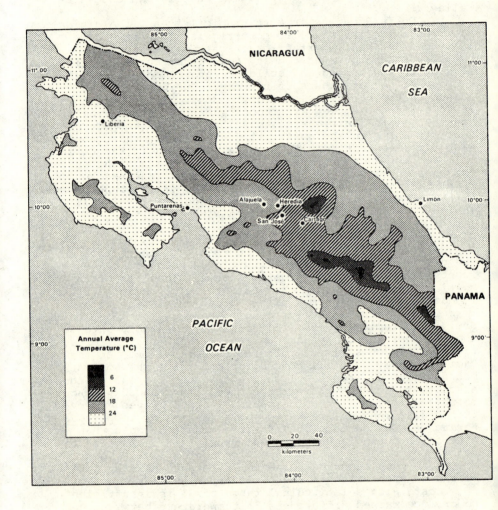

Figure 1.7 Annual average temperatures
<u>Source</u>: IPGH 1976.

12 to 24°C. On the higher slopes and summits of the Cordillera Central and Cordillera de Talamanca, the annual
average is less than 12°C, and temperatures occasionally
fall to freezing point in exposed areas. The cool mountain climates modify the natural vegetation and permit the
cultivation of a wide variety of subtropical and temperate
crops that could not otherwise be grown at these latitudes.
    As in all tropical regions, seasonal variations in
temperature are minimal, averaging 2 to 3°C difference between the warmest and coolest months. This pattern is not
modified by altitude, so it is misleading to think of upland climates in the tropics as similar to those of the
temperate regions, where there are marked variations in
temperature between winter and summer. The physiological
temperature range in Costa Rica is greatest in areas with
a marked dry season. Strong winds, dry air, and slightly
lower temperatures produce a relatively cool season at the
turn of the year. As the trade winds weaken, the weather
becomes hot and hazy in March and early April. The onset
of the rains marks the beginning of a warm, humid season
in the middle of the year, followed by slightly cooler,
very wet weather in September and October.
    Throughout the country, diurnal temperature range ex-
ceeds seasonal variation. Closely related to cloud cover,
it may span 8 to 10°C. The range is greatest during the
dry season, when the absence of clouds permits high insolation by day and intense radiation from the earth's surface at night. In the upland regions, nights are pleas-
antly cool, but heating is required in buildings only at
very high elevations, well above the main areas of settlement.
    Costa Rica's natural vegetation reflects the intrica-
cy of her climate. Just as temperature decreases with
elevation, vegetation changes from luxuriant selva in the
regions close to sea level with no pronounced dry season
to paramos above the tree line on the highest mountain
summits. Between these extremes lies a complex series of
montane forests.
    The country's flora is extraordinarily rich. It in-
cludes North American, South American, and endemic species.
1,260 species of trees have been recorded, and there may
be more, as yet, unclassified (Holdridge 1953). Plant
dispersion between North and South America has been particularly active at lower elevations. Both the Pacific and
Caribbean lowlands of Costa Rica form part of extensive,
transitional floral regions linking the two continents.
The high mountains, on the other hand, are isolated from
similar areas in northern Central America by the Nicaragua
Depression, and from the Colombian Andes by the lowlands
of central Panama and the Darién Peninsula. These lowlands have acted as barriers to the dispersal of plants
adapted to cooler climates. Many species are therefore
endemic to the mountains of Costa Rica and the neighboring
Chiriquí volcano in western Panama. Oaks are abundant,

but junipers, firs, maples, sycamores, and pines, found in the mountains of northern Central America, are absent from the uplands of Costa Rica. There are probably more South American than North American genera, and the northernmost outliers of Andean paramo vegetation are found on the summits of the Cordillera de Talamanca (Skutch 1971, 7-8, 88; Standley 1937-1938, 1:1-62).

Forest is the natural vegetation in nearly all of Costa Rica, attaining its maximum development in the warmest and wettest regions. No area is too dry to support trees. Less than 30 square kilometers lie above the tree line, where low temperatures limit the natural vegetation to bushes and herbaceous plants. The savannas in the General-Coto Brus depression and Guanacaste are manmade features, the result of recurrent burning for shifting cultivation and pastures (Barrantes Ferrero 1965). During the pre-Columbian era, indigenous land use permitted constant regeneration of most of the forests. Not until the present century did Hispanic American colonists accelerate the process of deforestation that threatens to destroy completely the natural vegetation within the next two or three decades. Man has already removed the natural plant cover from two-thirds of the country. It is almost impossible to estimate how much of the remaining vegetation is primary forest. Some formations have virtually disappeared and are only shown hypothetically on modern maps.

Although much early botanical work in Costa Rica concentrated on the identification of individual species, there could never be any attempt to classify natural vegetation on this basis. Tropical forests have a very heterogeneous floral composition. They contain an enormous variety of plants, including trees, shrubs, and epiphytes. There are few stands of single species of trees, such as those found in temperate latitudes. Standley's (1937-1938) catalogue of the flora of Costa Rica, which he himself acknowledged was by no means exhaustive, ran to four large volumes. Climate was the only feasible basis for classifying vegetation.

Conventional classification systems, such as those of Köppen and Thornthwaite, bring out few of the regional variations in Costa Rica's climates and natural vegetation, because they fail to take into account the peculiar characteristics of high elevation zones in tropical latitudes. These zones are classified by Köppen and Thornthwaite in the same categories as temperate climates of the middle latitudes: Köppen's "C" climates and Thornthwaite's Mesothermal "B" and Microthermal "C" climates are identified in Costa Rica's mountains, although these regions exhibit no pronounced seasonal variation in temperature.[1] Botan-

---

[1] See AID (1965) for a map of Costa Rica's climates according to Köppen's classification, and IPGH (1976) for an application of Thornthwaite's classification.

ists and climatologists, including Pittier (1908), Wercklé (1909), Standley (1937-1938), Coen (1953), and Scott (1966), all recognized that elevation was the principal differentiating factor in Costa Rica's climate and natural vegetation. They used a threefold classification, <u>tierra caliente</u>, <u>tierra templada</u>, and <u>tierra fría</u>, similar to that applied to the Andes of South America. These elevational zones were subdivided according to the pattern of precipitation.

LIFE ZONES

The concept of elevational temperature zones, subdivided according to rainfall regimes, has been incorporated into a precise and sophisticated bioclimatic classification by Holdridge (1967), whose system of life zone ecology forms the basis of most modern analyses of Costa Rica's climate and natural vegetation.[1] Although envisaged as a world classification, this scheme differs from those of Köppen and Thornthwaite because it takes into account not only variations caused by latitude, but also those related to elevation. It is, therefore, particularly useful for mountainous, tropical countries.

Twelve life zones are present in Costa Rica (Figure 1.8). The most extensive occupies nearly one-quarter of the country, the most restricted, only a few square kilometers (Table 1.1). Tosi (1969) has mapped the life zones at 1:750,000. At this scale, it is possible to show all twelve zones and the transitional areas between them. Figure 1.9 is a simplified version of this map, eliminating the transitional areas and simplifying the pattern at

---

[1]Life zones are defined by three parameters: heat, precipitation, and moisture. Heat is expressed as the mean annual biotemperature, that is, the heat effective for plant growth. The concept eliminates temperatures below freezing and in excess of 30°C. Precipitation is measured by the mean annual total, and moisture by the potential evapotranspiration ratio. Potential evapotranspiration is the amount of water returning to the atmosphere via evaporation from the earth's surface and transpiration from plants. This quantity is calculated by multiplying the mean annual biotemperature by an empirically derived factor of 58.93 and dividing this figure by the mean annual precipitation in millimeters. A ratio greater than unity indicates a dry climate, where potential evapotranspiration exceeds precipitation; the ratio is less than unity in humid areas, where precipitation exceeds potential evapotranspiration. Fieldwork in Costa Rica and elsewhere in the American tropics has indicated a logarithmic progression in the increase of heat and precipitation required to produce significant changes in natural vegetation. Life zone boundaries occur along isotherms of 3, 6, 12, and 24°C mean annual biotemperature, and isohyets of 1,000, 2,000, 4,000, and 8,000 millimeters mean annual precipitation.

24

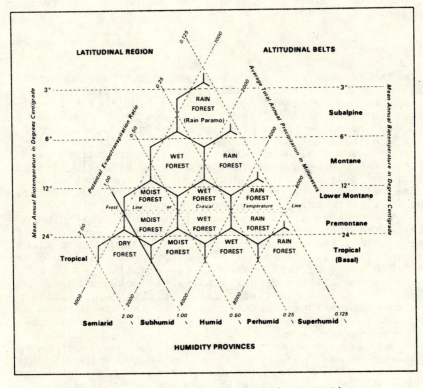

Figure 1.8 Chart of life zones in Costa Rica
Adapted from Holdridge 1967.

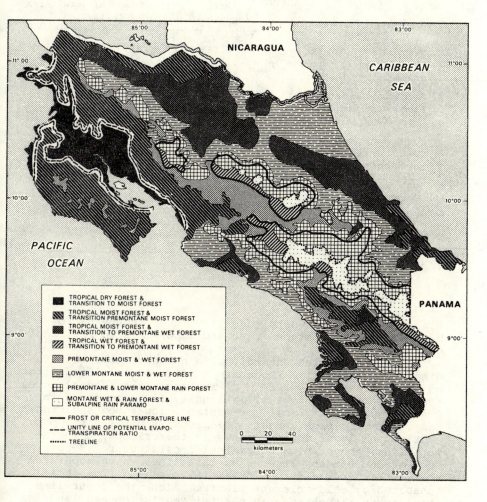

Figure 1.9 Life zones

Source: Nuhn 1978b (Reprinted with the permission of the
Instituto Geográfico Nacional).

TABLE 1.1
Area of life zones

Life Zone	Area (square km)	Percentage of Total Area of Costa Rica	
1. Tropical dry forest	5,263	10.3	
2. Tropical moist forest	12,366	24.2	57.1
3. Tropical wet forest	11,549	22.6	
4. Premontane moist forest	2,402	4.7	
5. Premontane wet forest	6,950	13.6	28.1
6. Premontane rain forest	5,008	9.8	
7. Lower montane moist forest	102	0.2	
8. Lower montane wet forest	767	1.5	9.1
9. Lower montane rain forest	3,781	7.4	
10. Montane wet forest	51	0.1	5.5
11. Montane rain forest	2,759	5.4	
12. Subalpine rain paramo	102	0.2	0.2
TOTAL	51,100	100.0	100.0

Source: Holdridge et al. 1971, 61.

higher elevations, where many life zones occupy narrow
bands on mountain slopes that are impossible to represent
on a small scale.
    Costa Rica lies entirely within the tropical latitu-
dinal zone. Its life zones are therefore classified first
on the basis of elevation. Of the seven elevational zones
that may occur in tropical latitudes, five are found in
Costa Rica: the tropical, premontane, lower montane, montane, and subalpine zones. The boundary between the premontane and lower montane zones is the critical temperature line, above which occasional frosts occur. 85 percent of the country lies below this line, which separates
the zones suitable for cold-sensitive plants from those
inhabited by cold-tolerant plants. Along the frost line
there are sharp changes in natural vegetation and land
use. Each elevational zone is subdivided into humidity
provinces, of which there are four in Costa Rica: dry,
moist, wet, and rain. Along the boundary between the dry
and moist provinces, the potential evapotranspiration ratio is unity. 90 percent of the country lies within humid
provinces, where precipitation exceeds potential evapotranspiration.
    More than half of Costa Rica lies in the basal tropi-
cal zone (or tierra caliente), from sea level up to 500
meters on the Caribbean slope and 700 meters on the Pacific

slope. The mean annual temperature exceeds 24°C. The tropical zone is subdivided into three humidity provinces. This area is the only elevational zone that contains a dry province: in the northwest of the country, where there are six rainless months, mean annual precipitation ranges from 1,400 to 2,000 millimeters. This dry zone has the pleasantest tropical climate for settlers of European origin and is the only lowland region that has been continuously occupied by non-Indians since the colonial period. In the tropical moist life zone on both the Pacific and Caribbean slopes, mean annual precipitation ranges from 2,000 to 3,000 millimeters and there is rainfall during much of the year. The tropical wet life zones in the Caribbean and south Pacific lowlands, with mean annual rainfall in excess of 4,000 millimeters, have hardly any dry season. The wetter tropical zones, successfully inhabited by the indigenous population, presented many difficulties to settlers of European descent and were not extensively colonized until the twentieth century.

The natural vegetation in the tropical zone ranges from semideciduous forest to dense selva. The tropical dry forest is relatively low and open. It contains an upper story of deciduous trees, 20 to 25 meters high, and an understory of semideciduous and evergreen trees and shrubs. Most of the canopy trees have flat, spreading crowns. There are approximately thirty species, including valuable hardwoods such as Mahogony (Swietenia humilis), Pochote (Bombacopsis quinatum), and Cenizaro (Pithecolobium saman). The tropical dry forest has been extensively cleared both for its timber and to make way for agriculture and cattle ranching. Only isolated patches of the formation are still intact. Many species of the tropical dry forest are also found in the semi-evergreen tropical moist forest, as well as trees such as Ceiba (Ceiba pentandra), Fruta Dorada (Virola koschnii), and Laurel (Cordia alliodora). This formation is taller, denser, and more complex than the tropical dry forest. Much of the tropical moist forest has also been cleared for cultivation, including the establishment of large banana plantations. The formation survives mainly in inaccessible areas close to the border with Nicaragua. The tropical wet forest, even on poor soils, is still more luxuriant than the dry and moist formations. It is the most heterogeneous of all the forests, containing up to a hundred species of trees, mainly evergreens. The tall, upper story trees, many over 50 meters high, have compact crowns and grow very close together. Some have gigantic buttressed trunks. The dense understory includes up to eighty-five species of palms, as well as broad-leaved herbaceous plants (Allen 1956). There has been some clearing for cultivation, but much of Costa Rica's surviving forest belongs to this formation.

More than a quarter of the country, including the intermontane depressions and the lower slopes of the cordilleras, is located in the premontane zone (or tierra

templada) between 500-700 and 1,500 meters above sea level.
Annual average temperatures range from 18 to 24°C. At
this elevation, total amounts of precipitation similar to
those of the three humidity provinces in the tropical zone
(1,000-2,000, 2,000-4,000, and over 4,000 millimeters)
produce moist, wet, and rain subtypes. The dry season is
pronounced in the moist province on the Pacific slope, but
weakly developed in the rest of the premontane zone. Some
of the drier parts of this zone have been densely settled
since the sixteenth century. They are still the most
heavily populated areas of the country, in spite of recent
migration down to the tropical zone.

The premontane moist forest resembles the tropical
dry formation. Its semideciduous upper story, 20 to 25
meters high, contains trees with stout trunks, heavy,
widespreading branches, and broad, flat crowns; the understory is composed mainly of evergreen trees and shrubs.
The premontane wet and rain forests are similar to the
tropical moist and wet forests. They comprise an upper
story of tall evergreens and understorys containing a wide
range of palms. Since many hillsides receive greater precipitation than adjacent lowlands, the premontane forests
are often denser than those in the tropical zone, although
the number of species is reduced to about fifty. Ferns,
mosses, and epiphytes typical of tropical mountains are
common in the premontane zone. Many of the premontane
moist and wet forests, particularly in the Valle Central,
have been almost entirely cleared for agriculture. Premontane forests survive mainly on the wetter mountain
slopes.

Above the frost line, the lower montane, montane, and
subalpine zones (or tierra fría) occupy approximately 15
percent of the country. Too cold and humid for most types
of land use, they have always been zones of relatively
sparse population. In the lower montane zone, located between 1,500 and 2,500 meters above sea level on the summits of the Cordillera de Guanacaste and the upper slopes
of the Cordillera Central and Cordillera de Talamanca,
mean annual temperature ranges from 12 to 18°C. The humidity provinces are identical to those in the premontane
zone. The lower montane moist and wet climates are found
only on the most sheltered Pacific slopes; the more extensive lower montane rain climate occurs on both sides of
the continental divide. The montane zone, at 2,500 to
3,500 meters above sea level and with mean annual temperatures between 6 and 12°C, is restricted to small areas in
the Cordillera Central and Cordillera de Talamanca. At
this elevation, even 1,000 millimeters of precipitation is
sufficient to produce a wet climate, and 2,000 millimeters
or more constitute a montane rain climate. The montane
wet zone is limited to a small area on the sheltered southwestern slope of Irazú volcano. All the other areas at
this elevation have a montane rain climate. The small
subalpine zone, located above 3,500 meters on the summits

of the Cordillera de Talamanca, has a mean annual temperature between 3 and 6°C and mean annual precipitation in
excess of 1,000 millimeters.

The small areas of lower montane moist and wet forests have now been largely cleared for farming. The more
extensive, lower montane rain forest is located in regions
frequently enveloped in drizzle, cloud, and fog. Low temperatures reduce the height of the trees, and there are
only twenty-five to thirty species. Broad-leaved evergreen shrubs predominate in the understory. The whole
forest carries a heavy load of epiphytes. The montane or
cloud forests, in areas of low temperature and high humidity, are composed mainly of evergreens. There are usually
less than twenty species, including oaks (Quercus costar-
ricensis) that predominate in the upper story. The understory contains many bamboos. Orchids, mosses, ferns, and
lichens occur throughout the montane zone (Hunter 1976;
Sawyer and Lindsey 1971). Only the subalpine zone lies
above the tree line. The natural vegetation is a paramo
similar to that of the Andes, although it contains less
variety of shrubs and herbaceous plants (Weber 1959).
Most of the species in the Costa Rican paramo are of Andean origin, but some are North American plants. At the
end of the dry season in 1976, much of the paramo and an
adjacent area of montane forest on Chirripó massif in the
Cordillera de Talamanca were destroyed by a fire, of unknown origins, that lasted for almost three weeks. The
regeneration of the vegetation will probably take many
years, and the paramo may never recover all its species
(Chaverri et al. 1976).

Costa Rica's large number of life zones permits the
cultivation of a much wider range of crops than would otherwise be possible at this latitude. The better soils and
more gently sloping land in the lower montane moist and
wet zones can be used for dairy farming and temperate horticulture, including the production of potatoes, cauliflowers, cabbages, carrots, celery, and lettuces. Subtropical crops, such as coffee, tobacco, pineapples, tomatoes, peppers, mangoes, avocadoes, and citrus fruits,
can be cultivated in the premontane moist zone and the
better soils of the premontane wet zone. The tropical dry
zone is well suited to beef cattle ranching. Its more
fertile soils can be sown in "dry" rice, cotton, sugar
cane, maize, sorghum, papaws, and cashews. The tropical
moist and wet zones are ideal for "wet" rice and tree
crops such as bananas, cocoa, coconuts, Manila hemp, rubber, African oil palm, breadfruit, and the pejibaye or
peach palm. These crops can be undersown with root crops
such as cassava, yams, and sweet potatoes (Hunter 1959).

All the life zones have now been affected by man's
occupation. In some, notably the tropical dry and premontane moist zones, little natural vegetation remains. The
life zone classification, however, is useful for analyzing
not only the natural environment, but also the complex

ecosystem in which man is the dominant species. Knowledge of climate and natural vegetation, even when little of the latter remains, is vital for future land use planning. By simulating the natural vegetation in forestry and farming, modern man could once again move towards the ecological equilibrium the indigenous population maintained in pre-Columbian times.

SOILS

Theoretically, it should be possible to include soils within the life zone framework, since both climate and vegetation are important soil-forming factors. In practice, particularly in mountainous countries, other factors vary over such small distances that each life zone contains a complex mosaic of soils (Holdridge et al. 1971, 578-579). Pérez Rosales et al. (1979) identified five principal soil-forming factors in Costa Rica: climate, vegetation, parent material, relief, and time.

Except in the tropical dry zone, precipitation exceeds potential evapotranspiration throughout the country. Under these humid conditions, the downward movement of water through the soil is greater than upward movement and loss through evaporation. Where there are neither steep slopes nor impeded drainage, leaching and ferrallitization are the dominant processes in soil formation, eventually producing deep latosols or ultisols. Soluble bases such as calcium, magnesium, potassium, and sodium are washed away, leaving an acid soil generally yellow or reddish in color, whose major components are iron and aluminium oxides. In the tropical dry zone, on the other hand, where there is a long dry season, potential evapotranspiration exceeds precipitation, and the upward movement of water through the soil produces an accumulation of salts in neutral or alkali vertisols. These soils are sticky in the wet season, but dry out and crack during the rainless months. In the lower elevational zones, constantly high temperatures foment rapid decomposition of the organic material in the soil. Humus content therefore tends to be low, except in areas of impeded drainage. In the montane and subalpine zones, by contrast, where temperatures are low throughout the year, organic material decomposes much more slowly. Soils in these zones tend to be acid and dark in color, with a thick layer of humus near the surface. Harris et al. (1969) identified podsols or spodosols in the montane zone above 2,500 meters.

In the tropical dry zone, where the natural vegetation is a deciduous forest, the soil contains relatively little organic material during most of the year. Leaves and other litter accumulate on the soil surface during the dry season and are rapidly mineralized with the onset of the rains. The semi-evergreen and evergreen forests in the remainder of the country provide a constant supply of organic litter to the soil. Permanently high temperatures and heavy rains, however, rapidly decompose this material and many valuable nutrients are washed away. In Costa Rica, as in many other humid tropical regions, the luxuriant natural vegetation deceived settlers of European descent into thinking that the underlying soil was extremely fertile. Once the dense natural forest is replaced by crops or pasture, the organic material available to the soil is greatly reduced; because of leaching, fertility declines so rapidly that the land may become sterile after only a few years' cultivation.

In a country geologically so complex as Costa Rica, parent rock is very diverse. Although similar soils can be produced from different parent materials, some of these produce specific types of soil. The active volcanoes of the Cordillera de Guanacaste and Cordillera Central intermittently deposit ash and lava over wide areas. Whereas lava initially produces only a lithic protosol, volcanic ash, composed of a variety of minerals normally leached out of humid tropical soils, produces deep, black and brown andosols. In some areas of the Caribbean lowlands to the east of the River Reventazón, and in parts of the Nicoya Peninsula, soils derived from limestone have a high calcareous content.

Relief affects both the accumulation and erosion of soils. Zonal soils, such as latosols and vertisols, develop only where there is gentle topography and unimpeded drainage. On steep slopes, where most precipitation is converted into surface run-off, little water is available for rock weathering and soil formation. Only shallow, coarse-grained lithosols develop. The natural vegetation protects these soils from excessive erosion; once the forest is removed, the torrential rains rapidly deplete the soil. Reverse conditions obtain in flat areas and hollows, where both weathered rock and organic material accumulate to form deep, waterlogged hydromorphic soils.

The time over which soils have developed is reflected in their structure. Many of the Cretaceous and Tertiary rocks of Costa Rica are covered with mature soils, including latosols that have reached the ultimate stage of weathering under the climatic conditions of the humid tropics. These are deep soils with distinct horizons. Many soils, however, particularly in regions of Quaternary surface geology, are recently formed inceptisols lacking a well-developed profile. Among these are volcanic and alluvial soils. Although they are subject to leaching, their periodic replenishment with ash or fluvial sediments counteracts the tendency towards the formation of latosols. Old alluvial deposits on river terraces no longer subject to flooding have gradually been converted into latosols (Dóndoli 1943).

Latosols occupy more than half the country. They are widespread in regions such as the General-Coto Brus depression, the central and southern Pacific lowlands, and

the northern plains, where there is gentle topography and
a humid climate. Vertisols and planosols, associated with
a drier climate, are restricted to sheltered, well-drained,
flat, or undulating areas in the northern Pacific lowlands.
Lithosols cover approximately 14 percent of the country.
They reach their maximum extent on the steep slopes of the
Cordillera de Talamanca, but they also occur in the other
cordilleras and in the hills of the western peninsulas.
Large areas of the Caribbean lowlands and smaller areas of
the Pacific lowlands contain poorly drained hydromorphic
soils. Near the coast, there are thin, unconsolidated,
sandy rhegosols. Alluvial soils occur in small areas on
the coastal lowlands and in the intermontane depressions.
Andosols, derived from volcanic ash, are found on and adjacent to the Cordillera de Guanacaste and Cordillera Central, and in the extreme south of the country, close to
Chiriquí volcano in Panama.

Most of Costa Rica is thus covered with relatively
infertile soils, subject to rapid depletion when poorly
managed. The mountain lithosols are unsuitable for cultivation both because of their inherent infertility, and because of the steep slopes on which they have developed.
The extensive latosols are poor in plant nutrients, lacking organic materials and many minerals. The hydromorphic
soils have a higher proportion of humus, but are poorly
drained. Less than one-fifth of the country contains fertile volcanic and alluvial soils (OPSA 1979a, 57). The
indigenous population preserved the soils by practicing
shifting cultivation, allowing long periods of natural regeneration under forest cover. Settlers of European descent, by contrast, deforested extensive zones of poor
soils, many of which, after a few years of crop production,
were exhausted and eroded and should ideally have been replanted with trees.

PRE-COLUMBIAN OCCUPATION OF THE LAND

The pre-Columbian peoples of Costa Rica developed no
form of writing. Our knowledge of them relies principally
on the archaeological record, supplemented by ethnohistorical sources dating from the time of the Spanish conquest
in the sixteenth century. Much of the prehistoric record
has already been irreparably damaged by the activities of
huaqueros--collectors and traders--who have removed thousands of artefacts, often without recording their prove-
nance and always irrevocably destroying the possibility of
accurate dating and the establishment of a cultural sequence (Baudez 1970, 25). Only a small number of archaeological sites have been scientifically excavated. They
are unevenly distributed both spatially and temporally,
and there are regions and periods about which little is
known. Many of the archaeological monographs are concerned principally with the establishment of ceramic

sequences and contain little interpretation of the economic, social, and political organization of the indigenous
population.

America was initially settled, perhaps as long as
30,000 years ago, by migrants of mongoloid Homo sapiens
from the Old World. It is not yet known when man first
arrived in Costa Rica. Stone projectile points, discovered
in the northwestern province of Guanacaste and in the Turrialba Valley on the eastern margin of the Valle Central,
are the earliest evidence of human occupation. They include fluted Clovis points, similar to those found in
North America, and fishtail points of South American design that probably date from 12,000-7,000 B.C. (Bosch-
Gimpera 1959; Snarskis 1976, 1977, 1981; Swauger and Mayer-
Oakes 1952). These lithic complexes suggest the country
was initially settled by Paleolithic hunters and gatherers
who subsisted on a flora and fauna that, in the period immediately after the last Pleistocene glaciation, included
species now extinct. There is no evidence of cultivation
during this early period. Population density must have
been very low. Sociopolitical organization was probably
limited to primitive bands.

The stratigraphical record has been traced back only
to the first millenium B.C. By this time, cultural development had reached the stage American archaeologists term
Formative, a rough equivalent to the Neolithic in the Old
World (Willey and Phillips 1958, 144-147). This stage
persisted in Costa Rica until the Spanish conquest. Hunting, fishing, and gathering persisted as essential elements of the economy. There was little or no domestication of animals, but man had mastered simple cultivation
techniques. How and when the transition from food collection to food production was accomplished is not yet clear.
There is no evidence of primary plant domestication; knowledge of agriculture was probably diffused from Meso-
America, the Central Andes, and the tropical lowlands of
northern South America.

Communally occupied lands around villages and hamlets
were cleared and cultivated with stone and wooden tools;
the use of iron was unknown in pre-Columbian America. On
the Pacific slope, the natural vegetation was burned in
the dry season. Indian policulture imitated the heterogeneous natural vegetation, and forest clearings were
rarely so extensive as to lead to serious depletion of
fauna, soils, and water resources. Plots were abandoned
after a few harvests and new patches of forest cleared for
temporary cultivation.

The Indians exploited a wide variety of natural resources. Wild plants provided fibers, recipients, dye-
stuffs, condiments, stimulants, and medicines, as well as
seeds and roots for cultivation. Temperatures permitted
plant growth throughout the year, except on the highest
mountain summits. Precipitation was everywhere sufficient
for one and, in many areas, for two or three harvests per

year of numerous tropical and subtropical crops. Even the
latosols yielded good harvests under swidden cultivation.
Wild animals, such as danta, deer, armadillos, monkeys,
tepezcuintles, and iguanas, provided meat in the Indian
diet (Ferrero 1975, 44-50). The rivers, coastal swamps,
and lagoons contained abundant supplies of fish and shellfish, and the lagoons were panned for salt. In nearly
every region excavated so far, archaeologists have noted a
marked preference for village sites near rivers and coasts
(Baudez 1970, 15-16). Timber, straw, stones, and other
materials were used for building.

The combination of cultivation, hunting, gathering,
and fishing supported only a relatively small population,
with most individuals engaged in producing and collecting
food. Sociopolitical organization took the form of tribes
and chiefdoms. There is no evidence in any part of the
country of the emergence of larger, more complex political
units, nor of Classic urban civilization. Monumental architecture was unknown, but the Indians showed great skill
in minor arts such as pottery, stone carving, and the
working of gold and jade.

Costa Rica was part of the region lying between the
advanced, urban civilizations of Meso-America and the Central Andes defined by archaeologists as the Intermediate
Area. Evidence is still insufficient to afford a conclu-
sive explanation of the retarded development of this region, although much recent research has been devoted to
the problem (Ekholm and Evans 1962) and two major hypotheses have been advanced (Helms 1975, 111-119). The first
hypothesis suggests that some cultural contacts between
Meso-America and the Central Andes were effected by sea,
skirting the Intermediate Area. Metallurgy, for example,
may have been diffused from coastal Peru or Ecuador to the
Pacific coast of Mexico, from whence it finally reached
Central America no earlier than 1,100 A.D. (Coe 1962). An
alternative hypothesis emphasizes the ecology of the Intermediate Area. In contrast to central Mexico and Peru,
it lacks arid regions conducive to the development of hy-
draulic agriculture and the emergence of complex, centralized states to organize and control such a system of cultivation. With ecological conditions suitable for swidden
cultivation in the tropical forest, the Intermediate Area
remained politically fragmented into tribes and chiefdoms
(Sanders and Price 1968, 172-173).

In spite of the general uniformity of Costa Rica's
indigenous cultures, archaeological research is providing
evidence of gradual changes over time in economic activities, sociopolitical organization, and population density.
These changes are similar to those noted in other parts of
the Intermediate Area (Willey 1971, 286-348). Economic
activities were gradually diversified by the introduction
of new crops, the exploitation of marine resources, the
diffusion of metallurgy, and the widening of trade. Sociopolitical organization evolved from small tribal groups

to the establishment of chiefdoms with populations of several thousands, elementary social stratification, and political control over fairly wide areas. The increase in the number and size of archaeological sites between 1000 B.C. and 1500 A.D. suggests a slow overall rise in population, although there were probably many short-term fluctuations. Settlements ranged from hamlets and small villages in the earlier phases to larger villages and perhaps even small towns during later periods (Baudez 1963). Population may have reached a temporary peak in some areas a few centuries before the Spanish conquest. Colonial documents of the 1520s recorded an Indian population of 27,200 (Thiel 1902), but this figure was based on a very incomplete reconnaissance. The total may well have been as high as 400,000 (Denevan 1976, 291), an average of about eight persons per square kilometer.

There was little settlement in the cold montane and subalpine areas. Over the rest of the country, there is evidence of indigenous occupation of every life zone. Research is not sufficiently advanced for detailed mapping of pre-Columbian settlement, but archaeologists have identified three major regions, separated by the high cordilleras: Nicoya, centered in the tropical dry zone in the northwest of the country; the Atlantic Watershed and Central Highlands, spanning a wide variety of humid environments on the Caribbean slope, from the tropical to lower montane zones; and the Diquis region, on the humid south Pacific slope (Figure 1.10) (D. Stone 1977). Their frontiers do not correspond with modern political boundaries, and all three continue into areas now occupied by neighboring republics. Regional variations became particularly pronounced from about 500 A.D. onwards (Snarskis 1981).

Nicoya formed part of a larger cultural province, the Greater Nicoya Subarea, which continued into Pacific Nicaragua (Norweb 1968). A circular oven near Culebra Bay, with a radiocarbon date of about 800 B.C., is the earliest evidence of permanent settlement (Snarskis 1981). Elsewhere, the relatively small number of sites dating from the Zoned Bichrome period, 300 B.C.-300 A.D., indicates a sparse population living in scattered villages close to water sources. Houses were probably constructed of perishable materials, such as canes and leaves, bound together with vines. Hunting and fishing were combined with shifting agriculture. Cassava (_Manihot utilissima_) was probably the main crop, with tiquisque (_Xanthosoma violaceum_), yams (_Dioscorea trifida_), and maize (_Zea mays_) as subsidiary staples. The Zoned Bichrome period was contemporary with the late Formative stage in Meso-America and the Central Andes. Archaeologists have suggested the existence at this time of a single Formative stage throughout Nuclear America, between central Mexico and Peru (Willey 1959).

The Early Polychrome period in Nicoya lasted from about 300 to 800 A.D. By this time, Classic urban civili-

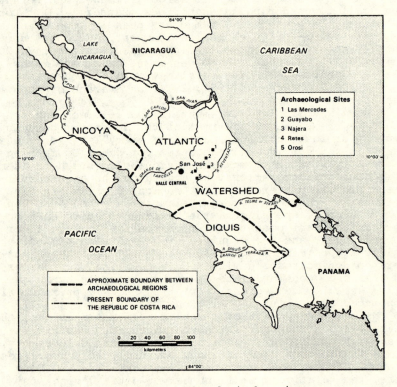

Figure 1.10 Archaeological regions

zations were flourishing in Meso-America and the Central Andes, while the Intermediate Area remained at the Formative stage. Settlements continued to be located mainly along rivers and coasts, but their greater size and abundance indicates an increase in population. The subsistence base was broadened by the exploitation of shellfish, the gathering of wild nuts and berries, and the cultivation of chillis (Capsicum sp.), a valuable source of vitamins. At one coastal site, the remains of tuna fish dating from about 400 A.D. indicate that at least some groups were able fishermen on the high seas.

During the Mid-Polychrome period, between 800 and 1200 A.D., there was a further rise in population as a result not only of natural increase, but also of the immigration of two groups of Mexican Indians, the Chorotega and the Nicarao. The large number of sites discovered in the Tempisque Valley and along the coast suggests that this period may have seen the maximum pre-Columbian population in Nicoya. Economic activities were further diversified. The Nicarao introduced the cultivation of cocoa (Theobroma cacao), which was mixed with cold water, maize, pepper, and vanilla to make a chocolate beverage. Cocoa beans also became a widely accepted medium of interchange. The Mid-Polychrome sites contain abundant shell middens, including remains of the mollusc Murex exploited for a purple dye used in the preparation of cotton textiles. Together with salt panned along the coast, this mollusc was an important item of trade in a commercial network linking Nicoya with a wide area stretching from the highlands of Guatemala in the north to the Diquis region in the south.

The Late Polychrome period, from 1200 to 1500 A.D., may have been a period of demographic decline or, alternatively, of population redistribution. The abundant sites in the Sapoa Valley, close to the present border with Nicaragua, are indicative of local population pressure on the land. Agriculture alone was unable to supply sufficient food, and there is evidence of increased consumption of molluscs and wild nuts. The absence of bones points to a decline in the wild game available for hunting. The extensive settlement of littoral sites suggests there was a gradual transfer of population from inland to coastal locations. These migrations may have reflected a growing reliance on fish and shellfish (Baudez 1967; Baudez and Coe 1962; Lange 1971b, 1976, 1977).

Early archaeologists regarded Nicoya as the southernmost extension of the Meso-American realm of seed agriculture (Kirchoff 1966). Ethnohistorical evidence dating from the early sixteenth century corroborates this interpretation. The conquistadores described the Nicarao and Chorotega as the most advanced cultural groups in the area now comprising the republic of Costa Rica. They practiced hoe cultivation, combining the production of maize and beans (Phaseolus vulgaris), complementary in their use of soil nutrients, with that of squashes (<u>Cucurbita</u> sp.), whose large leaves afforded protection from evaporation and erosion. Maize was irrigated manually during the dry season. Grains were stored in warehouses. Artesans produced a wide variety of manufactured goods for sale, of which cotton textiles and pottery were among the most important. The largest villages, some of which may have had several thousand inhabitants, contained central functions such as markets, temples, and political meeting houses located around plazas. There were three social classes: nobles who received tribute, common people who paid tribute, and slaves (Chapman 1974; Ferrero 1975, 111-123).

In spite of the ethnohistorical evidence of three Meso-American enclaves in Costa Rica at the time of the Spanish conquest--the Chorotega, the Nicarao, and a recently arrived Aztec group, the Sigua, who lived in the southeastern foothills of the Cordillera de Talamanca--modern archaeologists place increasing emphasis on South American influences. They stress the fact that cultural boundaries fluctuate over time, often spanning extensive transitional zones, and consider that Nicoya does not show clear Meso-American affiliations until the arrival of the northern migrants (Baudez 1967, 205-212; Willey 1966, 168-169). These groups may have been responsible for no more than a temporary and indirect florescence of Mayan traits during the Mid-Polychrome period, which by no means obliterated South American influences (Lange 1971a; Snarskis 1975). Had the European discovery of America been delayed, however, Costa Rica might have fallen increasingly within the Meso-American sphere (D. Stone 1949, 1968).

While the cultural affinities of Nicoya are still the subject of debate, there is general agreement that South American influences were dominant in the rest of the country. Most of the staple crops cultivated in the Atlantic Watershed and Diquis regions were natives of the tropical forest zone of northern South America. They included roots such as cassava and tiquisque, as well as the highly nutritious fruit of the pejibaye or peach palm (<u>Gulielma utilis oerst</u>.), diffused from the Orinoco Valley. Cocoa may also have been introduced from South America for use in religious ceremonies, following the Amazon and Orinoco tradition, rather than as a medium of exchange in the Meso-American fashion (D. Stone 1977, 7). Until recently, it was presumed that maize was diffused from Meso-America. Excavations in the Linea Vieja area of the Atlantic Watershed, however, have uncovered charred remnants of corn cobs of a South American type dating from the early centuries A.D. (Snarskis 1975). Maize probably remained subsidiary to cassava and the pejibaye. It may have been used mainly for the manufacture of <u>chicha</u>, a fermented beverage (Ferrero 1975, 52-54). Maize is not suited to the humid climate of the Caribbean and south Pacific regions, and storage must have presented serious problems. Root crops such as cassava, by contrast, produce throughout the year and can be harvested as required.

The Atlantic Watershed and Central Highlands constitute the largest and most disparate of the archaeological regions. There are several subregions, but artefacts display stylistic similarities throughout the region, suggesting common cultural traditions (Snarskis 1981). There is evidence of pre-Columbian settlement in the Caribbean lowlands, the Valle Central, and adjacent slopes of the Cordillera Central up to an altitude of about 2,700 meters above sea level.

The cultural sequence in the Valle Central can be closely correlated with that of Nicoya. Once again, the increasing number of sites for each successive period points to gradual population growth. During the Pavas phase, between 300 B.C. and 300 A.D., population was sparse. Settlements were small and scattered; many were no more than hamlets occupied by one or two families. Cultivation of cassava and maize was supplemented by wild game and freshwater fish. In the Curridabat phase, from 300 to 850 A.D., there is evidence of an incipient differentiation between residential and ceremonial settlements. By the Cartago phase, from 850 to 1500 A.D., the political and ceremonial centers of the chiefdoms were large villages, with populations of several hundred people (Aguilar Piedra 1974; Kennedy 1968). At Guayabo de Turrialba, a well-protected site lying 1,100 meters above sea level in the eastern Valle Central, cane and wooden buildings were constructed on foundations of stones collected from nearby river beds. The village had paved paths and aqueducts. Guayabo reached its maximum development about one hundred years before the arrival of Europeans and was in decline by the time of the Spanish conquest (Aguilar Piedra 1972). Similar ceremonial centers existed at Najerra and Orosi in the upper Reventazón Valley, Retes on the slopes of Irazú volcano, and Las Mercedes in the Caribbean lowlands. Many of these villages were interconnected by stone causeways. The whole of the Atlantic Watershed was an important trade area. Among the items exchanged with other regions of Costa Rica and beyond were tapirs, wild pigs, salt, cocoa, honey, cotton cloth, hammocks, and gold artefacts (D. Stone 1977, 168-204).

The scattered excavations undertaken in the Caribbean lowlands reveal a culture complex similar to that of northern South America. Both pottery styles and the subsistence base of cassava and pejibayes show marked affinities with those of the coastal lowlands of Colombia. A single Tropical Forest Culture probably extended from the Amazon and Orinoco basins along the Caribbean coast as far as Honduras. In the Linea Vieja area, there are numerous tombs and cemeteries dating from the El Bosque phase, between 300 B.C. and 500 A.D., although there are no remains of surface architecture. A trend towards increasingly nucleated settlements is apparent by the Late Ceramic phase, between 900 and 1500 A.D. The fact that many of these villages were located on easily defended sites suggests that the militarism that characterized the contemporary Post-Classic civilizations in Meso-America and the Central Andes permeated the Intermediate Area (Snarskis 1975, 1976).

The Diquis region was part of the larger cultural province known as Gran Chiriquí, which continued into western Panama. This region is archaeologically the least known in Costa Rica. There are no radiocarbon dates and only a tentative cultural sequence has been established. There were significant local variations in settlement patterns. In the Térraba delta, many of the small, scattered settlements were ephemeral not only because of the nature of indigenous shifting agriculture, but also because of the constant threat of flooding in low-lying regions. Houses were built on stilts to provide protection from the swollen rivers (Lothrop 1963). Inland, by contrast, in the General-Coto Brus depression, the particularly large number of tumuli dating from 1000 to 1500 A.D. indicates fairly dense settlement in the centuries prior to the Spanish conquest (Haberland 1961). Ethnohistorical sources record the existence of large, fortified villages and of constant intertribal warfare, in order to take captives and to control rivers that contained placer deposits of gold (D. Stone 1977, 133). Local pressure on the land was such that excessive burning and short fallows in the cycle of shifting cultivation led to the development of savannas.

This degradation of the natural environment in pre-Columbian Costa Rica, however, was probably the exception rather than the rule. The overall density of population was still low in the early sixteenth century. The clearings made for villages and shifting cultivation cannot have occupied more than a fraction of the country. The Spaniards discovered a land almost entirely covered with the forest that was key to the Indians' livelihood.

SURVIVING INDIAN COMMUNITIES

In the Meso-American republics of Mexico and Guatemala and the Andean republics of Peru, Ecuador, and Bolivia where there were sophisticated pre-Columbian civilizations, large Indian communities have survived to the present day, retaining many of their cultural traditions including the use of native languages. The tribes and chiefdoms of the Intermediate Area put up prolonged resistance to European rule, but, once they had been subdued, their small numbers and relatively primitive culture doomed them to assimilation into colonial Hispanic American society. High mortality rates, miscegenation, and acculturation reduced the Indian population of Costa Rica to an ethnic minority that by the early nineteenth century accounted for less than one-fifth of the population and, today, comprises under 1 percent of the nation's inhabitants.

The native population was one of the most prized

resources of the Spanish empire. The exploitation of precious metals and fertile farmlands required a servile labor force, initially provided by the conquered peoples. The Spanish frontier of settlement in most of the New World was a "frontier of inclusion"; the Indians were integrated into colonial society rather than deliberately exterminated as an impediment to European settlement (Hennessy 1978, 19-20).

A variety of institutions was employed to subjugate the native population. In Nicoya, incorporated into the Spanish province of Nicaragua in 1527, the Indians were enslaved. Many were exported for sale in Panama and Peru (Macleod 1973, 49-55; Sherman 1979, 53-60). By 1569 the region's native population had declined to 3,300 (Thiel 1902).

By the time the Spaniards began to colonize the interior of Costa Rica in the 1560s, the New Laws of 1542 had prohibited enslavement of the native population, and the encomienda was the principal mechanism for incorporating the Indians into the colonial system. During the late sixteenth and early seventeenth centuries, virtually all the tribes known to the Spaniards were distributed among encomenderos, entrusted with the Indians' well-being and their conversion to Christianity (Thiel 1940). The Indians were obliged to pay tribute; many Spanish colonists also illegally used encomienda Indians as an unpaid labor force. The encomienda system functioned in the major areas of European settlement, particularly the Valle Central where Indians were forced to settle in reducciones or nucleated villages and adopt Spanish culture (Meléndez 1977a, 47-56). After a transitional phase during the early decades of colonial rule, pacified Indians spoke Spanish, and their native tongues fell into disuse. Each Indian village had a Christian church where pagan ceremonies survived only if they could be woven into the rituals of catholicism.

In outlying regions, the encomienda was ineffective, and the colonial authorities resorted to other means of controlling the native population. By the seventeenth century, the pacification of southern Costa Rica had been delegated to Franciscan missionaries, supported from time to time by military escorts provided by the provincial governor in Cartago. The most successful mission settlements were those on the Pacific slope, in the General and Térraba valleys, where Spain never faced serious competition from rival imperial powers. On the Caribbean slope, the missionaries encountered hostile tribes who, in turn, were harassed by the Zambos Mosquitos, descendents of Miskito Indians and shipwrecked Negro slaves who inhabited eastern Nicaragua. The Zambos Mosquitos, in league with English pirates, captured Costa Rican Indians to sell as slaves in the British colony of Jamaica, provoking the virtual extinction of tribes such as the Changüenes (Meléndez 1977a, 129-140). By the eighteenth century, the

missionaries resorted to removing the Indians by force
from the Talamanca region and resettling them in areas under Spanish control. Some were taken to the Térraba Valley, others as far away as the Nicoya peninsula, and some
to the Valle Central where several new villages were founded to accommodate them (Floyd 1967, 87-100; Prado 1925,
63-70). The Indians who lived in mission villages in the
peripheral regions acquired a veneer of Spanish culture
but never entirely abandoned their traditional way of life.
The missions were in decline by the end of the colonial
period, and, in 1829, the federal government of Central
America abolished monastic orders throughout the isthmus.

In Costa Rica, as in other parts of America, the Indians reacted in three ways to European colonization (Ribeiro 1971, 20-21). Many fled into regions such as the
northern plains and the Cordillera de Talamanca, over
which the Spaniards never established permanent control
(Floyd 1967, 41-53, 97-100). In these refuges, native
cultures survived into the republican period. The second
reaction was armed resistance, a process that continued
intermittently throughout the colonial period. Rebellions
in Talamanca in 1610 and again in 1709 forced the Spaniards to retreat for many years (Fernández Guardia 1968,
46-51, 81-83; López Leal 1973). In the long term, however,
the contact between Indian and European resulted in either
assimilation or extermination for the majority of the native population.

The Spaniards failed to maintain a strict apartheid
system, in spite of the original confinement of the Indians to reducciones whose only non-Indian inhabitants
were Spanish priests. From the sixteenth century onwards,
mestizaje or miscegenation was one of the two major processes by which the Indian population declined. The other
process was the high mortality rate among the native population caused by the introduction of Old World diseases
such as smallpox, measles, typhus, whooping cough, influ-
enza, and the common cold to which they had no immunity.
Assuming there were several hundred thousand Indians in
Costa Rica on the eve of the Spanish conquest (Denevan
1976), their decline was as catastrophic as in other parts
of the continent. The colonial authorities recorded 17,000
Indians in the province in 1569 and 8,000 in 1801, though
these figures may have underestimated the native population in the regions outside effective Spanish control.
The Indians' share of the total population declined over
the same period from 98 to 16 percent (Table 1.2). In
Nicoya and the Valle Central, Indians comprised only 13
and 8 percent, respectively, of the population in 1801
(Table 1.3). They were still the dominant racial group in
the northern plains and throughout the south of the country, although in both areas population was extremely
sparse, averaging less than one person per square kilometer.

Only in these peripheral regions, located mainly in

TABLE 1.2
Indian population, c. 1500-1978

Year	Number of Indians	Indians As a Percentage of the Total Population
c. 1500	400,000?	100.0
1569	17,166	98.0
1611	14,908	96.0
1700	15,489	80.0
1720	13,269	68.0
1741	12,716	53.0
1751	10,109	42.0
1778	8,104	24.0
1801	8,281	16.0
1927	4,197	.9
1950	2,692	.3
1978	15,000-20,000	less than 1

Sources: c. 1500: Denevan 1976; 1569-1801: Thiel 1902; 1927: DGEC 1960; 1950: DGEC 1953a; 1978: estimate of the Departamento de Reservas Indígenas, Instituto de Tierras y Colonización, San José.

TABLE 1.3
Regional distribution of Indian population, 1801

Region	Number of Indians	Indians As a Percentage of the Total Population
Valle Central	3,542	8
Nicoya, Guanacaste, and Esparza	709	13
Northern plains	800	100
South	3,230	100
Costa Rica	8,281	16

Source: Thiel 1902

the tropical and premontane moist and wet life zones where there was little Hispanic American settlement before the twentieth century, did Indian communities retain their racial and cultural identity after Costa Rica attained independence from Spain in 1821. Elsewhere, the surviving Indians were absorbed into Hispanic American society during the nineteenth century. Legislation promulgated during the first two decades of the republican period abolished racially segregated settlements and converted the remaining Indian villages into barrios or suburbs of nearby Hispanic American towns (Meléndez 1957, 14-15). Today, Indian racial features and cultural traits persist in only a handful of villages in Guanacaste and the Valle Central: Matambú and Santa Bárbara in the Nicoya peninsula, Quitirrisi to the southwest of San José, and Cot near the town of Cartago (Figure 1.11) (Bozzoli 1975, 12).

The northern plains and the whole area south of the Valle Central were extremely isolated during the early decades of the republican period. The majority of Costa Ricans lived in ignorance of the Indian cultures surviving in these forested regions (Ferrero 1978, xx). Towards the end of the nineteenth century, explorers such as William Gabb (1875) and Bishop Thiel (1896) (the first Catholic priest to visit many Indian regions since the departure of the Franciscan missionaries) undertook the virtual rediscovery of the indigenous communities and wrote the first modern ethnological accounts of the Indian population.

By this time, the Guatusos were the only surviving tribe in northern Costa Rica. Shortly before Thiel's arrival in 1882, they had been harassed by rubber trappers who had killed their chief, enslaved their children for sale in Nicaragua, and driven most of the remaining population into hiding in the forest. Thiel's expedition nevertheless discovered some palenques or communal houses built of cane, straw, and leaves. The Guatuso economy had altered little since pre-Columbian times except for the adoption of a few Old World crops and iron tools; shifting cultivation of cassava, plantains, pejibayes, maize, sugar cane, and cocoa was complemented by hunting and fishing. All the other Indian tribes inhabited the south of Costa Rica. Hispanic American influences were strongest on the Pacific slope, where contact with the colonial missions had been most prolonged; the Borucas and Térrabas lived according to Costa Rican law and the precepts of Roman Catholicism. By contrast, the Cabécares and Bribris on the Caribbean slope retained their chief, the Cacique of Talamanca, recognized by the Costa Rican government in 1867 as the local jefe político. They were fearful of becoming Christians lest they be forced to migrate to the Valle Central like their predecessors in the colonial period. The Cabécares and Térrabas still inhabited palenques. They had adopted some European tools and Old World crops such as rice and sugar cane.

At the end of the last century, the surviving native communities were regarded as remnants of a backward and inferior race, doomed to extinction. At the prompting of Thiel, the government passed a law in 1882 prohibiting persecution of the Indians and extraction of rubber and timber from the northern plains. This legislation was never enforced, and official indifference towards the Indian communities persisted well into the twentieth century (Meléndez 1957, 15).

Contrary to the explorers' premonitions, however, the tribes they visited not only survived, but multiplied as they came into more permanent contact with Hispanic American society. There are no estimates of the Indian population between 1801 and 1927, when the census recorded slightly more than 4,000 individuals (Table 1.2). The considerable increase registered since 1950 probably reflects both underestimates in the censuses of 1927 and 1950 and natural population growth in recent years. Today, when Costa Rica's total population is slightly more than 2 million, that of the five principal Indian groups--Guatusos, Borucas, Térrabas, Cabécares, and Bribris--is thought to number between 15,000 and 20,000 (Rafael Ocampo, personal communication). Of these, probably only 5,000-6,000 retain a predominantly indigenous culture, including knowledge of a native language (La Nación, 13 February 1979). All the areas occupied by Indians are now being integrated by modern modes of transport with the rest of the country. The lands of the Borucas and Térrabas are close to the Pan-American Highway; dirt roads and local air services give access to Guatuso, Cabécar, and Bribri territory.

In recent decades, Costa Rica's surviving Indian population, in common with that in other parts of tropical America, has undergone a rapid transition from tribal to peasant society. Traditional forms of political organization have largely disappeared. Indians vote in national elections, although they pay no taxes to the central government. Most have access to a Catholic church and to state schools where Spanish is the principal language. Not only official buildings, but also houses are now constructed of wood and corrugated iron instead of cane and thatch. The native economy has been profoundly modified. Some Indians still practice rotational bush fallowing, but the encroachment of Hispanic American colonists has obliged the majority to become permanent cultivators. Primitive vegeculture has given way to seed agriculture (Grigg 1974, 11). Rice and beans are now the staples for the Indians, as for the Hispanic American peasant. Tractors and ploughs have not yet been adopted, but the use of machetes and firearms is ubiquitous. Wild plants, freshwater fish, and game have been severely depleted. The Indians have compensated for the decline in wild sources of protein by adopting domestic animals, particularly chickens and pigs, and by purchasing tinned meat and fish. Few if any Indians are totally isolated from the capitalist market economy. Many are still predominantly subsistence farmers, but they also produce goods for sale. Among the Cabécares, for example, pigs are the main commercial commodity, sold to obtain items such as salt, coffee, clothing, paraffin, and matches in non-Indian village stores (Bozzoli 1975; Camacho Zamora 1974; Hill 1973; López de Piza 1974).

The surviving Indian communities rank among the poorest in contemporary Costa Rica. Their future has been the

subject of considerable debate in recent years (Ornes 1980).
Many people, including some of the Indians themselves, favor total integration, arguing that because of their small
numbers the Indians could soon be completely assimilated
into Hispanic American society (La Nación, 23 June 1978).
Anthropologists, while recognizing Indian rights to the
same social services the rest of the population enjoys,
have warned that native cultures may soon completely disappear (Bozzoli 1973).

Modern government intervention to protect Indian communities and their access to land dates back to 1939, when
the Ley General sobre Terrenos Baldíos recognized as an
inalienable and exclusive property of the Indians "a zone
deemed suitable by the Executive Power, with the aim of
conserving our native races, and liberating them from future injustices" (Salas Marrero and Barahona 1973, 263).
This nebulous legislation was little more than a declara-
tion of intent, since no specific delimitations of Indian
lands were made. In 1945, the Junta de Protección de las
Razas Aborígenes de la Nación was created to establish Indian reserves and to raise the standards of health and education among the native population. The first reserves--
Boruca y Térraba, Salitre, and China Kiché--were delimited
in 1956 among the Pacific tribes that had been in permanent contact with Europeans and their descendents since the
colonial period (Figure 1.11). In 1961, the Ley de Tierras y Colonización transferred the administration of Indian lands to a new government agency, the Instituto de
Tierras y Colonización, ITCO. This legislation perpetuated the colonial principle of "reducing" the native population to small areas in which they would be settled in
nucleated villages and provided with adjacent farmlands
(Meléndez 1977a, 65-98; Salas Marrero and Barahona 1973).
Several new reserves were established: Guaymí in the southwest of the country, Telire, Estrella, Chirripó, and Talamanca in the east, and Guatuso in the north. By the time
these reserves were created, Hispanic American colonization had already forced the native population to retreat
to poor, infertile lands. Most of the reserves are areas
of rugged terrain; only an estimated 10 percent of their
total area of 268,074 hectares is suitable for cultivation
(La Nación, 14 February 1979; Tosi 1967a). Most Indians
have little notion of the commercial value of land and are
easy prey for unscrupulous Hispanic American colonists who
are settling illegally within the reserves and buying out
the Indians at very low prices (Bozzoli 1975, 23).

In 1973, the government created the Comisión Nacional
de Asuntos Indígenas (CONAI) to promote scientific research of Indian cultures, particularly the study and use
of native languages, and to raise the Indians' standard of
living by establishing agricultural cooperatives, health
centers, and improved educational facilities in the reserves (CONAI 1973). So far, little has been achieved in
these fields. In collaboration with the ITCO, the CONAI

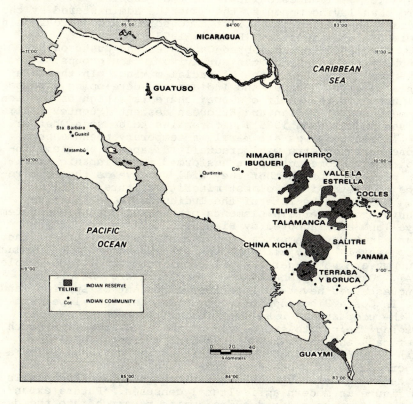

Figure 1.11 Present-day Indian communities and reserves
Sources: IGN 1973; ITCO 1979.

has been concerned mainly with protecting the Indians' access to land (CONAI 1977). This action in itself is insufficient to ensure that the Indians survive as a distinctive cultural group; it merely gives them the opportunity to develop a peasant economy similar to that of Hispanic American colonists. If the reserves are to be more than living museums, they must be administered by the Indians themselves as part of a conscious effort to retain their cultural identity (Bozzoli 1973).

The isolated and inbred Cabécares and Guatusos are probably the purest of the surviving Indian groups. The others already show signs of racial mixing. In the Talamanca reserve, Negroes and Indians are developing a zambo culture. On the Pacific slope, there is a high proportion of mestizos of Indian and European descent (Fuentes 1961; Matson and Swanson 1965). It remains to be seen whether the Indian reserves are merely a temporary phenomenon whose raison d'être will gradually disappear as their inhabitants become totally transformed into Hispanic American peasants, or whether they will survive as the last refuge of Costa Rica's oldest minority culture.

Whatever the fate of the Indians as a distinctive ethnic group, certain elements of the indigenous ecosystem have long been adopted by Hispanic American society. Plants native to America occupied nearly one-third of the crop area in 1973, although the staples of the pre-Columbian economy are no longer the principal sources of food (Table 1.4). Cassava, probably the major food crop before the conquest, was never an important component of Spanish land use in Costa Rica and today occupies less than 1 percent of the crop area. Like most indigenous root crops, including the potato introduced by the Spaniards from South America, cassava is now consumed as a vegetable rather than as a staple food. The fruit of the pejibaye palm, a major source of protein in pre-Columbian times, is now prized as a delicacy. The area sown is so small it fails to figure in modern agricultural censuses. Future expansion of commercial production awaits research into the development of new varieties and improved methods of transplanting suckers and handling the harvested fruit (Hunter 1969). Maize and beans, probably subsidiary to cassava and pejibayes in the pre-Columbian diet, are the most important indigenous crops in Costa Rica today. Both were grown by the Spaniards during the colonial period and are now widely distributed throughout the country, even in ecologically marginal areas. Many native fruits continue to be cultivated, though most are unrecorded in the agricultural censuses. They include pineapples, now diffused throughout the world, as well as an enormous variety of fruits little known outside tropical America. Several indigenous plants have been produced as specialized cash crops. Cocoa and tobacco were cultivated commercially on a small scale during the colonial period and persisted as secondary export crops after independence. Several attempts

TABLE 1.4
Area sown in crops native to America, 1973

Crops	Area (in ha.)	Percentage Total Crop Area (excluding fallows)
Root crops:		
Cassava	2,076.8	0.57
Sweet potato	109.0	0.03
Potato	2,001.0	0.55
Grains & legumes:		
Maize	51,888.3	14.19
Beans	26,680.9	7.30
Fruits & vegetables:		
Pineapple	738.0	0.20
Tomato	494.4	0.14
Avocado pear	221.0	0.06
Papaw	166.0	0.05
Cash crops:		
Cocoa	20,305.0	5.55
Tobacco	1,505.7	0.41
Cotton	73.5	0.02
TOTAL	106,259.6	29.07

Source: DGEC 1974b.

have been made in recent years, in Costa Rica and in neighboring republics, to develop commercial cotton cultivation.
    Potentially still more valuable than the heritage of individual crops is the whole native tradition of man-land relationships. The Indians developed a profound empirical knowledge of their physical environment, allowing them to exploit its resources without seriously disrupting its underlying equilibrium. The forest provided shelter for game, yielded edible plants, protected fish and water resources, and helped regenerate the soil after periods of cultivation. The native crop complex included a great variety of plants, often grown together in imitation of the heterogeneous natural vegetation. Whereas indigenous society was integrated into the natural environment, Hispanic American society radically transformed it, removing the forest, replacing polyculture by monoculture, and introducing alien patterns of land use (Meggers 1971, 150-153; Tosi and Voertman 1964; Varese 1973). Hispanic American farmers learned little from the Indians about land management and resource conservation. The solution of the grave ecological problems Costa Rica faces today--the depletion of forest resources, severe soil erosion, and the alteration of river regimes--calls for a reevaluation of

the ways in which the indigenous population successfully
occupied over thousands of years a tropical environment
that Europeans and their descendents have exploited so de-
structively in recent decades.

2
The Legacy of European Colonization

European imperial expansion between the fifteenth and twentieth centuries radically transformed the geography of vast regions of the world. Central and South America, the first entire continent overseas to which Europeans laid claim, remained under colonial rule for three centuries. Out of this prolonged period of contact emerged a new culture realm, Latin America, today the most westernized continent of the third world.

In Costa Rica, the legacy of European colonization has been out of all proportion to the number of immigrants from Spain. No more than a few thousand Spaniards settled permanently during the colonial period from 1502 to 1821. Yet, as representatives of an imperial power with a more advanced material culture than that of the indigenous population, they instigated profound structural changes whose impact persists to the present day. A new geopolitical system was imposed upon the Central American isthmus, and the nation-state of Costa Rica evolved from the colonial province of the same name. The heterogeneous native tribes were replaced by an Hispanic American society, racially mixed but culturally homogeneous. Costa Rica's incorporation into the world economy as a primary export producer prolonged a colonial pattern of underdevelopment long after political independence. European concepts of the relationship between man and the land transformed the ecosystem: forest gave way to permanent, privately owned farms in which Old World crops, animals, and techniques were of prime importance.

THE NATION-STATE OF COSTA RICA

In contrast to the Aztec and Inca empires, which became the core areas of Spanish viceroyalties and subsequently of the independent republics of Mexico and Peru, the tribes and chiefdoms of the Intermediate Area were never adopted as a basis for colonial administration. That the Spaniards found the indigenous political geography of

51

Costa Rica extremely complex and confusing is evident from the innumerable versions of the names they gave the Indian tribes in early colonial documents (Ferrero 1978, xxi-xxii). More than a dozen "naciones" or chiefdoms had to be conquered one by one (Peralta 1896).

Spain claimed possession of the whole Central American isthmus and took advantage of alliances with one tribe in order to overrun another, but large areas, particularly on the Caribbean slope, were never brought under effective control. Spanish colonization in southern Central America was particularly patchy. It was concentrated in several small, separate areas, one of which was the Valle Central of Costa Rica. These areas of control became the cores of colonial provinces, separated by extensive frontier zones inhabited by unconquered Indian tribes. The political fragmentation inherent in the colonial system impeded the establishment after independence of a single Central American state, and the former Spanish provinces became a series of independent republics that have persisted to the present day (Figure 2.1).

Spanish exploration of the Central American isthmus, undertaken from colonies recently founded in the Caribbean islands, was initially a littoral process. It had two principal objectives: the discovery of a maritime route linking Europe westwards with Asia, and the search for wealth within the isthmus itself. The east coast was reconnoitered during the first decade of the sixteenth century; Balboa's fortuitous discovery of the Pacific Ocean in 1513 was followed by voyages along the west coast. Southern Central America was initially divided into a series of coastal provinces, separated by large, unexplored hinterlands in the interior of the isthmus. Veragua occupied the Caribbean slope; the Pacific slope, including what was later to become Costa Rica, was divided between Castilla del Oro, centered on Panama, and the province of Nicaragua, created in 1527. Nicoya, which had the strongest links with Meso-American indigenous cultures of all the regions of Costa Rica, was associated with Nicaragua throughout the colonial period and retains distinctive cultural traditions to the present day (Wagner 1958). During the early sixteenth century, Panama and Nicaragua, containing the two principal lowland routes across the isthmus, were the major foci of Spanish exploration and settlement. After the discovery in the 1520s and 1530s of the rich Inca empire in South America, many Spaniards left Central America for Peru, and the interior of the zone between Nicaragua and Panama remained largely unexplored.

The name Costa Rica--reflecting Spanish illusions, never realized, of discovering rich deposits of gold on the Caribbean slope--was first used in 1539 to denominate the whole uncolonized area south of Cape Honduras. In the 1560s, when expeditions from Nicaragua finally began the permanent colonization of Costa Rica, the area to the

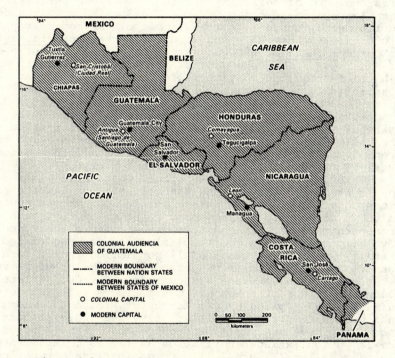

Figure 2.1 Geopolitical structure of Central America

north of the Desaguadero or River San Juan was segregated
from the province (Figure 2.2). The territory left to
Costa Rica was defined in the <u>capitulación</u> or settlement
contract signed between the king of Spain and Diego de
Artieda in 1573 and remained unaltered for the rest of the
colonial period. The province was bordered to the north
by Nicaragua and the Desaguadero, to the south by the
<u>Audiencia</u> of Panama (Sibaja 1974, 7-95).

Since the sixteenth century, Costa Rica has thus comprised a band of territory stretching between the Caribbean Sea and the Pacific Ocean. The Spanish province occupied mainly humid life zones; most of the modern republic's tropical dry zone was located in the <u>Alcaldía Mayor</u>
or <u>Corregimiento</u> of Nicoya, associated with the province
of Nicaragua. The core area of the province of Costa Rica
was the fertile, premontane Valle Central, where most
Spanish immigrants settled. This region contains the
former colonial capital, Cartago, and the city of San José,
which has been the republican capital since 1823. In
spite of its nodal location within Costa Rican territory,
the Valle Central's interior position condemned it to extreme isolation until the construction of modern modes of
overland transport in the nineteenth century.

Throughout the colonial period, Costa Rica was a minor frontier province of the Spanish empire. Lacking precious metals and a large native population, it was never a
valuable colony from an economic point of view, though its
transisthmian position enhanced its strategic importance.
Rival imperial powers, particularly Britain, recognized
that its weak defences and small population (never more
than 60,000 in the colonial period) made the province vulnerable and tried on several occasions to wrest an interoceanic corridor from Spain. Costa Rica's religious affairs were controlled by the Bishop of Nicaragua, whose
seat was in León. For administrative and judicial purposes, the province was appended to the <u>Audiencia</u> of Guatemala, which extended northwards as far as Chiapas, now a
state of Mexico (Figure 2.1). Communications between colonial officials and their superiors in Guatemala and
Spain took months or even years. The province's economic
development was severely hampered by the cumbersome administrative system of the empire. Intermittently during the
sixteenth and seventeenth centuries, Spanish settlers un-
successfully petitioned the colonial authorities to transfer Costa Rica to the <u>Audiencia</u> of Panama, where there was
a ready market for the province's agricultural produce.
When trade with Panama contracted in the late seventeenth
century, its partial replacement by contraband in the Caribbean reflected the same centrifugal tendencies (Cardoso
and Pérez 1977, 62).

The crisis in the Spanish monarchy provoked by Napo-
leonic expansion provided the opportunity for Spain's
American colonies to declare their independence. The
<u>Audiencia</u> of Guatemala became independent in 1821. In

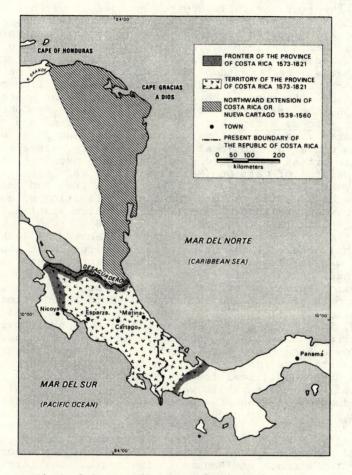

Figure 2.2   The Spanish province of Costa Rica
Sources: IGN 1972; Sibaja 1968.

Costa Rica, there was no armed struggle against the colonial authorities and the news of independence reached the remote province with several weeks' delay. The early years of independence were a period of confusion and civil strife. In 1823 and again in 1835, residents of the principal towns of the Valle Central engaged in pitched battles to determine Costa Rica's new political status and the location of its capital. After ephemeral annexation to Iturbide's Mexican empire, the former Audiencia of Guatemala became a federal republic within which each province had a jefe de estado. Costa Rica's location on the southern margin of the federation isolated her from most of the power struggles between the other member states. In 1838, the assumption of dictatorial powers by Costa Rica's jefe de estado ended municipal rivalries and consolidated a strong national government in San José, which, as the center of the local tobacco industry, was already a more important and populous town than the decadent colonial capital of Cartago (Meléndez 1977a, 183-199). In the same year, Costa Rica declared herself a free and independent state, paving the way for the proclamation of a republic when the Central American federation was finally dissolved in 1848 (Meléndez 1979a, 95-98).

The failure of the federation reflected the lack of internal coherence in the colonial institution it replaced. There was little socioeconomic integration between the provinces of the Audiencia of Guatemala. The prolonged economic depression of the seventeenth century had stifled the growth of towns and exacerbated the fragmentation and isolation of colonial settlements (Cardoso and Pérez 1977, 70-73, 151). The core areas of the five Central American republics--Guatemala, El Salvador, Honduras, Nicaragua, and Costa Rica--were but islands of settlement, separated by several days' journey through thickly forested country. Costa Rica's political frontiers were still largely uninhabited when the republic was proclaimed. As colonization proceeded during the nineteenth and twentieth centuries and the effectively occupied area of each state expanded, it became necessary to delimit precise boundaries (Meléndez 1971; Stanger 1932). Costa Rica was involved in prolonged border disputes both with Nicaragua to the north and with Colombia and Panama to the south. Her territory was not finally delimited until 120 years after independence (Figure 2.3).

In a plebiscite held in 1824, the population of the Partido of Nicoya voted in favor of annexation to Costa Rica. The peninsula had developed economic ties with Costa Rica across the Gulf of Nicoya, although the northern part of the Partido, centered on Liberia, had been colonized from the Nicaraguan town of Rivas (Meléndez 1977a, 201-211). Nicaragua resented the loss of territory. The border dispute between the two states was complicated in the midnineteenth century by controversy over delimitation of the boundary on the Caribbean slope. The area to

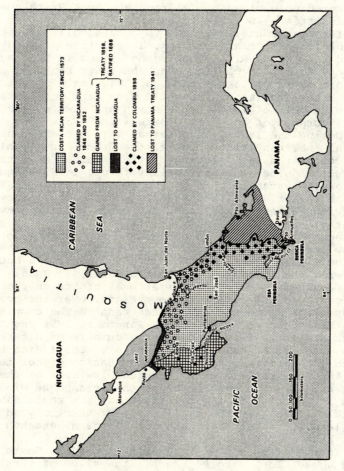

Figure 2.3 Territorial evolution of the republic of Costa Rica

Sources: IGN 1972; Sibaja 1968, 1974.

the east of Lake Nicaragua remained sparsely populated throughout the colonial period, and the frontier along the Desaguadero was undisputed. After independence, Costa Rica planned to develop navigation on the River San Juan and its tributary, the Sarapiquí, in order to export coffee from the Caribbean port of San Juan del Norte or Greytown to European markets; Nicaragua was interested in the construction of an interoceanic canal to transport passengers traveling from the eastern United States to the newly discovered gold mines of California. Both Britain and the United States also tried to establish hegemony over the transisthmian route. Nicoya, topographically unsuitable for interoceanic transport and, in practice, already integrated into Costa Rica, took second place in Nicaragua's strategy to obtain control over the River San Juan and the southern shore of Lake Nicaragua. Nicaragua's most exaggerated territorial claims would have deprived Costa Rica of a wide belt of land in the north and east of the country, incorporated into the province in 1573.

During the 1850s, an external threat to the entire Central American isthmus united the fractious republics and accelerated the solution of their border dispute. Costa Rica joined the nationalist forces in Nicaragua who opposed the establishment by the North American filibuster, William Walker, of a racist society based on slavery. Following Walker's expulsion, the two republics drew up in 1858 the Cañas-Jeréz treaty, ratified thirty years later. Nicaragua ceded Nicoya to Costa Rica in exchange for a narrow strip of land along the southern shore of the lake, for the middle course of the San Juan, and for a boundary following the southern bank of the lower San Juan. Costa Rica retained commercial navigational rights on the river, but renounced all claims to sovereignty over the port of San Juan del Norte and any future canal. The completion of interoceanic railways across Panama in 1856 and the United States in 1869 rendered the cumbersome Nicaraguan route obsolete (Sibaja 1974, 110-126). Costa Rica has probably benefited more from the extension of her territory into the fertile, dry, tropical lowlands of the northwest, capable of producing crops that cannot be widely grown in the rest of the country, than she would have received by retaining the small strip of territory adjacent to a lake and river that, since the late nineteenth century, have only been used for local traffic.

In the dispute over her southern border, Costa Rica fared worse, losing to Panama a large slice of territory containing mountains with valuable timber and mineral resources, fertile alluvial lowlands, and ports on both coasts. Until the late nineteenth century, the frontier zone between Costa Rica and Colombia (from which the independent republic of Panama was segregated in 1903) was sparsely populated and isolated from the principal regions of settlement in both republics. A series of treaties rejected by one or both governments during the nineteenth century would each have given Costa Rica considerably more territory than she eventually acquired. By 1898, Colombia, on the basis of an ephemeral colonial disposition, claimed not only the Caribbean coast of Costa Rica, but also Mosquitia to the north. Banana plantations had been established in the frontier zone, and Colombia proposed to grant land within the disputed area to the French entrepreneurs who had been contracted to build the Panama Canal. During the early decades of the twentieth century, a succession of international arbiters proposed boundaries similar to that finally established in 1941, stretching from the River Sixaola in the north to the Burica peninsula in the south (Sibaja 1968). Costa Rica retained the whole Golfo Dulce, including the magnificent natural harbor of Golfito.

Since 1941, the republic has comprised an area of 51,100 square kilometers, most of which has now been incorporated into the Hispanic American oecumene. The destruction of indigenous tribal organization and the evolution of a culturally homogeneous Hispanic American society during the long period of colonial rule laid the foundations for a nation-state that has never been challenged by ethnic minorities or centrifugal tendencies towards regional autonomy and secession. Costa Rica is small by American standards, although it exceeds in area several European states, including Belgium, Holland, Denmark, and Switzerland. Size imposes certain diseconomies of scale, but these have been offset by the diversity of the physical environment, the wide range of natural resources, and the growth of population. No part of the country is more than 200 kilometers from the sea; direct access to two oceans places Costa Rica in a very favorable position for international trade. Her relatively compact territory forms an elongated trapezoid to which are appended on the Pacific slope three peninsulas--Nicoya, Osa, and Burica-- and several small, mainly uninhabited islands, including Coco Island 293 nautical miles to the southwest of the Pacific port of Puntarenas.

As former members of the same European empire, all the Central American republics except Belize share their language, religion, and a basically Hispanic American culture, although Guatemala in particular still contains large Indian communities. In spite of this common heritage, the republics have consolidated strong national sentiments. It is highly unlikely that they will reunite in the foreseeable future to form a single state. Over the past century and a half, they have diverged both in socioeconomic development and political organization.

Costa Rica, the poorest Spanish colony, became the most prosperous independent republic. Her population enjoys a higher level of living than found in most of the neighboring countries, where there is a larger gap between rich and poor and a smaller middle class. The Central American economies, traditionally oriented towards primary

export production, have been competitive rather than complementary. Each republic established stronger economic
ties with Europe and North America than with the other
countries of the isthmus. Not until the late 1950s and
early 1960s did Guatemala, El Salvador, Honduras, Nicaragua, and Costa Rica form the Central American Common Market, conceived not only as a free trade area but also as a
unit for integrated industrial development. The market,
still in operation, has had a chequered existence and has
never pretended to promote political union.

In most of the isthmus, a conservative alliance between the upper class and the army monopolized political
power for many decades. Widespread unrest in recent years
culminated in the establishment of a Marxist government in
Nicaragua and left-wing guerrilla movements in El Salvador
and Guatemala. Costa Rica, by contrast, developed one of
the most stable parliamentary democracies, not only in Latin America, but in the whole third world. Liberal reforms in the nineteenth century strengthened the control
of the central government, reduced the power of the church,
promoted public education and a free press, and paved the
way for the establishment of political parties and a parliamentary system modeled on those of Europe and North
America, though electoral fraud and coups d'état persisted
during the first half of the twentieth century (Cardoso
and Pérez 1977, 295-318). Direct suffrage was introduced
in 1913, the secret vote in 1928, and votes for women in
1949 (S. Stone 1975, 126, 236). The administration of
Alfredo González Flores (1914-1917) made a first, premature attempt to increase the role of the state in socioeconomic development. Its proposals to establish direct
taxation provoked a reactionary coup d'état, but new political parties and groups continued during the 1920s and
1930s to advocate comprehensive reforms and, in some cases,
revolutionary change. All the governments since 1940 have
to a greater or lesser extent espoused reformismo, the
pursuit of development via reform rather than revolution.
Costa Rica has consolidated a mixed economy and one of the
most advanced welfare states in Latin America (Salazar
1981).

HISPANIC AMERICAN SOCIETY

The nature of the pre-Columbian cultures in Latin
America to a large extent determined the type of colonial
society that replaced them, establishing fundamental regional variations in the continent's geography that have
persisted to the present day. Service (1955) postulated a
threefold typology of Latin American societies: Indo-
American, in regions where there were dense populations
and sophisticated civilizations in pre-Columbian times and
where, today, large Indian communities retain their racial
and cultural identity; Mestizo-American, in regions where

smaller native populations who had attained an intermediate stage of development, characterized by tropical forest agriculture and tribal organization, were absorbed into colonial society; and Euro-American, in marginal regions where sparse populations of hunters and gatherers were virtually exterminated by white settlers. Service accepted the "myth" of Costa Rica's predominantly white population and classified it as Euro-American. Historical evidence and modern anthropological research, however, suggest that, together with the rest of southern Central America and adjacent regions in Colombia and Venezuela, Costa Rica falls rather into the category of Mestizo-American, where profound racial mixing was accompanied by the implantation of a European way of life and the development of a culturally homogeneous, Hispanic American society (Adams 1956).

The racial transformation of the population during the colonial period was the result of two processes: immigration and miscegenation. Permanent Spanish settlement in the province of Costa Rica began in the 1560s. Most of the early colonists accompanied conquistadores who had signed contracts with the Crown to pacify and settle the country (Sanabria 1977). Some had already been living in America for several years, but most were natives of Spain. Their surnames suggest that Sephardic Jews may have been prominent. Among the conquistadores were hidalgos of the provincial nobility of Spain, who quickly constituted an elite in Costa Rica. S. Stone (1975, 54-71) has argued that their descendents continued to dominate politics and economic activities until the twentieth century. Little is known about the magnitude and origin of Spanish immigration in the seventeenth and eighteenth centuries. To the prospective settler, Costa Rica was certainly one of the least attractive provinces of the empire, since it contained neither a large native population nor known deposits of precious metals. Immigrants included government officials, soldiers, and adventurers (González Víquez 1921), some of whom joined the elite descended from the conquistadores. According to colonial censuses, the white population never exceeded 10,000 (Table 2.1). The fluctuations from one census to another are probably due partly to inconsistencies in distinguishing between whites and persons of mixed blood.

The Spanish expeditions that explored and colonized America included a second immigrant group, Negro slaves, who partially replaced the dwindling Indian population. The small number and poverty of the European settlers in Costa Rica limited their capacity to purchase slaves; probably no more than a few thousand Negroes were brought to the province in the course of the colonial period. Few settlers possessed more than ten or fifteen slaves. They worked as domestic servants and artesans in the towns and as farm laborers in the countryside, particularly in the tropical zone. Colonial censuses never registered more

TABLE 2.1
Racial composition of the population during the colonial period

Year	Indians	Whites	Negroes	Total Pure Races	Mestizos	Mulattos & Zambos	Total Mixed Races
1569	17,166 (98%)	113 (1%)	30 (trace)	17,309 (99%)	--	170 (1%)	170 (1%)
1611	14,908 (96%)	330 (2%)	25 (trace)	15,263 (98%)	25 (trace)	250 (2%)	275 (2%)
1700	15,489 (76%)	2,146 (11%)	154 (1%)	17,789 (88%)	213 (1%)	2,291 (11%)	2,504 (12%)
1720	13,269 (68%)	3,059 (16%)	168 (1%)	16,496 (85%)	748 (4%)	2,193 (11%)	2,941 (15%)
1741	12,716 (53%)	4,689 (19%)	200 (1%)	17,605 (73%)	3,458 (14%)	3,065 (13%)	6,521 (27%)
1751	10,109 (42%)	7,807 (33%)	62 (trace)	17,908 (75%)	3,057 (13%)	2,987 (12%)	6,042 (25%)
1778	8,104 (24%)	6,046 (18%)	94 (trace)	14,244 (42%)	13,915 (40%)	6,053 (18%)	19,968 (58%)
1801	8,281 (16%)	4,942 (9%)	30 (trace)	13,253 (25%)	30,413 (58%)	8,925 (17%)	39,338 (75%)

Source: Thiel 1902.

than 200 Negroes (Table 2.1), but, in some years, over a hundred slaves were acquired, so census data may underestimate the number of Negroes in the eighteenth century. As a result of manumission and miscegenation, slavery was in decline before its abolition by the Central American federal assembly in 1823, when only 89 slaves remained in Costa Rica (Aguilar Bulgarelli 1973; Gudmundson 1978, 17-78; Meléndez 1967; Meléndez and Duncan 1972).

The Spaniards attempted to create a social structure based on racial segregation. Initially, there were three classes: Spanish vecinos, and servile laboring classes of Indians and Negro slaves. The spatial expression of apartheid was the establishment of exclusive settlements for each racial group (Figure 2.4a). The Indians, whose principal occupation was still agriculture, continued to be a predominantly rural population, but were forced to live in nucleated reducciones or pueblos. Spaniards inhabited a new type of settlement, the ciudad or town, whose population was predominantly nonagricultural. From the midseventeenth century onwards, suburbs known as pueblas were set aside on the margins of the towns for the colored population.

Social and spatial segregation failed to prevent miscegenation. After the decimation of the Indians, the few thousand Spanish and Negro immigrants were sufficient to transform the racial composition of the population. It was probably natural population growth and racial mixing, rather than immigration, that finally halted the demographic decline during the seventeenth century. Few European women participated in the Spanish expeditions to America. Illegal unions between conquistadores and Indian women gave rise to the first mestizos. In the principal areas of colonial settlement, economic activities brought all races together, and miscegenation produced a great variety of persons of mixed blood known collectively as the castas. The initial threefold division of colonial society was replaced by a much more complex hierarchy whose major components, in order of declining status, were peninsulares (Spaniards born in Spain); criollos (whites born in America); mestizos (descended from whites and Indians); free Negroes, mulattos (descended from whites and Negroes), and zambos (descended from Indians and Negroes); Negro and mulatto slaves; and Indians. Miscegenation in Costa Rica was but a part of the great process that took place throughout Latin America to produce, by the nineteenth century, the largest racially mixed population in the world (Mörner 1969).

The colonial censuses leave no doubt about the failure of the apartheid system (Figure 2.1). Mulattos were registered as early as 1569. In all the censuses, they greatly outnumbered pure Negroes. Many slaves were mulattos. From the early seventeenth century onwards, the censuses recorded an ever-increasing number of mestizos. No separate mention was made of zambos, but these existed,

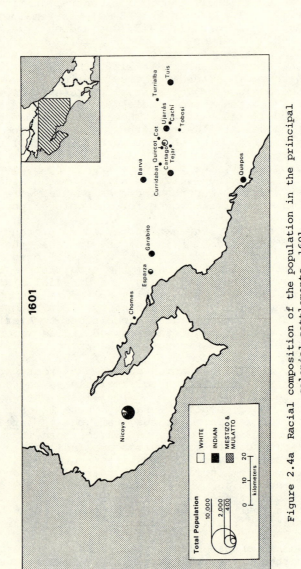

Figure 2.4a Racial composition of the population in the principal
colonial settlements, 1601

Source: Thiel 1902.

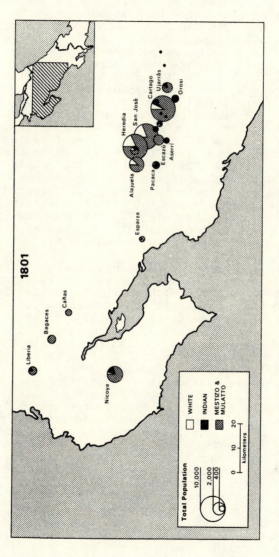

Figure 2.4b Racial composition of the population in the principal
colonial settlements, 1801

Source: Thiel 1902.

particularly in the coastal lowlands. By the third quarter of the eighteenth century, persons of mixed blood outnumbered those of the three primary races. In the census of 1801, the last of the colonial period containing a racial breakdown of the population, three-quarters of the individuals were classified as mestizo, mulatto, or zambo. Indians were still the largest primary racial group, but they now accounted for only 16 percent of the population. Fewer than one in ten Costa Ricans were of entirely Spanish descent, and pure Negroes had almost disappeared.

In the unconquered peripheral regions and the Térraba mission field, Indians still lived apart from other races. A few villages in the Valle Central were also inhabited exclusively by Indians, but most settlements were racially mixed (Figure 2.4b). Pueblos such as Barva, Tres Ríos, Ujarras, and Nicoya had substantial non-Indian populations. A recent analysis of the parish archives of Cartago shows how profound was the process of racial mixing in the province's major town: less than 6 percent of those baptized between 1771 and 1820 were white; the remainder belonged to the castas. Illegitimacy, which increased substantially during the eighteenth century, contributed to miscegenation; more than 98 percent of the illegitimate births recorded in Cartago between 1771 and 1820 involved racial mixing (Pérez Brignoli 1981a). By the end of the colonial period, mestizos and mulattos outnumbered whites in all the ciudades.

Traditional Costa Rican historiography portrayed colonial society as an impoverished but egalitarian "rural democracy," in which each family cultivated its own small farm and there were neither servants nor slaves (Monge 1974a, 146-147; Rodríguez Vega 1977, 93). Costa Rica was undoubtedly one of the poorest, most isolated and abandoned provinces in the Spanish empire, but there was incipient socioeconomic stratification of the population in the colonial period. Descendents of the earliest settlers, who had received land grants from the Crown, comprised an upper class into which some members of the colonial bureaucracy, military, and clergy were gradually assimilated. By the early nineteenth century, an embryonic middle class was also distinguishable (Fonseca Corrales 1981, 316; S. Stone 1975, 72-73). Gudmundson's (1978) detailed study of the village of Barva in 1838 has shown how wealth was concentrated in the hands of about one-quarter of the community's families, the landowners.

During the nineteenth and twentieth centuries, there was no major change in the racial composition of the Hispanic American society that had been consolidated by the end of the colonial period. After independence, the former Spanish colonies were opened to foreign immigration. Costa Rica, whose population in 1824 was 65,393 (Thiel 1902), tried in vain to emulate other sparsely populated American states that were gradually occupying their territories with European colonists. In spite of the fact that

most Costa Ricans were racially mixed, prejudice dictated
a preference for white settlers. Numerous immigration
contracts were drawn up in the nineteenth and early twentieth centuries. Some stipulated that as many as a thousand Europeans be brought to Costa Rica. Given the republic's small population, the success of these projects
would have significantly modified its culture and racial
composition. Since most of the colonists were expected to
settle in isolated, undeveloped regions of dense tropical
forest, however, Costa Rica held out few attractions in
comparison with the temperate lands of North America and
the southern cone of South America, where railways were
opening up large areas for commercial exploitation (Hall
1976a, 56-57). Europeans never comprised more than 1 percent of the population. Most arrived not under official
contracts, but as independent traders, adventurers, or
teachers. They quickly played a leading role in economic
and cultural activities and, within one or two generations,
were socially and politically integrated into the nation
(González Flores 1976). The only Europeans who immigrated
to Costa Rica primarily as manual laborers were Italians,
who worked as railway navvies in the 1880s (Stewart 1967,
75) and were easily assimilated into Hispanic American society.

The most important wave of immigration in the republican period was the influx of Negroes, who settled in the
Caribbean lowlands. In the early nineteenth century,
small groups of Negroes from Nicaragua and Panama settled
the Caribbean coast (Palmer 1977). At the turn of the
century, after the completion of the Atlantic railway,
West Indian Negroes were the principal laborers of the
North American and English companies that controlled the
plantations, transport, and export trade of the province
of Limón. The West Indians arrived as temporary migrants,
hoping soon to return with their savings to the Antilles.
In common with most groups of immigrant plantation workers,
slave or free, they were predominantly men of working age.
The poor development of family life stimulated delinquency
and prostitution and retarded natural population growth.
Until the 1920s, the Negro labor force was maintained
largely through continued immigration. The West Indians
despised Hispanic American culture and for many years had
no desire to become integrated into Costa Rican society.
The government likewise opposed assimilation of a racial
group that retained an alien culture on Costa Rican soil.
In the early twentieth century, the province of Limón was
more akin to a Caribbean island than to the highlands of
Costa Rica. English was the dominant language, and most
of the population belonged to Protestant sects. The Negro's material culture and way of life were in marked contrast to those of the Hispanic American peasant. Cassava
and yams were their staple foods; their unpainted wooden
houses on stilts owed nothing to the Costa Rican tradition
of whitewashed adobe and tile houses that predominated in

the old areas of Spanish settlement. In 1927, the 18,000
Negroes in Limón--most still registered as foreigners--ac-
counted for 56 percent of the population. Not until the
midtwentieth century did the province's population growth
rate and age and sex structure resemble that of the rest
of Costa Rica. By 1950, less than 14,000 Negroes remained.
They comprised only one-third of Limón's population. Half
were Costa Rican citizens, and the process of miscegenation with migrants from the interior of the country was
already underway (Casey 1979, 223-276; Meléndez and Duncan
1972).

Three other immigrant groups formed small ethnic minorities in the late nineteenth and early twentieth centuries. In common with other Latin American countries, notably Peru, Chile, and Cuba, Costa Rica authorized the immigration of Chinese coolies. From 1873 onwards, several
hundred Chinese worked as railway navvies and farm laborers.
Like the West Indians, they were harshly exploited (Casey
1975). In contrast to the Negroes, however, the Chinese
were not confined to the Caribbean lowlands. In 1950, of
the 933 people classified in the population census as
"yellow," 83 percent lived in the coastal provinces of
Limón, Puntarenas, and Guanacaste, and 14 percent in San
José. In all the areas where they settled, the Chinese
gradually established themselves as shopkeepers, innkeep-
ers, and restauranteurs.

Small numbers of Christian Lebanese began to settle
in Costa Rica during the 1890s, continuing a tradition of
emigration that had started in 1861 because of religious
conflict in their native country. In 1968, the Lebanese
community comprised at least 166 families; the number may
have been considerably higher. Most Lebanese immigrants
worked in the tertiary sector of the economy. Many became
wealthy traders and industrialists; some of their descendents have held high political office (S. Stone 1975, 341).

Sephardic Jews have been living in Costa Rica since
the colonial period and are entirely assimilated into Hispanic American society. Before and immediately after the
Second World War, an estimated 650-800 Askenak Jews arrived in the country as refugees from Nazi persecution in
Poland. Many originally earned their living as door-to-
door salesmen (giving rise to the local expression "pola-
queando"). Some are now prosperous traders and industrialists, and their descendents have entered the liberal professions (Schifter et al. 1979).

The proportion of foreigners in the population reached
a maximum of nearly 10 percent in 1927. By 1973, it had
fallen to less than 2 percent (Table 2.2). Whereas in
1927 more than one-third of the foreigners were Jamaicans,
at the present time, most are citizens of other Latin
American countries whose cultures are similar to that of
Costa Ricans. In 1973, Nicaraguans and Panamaneans, many
of whom work as agricultural laborers, together accounted
for 59 percent of foreign residents; since then, an

TABLE 2.2
Foreigners in the population, 1864-1973

Year	Total Population of Costa Rica	Foreigners Living in Costa Rica	Foreigners As a Percentage of the Total Population
1864	120,499	2,653	2.20
1883	182,073	4,556	2.50
1892	243,205	6,289	2.59
1927	471,524	44,340	9.40
1950	870,875	34,821	4.00
1963	1,336,274	30,128	2.25
1973	1,871,780	34,857	1.86

Sources: DGEC 1885, 1893, 1953a, 1960, 1966a, 1974a.

estimated 3,000 Chileans, some of whom are political exiles, have settled in the country. The largest non-
Hispanic group are United States citizens, who accounted
for 8 percent of the foreigners registered in 1973. They
include employees of multinational companies and pension-
ers who have taken advantage of legislation passed in 1965
to attract settlers with regular, hard currency incomes
(Schmidt 1979).

Except locally for the West Indian Negroes, none of
the immigrant groups that arrived after independence was
sufficiently large to effect any significant change in the
racial composition of the population. Only two censuses
of the republican period, those of 1927 and 1950, recorded
race (Table 2.3). Data were published only by province,
precluding detailed mapping. Pure Indians had been reduced to a very small minority, although their numbers may
have been underestimated. They were confined mainly to
isolated, sparsely populated, peripheral regions: the Guatuso plain in the north and the Cordillera de Talamanca
and adjacent valleys in the south. Pure Negroes, descended from West Indian immigrants, lived mainly in the province of Limón on the Caribbean lowlands. Both censuses
classified the majority of the population as white or mestizo. In 1927, an attempt was made to distinguish between
them. 80 percent of the population was classified as
white, but this group probably included many mestizos and
mulattos. In 1950, whites and mestizos (the latter term
being used to describe all those of mixed blood) were
placed in a single category that comprised 98 percent of
the population. Because all Costa Ricans, regardless of
their color, are equal citizens before the law, the population censuses taken since 1950 have not included data on
race.

TABLE 2.3
Racial composition of the population, 1927 and 1950

| Racial Group | 1927 | | 1950 | |
	Number of People	Percentage	Number of People	Percentage
Indians	4,197	0.89	2,692	0.33
Whites	377,994	80.16	782,041	97.65
Mestizos	66,612	14.13		
Negroes	19,136	4.06	15,118	1.89
"Yellows"	3,585	0.76	933	0.12
Others			91	0.01
TOTAL	471,524	100.00	800,875	100.00

Sources: DGEC 1953a, 1960.

Modern anthropological research confirms that Costa Rica has a triracial population, although the evidence concerning the contribution of each primary race is conflicting. On the basis of blood groups, P. O. Roberts (1978) has calculated that the population is approximately 40 percent European, 48 percent Negro, and 12 percent Indian in origin. Physical traits, however, suggest that typically Negro blood groups are overrepresented. Most Costa Ricans are probably of mixed blood, descended from two or three of the primary races present since the sixteenth century.

The significant and interesting outcome of four centuries of miscegenation is that both Costa Ricans themselves and many foreign scholars (Waibel 1939) have regarded the population as "white" because its culture is derived almost entirely from European, and more recently, North American models. With the exception of some Indians, Negroes, and Askenak Jews, all Costa Ricans are Hispanic Americans, irrespective of whether their ancestors were Indian, European, or Negro. Whereas in many former colonies in Asia and Africa European culture is but a veneer superimposed on traditional values and ways of life, in Costa Rica Spanish colonialism largely destroyed both the native cultures and those of the Negro slaves. Indian and Negro beliefs and languages virtually disappeared. Today, use of the Spanish language is almost universal and nominal adherence to Roman Catholicism very widespread. Traditional material cultures were replaced by European costume, architecture, and artefacts. Spain is revered as the Madre Patria, though few Costa Ricans today have family ties

in Europe; most belong to families born and bred for many
generations in the tropics. Imperial Spain tried to prevent intellectual and commercial contacts between her colonies and foreign countries, but in practice they occurred,
particularly towards the end of the colonial period. Contraband trade flourished in the circum-Caribbean region,
and the ideas of the Enlightenment circulated in eighteenth-
century Central America (Meléndez 1970). After independence, England replaced Spain as Costa Rica's economic and
financial metropolis, and France provided the model for
the republic's legal code and educational system. The
diffusion from the industrial countries of scientific and
technological achievements--mass-produced factory goods,
new modes of transport and communications, new sources of
energy, and advances in medicine and public health--played
a major role in the modernization of Costa Rica during the
nineteenth and twentieth centuries. In recent decades,
North American patterns of consumption have permeated many
sectors of society. The model of a dual society, composed
of a native and a Europeanized sector, has little application to contemporary Costa Rica. Modes of thought, systems of values, and patterns of behavior are culturally
homogeneous, varying if at all according to economic status and social class and between the urban and rural population (Seligson 1977).

The small groups retaining traits of distinctive minority cultures probably constitute no more than 2 percent
of the population, though their spatial concentration
makes them locally more important. All are gradually becoming assimilated into Hispanic American society. The
future of the surviving Indian communities is uncertain;
racial mixing and acculturation is taking place to a
greater or lesser extent in all the reserves. Most of the
Negroes in Limón province are today Spanish-speaking,
Costa Rican citizens (Meléndez and Duncan 1972). Hispanic
American migration into the Caribbean lowlands has accelerated miscegenation and acculturation in the core area of
West Indian settlement. Within a few generations, the
second wave of Negro immigrants may become as profoundly
absorbed into the Hispanic American population as are the
descendents of the colonial slaves. The descendents of
the Chinese, Lebanese, and Askenak Jewish immigrants speak
Spanish and are economically indistinguishable from other
Costa Ricans. The Lebanese and Chinese have intermarried
with Hispanic Americans. The Askenaks are a more endoga-
mous social group, adhering to Jewish religion and customs.
It remains to be seen whether the incipient process of in-
termarriage and the incorporation of Jews into the professional classes will eventually lead to their complete acculturation (Schifter et al. 1979).

Although contemporary Costa Rican society is largely
free of the racial tensions besetting so many former European colonies and is less polarized than many other Latin
American republics, it nevertheless contains well-defined

classes, all of which are racially mixed and culturally
Hispanic American. Between 5 and 7 percent of the population belongs to the upper class, which S. Stone (1975) has
defined primarily by its family ties and its access to
power via the principal political parties. This group includes large landowners, industrialists, and members of
the liberal professions. Many members of the upper class
are very rich, but social prestige is usually unaffected
by economic misfortune. The middle class, embracing about
15 percent of the population, is one of the most dynamic
groups in Latin America. It lacks close family bonds with
the upper class, but enjoys a higher level of living than
does the lower class. It includes small farmers and busi-
nessmen, office workers, and poorly paid professional
groups. Both the upper and middle classes are concentrated in the towns, particularly the metropolitan area of San
José. The rest of the population still belongs to the
lower class and is engaged mainly in manual labor in both
urban and rural areas (Biesanz and Zubris 1979, 231-260;
S. Stone 1975, 196-200).

ECONOMIC UNDERDEVELOPMENT

     Costa Rica's incorporation into the world economic
system as the colony of a mercantilist European empire
initiated the long process of underdevelopment that has
persisted to the present day. From the moment of its discovery by Columbus in 1502, Costa Rica, the Rich Coast,
was famed as a region of great mineral wealth. Lured by
the Indians' gold and copper ornaments, the Spaniards
searched avidly for mines and placers. They had virtually
no geological knowledge of the country and relied mainly
on bullying the Indians into leading them to sources of
precious metals. The Cordillera de Tilarán and the Cerros
de Abangares contain veins of auriferous quartz, but these
were unknown to the Indians who obtained gold by trade and
from small placers in the south of the country. The Spaniards never discovered any mineral resources of commercial
value. Nor did Costa Rica contain a large native labor
force to produce exotic tropical crops for export to Europe. Although the early Spanish explorers were able to
acquire food from the Indians by amicable barter and the
Nicoya peninsula provided supplies for the expeditions into the Valle Central, the conquistadores in the interior
of Costa Rica were reduced by the 1560s to pillaging the
natives' crops and were soon obliged to take up farming
themselves. Isolated, sparsely populated, and abandoned
by the colonial authorities, the province was one of the
poorest in America. Most of its production was destined
for subsistence consumption. Exports were limited to agricultural commodities sold officially to other Spanish
colonies in America and illegally to English smugglers in
the Caribbean (Brenes Castillo 1978).

Neighboring Panama, which contained the principal transisthmian route between the Atlantic and Pacific oceans, was the earliest market for Costa Rican goods, and the province would probably have enjoyed greater prosperity had it belonged to the Audiencia of Panama instead of constituting the remote southern frontier of the Audiencia of Guatemala (Facio 1972, 29). During the sixteenth and seventeenth centuries, biscuits, flour, maize, onions, garlic, pigs, chickens, tallow, suet, and hides were exported in small quantities for sale to the resident population and visiting ships' crews in Panama. Costa Rica was also an important intermediary in the overland mule trade that provided animals for transisthmian transport; mules bred in Honduras and Nicaragua stopped for grazing in the Valle Central en route to Panama, and Costa Rica was authorized to levy a tax on each animal traversing the province. Trade with Panama decreased during the seventeenth century as a result of overgrazing and indiscriminate slaughtering on Costa Rican cattle ranches, pirate attacks on the boats transporting provisions, the economic depression, which reduced the volume of international trade in Panama, and, above all, the growth of agriculture along the coast of Peru, which by about 1680 had replaced Costa Rica as the major supplier to Panama (Macleod 1973, 274-275).

The declining provisions trade was partially compensated for by a new activity: specialized production of tropical and subtropical crops. During the seventeenth and eighteenth centuries, cocoa (Theobroma cacao) was grown in the Caribbean lowlands. The crop's official market was the neighboring province of Nicaragua, to which it was transported by expensive mule trains; however, in practice, much of the harvest found its way into British hands as a result of piracy and contraband in the Caribbean (Rosés 1975). A second cash crop, tobacco (Nicotiana tobacum), was grown in the Valle Central. In 1766, the colonial authorities established an estanco under which they controlled tobacco cultivation and marketing. The industry reached its zenith between 1787 and 1792, when Costa Rica was the monopoly supplier to the whole of the Audiencia of Guatemala. Except for this brief period, Costa Rican tobacco was sold only within the province and to the Factoría in León, Nicaragua (Acuña Ortega 1978). Neither the cocoa nor the tobacco industries sustained a flourishing export economy. They were hampered by labor shortages, Spanish prohibitions on sales to external markets, the competition of better-quality crops produced in other colonies, isolation, and the expense and delays of overland transport by mule. Both industries were in decline by the end of the colonial period. They were, nevertheless, the precursors of the agro-export economy Costa Rica consolidated after independence (Vega 1980a, 21-35). They generated some internal capital accumulation, and the income from its monopoly of tobacco sales sustained the

Costa Rican government until the midnineteenth century, providing funds for public works (Araya 1981; Cardoso and Pérez 1977).

Ironically, Costa Rica achieved political independence before she consolidated a typically colonial economy of desarrollo hacia afuera (or externally oriented development) based on the export of one or two primary products and the import of a wide range of manufactured goods and raw materials. Costa Rica's relatively early stabilization of republican government, and her very condition as one of the least developed and emptiest areas of Latin America--unhampered by the social and economic problems of large Indian communities or former slave populations--enabled her to be one of the first countries of the continent to establish a neocolonial export economy (Cardoso and Pérez 1977, 145; Halperín 1970, 160).

Immediately after independence, gold, which had proved so elusive to the Spaniards, appeared to be the most promising export commodity. The veins in the Cerros de Aguacate were discovered in 1815 and mined during the 1820s and 1830s. Although technology was primitive and many of the mines were soon abandoned because of flooding and exhaustion, the value of the gold extracted probably reached 7 to 8 million pesos, a large sum at that time and an internal source of capital for the future development of export agriculture. Gold mining was one of the first activities in which foreign immigrants were important entrepreneurs; many of them subsequently moved into coffee production. The first mining cycle, however, occurred too early to attract large quantities of British capital (still being used primarily to finance the industrial revolution at home), and the political instability of the Central American federation also deterred foreign investment (Araya 1973).

Subtropical and tropical crops, of which coffee (Coffea sp.) and bananas (Musa sapientum) were by far the most important, replaced minerals as the major items of foreign trade, and the impact of the agro-export economy on land use and spatial organization has persisted to the present day. Export crops occupied many of the most fertile and accessible lands, often as monocultures. The desire to open up new lands for coffee and banana production was one of the driving forces behind agricultural colonization after independence. Much of the modern transport network was designed to link areas of export agriculture to coastal ports, neglecting the need to interconnect different regions within the country.

Coffee, a subtropical crop cultivated in the premontane zone, emerged in the 1840s as the country's principal export commodity. Neither railways nor steam navigation had yet reached Central America; processed coffee had the advantage of being an unperishable commodity that could withstand slow and costly transport by ox cart and sailing ship. It found a ready market in western Europe, particularly Britain and Germany, and for nearly fifty years was, virtually, Costa Rica's only export. In common with most of the early export sectors in Latin America (Sunkel and Paz 1973, 320), coffee production remained largely in national hands. The major cafetaleros were descended from important colonial families (S. Stone 1975, 74). Their modest capital, accumulated from earlier activities such as the production of cocoa, tobacco, and gold, was invested in the new export industry. Advance payments from importing houses in Europe and North America provided a complementary source of finance to exporters and millers, who in turn supplied credit to the small growers whose harvest they handled (Cardoso 1973; Hall 1976a, 33-39). The coffee processors and exporters formed an elite within the industry, but they never established a monopoly over the cultivation of the crop. The volume of coffee exported fluctuated considerably from year to year, reflecting variations in harvest yields, but the overall trend from the midnineteenth to the midtwentieth centuries was a gradual increase in output, achieved mainly by expanding the area under cultivation (Figure 2.5). After 1950, cultivation was intensified and the volume of exports tripled (Hall 1976a, 152-166).

In the late nineteenth century, bananas, grown in the tropical moist and wet life zones, were established as a second export crop sold mainly to the United States. Since bananas are highly perishable, their production relied on rail transport within Costa Rica and refrigerated steamships to carry the fruit to foreign markets. Some of the early plantations were established with Costa Rican capital, but, in contrast to the coffee sector where the role of Britain and other countries was limited to indirect financing, North American capital controlled production in the banana industry. First the United Fruit Company and then other multinational corporations established a vertically integrated industry, controlling transport and marketing and cultivating a substantial proportion of the crop. Exports began in the 1870s and rose sharply during the late nineteenth and early twentieth centuries, until by 1905 bananas were earning more foreign exchange than coffee and Costa Rica was producing one-fifth of the fruit entering world trade (Casey 1979). Since bananas were harvested throughout the year, they were less susceptible than coffee to annual fluctuations in yields. In the longer term, however, they proved to be an unstable crop. The Gros Michel variety, cultivated until the midtwentieth century, was vulnerable to Panama disease (Fusarium oxysporum f. cubense) and Sigatoka (Mycosphaerella musicola), which wiped out whole regions of plantations. The sharp reduction in the volume of exports during the second quarter of the twentieth century reflects the time lag between the decline and eventual abandonment of production on the Caribbean lowlands, and the establishment of new plantations on the Pacific lowlands. The

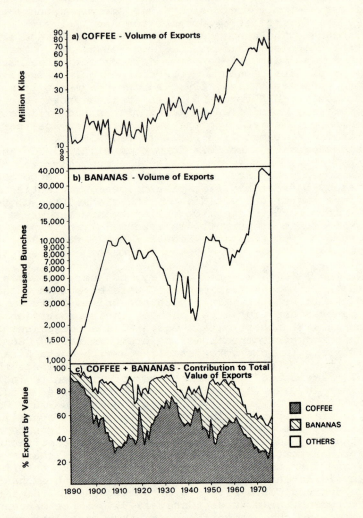

Figure 2.5 Exports of coffee and bananas, 1890–1977

Source: DGEC

control of Sigatoka by crop spraying and the introduction
of the high-yielding Giant Cavendish variety, resistant to
Panama disease, permitted a vast redevelopment of banana
cultivation in the Caribbean lowlands during the second
half of the twentieth century. The volume of exports increased approximately seven times during the 1960s and
1970s, an increase even more dramatic than that of coffee.

No other export product seriously challenged the hegemony of coffee and bananas until the 1960s. Gold and
silver mining was temporarily revived at the turn of the
century in the Cerros de Abangares, geologically a continuation of the Cerros de Aguacate. Local entrepreneurs
were quickly replaced by North American investors. At the
height of production during the second decade of the twentieth century, gold accounted in some years for 10 percent
of the value of exports. By the 1930s, as a result both
of the depression and the exhaustion of easily accessible
veins, the second mining cycle came to an end (Araya 1977).
For a short time during and immediately after the First
World War, Costa Rica exported small quantities of manganese, used in the fabrication of steel for armaments.
Manganese was mined in the Nicoya peninsula by a Costa
Rican and North American company that installed an elementary infrastructure of rails and wharves, now derelict
(R. Roberts 1944). Sugar and cocoa made sporadic contri-
butions to foreign trade. During the Second World War,
when the Japanese occupation cut off traditional sources
of supply in Southeast Asia, North American companies cultivated the quinine tree (Cinchona sp.) at Vara Blanca in
the Cordillera Central, and rubber (Hevea brasiliensis)
and Manila hemp (Musa textilis) in the Caribbean lowlands
on abandoned banana lands. After the war, the plantations
quickly became uneconomical, and all three crops were
abandoned (L. E. Peterson 1947, 41-55; Stouse 1970). Not
until after the slump in coffee prices in 1958 did sugar,
beef, and to a lesser extent cocoa finally diversify primary exports. In 1976, these three commodities accounted
for 13 percent of the value of exports, and the share of
coffee and bananas had declined to 53 percent.

A corollary of export agriculture, in Costa Rica as
in many other underdeveloped countries, was the relegation
of food production to areas both ecologically and economically marginal. Coffee replaced food crops and stock
rearing in the Valle Central. Both coffee and bananas occupied accessible, newly colonized lands, also suitable
ecologically for grains, root crops, fruits, and vegetables. Home-produced wheat was replaced entirely by imported supplies. Other basic food crops survived the establishment of the coffee economy, but cultivation methods
were primitive and harvests unreliable. From the midnineteenth century onwards, there was a series of subsistence crises. In many years, Costa Rica imported substantial quantities of rice, beans, maize, animal fats, and
vegetable oils that could have been produced at home

(Cardoso and Pérez 1977, 270-272; Facio 1972, 109-126; May et al. 1952, 44-47).

Local manufacturing was also stifled by the agro-export economy. England was the major supplier, not only of machinery and tools for the coffee industry, but also of a wide range of consumer goods, particularly textiles (Vega 1980a, 119-120). In the midnineteenth century, with the exception of the national liquor factory in San José, manufacturing was carried out entirely by artesans, seam-stresses being the largest single group. Some small factories were in operation by the turn of the century, but they produced only a limited range of consumer goods such as soap, candles, cigarettes, brooms, shoes, soft drinks, and bricks (Samper 1979, 90, 137).

The second half of the nineteenth century was never-theless a period of progress and economic growth. Cart roads were constructed, a postal service was established, domestic comforts multiplied, and towns were embellished (González Flores 1974). Small farmers grew a substantial share of the coffee crop, and export production gave rise to many ancillary activities such as cart building, iron-mongery, transport, and communications. Not only, there-fore, did the new industry provide a solid economic base for the upper class, it also enabled the majority of the population to raise their level of living (Facio 1972, 46-47; Vega 1980a, 94).

Heavy reliance on one or two exports, however, ex-poses any country to the risks of economic depression and ecological hazards. Small nations, unable to dominate the world markets of the commodities they produce, are parti-cularly vulnerable (Selwyn 1975, 8-10). Recurrent crises in the coffee economy culminated in a prolonged period of depression between 1897 and 1907, when overproduction in Brazil, the world's leading producer, glutted the market and greatly reduced prices (Cardoso 1973). The early twentieth century has been interpreted as the turning point, when the agro-export economy ceased to bring con-tinuous growth and prosperity to Costa Rica. Export pro-duction failed to keep pace with population growth, which found an outlet in the subsistence economy of frontier colonization (Sáenz Pacheco 1969, 42-48). The world de-pression that began in 1929 affected Costa Rica still more severely than the crisis at the turn of the century. Cof-fee prices again descended rapidly, not fully recovering until after the Second World War. Disease hit the banana industry, and output did not surpass the previous record harvest of 1913 until 1952.

There were no major changes in the structure of the economy, however, until the second half of the twentieth century, when successive governments adopted a policy of desarrollo hacia adentro (or internally oriented develop-ment) in an attempt to lessen the country's dependence on international trade. Three principal factors encouraged the establishment of modern manufacturing industries.

First, the sharp decline in coffee prices from 1958 reduced the ability to import manufactured goods. Second, there were fears of rising unemployment since the crisis in the agro-export economy coincided with very high rates of population growth; with full employment, the population explosion could be turned into an advantage, since it led to a rapid expansion of the potential home market for industrial goods. Third, progress had been made during the 1950s towards integrating the economies of the five Central American republics, excluding Panama. Guatemala and El Salvador had already begun a process of industrialization, and Costa Rica would have been at a disadvantage had she not followed suit. An initial free trade agreement was signed in 1958, and Costa Rica became a full member of the Central American Common Market in 1963 (Carvajal et al. 1977a, 91; Weisenfeld 1969). Most of the factories established during the 1960s and 1970s produced consumer goods for home and Central American markets. Between 1950 and 1973, the secondary sector of the economy gradually increased its contribution to employment and GNP, and by 1973 manufactured goods accounted for one-quarter of the value of exports (Table 2.4). The decline in the import of consumer goods, however, was less than the increase in that of capital goods, industrial raw materials, and semi-finished products. The impact of desarrollo hacia adentro was smaller than had been anticipated, and the most rapid expansion in both GNP and employment occurred in the tertiary rather than in the secondary sector of the economy.

Costa Rica's basic role within the world economy remains that of a primary commodity producer. The volume of international trade has risen sharply in recent years. Its composition is typical of a developing country: exports are dominated by a small number of primary products whereas imports are extremely diverse, ranging from foodstuffs and raw materials to finished manufactured goods (Figure 2.6). Commerce with Spain is insignificant, but

TABLE 2.4
Structure of the economy, 1950, 1963, and 1973

Economic Sector	GNP (%)			Employment (%)			Value of Exports (%)	
	1	2	3	1	2	3	Primary Products	Manufactured Goods
1950	45.00	11.42	43.58	55.00	15.26	29.74	99.25	0.75
1963	26.76	12.80	60.44	49.44	17.37	33.19	94.61	5.39
1973	22.28	15.88	61.84	36.70	18.62	44.68	74.83	25.17

Sources: BCCR 1963, 1978; DGEC 1953a, 1953c, 1964a, 1966a, 1974a, 1974e.

80

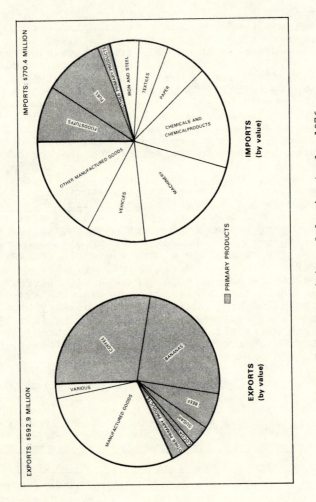

IMPORTS: $770 4 MILLION

OTHER PRIMARY PRODUCTS
IRON AND STEEL
TEXTILES
PAPER
FUEL
FOODSTUFFS
CHEMICALS AND CHEMICALPRODUCTS
OTHER MANUFACTURED GOODS
VEHICLES
MACHINERY

IMPORTS
(by value)

PRIMARY PRODUCTS

EXPORTS: $592 9 MILLION

COFFEE
VARIOUS
BANANAS
BEEF
SUGAR
COCOA
OTHER PRIMARY PRODUCTS
MANUFACTURED GOODS

EXPORTS
(by value)

Figure 2.6 Composition of foreign trade, 1976
Source: DGEC 1978.

industrialized countries are still Costa Rica's major
trading partners (Figure 2.7). The principal markets for
coffee and bananas are the developed countries of the temperate latitudes, from which manufactured goods are imported. Trade with other developing countries is limited
mainly to the interchange of consumer goods within the
Central American Common Market and to the purchase of petroleum from Mexico and Venezuela.

ECOLOGICAL CHANGES

The consolidation of the colonial economic system im-
plied fundamental changes in the relationship between man
and the land. The pre-Columbian communities produced
mainly for their own subsistence, trading by barter to acquire items such as dyes, metals, or salt unobtainable in
their immediate environment. The colonies of imperial
Spain, in addition to maintaining the surviving Indian
population, had to support the intruding settlers and produce commodities for export to other parts of the empire.
Costa Rica's native economy of shifting cultivation, hunting, gathering, and fishing was unable to comply with
these demands upon its output. Its gradual replacement by
more intensive systems of production led to profound ecological changes.
The Spaniards in America pioneered European settlement in the tropics. Whereas previous European expansion
overseas, notably by the Portuguese, had been concerned
mainly with the establishment of coastal trading stations,
the Spaniards in the sixteenth century settled extensive
areas in the tropical and subtropical latitudes of the New
World. Although they failed effectively to occupy the
whole of the immense territories they claimed within their
empire, they nevertheless transformed the landscape in
many parts of America and introduced alien ecological concepts that have persisted to the present day.
In Costa Rica, the Spaniards were confronted with a
natural environment totally different from that of their
homeland and with patterns of settlement and land use with
which they were wholly unfamiliar. Nearly all of Costa
Rica is wetter than any part of Spain. There is no pronounced seasonal variation in temperature. In much of the
country, there is no marked dry season either. Whereas in
Spain land use had to be adapted to draught, most of Costa
Rica is too wet for the types of farming suited to the
Iberian Peninsula. Costa Rica's topography is, on the
whole, much more rugged than that of Spain. The problem
of soil erosion (by no means absent in Spain) are exacerbated in Costa Rica by the combination of irregular topography and torrential rain. When the Spaniards arrived in
America, Costa Rica was almost entirely covered with forest. Patches of manmade savanna and scattered, temporary
clearings for cultivation occupied only a fraction of the

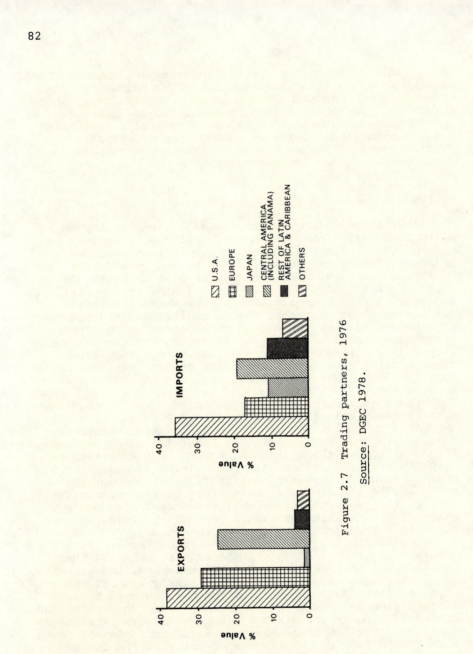

Figure 2.7 Trading partners, 1976

Source: DGEC 1978.

country. The luxuriance of the forests belied the inherent infertility of many of the soils. The Indians solved this problem with their system of shifting cultivation: as yields declined after one or two harvests, crop land was allowed to revert to forest and a new patch was cleared for cultivation. In this way, both soil exhaustion and soil erosion were controlled. The forest, in addition to protecting the soil, contained wild plants and animals that, together with fish and shellfish, provided the Indians with valuable sources of protein, compensating for the absence of stock rearing in pre-Columbian America. Pasture, which covered so large a part of late medieval Spain, had no place in the indigenous ecosystem of Costa Rica. Root crops and palm fruits, not grains, were the staple foodstuffs. There was no specialized commercial farming on the scale of Spanish sheep rearing; Indian polyculture was designed principally to produce a wide variety of subsistence crops.

The Spaniards were well aware of these enormous differences between their homeland and the province of Costa Rica. Like other European imperialists, however, they regarded the native systems of land use in their tropical colonies as backward and primitive and embarked upon the process that has been aptly described as "ecological colonialism": the replacement of the indigenous ecosystem by their own farming systems and by patterns of land use adapted to the dry, warm, temperate zone, but alien to the humid tropics (Varese 1973).

Central to this process were fundamental changes regarding access to the land. In the pre-Columbian system of shifting cultivation, each community had access to a large area of forest. When the Spaniards took possession of Costa Rica, all land became the property of the Crown. The reduced extent of the village lands over which the Indians retained communal rights obliged them to become permanent cultivators. Following the Spanish tradition, pastures and stubble were initially designated as public lands; in practice, many were gradually appropriated as private property. During the second half of the sixteenth century, the monarch distributed to the first generation of Spanish settlers solares, or building plots on which to construct their houses in the towns, and mercedes of individual grants of land in the surrounding rural areas for the development of farms. In 1591, the colonial authorities established the system of composiciones, whereby colonists could acquire legal title to farmland on payment to the Crown. Expense and bureaucratic problems deterred many settlers from making composiciones, but the lands they occupied were treated as private property and changed hands via sales and inheritances (Fonseca Corrales 1981, 33-89; Meléndez 1977a, 21-46). At independence in 1821, unoccupied realengas or royal lands became tierras baldías belonging to the state. As Hispanic American settlement expanded during the nineteenth and twentieth centuries, vast areas of _tierras baldías_ were appropriated by individual colonists. Today, with the exceptions of the Indian reserves, of the public lands retained by the state, and of a small number of collective farms, land tenure throughout Costa Rica is based on the concept of private property.

The Spaniards established farming systems that, in modified forms, have survived to the present day. They included variants on those systems already developed in the Iberian Peninsula, as well as new colonial systems. Meléndez (1977a, 65-98) has postulated a threefold typology of the farming systems established in the colonial period. The _chacra_ was a peasant farm producing a variety of crops and animals, mainly for subsistence consumption. It gradually evolved into a variety of subtypes, differing in size and land use. Some family farms were fragmented by inheritance, creating subfamily _minifundios_; others were enlarged, usually by piecemeal purchases, to form medium-sized farms employing wage labor. During the nineteenth and twentieth centuries, _chacras_ were transformed from predominantly subsistence to predominantly commercial enterprises, producing for both home and export markets. The second system was the hacienda, a large estate that in more densely settled parts of the Spanish empire contained both arable and pasture land, but in the sparsely populated province of Costa Rica was devoted almost entirely to extensive cattle ranching. After independence, haciendas were widely established throughout the peripheries of the country, but the system underwent few fundamental structural changes until the second half of the twentieth century. The plantation was the most novel Hispanic American farming system, designed for intensive, specialized production of tropical and subtropical commodities that could not be produced in the metropolis. The colonial plantation, which generally relied on slave labor, was weakly developed in Costa Rica. After independence, plantations using free labor became important producers of export crops.

All these farming systems involved permanent cultivation and, therefore, for the first time in Costa Rica, widespread deforestation. The Spaniards introduced iron agricultural implements, which were more efficacious than the native stone and wooden tools. Iron axes were particularly valuable for felling trees. The land was then cleared and cultivated with machetes and hoes, although there was little use of ploughs (Meléndez 1953, 19-33). The felled timber was used, if at all, for firewood and construction materials; a product as heavy and bulky as tropical hardwood could never become a major export commodity at a time when overland transport in Costa Rica was effected by mules and potential European markets could be reached only by sailing vessels. Much of the timber was either burned or left to rot on the ground. Since the rate of land clearance during the colonial period was very slow, the remaining natural forests ensured ample supplies of timber. There was no reforestation, and forestry was never incorporated into Hispanic American farming systems.

Agricultural colonization accelerated after independence. There were few prior scientific studies of the natural environment. Many potential resources remained unexplored, but those that were utilized were often exploited with a mining mentality. While a small population occupied only a fraction of the national territory, few people were conscious of the need to protect and conserve resources that are renewable if properly managed. When the output of timber and crops in one area declined, the natural forests and virgin soils of yet another frontier of colonization were brought under production (Vogt 1946).

Indiscriminate deforestation on steep slopes and in areas of heavy rainfall created grave ecological problems. The forests regulated the water supply to the drainage system and protected the soil from erosion. When the forest was removed, less water was stored in the vegetation, and moisture quickly evaporated from the exposed soil surface. Soil erosion in the upper parts of river basins produced heavy sedimentation along the lower courses of rivers. Surface run-off, transporting eroded topsoil, increased during the rainy season, sometimes to the point of causing floods in the lower parts of drainage basins. In the dry season, with rapidly diminished run-off, rivers and streams were reduced to a trickle and soils exposed to eolian erosion by the strong trade winds. Ecologists estimate that serious erosion by water and wind now affects at least 30 percent of Costa Rica (Tosi 1974).

Hispanic American farmers exploited a much narrower range of natural resources than did their Indian predecessors. Hunting, gathering, and freshwater fishing paled into insignificance as the natural flora and fauna were depleted. The Spaniards imitated the land use of their homeland with relatively few concessions to the tropical environment. They adopted the native maize and beans, being familiar in Europe with the cultivation of grains and legumes, but the principal Indian foodstuffs of Costa Rica, such as pejibayes, cassava, and a wide variety of other root crops, fruits, and vegetables, were largely ignored by Hispanic American cultivators. Plants such as the olive and vine failed to prosper even in the driest parts of Costa Rica, but other Spanish crops were successfully cultivated in the center and northwest of the country where the alternating wet and dry seasons most nearly resembled Mediterranean conditions. Wheat was one of the principal crops in the Valle Central until its displacement by coffee in the nineteenth century (Meléndez 1977a, 99-127). Rice, sugar cane, bananas, and citrus fruits, plants that had been diffused by the Arabs from Asia to the Iberian Peninsula, were in turn cultivated by the Spaniards in their American colonies. Arabica coffee, native to Ethiopia and first domesticated in Arabia, was introduced into Costa Rica from the Antilles in the late

TABLE 2.5
Area sown in Old World crops, 1973

Crop	Area in Hectares	Percentage of Total Crop Area (excluding fallows)
Grains		
Rice	65,458.4	17.90
Sorghum	3,752.5	1.03
Fruit and vegetables		
Plantains	6,429.1	1.76
Guineos	3,507.1	0.96
Vegetables[1]	890.0	0.24
Oranges	408.9	0.11
Cash crops		
Coffee	83,406.8	22.81
Sugar cane	38,762.9	10.60
Bananas	36,154.9	9.89
Coconuts	1,088.6	0.30
TOTAL	239,859.2	65.60

Source: DGEC (1976b)

[1]Includes garlic, onions, lettuce, carrots, cabbages, beetroot, and French beans.

eighteenth century (Grigg 1974, 26-33). These crops were grown on a small scale for local consumption during the colonial period. Rice is now a staple food; coffee, bananas, and, to a lesser extent, sugar cane were developed as export crops after independence. In 1973, Old World plants occupied approximately two-thirds of the crop areas (Table 2.5).

Still more profound were the ecological changes resulting from the introduction of domestic animals, which replaced wild game as the principal source of meat. The Spanish expeditions that entered Costa Rica from Nicaragua in the 1560s and 1570s brought cattle, horses, donkeys, pigs, goats, and chickens. Many were slaughtered to provide emergency food supplies, but enough survived to form the basis of the new stock-rearing industry (Jiménez Oreamuno 1931). Sheep farming, the most important livestock industry in medieval Spain, was never successfully established in the humid tropics. Pigs and chickens were largely confined to the peasant subsistence economy. Cattle rearing, on the other hand, was one of the principal economic activities of colonial Costa Rica, and, for the first time, pastures were a dominant feature of the landscape. Even the pacified Indian communities kept small

herds of cattle (Chacón de Umaña 1974). Draught animals
such as mules, oxen, and horses were the basis of colonial
modes of overland transport and provided energy for simple
agricultural processing plants such as sugar trapiches.
Animal traction is still important in the more isolated
areas. In recent decades, beef cattle ranching has expanded into a major industry. Pasture now occupies half
the farm area and one-third of Costa Rican territory (DGEC
1974b).

The replacement of forest by extensive, manmade savannas used as rough cattle pastures--a process still taking place in peripheral regions--causes profound, probably
irreversible, ecological changes. Savanna soils contain
much less humus than forest soils, which are regularly replenished with abundant leaf litter and twigs. They also
contain fewer of the invertebrates that preserve porosity
in the soil. Water infiltrates more easily into forest
than savanna soils, which are compacted by the trampling
of cattle. The greater surface run-off on savannas contributes to rapid rises in stream and river levels during
and after aguaceros; conversely, in dry weather, savanna
soils crack and dry out to greater depths than forest
soils. Perhaps the most significant change of all is the
acceleration of erosion on savannas, even on gentle slopes.
From the evidence of pedestaled plants in a savanna with a
9 percent slope near Cañas, Guanacaste, Daubenmire (1972)
calculated that 11 centimeters of topsoil had been lost in
just twenty-two years following forest clearance.

The "grain and pasture" system the Spaniards introduced into Costa Rica is best suited to flat and undulating lands in the life zones close to the unity line of
evapotranspiration. In the center and northwest of the
country, beef cattle, maize, rice, and sorghum can be produced in the tropical zone, and dairy cattle, maize, and
wheat in the premontane and lower montane zones. When
Hispanic American colonists in the nineteenth and twentieth centuries introduced this type of farming into more
humid life zones and rugged, mountainous areas, severe
ecological restrictions were encountered. In regions
where there was heavy rainfall throughout the year, constant leaching removed nutrients from the soil, and it was
difficult to maintain fertility for grain cultivation.
Unpalatable woody plants and weeds quickly invaded pastures, and cattle were vulnerable to parasites and diseases. The shallow lithosols of steep slopes are natural-
ly infertile, and neither annual crops nor pastures provided sufficient protection from soil erosion. In recent
years, ecologists have advocated the development of new
systems of land use that, like those of the pre-Columbian
era, simulate the heterogeneous, multistory, natural vegetation of the humid tropical ecosystem (Tosi and Voertman
1964).

Although most colonial farms practiced mixed land
use, often combining crops and stock rearing, there was

already an incipient tendency towards monoculture that expanded rapidly in the nineteenth and twentieth centuries. Many of the cattle ranches in the tropical dry zone contained little and poor pasture; cocoa was grown as a monoculture in the Caribbean lowlands. After independence, many of the most fertile and accessible lands were devoted to the cultivation of specialized cash crops, particularly coffee and bananas, but also sugar cane, cocoa, and, more recently, African oil palm. Commercial monoculture involves land use patterns totally at variance with the heterogeneous natural vegetation of the humid tropics and has exposed modern Costa Rica to many ecological and economic problems: soil exhaustion, vulnerability to diseases and pests, the vicissitudes of commodity prices, and heavy reliance on the export of one or two crops to a limited number of foreign markets.

The problems derived from the ecological changes begun in the sixteenth century and accelerated during the past 150 years have now reached a critical level. Although the average population density is only forty-two persons per square kilometer and the country cannot by any means be described as overpopulated, the destruction of potentially renewable resources is proceeding at an alarming rate. Fifty years ago, natural forests still covered more than two-thirds of the country. Today, scarcely one-third remains forested. If deforestation continues unabated, the natural vegetation will completely disappear by the end of the century. Many of the cleared lands are too steep or too wet for permanent crop production and, after two or three harvests, are used only for rough pasture. Accelerated erosion on deforested lands is washing away thousands of hectares of topsoil that may never be replenished. The alteration of the hydrological cycle in many river basins provokes wet season floods and dry season draught. Contamination by uncontrolled rubbish disposal, untreated sewage, smoke, and petrol exhaust is deteriorating the environment in both urban and rural areas.

The preparation of detailed inventories is a prerequisite for improved resource management. By the mid-1960s, Costa Rica was one of the few countries in Latin America possessing topographical maps at scales of 1:200,000 and 1:50,000 of its whole territory. Some areas have been mapped at 1:25,000 and 1:10,000 (Barrantes Ferrero 1975a). There is also complete coverage in aerial photographs and satellite images. Detailed resource inventories, however, have only been made for small areas (e.g. Tosi 1967a, 1967b; Vargas Ulate 1978). A great deal of local exploration remains to be carried out. There are few analyses of land capability or subsoil resources at scales large enough to provide a basis for exploitation. In fields such as geomorphology, climatology, ecology, and mineralogy there is an acute shortage of Costa Rican research scientists.

Many public and private organizations are now engaged

in the exploration and exploitation of specific resources,
but no government department has overall responsibility
for natural resources and the environment. A private organization, the Asociación Costarricense para la Conservación de la Naturaleza, has acted as an ecological pressure
group since 1972. There have been several proposals to
establish an Institute or Ministry of Natural Resources
responsible for all aspects of the conservation and exploitation of natural resources, including the conditions
under which foreign entrepreneurs would be allowed to participate (Barrantes Ferrero 1975a; Dengo Obregón et al.
1977). Current legislation referring to natural resources
is fragmentary and its implementation halfhearted. Effective control over the use of resources would require a
permanent cadastral survey covering the whole country.
Cadastral surveys have been carried out in several regions
over the past fifteen years, but most are now out of date
(Sr. Alvaro Morera, personal communication).

Current knowledge suggests that the natural resource
endowment, if not spectacularly rich, is nevertheless extremely varied and sufficient to support a population several times larger than the present 2.2 million (Rosero
1978, 30-35). The crucial ecological problem, inherent in
the historical process of underdevelopment, is not a paucity of resources but, rather, the paradoxical coexistence
of underutilization and overexploitation of the physical
environment. There has been much debate in recent years
about the ecological crisis and the contribution of natural resources to economic development. The time has come
to replace debate by action if environmental deterioration
is to be halted and natural resources preserved for future
generations.

3
The Expansion of the
Hispanic American Oecumene

The expansion of the Hispanic and Luso-American oecumene at the expense of the indigenous oecumene in Latin
America has spanned more than four hundred years and is
only now drawing to a close. During the colonial period
in Costa Rica, this process was not only extremely slow,
but was characterized by alternating phases of expansion
and retreat. Permanent Spanish settlement was limited to
very small areas. Most of Costa Rica continued to be occupied, if at all, by the sparse Indian population that
resisted the European conquest. Many regions were never
thoroughly explored by the Spaniards; in others, disheart-
ened by the lack of precious metals and native labor or
repulsed by belligerent tribesmen and the hostile tropical
environment, the Europeans abandoned all attempts at permanent colonization. In 1821, most of the country was
still covered with forest. Colonial settlement patterns
are nevertheless vital to an understanding of the geography of contemporary Costa Rica, because they were the
foundation upon which the Hispanic American oecumene expanded after independence.

In the nineteenth and twentieth centuries, desarrollo
hacia afuera involved not only orienting the economy towards foreign markets but also a process of spatial expansion from the center to the peripheries of the country.
Accelerated population growth found an outlet in internal
migration into the vast forested zones that surrounded the
small cores of colonial settlement. Vigorous agricultural
colonization opened up new lands for both food production
and the cultivation of export crops. The development of
transport integrated Costa Rica more effectively into the
world economy and afforded access to the frontiers of settlement. The foundation of villages and towns created an
embryonic hierarchy of central places, the basis for subsequent urban expansion.

COLONIAL SETTLEMENT

For more than a hundred years after Columbus's discovery of Costa Rica in 1502, the immigration of Europeans and Negro slaves was offset by such a high rate of mortality among the Indians that the total population fell to 17,479 in 1569 and 15,538 in 1611. In the course of the seventeenth century, this trend was replaced by a steady, if slow and fluctuating, rate of population growth. An annual average increase of 1 percent during the eighteenth century produced a population of 52,591 by 1801 (Thiel 1902). This figure still represented an average density of only one person per square kilometer. Although more than nine-tenths of the population by this time had been assimilated into Hispanic American society, they occupied only small, fragmented areas, together covering less than 5 percent of the country (Figure 3.1).

Three interrelated frontiers persisted throughout the colonial period. First, the shifting frontier between Spaniard and Indian was never eradicated. With only small military forces at their command, the colonial authorities in Cartago were in no position to impose their rule over a largely forested territory occupied by hostile tribes. Not until the eighteenth century did the population in the areas of Spanish settlement exceed that of the unconquered Indians in the regions beyond imperial control (Figure 3.2). Second, the province's southern boundary separated not only the audiencias of Guatemala and Panama, but also the viceroyalty of New Spain to the north from that of Peru, and later Nueva Granada, to the south. Far from the major administrative centers of the empire, Costa Rica was one of the most neglected provinces in Spanish America. Third, it laid along the frontier between two rival imperial powers. Britain failed to gain control over an interoceanic route across the Central American isthmus, but most of the Caribbean lowlands fell within her sphere of influence and were never effectively controlled by Spain. In Mosquitia in eastern Nicaragua, the British protected a puppet native king; from this base, they constantly harassed the Spaniards in Costa Rica.

During the sixteenth and early seventeenth centuries, the Spaniards attempted to colonize all the principal regions in the tropical and premontane life zones except the northern plains. This period was one of optimism and spatial expansion during which the conquistadores still hoped to chance upon precious metals. Three phases of exploration and attempted settlement can be distinguished: from 1502 to about 1560, a prolonged period of sporadic peripheral exploration along both coasts, the only permanent result being the subjugation of the population in the region around the Gulf of Nicoya; during the 1560s, the conquest from bases in Nicaragua and Nicoya of the Valle Central; and from the 1560s until 1610, a series of attempts to establish civilian settlements in the south of Costa Rica, both in the General-Coto Brus depression on the Pacific slope and in the Talamanca or Sixaola Valley on the Caribbean slope (Rivas 1979, 272). Spanish claims to

Figure 3.1 Colonial settlement

<u>Sources</u>: IGN 1972; Meléndez 1977a; Ministerio de
Transportes 1967.

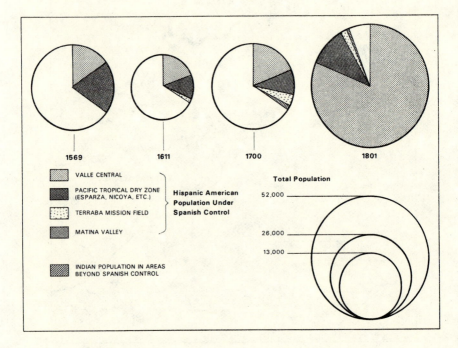

Figure 3.2 Regional distribution of population during the
colonial period

Source: Thiel 1902.

successive regions began with the foundation of towns and
continued with grants of <u>encomiendas</u> and the distribution
of land titles to European settlers. By 1610, no fewer
than sixteen towns were founded in Costa Rica (Meléndez
1977b). Indian hostility, isolation from established colonial settlements, the rigors of the tropical environment,
and the inability to make the new towns self-supporting
quickly forced the abandonment of all but two, Cartago and
Esparza. How different the subsequent geographical evolution of Costa Rica would have been if even some of the
others had survived! As it was, the expansion of the colonial oecumene was much slower after the first decade of
the seventeenth century, and many of the areas the Spaniards had attempted to settle in the sixteenth century
were not finally colonized by Hispanic Americans until after independence.

Only two regions were effectively governed and permanently occupied by the Spaniards during the colonial period: the central section of the Valle Central, roughly
from Ujarras in the east to Alajuela in the west; and the
zone bordering the Gulf of Nicoya, from Esparza in the
east, across the frontier between the provinces of Costa
Rica and Nicaragua, and around to the village of Nicoya in
the west. The intervening and surrounding areas remained
largely unsettled until the nineteenth and twentieth centuries. Both the major regions of colonial settlement
laid beyond the British sphere of influence in the circum-
Caribbean area. They were also located mainly in the
tropical dry and premontane moist life zones, the driest
parts of Costa Rica, where the climate is most suitable to
Iberian patterns of land use. The concentration of settlement in the center and west of the isthmus, not only in
Costa Rica but throughout the <u>Audiencia</u> of Guatemala, had
the disadvantage, however, of isolating the Central American colonies from the Atlantic trade routes that were the
economic lifelines of the Spanish empire. The more humid
life zones, with their dense, evergreen vegetation, were
difficult to clear for agriculture and unpleasant, un-
healthy regions for European settlers at a time of little
knowledge or control of tropical diseases. The Matina
Valley was the only area on the Caribbean lowlands occupied for any length of time. The Térraba mission field on
the southern Pacific slope constituted a second area of
peripheral colonial settlement. Neither the Matina nor
the Térraba valleys ever contained more than 5 percent of
the province's population, and Hispanic American settlement in both areas was in decline by the early nineteenth
century. Whereas the Valle Central and, to a lesser extent, the Nicoya region were areas of expanding settlement
from which pioneers emigrated after independence to cultivate surrounding forested lands, colonization in the Matina and Térraba valleys stagnated until they were reset-
tled by immigrants in the late nineteenth and twentieth
centuries.

With the foundation in 1564 of the colonial capital of Cartago, the Valle Central acquired a hegemony it has never relinquished. The center-periphery dichotomy that is such a marked feature of Costa Rica's contemporary spatial structure has its origin in the concentration of colonial settlement in one small region of the country. This fertile depression in the premontane life zone occupies only 3,246 square kilometers, 6 percent of the area of the republic of Costa Rica (DGEC 1979a). Since the eighteenth century, it has contained the majority of the country's population and most of its principal towns.

The interior location of the Valle Central at about 1,000 meters above sea level made it relatively cool and pleasant for European settlement, but it was very isolated both from the colonial ports of Caldera, Suerre, and Matina on the coasts and from the major centers of Spanish colonization in neighboring provinces. Although distances are short (less than 150 kilometers to the sea and under 300 to the frontiers of the province), overland transport was extremely primitive until the midnineteenth century. The Spaniards replaced the human porters of the pre-Columbian period with draught animals and wheeled carts, but the latter were used only over short distances within the principal areas of settlement. Long-distance transport overland was effected by horses and mules that with great difficulty, particularly in the rainy season when the unbridged rivers were full and the ground muddy and slippery, traversed narrow tracks cleared through the forest. The most important path, opened in 1601, received the grandiose title of Camino Real. It followed a northwest-southeast route along the Pacific slope, traversing the Alcaldía Mayor of Nicoya, climbing from Esparza on the coastal lowlands up to the Valle Central, and then continuing south to Panama via the Térraba Valley. The precise location of this trail probably varied over time. On many occasions, it had to be completely recleared because of landslides or because it had become overgrown with secondary bush. Two trails led eastwards, from the Valle Central along either side of the Reventazón Valley to Matina and Talamanca. Travel was extremely slow, and the Valle Central was several days' journey from the nearest colonial settlements.

The initial colonization of the Valle Central may have been a response to the decimation of the native population of Nicaragua by the slave trade and by disease. The Indians of the Valle Central were distributed in encomiendas, and extensive mercedes of land were granted to the original settlers. In Costa Rica too, however, the Indian population rapidly declined and the shortage of labor and capital precluded the consolidation of large estates (Fonseca Corrales 1981, 289). The Spaniards did not emigrate to America with the intention of undertaking manual labor, but in frontier provinces where no mining industry developed and the native population was sparse, they were soon obliged to move out of the towns and work on farmsteads in the countryside.

The Indian <u>reducciones</u> were located on the peripheries of the Valle Central, leaving the flatter central areas for European colonization (Meléndez 1977a, 47-56). The dominant Hispanic American agricultural system was the <u>chacra</u>, a mixed family farm producing wheat, maize, beans, sugar cane, potatoes, vegetables, fruit trees, and live-stock mainly for subsistence and small sales on local mar-kets (Meléndez 1975). The export of provisions from these farms to Panama during the early colonial period and the expansion of tobacco as a cash crop during the second half of the eighteenth century mark the tentative beginnings of the transformation of the colonial <u>chacra</u> into a special-ized commercial farm.

Cartago was the only urban settlement in the Valle Central until the eighteenth century, when Hispanic Amer-ican farmers began to congregate in the new settlements of Heredia, San José, and Alajuela. None of these towns had a population of more than 4,000 at independence, but the development of the tobacco industry consolidated the hege-mony of San José and of the western over the eastern sec-tion of the Valle Central, which by 1824 contained only one-quarter of the region's population (Cardoso and Pérez 1977, 125; Meléndez 1977a, 183-199).

The zone around the Gulf of Nicoya was the only other region the Spaniards controlled throughout the colonial period. The peninsula of Nicoya, incorporated into the province of Nicaragua in 1527, was the first area of mod-ern Costa Rica to come under imperial rule. It was not initially a region of Spanish urban settlement but, rather, a source first of slaves and then of tribute. As a tran-sit zone providing porters, muleteers, and provisions, it played a vital role in the conquest of the interior of Costa Rica (Rivas 1979, 32-132). During the midsixteenth century, the Spaniards subjugated the population along the eastern shore of the gulf. Esparza, founded in 1574 ten years after the establishment of Cartago, was the first permanent Spanish town on the Pacific lowlands. Virtually destroyed by pirates in the 1680s, its population during the colonial period never surpassed 500. The population of the entire tropical dry life zone never exceeded 6,000, and this area's share of the total population inhabiting the territory now belonging to the republic of Costa Rica dropped from 20 percent in 1569 to 10 percent in 1801. Partly for defense, partly because their livelihood was derived from the land, many Hispanic Americans lived in dispersed, rural settlements, colonizing both the area around the town of Esparza and the valleys of Abangares and Bagaces to the north. In the eighteenth century, new towns were founded along the Camino Real at Liberia, Cañas, and Bagaces.

Throughout the region bordering the Gulf of Nicoya, the prolonged dry season placed severe restrictions on land use. The dominant agricultural system was the hacienda, a cattle ranch extending over several hundred hectares. It was often owned by an absentee landlord and employed only a handful of Indian and Negro workers. The hacienda's products included cheese, hides, tallow, meat, and subsistence crops, but only the nonperishable commodities and live cattle could be transported any distance to market. In the sixteenth and seventeenth centuries, hides and tallow were exported to Panama. During the eighteenth century, live cattle destined for Guatemala were driven in the dry season to markets in Nicaragua (Gudmundson 1978, 79-125; Matarrita 1980b; Meléndez 1975). Towards the end of the colonial period, cattle farmers near Esparza produced meat for sale in Cartago, and the cheeses of the Bagaces Valley were sold in the Nicaraguan towns of Rivas and León (Quiros Vargas 1976, 174-197).

In the Caribbean lowlands, the abandonment by Spanish colonists of the town of Santiago de Talamanca in the face of Indian hostility in 1610 marked the end of European attempts to establish urban settlements in the tropical moist and wet life zones. Not until nearly three centuries later were towns again established in this region. Throughout the colonial period, the Caribbean lowlands were nominally part of the Spanish empire, but, in practice, they fell within the broad frontier zone that separated the core areas of the Spanish colonies in the center and west of Central America from the British sphere of influence in the Caribbean. The principal foci of Spanish activities were the fertile Matina, Barbilla, and lower Reventazón valleys, where there were cocoa plantations from the midseventeenth to early nineteenth centuries. Owned by Spaniards and criollos who lived in Cartago, the farms were worked by Talamanca Indians and Negro slaves. Most of the region's few hundred inhabitants were men, and there was little development of family life. Even though cocoa cultivation requires relatively little labor, the shortage of workers was one of the major restrictions on plantation expansion. Few plantations contained more than 3,000 trees, and most only about 1,000 (Meléndez 1977a, 65-98).

The fourth region of colonial settlement was the Térraba mission field in the tropical moist and wet life zones on the Pacific slope. In this region, too, the Spaniards attempted to found towns and implant the encomienda system during the second half of the sixteenth century. Neither Nueva Cartago, founded in 1564, nor Nombre de Jesús, established in 1571, however, survived more than a few months because of continuous Indian hostility and severe shortages of basic supplies. After the opening of the Camino Real, the necessity of ensuring unhindered transport across what was still a frontier zone between Spaniard and Indian prompted official support for the Franciscan missions in the Térraba Valley. Boruca was founded in the early seventeenth century, Térraba, Cabagra, and Guadalupe in the late seventeenth and eighteenth centuries. The region's population never exceeded 1,000 throughout the colonial period, and the mission villages and farmlands were in decline by the early nineteenth century. Most of the surviving indigenous population of this region now lives in the Indian reserves, and it is uncertain whether any of the modern villages occupy the original sites of the missions.

POPULATION GROWTH AND CENTRIFUGAL MIGRATION

At independence, the population of Costa Rica was approximately 65,000. The Valle Central contained 84 percent of the population, and 9 percent lived in the zone around the Gulf of Nicoya; the remaining 7 percent, mostly Indians, were scattered over the rest of the country. A pattern of relatively slow population growth, fluctuating between 1 and 2 percent per year, persisted into the first quarter of the twentieth century. The population reached about 100,000 by 1850, 250,000 by the turn of the century, and nearly 500,000 by 1927 (Figure 3.3). No birth and death rates for the whole country are available for the earlier part of this period. Between 1885 and 1930, a high birth rate, averaging slightly over 40 percent, combined with an average death rate of 24 percent gave an overall rate of natural population growth of 1.68 percent per year (Fernández Arias et al. 1976, 17) (Figure 3.4).

The last major demographic disaster was the outbreak of cholera, introduced in 1856 by soldiers returning from the war in Nicaragua against the North American filibuster, William Walker. The disease killed an estimated 7,000-10,000 people, about one-tenth of the population. The very gradual rise in the natural population growth rate during the remainder of the nineteenth and the early twentieth centuries can be attributed to two major factors: the eradication of epidemics and a slow increase in the fertility rate. These changes were associated with improvements following consolidation of the agro-export economy. In the long term, there was virtually full employment, and, in a country where agricultural workers were scarce, the importance of children's labor put a premium on large families. The level of living rose among all social classes. Hospitals and piped water supplies began to be installed in the major towns (Pérez Brignoli 1978, 1979). Nevertheless, parasitical and infectious diseases including malaria, prevalent on the coastal lowlands and occasionally breaking out in the intermontane depressions, still caused nearly half of all deaths in 1930 (Fernández Arias et al. 1976, 44; Kumm and Ruiz 1940).

Natural increase accounted for most population growth. During the period of maximum immigration at the turn of the century, when West Indians, Chinese, Lebanese, and small numbers of Europeans were entering the country,

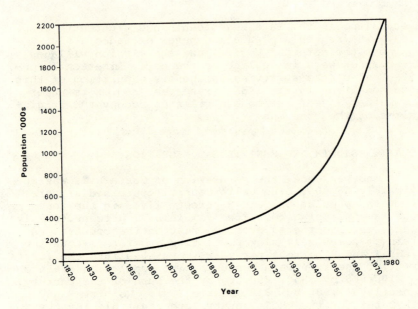

Figure 3.3 Population growth, 1824-1979

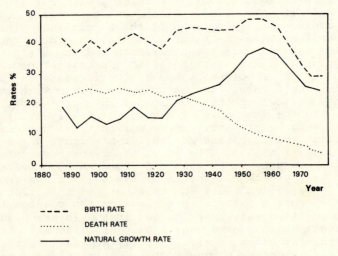

Figure 3.4 Birth, death, and natural population growth
rates, 1885-1977

<u>Sources</u>: DGEC 1979b; Fernández Arias et al. 1976.

about one-quarter of the total growth was attributable to the influx of foreign labor (Fernández Arias et al. 1976, 19). Immigration was insignificant after the first quarter of the twentieth century.

At about this time, however, the population entered a period of unprecedented natural increase, inconceivable to the nineteenth-century statesmen who had considered mass European immigration the only hope of rapid demographic growth. The population rose from just under half a million in 1927 to one million in 1957 and two million in 1977 (DGEC 1979b). By the late 1950s, the rate of growth—almost 4 percent per year—was among the highest in the world, exceeding what the industrialized countries had experienced in the nineteenth and early twentieth centuries. By the end of the 1970s, it still stood at 2.7 percent (OFIPLAN 1980a).

Such rapid population growth is an historically exceptional phenomenon, the result of transitions in the patterns of mortality and fertility. The death rate fell from more than 20 percent in the early 1930s to only 5 percent in the late 1970s (Fernández Arias et al. 1976, 17). This rate is one of the lowest in Latin America, comparable to that of the most advanced countries of the world (Sánchez-Albornoz 1974, 190). Life expectancy rose from an average of 41 years in 1927 to 68 in 1973. By 1977, infectious and parasitical diseases were responsible for only 7 percent of deaths. The principal causes of deaths were endogenous: 48 percent were attributable to tumors or to circulatory and respiratory diseases (DGEC 1980). These changes were achieved mainly by the eradication of infectious diseases, and the spread of preventive medicine and public health services. In 1915, with the support of the Rockefeller Foundation, a campaign was launched against hookworm, a parasitical disease gradually controlled by the use of latrines and shoes among the rural population. This project was followed by campaigns to eradicate smallpox, tiphoid fever, and malaria. The first maternity clinics were set up in 1920. These projects culminated in 1927 with the creation of the Secretaría de Salubridad Pública y Protección Social, which later became the Ministerio de Salud (Ministerio de Salud 1977; Pérez Brignoli 1979). The Caja Costarricense de Seguro Social, founded in 1941, accelerated the spread of medical services to large sectors of the population and now controls all but one of the country's public hospitals. Following the establishment of the Faculty of Medicine in the University of Costa Rica, the ratio of medical doctors per 10,000 population, which had stood at 3.3 in 1950, rose to 6.5 by 1973 (Bogan and Orlich 1979).

As the death rate fell, there was initially a slight rise in the birth rate, already high before 1930. During the 1950s, it reached the exceptional level of 48 percent. In the 1960s and 1970s, voluntary birth control was widely diffused, first by private family planning and then by the government-sponsored Programa Nacional de Planificación Familiar y Educación Sexual, launched in 1968 and generally recognized as one of the best organized and most successful projects of its kind in Latin America. In spite of the nominal adherence of the majority of the population to Roman Catholicism, contraceptive methods of all kinds found wide acceptance, diffusing from the urban to the rural population and from the upper and middle to the lower classes. Costa Rica experienced one of the most pronounced declines in fertility not only in Latin America but in the whole world, surpassed only by Formosa and Singapore. In absolute terms, population increase between 1961 and 1977 was approximately half a million less than it would have been had the demographic explosion continued unabated. In just fourteen years, between 1959 and 1973, the birth rate fell by one-third, from 48 to 29 percent. Since 1973, there has been a slight rise due to the demographic inertia inherent in the large number of women entering the reproductive age groups. The fertility rate, however, fell from 7.3 in 1960 to 3.7 in 1976.

The demographic transition is part of the wider process of modernization that in recent decades has profoundly changed the nature of Costa Rican society. Technology introduced from the more-developed countries permitted the rapid decline in mortality. The fall in fertility is related to socioeconomic changes. Improvements in education, the spread of public health services, and increased participation of women in the labor force all contributed to the desire for smaller families. Children are no longer evaluated primarily as a source of labor nor, eventually, of subsistence for their parents in old age. The fewer children per family the better they can be fed, housed, and educated, and the more money is available to satisfy material aspirations modeled on the consumption patterns of the developed, capitalist countries (G. González et al. 1978).

In absolute terms, the increase in the population during the last half century has been quite small, both in relation to the area of the republic and in comparison with the population growth in many other developing countries. Costa Rica does not face the problems of overpopulation that beset many countries of Asia and the Central American republic of El Salvador. It is the exceptionally high rate of increase that has made the population explosion such an important catalyst of change, first accelerating pioneer settlement on the frontiers of colonization and then nourishing a process of rapid urbanization. In the long term, the exhaustion of the settlement frontiers and the trend towards urbanization would probably have occurred without the population explosion, but they would have taken place more slowly, allowing a more gradual adaptation to new social and economic circumstances.

The demographic or, more precisely, the vital transition (since it does not deal with all aspects of population

change) provoked in Costa Rica, as in other countries,
what Zelinsky (1971) has termed the mobility transition.
Until the midtwentieth century, local population pressure
was relieved almost entirely by migration to sparsely populated peripheral regions. Emigration to foreign countries was insignificant. Urban areas did not begin to replace the frontiers of colonization as a major destination
of internal migrants until the 1940s and 1950s. For more
than a hundred years, population growth was paralleled by
constant expansion of the Hispanic American oecumene (Figure 3.5). In 1840, Hispanic American colonization comprised barely 5 percent of Costa Rica. Nearly a fifth of
the country had been colonized by 1880, a third by 1930,
and more than two-thirds by the late 1970s. The Indian
reserves contain 5 percent of the nation's territory, and
only the remaining 28 percent, most of which is now designated forest reserves, is still virtually uninhabited.

James (1941) pointed out many years ago that Costa
Rica is one of the few regions of Latin America where expansion of the oecumene was achieved largely by internal
migration (with a few local exceptions, the most important
being the West Indian migration into the Caribbean lowlands) and was accompanied by continuous occupation of the
older areas of settlement. Countries such as Argentina,
Uruguay, and Brazil depended heavily on foreign immigration in order to expand their areas of non-Indian settlement. James identified only four regions of Latin Amer-
ica--the Antioquia Highlands of Colombia, middle Chile,
the three southern states of Brazil, and Costa Rica--that
lacked a hollow frontier where colonization was followed
by abandonment and depopulation. Although some of the
older areas of settlement in Costa Rica registered net
emigration as new frontiers of colonization were opened,
very few cantons experienced an absolute decline in population, and the Valle Central always contained a heavy
concentration of population and economic activities.

In contrast to many parts of Latin America, Africa,
and Asia colonized by Europeans from the coast towards the
interior, the core area from which most expansion of the
Hispanic American oecumene took place is almost equidis-
tant from the Pacific and Caribbean. Colonists moved out
of the Valle Central in all directions. There was some
settlement in the lower montane and montane zones, but
most pioneers moved into other parts of the premontane
zone or down to lower altitudes, eventually settling extensive areas in the humid tropical life zones. Costa
Rica, like other Latin American countries, had no single
frontier comparable to the West of the United States but,
rather, many separate frontiers, initially isolated one
from another, in which there were several different types
of agricultural colonization (Hennessy 1978, 6).

Until the 1880s, most internal migration took place
within the Valle Central, of which only the central part
had been intensively settled during the colonial period.

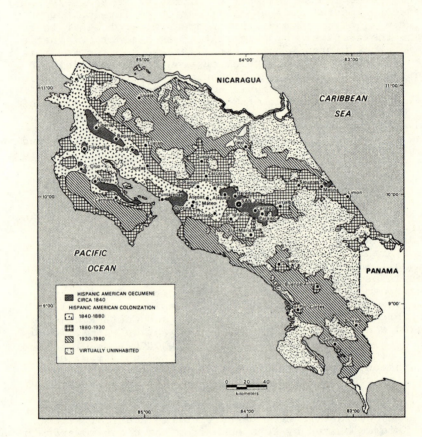

Figure 3.5 Expansion of the Hispanic American oecumene,
c. 1840-1980

Source: Adapted from Nuhn 1978b.

Throughout the nineteenth century, this region contained more than four-fifths of the country's population (Figure 3.6). A few pioneers crossed the mountains surrounding the Valle Central to settle in the Cerros de Aguacate to the west, the San Carlos and Sarapiquí valleys to the north, and the rugged mountains of Puriscal, Acosta, and Dota to the south. There was little expansion of the settled area in Guanacaste, still separated by extensive tracts of forest from the farmlands of the Valle Central.

During the next half century, from the 1880s to the 1930s, colonization continued in the Valle Central. Pioneers also pushed the settlement frontiers south from Puriscal, Acosta, and Dota to Turrubares and the upper General Valley, and north over the Cordillera Central into the tropical plains of San Carlos and Sarapiquí. Pockets of settlement were established by "cartagos," or migrants from the Valle Central, near Nicoya, Tilarán, and Abangares in the upland peripheries of Guanacaste. The Caribbean lowlands, also extensively colonized during this period, was the only region where foreign laborers, mainly West Indians, initially outnumbered internal migrants. By 1927, the proportion of the population living in the Valle Central had dropped to 71 percent, and the formerly isolated areas of settlement had coalesced into a single zone stretching from the Nicoya peninsula in the west to Limón in the east.

Most of the Valle Central had been settled by 1930. During the next twenty years, its proportion of the population fell yet again to 66 percent in 1950. Most of the expansion of the Hispanic American oecumene in this period took place on the Pacific slope, both on the coastal lowlands in the hinterlands of the ports of Quepos and Golfito and in the interior General Valley. These initially isolated foci of colonization eventually merged to form an extensive zone of settlement in the southwest. Colonization also continued on the northern plains and in the Nicoya peninsula (Jiménez Castro 1956; Nunley 1960; Sandner 1962-1964).

In 1950, when migration statistics were first compiled at a cantonal level, most of the areas colonized during the twentieth century--the Caribbean lowlands, San Carlos, the peripheries of Guanacaste, and the south Pacific region--still registered net immigration. Only the older areas of settlement in central Guanacaste and the Valle Central (excluding the metropolitan area of San José) were regions of net emigration (Figure 3.7a). During the intercensorial period between 1950 and 1963, the oecumene continued to expand in almost all directions. Italians pioneered settlement in the Coto Brus Valley, opening up a new frontier for internal migrants. Vigorous colonization on the Caribbean slope pushed the settlement frontier to the border with Nicaragua in the districts of Upala and Los Chiles. Most of the settled regions in the tropical zone registered net immigration in 1963, although the

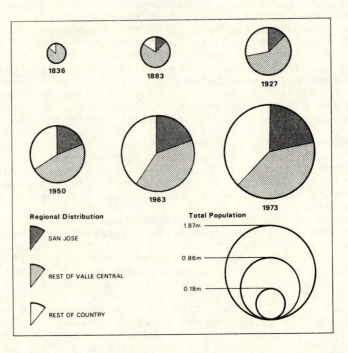

Figure 3.6 Changes in the regional distribution of
population, 1836-1973

Sources: DGEC 1885, 1893, 1953a, 1960, 1966a, 1974a.

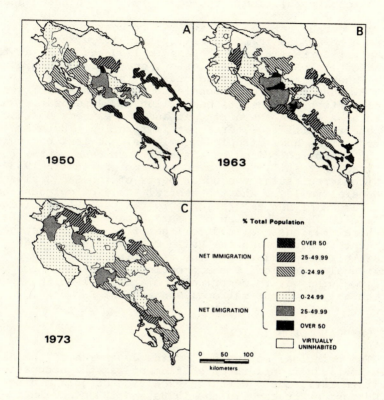

Figure 3.7   Internal migration, 1950, 1963, and 1973
Sources: DGEC 1953a, 1966a, 1974a.

proportion of migrants had in many cases declined since
1950. Guanacaste, still a region of extensive cattle
ranching that offered few opportunities for rural employment, was the only peripheral area of net emigration. Migration also continued out of the rural areas of the Valle
Central. In 1963, this region contained only 60 percent
of the total population (Figure 3.7b) (Buarque and Raabe
1975).

The decade between the two most recent censuses
marked a new phase in the mobility transition, as it did
in the vital transition. Whereas in 1950 and 1963, at the
height of the population explosion, one-third of the country's inhabitants were living outside their native canton,
by 1973, when the rate of population growth had declined,
the proportion of migrants had fallen to 14 percent. Only
two rural areas in the northeast and the extreme south of
the country still registered net immigration. Both are
located in the humid tropical lowlands, the last ecological zone to be colonized by Hispanic Americans. Many rural areas that still registered net immigration in 1963--
the Nicoya peninsula, the upper parts of the San Carlos
and General valleys, and the central Pacific lowlands--had
become areas of net emigration only ten years later (Figure 3.7c). The proportion of Costa Ricans living in the
peripheral regions declined for the first time since the
eighteenth century, and the Valle Central contained 63
percent of the population. The traditional process of
centrifugal migration to the frontiers of colonization was
rapidly giving way to centripetal migration into the towns,
particularly into the metropolitan area of San José.

AGRICULTURAL COLONIZATION

The principal motive behind the expansion of the Hispanic American frontiers of settlement was the occupation
of virgin farmlands. With the exception of gold mining in
the Cerros de Aguacate in the 1820s and 1830s and in the
Cerros de Abangares during the late nineteenth and early
twentieth centuries, extractive industries played little
part in the process of colonization. The forests that
surrounded the major areas of colonial settlement were
perceived not as renewable resources to be brought under
permanent economic production but as obstacles to agricultural colonization. As late as 1961, the Ley de Tierras y
Colonización imposed sanctions on landowners retaining
"tierras incultas" within their properties (MAG 1961).
Most Hispanic American colonists regarded the forested
areas as empty and unoccupied, although in some there was
a sparse Indian population practicing shifting agriculture,
hunting, fishing, and gathering.

There were three principal types of agricultural colonization after independence (Figure 3.8). The most important was spontaneous, unorganized colonization by

Figure 3.8 Agricultural colonization, nineteenth and
twentieth centuries

internal migrants. This process began in the midnineteenth century in the Valle Central and spread over a large part of the country. Landless laborers, peasants, and speculators were all attracted to the peripheral frontier regions, in spite of the initial isolation that often precluded the development of commercial agriculture. Once transport was improved, coffee was usually the major export crop. The plantation enclaves in the humid tropical lowlands constituted a second, quite different, type of colonization. They were initially isolated from the Valle Central, but their coastal location facilitated export agriculture (particularly banana cultivation) as soon as the forest had been removed. Foreign immigrants accounted for a substantial part of the initial labor force. North American companies supplied the capital and technology for land clearance, drainage, and the construction of railways, ports, and estate villages. Planned colonies of family farms were much less important than the other two types of pioneer settlement. Most of the projects involving foreign agricultural colonists were dismal failures. Planned colonization by Costa Rican families began on a small scale in the late nineteenth and early twentieth centuries and gained impetus under the auspices of the Instituto de Tierras y Colonización, founded in 1962.

Spontaneous Colonization

After independence, profound changes took place in the major area of colonial settlement between Alajuela in the west and Cartago in the east. Following the consolidation of foreign markets and credit supplies and the construction of a cart road down to the Pacific port of Puntarenas, coffee became the region's major export product, replacing the basic food crops and livestock of the colonial chacra. Wheat disappeared entirely from the Costa Rican landscape. The cultivation of maize and beans also decreased in the center of the Valle Central, although these grains continued to be produced on the frontiers of colonization. Many farms evolved a virtual monoculture of coffee; only pasture and sugar cane, both supplying fodder for oxen, were retained from the earlier mixed farming system. As population grew and coffee cultivation expanded, there were important changes in the pattern of land tenure. Many family farms were subdivided by inheritances among several sons and daughters, creating numerous minifundios of only one or two hectares. Even when planted with coffee, farms of this size were too small to support a family. In this densely populated region where little, if any, land was left for primary colonization by the midnineteenth century, the formation of latifundios was limited. Some large coffee estates were established, although many were spatially fragmented. Landless peones and minifundistas comprised the permanent labor force on

the larger coffee farms; during the harvest period, peasant farmers and their families worked on piece rates to
pick the crop (Hall 1976a, 33-38).

The growth of population and the proliferation of
minifundistas and landless laborers created a process of
spontaneous colonization only now coming to an end. This
colonization was, in effect, a substitute for agrarian reform, providing for more than a century partial, temporary
solutions to social and economic problems in the more
densely settled regions. Tierras baldías could be cheaply
purchased by prospective colonists. The area each colonist could claim was gradually reduced from 450 hectares in
1852 to 30 in 1939, but this amount was still ample in
most regions for the formation of family homesteads. Legal title could be obtained once the land had been brought
under cultivation. Services rendered to the state were
also often rewarded with grants of tierras baldías many
times more extensive than those individual colonists could
claim.

In practice, many settlers occupied tierras baldías
without petitioning for legal title. Abuse of the home-
stead legislation led over the years to the sale of usufruct rights, land speculation, the accumulation of large,
individual properties, and the emergence of a serious
squatter problem. The Ley de Poseedores en Precario,
passed in 1942, attempted to eliminate squatting, but, in
reality, it exacerbated tenure problems by stimulating
still further accumulation of land by absentee owners.
Squatters could obtain title to occupied lands, and the
former landowners were compensated by a further grant of
tierras baldías, equivalent in value to the expropriated
land. Since cleared land was worth much more than forested tierras baldías, the landlord received a larger area
than was lost. While this legislation was in force, until
1951, landlords actually encouraged squatters to occupy
uncultivated lands on their farms. The Ley de Tierras y
Colonización of 1961 brought back most of the earlier legislation in favor of squatters, although landlords were no
longer granted tierras baldías in compensation for expropriated land. This law also prohibited further spontaneous colonization of state lands, but in practice this settlement continued, as did squatting on privately owned
lands (Sáenz Pacheco and Knight 1971; Salas Marrero and
Barahona 1973, 324-329).

During the early decades of the republican period,
spontaneous colonization took place mainly in the Valle
Central. Only the central part of this region had been
intensively settled and farmed during the colonial period;
to the west of Alajuela and the east of Paraíso population
was sparse, and there were still extensive zones of tierras baldías. There was some pioneer settlement prior to
the improvement of transport, but the majority of colonists arrived after the construction of roads and railways
not only linked the central coffee region with the coastal

ports but also opened up new areas for intensive, commercial agriculture. Settlement between Alajuela and San Ramón accelerated after the completion of the cart road to
Puntarenas in 1846. On farms ranging from peasant small
holdings to large estates forest gave way to coffee, sugar
cane, grains, and pasture. Speculative land claims in the
eastern Valle Central date back to the early nineteenth
century, but most colonization took place after the completion of the Atlantic railway in 1890. Here, too, the
principal products were coffee, sugar cane, and cattle,
but, in contrast to the remainder of the Valle Central,
large estates predominated (Hall 1976a, 88-119). Primary
colonization in the Valle Central had come to an end by
about 1930, and, in many respects, the landscape of the
newly settled zones resembled that of the old area of colonial settlement (Sandner 1961, 1).

From the midnineteenth century onwards, settlers also
moved out of the Valle Central in all directions, simultaneously colonizing several separate frontiers. In many
families, successive generations migrated in stepwise
fashion, gradually settling farther and farther from the
Valle Central. In these peripheral regions, the process
of spontaneous colonization was quite different from that
in the Valle Central. Puriscal, Turrubares, Acosta and
Dota, the plains of San Carlos and Sarapiquí, the Cordillera de Guanacaste and the Cordillera de Tilarán, the
south and west of the Nicoya peninsula, and the General-
Coto Brus depression were all separated from coastal ports
and the Valle Central by rugged hills and mountains, which
for many decades remained virtually uninhabited and untraversed by all-weather roads. Pioneer colonization preceded the development of central places, the construction of
local roads, and the establishment of marketing facilities
for cash crops. The early stages in landscape change were
therefore rather similar on nearly all the frontiers, in
spite of the considerable ecological variations between
one region and another (Sandner 1961, 23).

There was often a time lag of many years between land
being claimed as private property and deforested for farming. Initial clearance was generally carried out by individual pioneers or small groups of colonists, whose
principal tools were axes and machetes. The larger trees
were chopped down, leaving the stumps and undergrowth to
dry out for subsequent burning. Commercial timber exploitation was restricted by the lack of transport, sawmills,
marketing facilities, and technology for using many of the
species found in tropical forests. Small amounts of wood
were consumed by the colonists themselves as building materials and fuel. Some timber was sold to local furniture
and construction industries. A few species of precious
hardwoods, such as Mahogany (Swietenia humilis), Cocobolo
(Dalbergia retusa), and Cenizaro (Pithecolobium saman),
were minor export commodities. The remaining timber--an
estimated 80 to 90 percent of the total in most regions--

was either burned or left to rot on the ground, virtually
eliminating many species of trees and destroying the seeds
of what eventually became nonrenewable resources (Tosi
1971, 1974).

Until the peripheral regions were penetrated by all-
weather roads, cleared lands were often no more than islands within the forest. There were two principal types
of farming. Peasant colonists established subsistence
farms similar to the colonial chacra in the Valle Central
(Sáenz Pacheco 1969, 4). Initially, many even reverted to
primitive shifting cultivation, resembling indigenous agriculture, until the increase in population and the development of large properties reduced the area available for
this extensive type of land use. Sandner (1959a) has estimated that between 60 and 80 percent of the area deforested between about 1860 and 1960 was initially used for
shifting cultivation. Colonists grew staples such as
rice, maize, plantains, and beans, small patches of coffee
and sugar cane for their own consumption, and a few fruits
and vegetables. Chickens, pigs, and perhaps one or two
cows were kept. Very little of this produce was sold, although even the most isolated pioneers were not totally
cut off from the market economy. Occasional local sales
of crops and animal produce, together with sporadic wage
labor on larger farms, provided a small cash income for
the purchase of indispensible manufactured goods such as
textiles, tools, matches, soap, and domestic accoutrements.

In many regions colonized by peasant farmers, ecological conditions were unsuitable for continuous cultivation.
Poor soils, steep slopes, or an excessively wet climate
led to soil exhaustion, erosion, and reduced yields. Many
colonists, therefore, moved on to new frontiers. Whereas
in the indigenous ecosystem, however, lands abandoned after a few harvests were left to revert to forest and re-
cuperate their fertility, many Hispanic American colonists
sold their lands to speculators who were thereby able to
accumulate much larger properties than those stipulated in
the homesteading laws.

A second type of farm thus developed side by side
with the peasant holdings and, to some extent, replaced
them, leading to the process Lambert (1969, 78) has described as "the premature destruction of the frontier."
On larger properties, the only viable land use prior to
the development of modern transport was extensive cattle
ranching (Sandner 1961). Repeated attempts to establish
plantation agriculture in inaccessible regions such as the
Sarapiquí Valley failed because of the lack of railways or
paved roads along which the harvests could be transported
to potential markets (León 1943b). Farms similar to the
colonial haciendas of Guanacaste and Esparza were established in other peripheral regions, including areas where
precipitation was excessive for good pastures and healthy
stock. Many of the lands bought from peasant colonists
had already been cleared of natural vegetation. Elsewhere,

the transformation from forest to pasture was usually very slow, a few hectares being cleared each year. Cattle ranching had the advantage over crop production of providing commodities that could withstand the slow and expensive transport out of the frontier regions. Live cattle could walk to their markets, although they lost weight and generally had to be fattened before sale. Hides and cheeses were high-value, relatively unperishable goods that could be taken by mule or ox cart to markets in the Valle Central. The cattle ranches employed little permanent labor; most of the work force was supplied by neighboring peasant colonists on piece rates (Hall 1977-1978).

This initial development of subsistence, often shifting, cultivation and extensive cattle ranching was a very wasteful process. Hundreds of thousands of hectares of forest were destroyed, but many of the areas cleared were so steep or infertile that their transformation into pasture or crop land ruined the soil. Productivity was low, and the increase in agricultural output lagged far behind the expansion of the area cleared for farming.

During the past fifty years, the construction of all-weather roads has removed the major economic restraint on the development of specialized, commercial farming. The Nicoya peninsula, the plains of San Carlos and Sarapiquí, Puriscal, Acosta, Dota, and the General and Coto Brus valleys are now linked both to the main internal market in the Valle Central and to coastal ports. The improvement in transport stimulated a process of secondary colonization on lands already partially deforested and settled. Sandner (1961) has estimated that as many as half of the colonists in regions such as the General Valley never actually reached the frontier of virgin lands. Population density increased, and land use was intensified as cash crops became increasingly important. Coffee was the principal export crop throughout the premontane zone. In Puriscal and the General Valley, colonists also produced tobacco for sale on the home market. Sugar cane was a major cash crop in the upper San Carlos Valley. Many of the regions also produced foodstuffs, such as grains, fruit, beef, and dairy products for sale in the Valle Central.

The transition from subsistence cultivation and cattle ranching to more intensive systems of land use, however, is far from complete. Many of the regions of spontaneous colonization beyond the Valle Central are too steep, too wet, or too infertile for continuous crop production and should ideally be used for forestry, not farming. In areas where export crops such as coffee have been established, ecological conditions rarely match those of the Valle Central (Hall 1976a, 121-149). The lack of wholesale markets and direct transportation between the peripheral regions has limited the production of foodstuffs for the home market (González Vega et al. 1970). Vast areas are still used principally for extensive stock rearing, and recent government support for the beef export

industry has encouraged large landowners to continue producing cattle rather than trees or crops (Spielman 1972).

Plantation Enclaves

In contrast to the regions of unorganized, spontaneous colonization, the plantation enclaves were developed
from the beginning as areas of specialized, commercial
farming. Isolated from the major zones of Hispanic American settlement, their economic links with the rest of the
country were initially very tenuous. North American fruit
companies colonized virtually unsettled regions, still the
principal areas of plantation agriculture today: the Caribbean lowlands in the hinterland of Port Limón; the area
between Parrita and Quepos in the central Pacific lowlands;
and the Térraba and Coto Colorado valleys in the south Pacific lowlands (Figure 3.8). These were but three of the
many areas in tropical America where plantation enclaves
were established in the late nineteenth and early twentieth centuries. They were very much a product of their
times, created during a period when extensive virgin lands
were available for cultivation and Latin American governments exercised little control over the activities of
multinational companies (Casey 1979, 10-11). International borders were disregarded, and the Sixaola and Coto Colorado valleys in the south of Costa Rica were administered
by the fruit companies as part of the divisions centered
on the Panamanean ports of Almirante and Armuelles.

The plantation enclaves had several geographical
characteristics in common. They were all located near the
coast, within easy access of oceanic shipping routes. By
the time the two Pacific enclaves were developed in the
1930s and 1940s, the Panama Canal provided a short cut to
ports on the Atlantic seaboard of North America. All the
enclaves were situated in the tropical moist and wet life
zones. Hispanic American settlers had previously shunned
these regions whose heavy precipitation, dense natural
vegetation, and diseases made them difficult to colonize
on a small scale with primitive technology. Insofar as
the foreign fruit companies cleared land for cultivation
and installed drainage, transportation, port facilities,
hospitals, and schools, they contributed to the development of areas previously almost uninhabited. Most profits
and wages were repatriated, however, and the Costa Rican
government derived relatively little benefit from the
plantation enclaves during the early decades of their operation (Casey 1979, 178-201). Monocultures of permanent
tree crops were established in all three regions. Bananas
were the principal crop, but, in contrast to the coffee
economy in the premontane zone where the oldest areas of
cultivation have always been the most important, the location of banana production fluctuated over time. The enclaves were characterized by rapid development from forest

to plantation, and equally rapid decline when the banana
industry was hit by disease and economic depression.

The first plantation enclave was established in the
hinterland of Port Limón. This area was the principal region of banana cultivation from the late nineteenth century until the 1930s. The North American entrepreneurs
who built the Atlantic railway from Alajuela to Limón
found that the coffee trade alone was insufficient to make
the line pay. From the 1870s, they planted small areas of
bananas, which provided both a staple food for the laborers building the railway and a return cargo for the foreign boats bringing construction materials and provisions
to Port Limón (Hall 1976b). The railway and its branch
lines opened up a zone stretching about 150 kilometers
from the Santa Clara plain in the northwest to the Sixaola
Valley in the southeast. Large areas of forest were
cleared near the railway lines, and the numerous streams
that traverse the coastal lowlands provided natural outlets for drainage ditches. Bananas were sown in Santa
Clara, Siquirres, and Zent during the 1890s; in the first
decade of the new century, cultivation was extended south
of Port Limón into the Banano, Estrella, and Sixaola valleys. The well-drained, sandy soils of the natural levees
proved to be the best banana lands; heavier clays back
from the rivers gradually became compacted and usually had
to be abandoned after a few years because of poor drainage
(C. F. Jones and Morrison 1952).

In contrast to coffee, bananas were produced mainly
on large plantations. The majority were owned and administered by foreigners, many of whom were English speaking.
The labor force was made up of West Indian Negroes and
Costa Rican migrants from the interior of the country.
The whole economy of the Limón region was dominated by the
activities of the United Fruit Company, founded in 1899.
For many years, the company owned more than 100,000 hectares of land, much of which originated in the concession
of tierras baldías received in 1884 by the North American
entrepreneur, Minor Keith, in recompense for the construction of the Atlantic railway. At the beginning of the
twentieth century, United Fruit cultivated about half the
bananas produced in the Caribbean lowlands; as plant diseases and soil exhaustion spread, the company's share in
total output fell to about one-quarter in 1928. The independent banana producers selling their harvests under contract to the United Fruit Company ranged from the Lindo
brothers, who owned more than 20,000 hectares of land, to
small growers, many of whom rented or squatted on lands
belonging to the company (Casey 1979). Because of the
ample resources of land available, large, uncultivated
areas were reserved within the plantations for future production as old lands wore out. There was little use of
fertilizers, so even good banana lands were exhausted after seven to ten years of monoculture and had to be rested
for a decade before being replanted.

While the banana industry was buoyant, the cultivation of subsistence crops was unimportant. Many of the foodstuffs consumed in the enclave were imported, and vegetables were brought down to the coastal lowlands from the premontane and lower montane zones in the interior of the country (C. F. Jones and Morrison 1952). Since the time they worked as railway navvies, however, the West Indians had introduced Afro-Caribbean patterns of subsistence production that assumed vital importance during the slack periods of railway construction and the subsequent depressions in the banana industry. Like Costa Rica's indigenous population, the Negroes practiced a polyculture that simulated the heterogeneous natural vegetation. Their tree crops included bread fruit, citrus fruits, and plantains for subsistence consumption and cocoa and coconuts for sale. As in the Indian economy, root crops such as cassava, yams, and sweet potatoes, well adapted to the humid tropics, prevailed over grains (Meléndez and Duncan 1972, 97-99).

Banana production began to decline after 1913. The First World War and the Great Depression reduced demand, and the low prices paid by the United Fruit Company to the independent producers were insufficient to combat Sigatoka, Panama disease, and soil exhaustion. By the 1930s, the company's enclaves in other circum-Caribbean countries were more profitable than those in Costa Rica, and the export of bananas from Limón ceased in 1942 (Casey 1979). The province entered a period of severe economic depression, only partially alleviated by the temporary cultivation of other plantation crops such as rubber and Manila hemp (Stouse 1970). Most small farmers and agricultural laborers remaining in Limón province during the 1940s and early 1950s turned to cocoa as a cash crop and produced a variety of subsistence foods. By this time, the volume of internal migration was approaching its zenith, and there was considerable spontaneous colonization by migrants from the interior of the country, both on tierras baldías and on abandoned United Fruit Company lands that had been invaded by secondary forest (Casey 1979, 257, 297-298). In 1956, the Standard Fruit Company pioneered the redevelopment of the banana industry, both in the old areas of production formerly cultivated by the United Fruit Company and in the Río Frío area to the northwest of Limón, opened up for commercial agriculture by the extension of the Old Line railway.

As banana exports from Limón declined, the United Fruit Company explored the possibility of colonizing other humid tropical areas for plantation agriculture. In 1926, it entered into negotiations with the Costa Rican government to extend production to the Sarapiquí Valley, where it proposed to sow 80,000 hectares of new plantations and to build a railway linking the region to Port Limón. The following year, however, the company's soil experts concluded that these lands would be unsuitable for cultivation without major drainage projects, and the Sarapiquí Valley remained a frontier for spontaneous colonization.

The humid tropical regions on the Pacific slope were still virtually uninhabited. In the 1920s, a German immigrant founded the Pirris Farm and Trading Company to produce bananas on the central Pacific lowlands, but he experienced great difficulties in transporting the fruit to the port of Puntarenas. Meanwhile, a subsidiary of the United Fruit Company, the Golfo Dulce Lands Company, was purchasing large areas of forested alluvial lands in the southern Pacific lowlands. The Cortés-Chittenden contract, signed in 1938 by the Costa Rican government and the Compañía Bananera (another subsidiary of United Fruit), allowed the company to develop new plantation enclaves on virgin lands in the Parrita, Térraba, and Coto Colorado valleys (Casey 1979, 43-46). Initially, there were no overland communications between the Pacific enclaves and the other settled areas of Costa Rica. They were, therefore, even more isolated than the Caribbean enclave, and, in contrast to Limón, Quepos and Golfito never developed into major national ports.

Its contracts with the Costa Rican government forbade the Compañía Bananera to transfer Negro workers from the Caribbean lowlands to the Pacific enclaves. These agreements were developed, however, at a time when Costa Rica's natural population growth rate was rising and the volume of internal migration increasing. Hispanic Americans from the Valle Central and Guanacaste, together with immigrants from the neighboring republics of Nicaragua and Panama, provided most of the labor force for the new plantations. The essential infrastructure of ports, railways, workers' housing, malarial control, and drainage was completed within a few years. Bananas were being exported from Quepos and Golfito by the early 1940s. By the early 1950s, 12,000 hectares of bananas had been sown on the coastal plain between Parrita and Quepos; a similar area was in production in the hinterland of Golfito a decade later.

Panama disease appeared in the Pacific lowlands soon after the establishment of the enclaves. Banana plantations were abandoned near Parrita as early as 1943, and commercial cultivation ended in the entire Parrita-Quepos enclave in 1956, after only eighteen years of production. Panama disease later affected the hinterland of Golfito, where severe floods in 1955 also destroyed many plantations. The area sown in bananas in this region declined by one-half during the intercensorial period from 1963-1973. In contrast to the Caribbean lowlands, however, where the United Fruit Company carried out very little secondary development for other crops, African oil palm, cocoa, teak, and cattle pastures replaced abandoned banana plantations first near Quepos and later near Golfito (Stouse 1967).

All the enclaves have gradually been integrated with the rest of the country. The formerly uninhabited, for-

ested lands that separated them from the principal areas
of settlement in the interior have been largely cleared
for spontaneous colonization. The enclaves are now connected to the national network of paved roads. Plantation
agriculture still predominates in all three regions, but
the system makes a greater contribution to the Costa Rican
economy than it did in the past. African oil palm, introduced in the 1940s, provides raw materials for the local
manufacture of margarine and soap, replacing imported supplies of vegetable oils. Independent producers grew an
increasing proportion of the banana crop. Most employees
of the multinational fruit companies, including technical
and administrative staff, are now Costa Ricans. The government receives in taxation U.S. 45¢ per box of bananas
exported and up to 45 percent of the companies' profits
(Gaceta Oficial, 5 December 1978).

Planned Colonies

Planned colonies of family farmers, whether Costa
Ricans or foreign immigrants, contributed much less than
either the plantation enclaves or spontaneous frontier
settlement to the expansion of the Hispanic American oecumene. Prior to 1961, the government played little part in
the organization of agricultural colonies, contracting the
establishment of these colonies to private entrepreneurs
(Salazar 1961, 232). A high proportion of the colonization projects, particularly those involving foreign immigration, were complete failures. The few successful colonies were located mainly in regions where the majority of
farmers were independent migrants (Figure 3.8).

Planned colonies constituted a type of settlement intermediate between the plantation enclaves and unorganized,
spontaneous colonization. In common with the plantations,
they were generally established around nucleated settlements that contained elementary social services, such as a
church and school. Many colonies also had sawmills and
simple agricultural processing plants, such as trapiches
for the manufacture of brown sugar. Nearly all, however,
initially lacked all-weather transport to the Valle Central and the coastal ports. They were often, therefore,
for many years reduced to predominantly subsistence cultivation, similar to that practiced by independent colonists.
This lack of essential infrastructure probably accounts,
more than any other single factor, for the failure of so
many of the colonies.

The early republican governments, eager to occupy all
the nation's territory, signed dozens of contracts with
entrepreneurs who undertook to introduce foreign immigrants and develop agricultural colonies. Most colonies
were to be established in peripheral regions beyond the
Valle Central, many in the tropical moist and wet life
zones. The hot, rainy climate, the prevalence of tropical

diseases, dense natural vegetation, and lack of communications deterred most prospective European immigrants. Many entrepreneurs failed to bring a single colonist to the country. La Mansión, a colony established in the Nicoya peninsula about 1890 with a hundred families of Cuban political exiles, was one of the very few projects that led to permanent settlement (Sandner 1962-1964, 1:125).

Two foreign colonies established in the 1950s were notable exceptions to the overall failure of immigrant colonization. An Italian colony was founded at San Vito de Java in the Coto Brus Valley, an area of fertile volcanic and alluvial soils in the premontane zone close to the border with Panama. In the early 1950s, it was envisaged that the Pan-American Highway would traverse this region, providing an outlet to the nearby plantation enclaves in both Costa Rica and Panama where there was a ready market for fresh fruit, vegetables, and dairy produce. When the highway was eventually constructed, however, it was located to the south of San Vito, and the Italian colony continued to rely on a dirt road. Coffee, a crop with which the immigrants were totally unfamiliar, was the only feasible commercial product. It soon came to dominate the landscape throughout the region. Most of the Italians left San Vito. They were replaced by Costa Rican colonists, who extended the settled area far beyond the 10,000 hectares initially set aside for the colony.

Contemporary with the settlement of the Coto Brus Valley was the foundation of a North American Quaker colony at Monteverde in the Cordillera de Tilarán, on the border between the premontane and lower montane zones. Whereas the Italian immigrants were commercially motivated, the Quakers, most of whom came from Alabama, emigrated mainly because of their opposition to the United States war economy. Hardly any colonists have abandoned Monteverde even though, like San Vito, it is linked to the Pan-American Highway only by a dirt road. The colony's principal commercial product is cheese. A variety of subsistence foodstuffs is also produced. The success of the colony lies not only in the stability of the Quaker settlement itself, but also in the stimulus it has given to independent Costa Rican colonists in the adjacent area to produce high-quality milk to sell to the Monteverde cheese factory (Masing 1964).

In addition to contracting foreign agricultural colonization, successive governments also planned the development of colonies of Costa Rican farmers in the peripheries of the country. A few of these projects, such as Aguas Zarcas in San Carlos established in 1896, Tilarán in Guanacaste planned between 1909 and 1912, and Colonia Carmona founded in the Nicoya peninsula in 1920, did lead to permanent settlement, although the colonists' attempts to develop intensive commercial agriculture were frustrated by the lack of all-weather roads. This problem led to the abandonment of many other colonies, such as El Salvador in

the Santa Clara plain to the northeast of the Cordillera
Central where seventy families who arrived in 1911 with
the illusion of producing coffee abandoned the region after two or three years of subsistence cultivation. By the
1930s, the combination of economic depression, rapid population growth, and an increasing squatter problem led to
some of the first experiments in planned colonization on
abandoned haciendas. The colony established in the old
estate of Guápiles, for example, on the Caribbean lowlands
provided family subsistence farms for former squatters,
though export agriculture was unsuccessful (Hall 1976a,
125-130; Sandner 1962-1964, 1:125).
     In 1961, it was estimated that one million hectares
of tierras baldías were still available for colonization
(Salazar 1961, 166), although not all of these lands were
suitable for farming. The Ley de Tierras y Colonización
of that year outlawed spontaneous colonization, and the
Instituto de Tierras y Colonización (ITCO) was thereafter
the only organization authorized to establish new agricultural colonies. Between 1962 and 1966, the ITCO set up
eleven colonies, occupying a total of 35,412 hectares of
virgin lands and providing farms for 1,222 peasant families. Most colonies were located in areas containing little socioeconomic infrastructure, so costs were high and
the opportunities for commercial farming extremely limited. Primary colonization projects ceased in 1966. Since
then, the ITCO has been concerned exclusively with the
solution of squatter conflicts and the implementation of
agrarian reforms (Salazar et al. 1977; Seligson 1978).
     Shortly after the establishment of the ITCO, govern-
ment control over agricultural colonization was complemented by legislation designed to protect the surviving
natural forests in areas ecologically unsuitable for farming. The Ley Forestal, promulgated in 1969, provided for
the establishment of national parks and of two types of
permanent forests: protective forests, in which no logging
would be allowed because of anticipated damage to soil and
water resources, and productive forest reserves, where
controlled exploitation would be permitted. A new department of the Ministerio de Agricultura y Ganadería, the
Dirección General Forestal (DGF), was authorized to make a
detailed survey of forest resources (a task it has never
carried out) and to control the exploitation of these as-
sets.
     Protective forests, forest reserves, and national
parks now encompass approximately 20 percent of the country.[1] Only 14,000 hectares, located mainly on the margins
of the Valle Central, have so far been designated as protective forests, whereas 900,000 hectares of forest reserves have been established. Situated principally in the

---

[1]There is no reliable, small-scale map of the protective forests and
forest reserves.

TABLE 3.1
Farm area, 1950, 1963, and 1973

Year	Farm Area (hectares)	Total Area of Costa Rica (%)
1950	1,794,693	35.12
1963	2,640,130	51.67
1973	3,122,456	61.10

Source: DGEC 1953b, 1965, 1974b.

montane zone, the latter include many watersheds and steep slopes where logging would create grave ecological problems. Some of these areas should be reclassified as protective forests. The 130,000 hectares of national parks include historic sites, such as the pre-Columbian remains at Guayabo near Turrialba and the old hacienda of Santa Rosa in Guanacaste, as well as coastal and mountain regions of outstanding scenic, biological, and geological interest (Boza 1978).

The Ley Forestal stipulated that a permit must be obtained from the DGF before any timber can be cut from private or public land. In practice, the DGF lacks the funds and trained personnel to enforce the law, and illegal Hispanic American colonization is still taking place. The rate of expansion of the farm area, however, declined from an average of 3.02 percent per year during the intercensorial period between 1950 and 1963 to 1.72 percent between 1963 and 1973 (Table 3.1). Since 1973, the agricultural expansion rate may have been still lower. The only large area still suitable for agricultural colonization is a zone of approximately 250,000 hectares on the Caribbean lowlands, most of which requires drainage before it can be used for farming (OPSA 1979a, 61).

THE DEVELOPMENT OF TRANSPORT

Isolation was one of the principal constraints on economic development throughout the colonial period. In the early nineteenth century, transport was still effected by mules overland and sailing vessels along the coast. After independence, Hispanic American colonization preceded in many regions the construction of roads and railways. Where there was no all-weather transport, most pioneer farmers lived in dispersed rural settlements and practiced a predominantly subsistence economy. Sandner (1960, 76-78) has suggested that isolation, rather than adversities in the natural environment, was the most important single factor in the economic and social stagnation of newly colonized areas. Improved transportation was indispensible for the development of commercial agriculture and central places and, in turn, attracted yet more colonists to cultivate virgin lands.

Most of the major roads and railways built during the nineteenth and twentieth centuries were individual projects, designed either to give regions of potential export agriculture outlets to coastal ports or to link regions of frontier settlement with the Valle Central. There was no coordinated development of the transport network as a whole, with the result that its spatial distribution was uneven and its integration poor.

In spite of her small size, Costa Rica's natural environment imposed many obstacles on the development of transport. Fluvial navigation was limited to short stretches along the rivers of the coastal lowlands, areas that remained sparsely populated until the twentieth century. Most of the population lived in the interior highlands where the rivers are unsuitable for navigation, although their valleys afford important natural routes. Road and railway construction was difficult in steep and rugged mountains and in the humid, densely forested lowlands, where crossing swamps and bridging wide, braiding rivers posed major problems. Torrential rains throughout the country caused frequent landslides, washing away roads, railway tracks, and bridges.

The country's physical structure imposed two basic axes on the transport network: a longitudinal northwest-southeast axis of about 400 kilometers following the predominant trend of the cordilleras, linking the country overland with the rest of the Central American isthmus; and a 200 kilometer east-west axis via the Valle Central crossing the continental divide in the Cerros de la Carpintera at approximately 1,550 meters above sea level. This interoceanic route was too long and high to compete for international trade with either the Panama railway and canal or the ephemeral San Juan-Lake Nicaragua route briefly exploited during the midnineteenth century. The roads and railways along the east-west axis were built to link the Valle Central with coastal ports rather than to transport cargo or passengers between the Pacific and Caribbean.

The process of transport expansion in nineteenth- and twentieth-century Costa Rica is an interesting variation on the well-known model for underdeveloped countries constructed by Taaffe, Morrill, and Gould (1963) and based on West African case studies. The differences observed in Costa Rica recur in other developing countries, providing the basis for constructing an alternative model (Figure 3.9) (Hall 1975).

Costa Rica's principal colonial settlements were located close together in the interior of the country. They imposed a single nucleus on the transport network that has persisted to the present day. The initial objective of transport development after independence was to construct

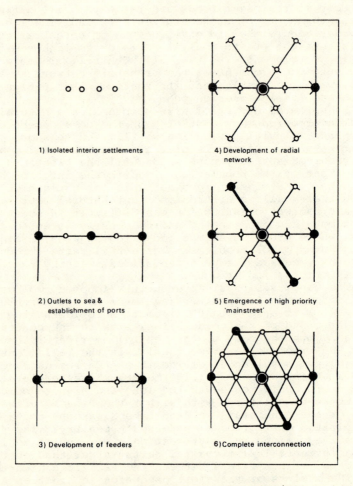

1) Isolated interior settlements

2) Outlets to sea & establishment of ports

3) Development of feeders

4) Development of radial network

5) Emergence of high priority 'mainstreet'

6) Complete interconnection

Figure 3.9 Model of transport expansion

routes providing outlets to the sea for the established Hispanic American population in the Valle Central, where the incipient coffee industry was hindered by lack of transportation. The construction of feeder routes followed shortly after the completion of each major outlet, so phases two and three were virtually simultaneous.

Between 1844 and 1846, the Sociedad Económica Itineraria, supported by the principal coffee growers, constructed a wide road for ox carts from Cartago in the Valle Central to the Pacific port of Puntarenas (Figure 3.10). Feeder roads linked the coffee regions of San Ramón and Grecia to the main road. Although the cart roads were not always kept in good repair and developed deep ruts during the rainy season, they revolutionized transport and made possible the transition from a predominantly subsistence to a primary export economy. Ox carts carried coffee from the Valle Central to Puntarenas and took back imported manufactured goods and foodstuffs (Hall 1976a, 59-61).

The cart road to Puntarenas had the disadvantage of leading to an ocean isolated from Costa Rica's major trading partners in Europe and eastern North America. In the 1840s, coffee exported from the west coast had to be taken in sailing ships around Cape Horn. The introduction of regular steamship transport along the Pacific coast and the completion in 1856 of a railway across the isthmus of Panama were only partial improvements; transport costs were high and railway administration deficient. Only after the opening of the Panama Canal in 1914 did the Cape Horn route finally become obsolete.

The Sarapiquí and San Juan rivers provided an outlet to the Caribbean port of Greytown or San Juan del Norte, in territory eventually adjudicated to Nicaragua, from whence boats sailed to Kingston, Jamaica, and on to London (Vega 1980a, 113). Navigation on both rivers was hazardous. This route was never a viable alternative to the Pacific cart road for exporting coffee, although for many years it was used to carry mail and newspapers to and from San José (González Villalobos 1976; Sibaja 1973). There were several projects in the nineteenth century to build cart roads between the Valle Central and the Caribbean coast, but none came to fruition.

The railways built during the late nineteenth and early twentieth centuries were the first improvements on ox carts for overland transport. They dominated transport for about fifty years until the diffusion of motor vehicles and the construction of paved roads provided a competitive, alternative mode of transport. Like the cart roads preceding them, the railways were designed mainly to carry export crops to coastal ports.

The two principal railway lines were originally constructed for transporting coffee. The Atlantic railway, built between 1871 and 1890 from Alajuela in the Valle Central to the new port of Limón on the Caribbean coast,

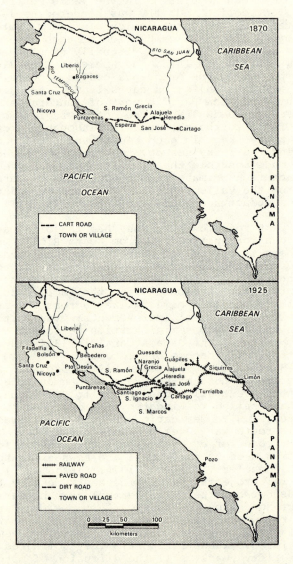

Figure 3.10a Evolution of the transport network,
1870 and 1925

Sources: MOPT 1980; Nuñez 1924; L. E. Peterson 1947.

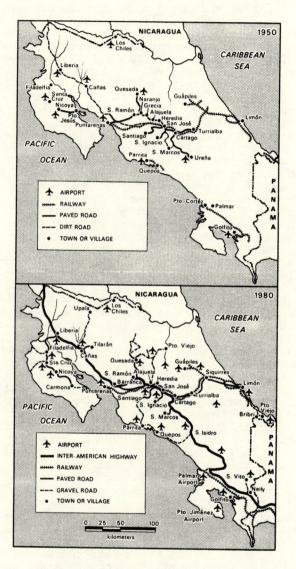

Figure 3.10b   Evolution of the transport network,
1950 and 1980

Sources: MOPT 1980; Nuñez 1924; L. E. Peterson 1947.

was constructed by North American entrepreneurs, financed by foreign capital and owned by a British company until nationalization in 1972. Initially, the railway was planned to run north of the Cordillera Central; the Old Line to Guápiles is a remnant of this route, which was never completed to San José. The main line was eventually built along the Reventazón Valley, between the Cordillera Central and the Cordillera de Talamanca. After 1890, the Atlantic railway--run initially on wood and coal and later on oil--replaced the cart road to Puntarenas as the major route for transporting coffee. It reduced traveling time between the Valle Central and the sea from several days to a few hours. Still more important, it provided an outlet to a much shorter oceanic route to Europe and eastern North America. By the end of the nineteenth century, it was being used not only to transport most of the coffee exports, but also to carry bananas from the plantation enclave established in the hinterland of Port Limón. Many branch lines were constructed on the Caribbean lowlands to open up new areas for banana cultivation (Kepner and Soothill 1949, 51-57; Stewart 1967). In this region where there were hardly any roads, the single-track, narrow-gauge railways were the backbone of the transport network until the 1970s.

Between 1897 and 1910, a railway was built between San José and Puntarenas. It occupied the valley of the River Tárcoles, parallel to the old cart road it replaced as the major route in the west of the country. The Pacific railway was built under contract with North American entrepreneurs, but, when completed, it was the property of the Costa Rican government. In contrast to the Atlantic railway, it traversed no humid tropical zones suitable for banana cultivation. No branch lines were constructed and the volume of traffic on the Pacific railway rarely surpassed that of the Atlantic line, which still provided the most direct route to Costa Rica's major trading partners. At first, the Pacific railway was run on firewood, then on coal and oil. The expense of importing fuel and the difficulty of transporting and storing oil persuaded the government to electrify the line between 1926 and 1930 (Castro Carazo 1933).

The construction of these outlets to the sea from a single nucleus in the Valle Central created an interoceanic axis running across the country between the ports of Puntarenas and Limón. Beyond this axis, the primitive transport systems that persisted into the twentieth century were totally inadequate for the development of specialized export production. The colonial Camino Real had fallen into disuse in the south of the country; the northwestern section, in the province of Guanacaste, was used only for animal transport. Local shipping on rivers and along the coasts facilitated the early expansion of the Hispanic American oecumene into the tropical zone, prior to the construction of railways and paved roads. Cabotaje or

TABLE 3.2
Length of road network, 1924-1977 (kilometers)

Year	Asphalt and Concrete	Macadam and Gravel	Dirt	Total
1924	--	c. 150	c. 700	c. 850
1940	365	423	n.d.	n.d.
1951	682	816	c. 6,000	c. 7,500
1965	1,120	4,322	n.d.	n.d.
1977	2,008	8,199	15,879	26,086

Sources: DGEC 1953a, 1966c, 1980; Ministerio de Fomento 1941; Ministerio de Transportes 1967.

coastal shipping was particularly important along the indented Pacific coast, which has a large number of sheltered inlets and bays suitable for small ports. Its peninsulas, separated from the mainland by large gulfs, are more accessible by sea than over land. Until the mid-twentieth century, the major route from the Valle Central to Guanacaste was by train to Puntarenas, then by boat up the Gulf of Nicoya and along the River Tempisque as far as the ports of Bolsón, Ballena, and Bebedero, and finally by horse or ox cart inland. The southwest of the country was reached via small ports such as Pozo (now Ciudad Cortés) on the banks of the River Térraba.

During the 1930s, the Compañía Bananera installed railways to link the banana plantations on the Pacific lowlands with newly constructed ports. In contrast to the branch lines of the Caribbean lowlands, which were linked to the main line between Limón and San José, the new Pacific railways were unconnected to the main line between Puntarenas and the capital. One ran parallel to the coast between Parrita and the port of Quepos. It fell into disuse when banana cultivation in the region was abandoned during the 1950s and was eventually taken up and replaced by a gravel road. The second line, known as the Southern Railway, linked the banana plantations of the Térraba and Coto Colorado valleys with the port of Golfito on the Golfo Dulce and is still in operation.

Road building was revitalized during the early twentieth century, following the introduction of motor vehicles. The total length of all-weather roads, built of asphalt, concrete, macadam, and gravel, increased from approximately 150 kilometers in the 1920s to more than 10,000 in the 1970s; dirt roads, passable by motor vehicles during the dry season, were extended over the same period from about 700 to nearly 16,000 kilometers (Table 3.2). This road building constituted a fourth phase of transport expansion, creating a radial network common in many underdeveloped countries, whether from a single coastal nucleus as in Uruguay or from an interior nucleus as in Costa Rica. The radial network reinforced the hegemony of the Valle Central at the hub of the transport system. It linked peripheral regions with the center of the country and indirectly with the international ports of Puntarenas and Limón, but it provided no direct routes from one peripheral region to another. Since the nineteenth century, dirt tracks had connected the frontiers of settlement with the Valle Central. During the first half of the twentieth century, these were gradually widened and their surfaces improved so that colonists in San Carlos, Sarapiquí, Tarrazú, Acosta, and Puriscal were able to produce both export crops and foodstuffs for selling in the principal regions of specialized coffee and banana cultivation.

The advent of aircraft, contemporary with the introduction of motor vehicles, extended the radial network still further, beyond the regions served by all-weather roads. Scheduled internal flights, operated by private companies, began in 1928, linking San José and Limón. During the 1930s, when all-weather roads were still limited to the Valle Central, regular flights were inaugurated from San José to San Ramón and Puntarenas, to Liberia, Tempisque, Santa Cruz, and Nicoya in the province of Guanacaste, and to several places close to the frontiers of agricultural colonization: Quesada in the San Carlos Valley, San Isidro and Buenos Aires in the General Valley, and Puerto Cortés in the Térraba Valley (Ministerio de Transportes 1967). Air transport reduced the isolation of pioneers on the frontiers of colonization, but it was too expensive for carrying most agricultural products to market. Because of the short distances involved, air transport declined as the radial road network expanded, though it is still vital in some of the more remote peripheral regions.

The emergence of a high-priority "main street" constitutes the fifth phase of the model. Costa Rica has not yet achieved the final phase: an integrated transport network knitting together the whole oecumene. During the 1940s, in response to the exigencies of the Second World War and the United States's interest in opening an overland route to the Panama Canal, construction began on the Pan-American Highway. This highway was the first modern route in Costa Rica to use the northwest-southeast axis previously occupied by the colonial Camino Real. The Pan-American Highway crossed Guanacaste via Liberia; at Barranca it joined the old road between Puntarenas and Cartago. From Cartago, a completely new route was opened over the Cerro de la Muerte at an altitude of more than 3,400 meters in the Cordillera de Talamanca, through the General Valley and the gorge of the River Térraba, and along the Pacific coastal lowlands to the border with Panama. This highway, completed in the 1960s, added two more

spokes to the radial transport network. The first improved overland route through the isthmus, it facilitated
the regional trade of the Central American Common Market.
It did not, however, eclipse the east-west route, reinforced in the 1970s by the construction of a paved road
between Turrialba and Limón. This road completes the interoceanic highway, parallel to the two major railways,
between Puntarenas and Limón.

THE FOUNDATION OF VILLAGES AND TOWNS

The expansion of the Hispanic American oecumene took
place within an agricultural economy, and, for more than a
century after independence, the rural areas absorbed over
four-fifths of the population growth (Fernández Arias et
al. 1976, 84-85). The processing of agricultural export
commodities was a predominantly rural activity, and there
was no large-scale development of mining or manufacturing
that might have promoted the growth of major urban areas.
During the nineteenth and early twentieth centuries, there
was no significant change in the ratio of rural to urban
dwellers. In 1927, only 19 percent of the population
lived in the country's seven towns (DGEC 1960).
    Of those founded during the colonial period, San José
alone experienced relatively rapid growth. The seat of
national government and the undisputed center of economic
and cultural activities, its population increased by an
annual average of 2.8 percent between 1864 and 1927, a period when Costa Rica's total population was growing between 1 and 2 percent per year. Natural increase must
have been reinforced by migration into the capital from
other parts of the country. Towards the turn of the century, San José began to acquire an infrastructure of im-
posing public buildings, electric lights, and tramways
similar to that installed in nearly all the Latin American
capitals at this time (Vega 1981a). By 1927, it was a
primary city with a population of approximately 50,000;
none of the country's other six towns had more than 8,000
inhabitants, and all the remaining central places were
villages and hamlets. With the exception of San José and
the principal ports, urban and rural places alike functioned simply as market, service, and administrative centers for the local farming population. When the urban
population did eventually enter a period of rapid growth
during the second third of the twentieth century, it was
associated not with the continuing expansion of the Hispanic American oecumene, but, rather, with the approaching
exhaustion of the frontiers of settlement and the replacement of centrifugal migration into the rural areas by a
new pattern of centripetal migration into towns.
    The foundation of villages and towns in the wake of
agricultural colonization was nevertheless a process of
cardinal importance because it laid the foundations of the

modern hierarchy of central places. The concept of urban
settlement had been introduced by the Spaniards, but only
four places--Cartago, Heredia, San José, and Alajuela, all
located in the Valle Central--retained the title of ciudad
in 1824. Their populations probably ranged between 1,000
and 4,000 (Meléndez 1977a, 183-199). The remaining nucleated settlements were villas and pueblos. A few of these
villages subsequently became urban settlements, but, of
the thirty-one towns registered in the most recent population census in 1973, more than two-thirds were founded after independence. Figure 3.11 indicates the periods during which the towns and principal villages of present-day
Costa Rica were founded. In most cases, the establishment
of a parish is taken to indicate the approximate date of
foundation; this installment usually preceded the creation
of a new administrative district. Much detailed historical research would be needed to assign accurate dates to
the foundation of the hundreds of small villages and hamlets that were also established on the frontiers of settlement.

The most dynamic central places in the expanding Hispanic American oecumene were the international ports,
linchpins of the agro-export economy. They were the only
new settlements that rapidly acquired urban status, and
the only central places, apart from the capital city, that
developed specialized functions serving the whole country.
During the colonial period, Costa Rica's exiguous maritime
trade relied on open roadsteads, and the lack of port installations was a major constraint on economic development.
After independence, the establishment first of the coffee
and then of the banana industries made it imperative to
build ports capable of handling both agricultural exports
and imported goods. In the century between the 1840s and
the 1940s, four ports were equipped for international
trade.

Puntarenas, founded during the eighteenth century and
opened to foreign traffic in 1814 (Meléndez 1977a, 173-
182), handled little cargo until the completion in 1846 of
the cart road from the Valle Central that facilitated the
export of large volumes of coffee. Its subsequent development was retarded by indecision about the best site for
a Pacific port. Located at the end of a long sand spit,
Puntarenas had no natural harbor, and ships had to contest
with a shifting seabed and adverse currents. Caldera,
Tárcoles, and Tivives to the south were all at various
times suggested as better sites, affording deeper, more
sheltered waters; they were also located closer to the
Valle Central and could be reached without crossing the
unbridged River Barranca that separated the peninsula of
Puntarenas from the mainland. In the midnineteenth century, Puntarenas still had no proper port installations;
lighters carried cargoes between the shallow estuary to
the north of the peninsula and ocean-going vessels an-
chored in the Gulf of Nicoya. The port was consolidated

Figure 3.11 Foundation of villages and towns, sixteenth to twentieth centuries

Sources: Estado del clero, 1972; Sandner 1962-1964.

during the 1870s with the construction of wharves and customs buildings. When the Pacific railway linked Puntarenas to San José in 1910, its hegemony on the west coast was no longer in dispute. An era of prosperity culminated in the late 1920s with the reconstruction of wharves, customs buildings, and lighthouses. By 1927, Puntarenas, with a population of more than 6,500, not only handled international trade but was also the principal commercial center for all the Pacific lowlands, linked to the port by cabotaje (González Víquez 1933).

Limón was the first town to be founded in the humid tropical lowlands since the unsuccessful Spanish settlements of the early colonial period. Originally developed as an alternative to Puntarenas for the export of coffee, it soon also became the country's principal banana exporting port. It was built in the 1880s on an uninhabited, swampy site, where a rocky outcrop and offshore island offered a minimum of shelter. It grew more rapidly than Puntarenas, attaining a population of over 7,000 by 1927. By the beginning of the twentieth century, the wharves were controlled by the United Fruit Company, and the town boasted the first macadam streets and the best water and sewerage systems in all Costa Rica. Because of the weak development of subsistence farming and manufacturing in its hinterland, Limón in its heyday was a great commercial center, second only to San José. Most of its trade was in the hands of foreigners: North Americans, Britons, Germans, Chinese, Jamaicans, Cubans, and Panamaneans (Casey 1979, 177-179). It was the first "company" town in Costa Rica. On the outskirts, the railway and banana companies built comfortable wooden houses for their Anglo-Saxon employees; the central pueblo civil, inhabited mainly by West Indians and Costa Rican migrants from the interior of the country, contained the commercial activities of the port. Limón's fortunes, however, were so closely tied to those of the banana industry that, when this industry disappeared from its hinterland, the town assumed an abandoned and run-down aspect it has not entirely lost to the present day, in spite of the resurgence of trade when banana cultivation was reestablished in the Caribbean lowlands in the 1950s.

When bananas first began being produced on the Pacific lowlands, the fruit was transported by boat to Puntarenas and, thence, across the country by rail for export from Limón. Efficient functioning of the new enclaves demanded the construction of ports close to the plantations, and the Cortés-Chittenden contract of 1938 authorized the Compañía Bananera to build Quepos and Golfito. Both were located on previously uninhabited sites, Quepos on a rather exposed section of the central Pacific coast requiring constant dredging, Golfito on a superb natural harbor in a sheltered, deep water inlet of the Golfo Dulce. Construction was completed in a few years. By 1950, Golfito with over 4,000 inhabitants and Quepos with more than 3,000 were among the major towns of Costa Rica. Both were laid

out as "company" towns, with separate areas for the fruit
company's upper echelon of employees, for its manual workers, and for the port installations. Adjacent to these
areas, the pueblos civiles contained independent traders
and services. When bananas were replaced in the 1950s by
African oil palm, destined for the home market, Quepos's
port functions declined, and it was the only town in the
whole country to register a decrease in population during
the second half of the twentieth century.

With the exception of the ports, all the new settlements in the expanding Hispanic American oecumene were
villages, none of which developed into a town until the
second third of the twentieth century. The distinction
between town and village is always somewhat arbitrary,
particularly in countries such as Costa Rica where successive censuses have used different definitions of "urban"
areas and populations. Sandner (1966) has suggested the
following criteria for the definition of a Costa Rican
town: a minimum population of 2,000, well-defined central
place functions, and a nucleated, built-up area physically
separate from other towns. Most of the villages established on the frontiers of settlement took many decades to
reach this stage of development.

The pattern of rural central places varied according
to the prevailing type of agricultural colonization. The
plans for organized colonies of immigrant or Costa Rican
farmers invariably included nucleated settlements, but,
since most of these projects failed, only a few villages
such as La Mansión, Aguas Zarcas, Monteverde, and San Vito
can trace their origins to the establishment of planned
agricultural colonies. In the plantation enclaves, the
banana companies built nucleated villages that followed a
standard design of two-story, wooden houses on stilts
around a central plaza. Some contained a church, store,
school, dispensary, and sports ground, but none was ever
the basis for subsequent urban development.

In the regions of unorganized, spontaneous colonization, most settlers lived on their own land, giving rise
to a predominantly dispersed pattern of settlement. There
was no planned network of central places. Some villages
from their inception were formally laid out with a plaza
and a gridiron pattern of streets; others evolved more
haphazardly, often from an original nucleus in a large
farm. Two functions in particular, religion and public
administration, seem to have acted as catalysts in village
development. Recent studies of the evolution of individual villages, such as San Pedro Poás and Santa Bárbara de
Heredia, have shown that they originally developed around
a small ermita or chapel. This chapel was replaced by a
larger church once a new parish was created (Salas Víquez
1979). In many places, the foundation of a parish preceded by several decades the establishment of a new administrative unit. The creation of a district or canton was
usually the result of petitions made by the local popula-

tion, aware that municipal status would attract other activities such as trade and services. As these functions proliferated and were diversified, the larger central places eventually acquired urban characteristics.

On the whole, villages were larger and more closely spaced in regions where improved transport permitted the establishment of specialized, labor-intensive, commercial agriculture than in areas where pioneer colonization stagnated at the stage of subsistence farming and cattle ranching. Following the completion of the Pacific cart road in the 1840s, villages grew up in the zone between Alajuela and Puntarenas. Along the road itself, the largest were Atenas and San Mateo, eclipsed by Orotina after the construction of the railway. In the coffee region to the north, the dense rural population supported central places every five to ten kilometers: San Pedro Poás, Grecia, Naranjo, Palmares, and San Ramón. All of these centers eventually developed into market towns during the mid-twentieth century. In the hinterland of the Atlantic railway, the prevalence of large farms producing both coffee and sugar cane in the upper Reventazón and Turrialba valleys and bananas on the coastal lowlands led to the formation of many estate villages, with workers' housing, elementary social services, and agricultural processing plants. Most villages never developed into towns, although one of the largest, Juan Viñas to the east of Cartago, evolved a pattern similar to that of the ports with an estate village adjacent to a pueblo civil. Turrialba and Siquirres, the principal settlements along the railway, were flourishing commercial centers by the early twentieth century.

Beyond the east-west axis between Limón and Puntarenas, where export agriculture was concentrated, village development was much less dynamic. The principal settlements in Guanacaste--Nicoya, Santa Cruz, Filadelfia, Liberia, Bagaces, Cañas, Tilarán, and Las Juntas--were regularly spaced every fifteen to twenty kilometers, but the sparse rural population limited their development as central places and only the provincial capital, Liberia, had a population of more than 2,000 in 1927. In the mountains to the south of the Valle Central, Santiago de Puriscal, San Ignacio de Acosta, San Marcos de Tarrazú, and Santa María de Dota, all founded during the second half of the nineteenth century, remained small villages with only a few hundred inhabitants. Colonists who crossed the cordilleras founded settlements at the foot of the mountains: Villa Quesada in the upper San Carlos Valley and Ureña, later San Isidro, in the upper General Valley (Sandner 1962). Sparsely populated frontier zones occupied mainly by subsistence farmers and cattle ranchers continue to be characterized to this day by a singular lack of towns. The principal central places in the most recently colonized peripheries--La Cruz, Upala, Los Chiles, Puerto Viejo, and San Miguel in the north, Hojancha and Carmona in the

Nicoya peninsula, Bribri and Buenos Aires in the south--
are still no more than villages.

Irrespective of their origins, the morphology of most
larger central places was rather similar and has left its
imprint on town plans to the present day. The gridiron
plan introduced by the Spaniards was retained after independence. No Costa Rican town was ever walled, so the
gridiron usually gave way on the outskirts to a pattern of
irregular streets and ribbon development along the main
roads. In the more densely settled regions, particularly
the Valle Central, there was rarely a sharp boundary between town and countryside.

Within the towns and villages, three categories of
land use were intermeshed. The central block was occupied
in smaller places by a simple grass plaza and in larger
places by a formal park with trees, lawns, a bandstand,
and benches, which constituted the main public meeting
place. Services, such as the church, school, and municipal offices, were usually located around the park. In
larger places, the central business district was concentrated around a covered market, generally located one or
two blocks away from the park. The residential area en-
circled the park and central business district. Until
well into the twentieth century, many town houses followed
the Spanish design (in turn a legacy of the Arab occupation of the Iberian Peninsula) of a walled frontage and
interior patio. The best houses were located close to the
park, the poorer relegated to the irregular, unpaved
streets on the outskirts. Few central functions inter-
vened in the residential areas except for pulperías or
general stores scattered at street corners and, in larger
places, one or two additional churches with their respective plazas.

Even in San José, the majority of buildings in the
early twentieth century were still single story. In the
older areas of settlement, the traditional building materials were stones for the foundations, adobe or rough earth
bricks for walls, and canes and tiles for roofs. Adobe
houses were cool and easily manufactured, but vulnerable
to seismic damage. Most of the buildings destroyed in
Cartago in the earthquake of 1910 were made of adobe, and
the material was forbidden in the subsequent reconstruction of the town. During the nineteenth century, adobes
had already begun to be replaced by a structure more resistant to seismic movements, bahareque: a cane frame was
filled in with mud, broken tiles, and manure, which dried
out to give a firmer, thinner wall. On the frontiers of
colonization, timber was the cheapest building material
available. The best wooden houses, with their insulated
double walls, tall rooms, and tiled roofs, were cool and
elegant. Wood had the advantage of being lighter than
adobe or bahareque, but it was vulnerable to damage by
fire, water, and rodents and the houses of many pioneer
farmers were little more than rough shacks (Sandner 1962-

1964, 2:27-32).

The agro-export economy generated a modern socioeconomic infrastructure in the principal areas of coffee and banana cultivation, in the towns of the Valle Central, and in the ports. During the nineteenth and early twentieth centuries, these centers acquired roads and railways, schools, hospitals, banks, electricity, and running water. Elsewhere, however, with a few notable exceptions such as primary education, curative medicine, and the postal and telegraph networks, the spatial diffusion of basic services lagged many decades behind the clearance of land. Cut off from access to all-weather transport and urban central places, colonists in the extensive peripheral regions of subsistence production and cattle ranching saw little improvement in their level of living until the middle of the twentieth century.

4
The Rural Areas

Costa Rica is now coming to the end of her frontier stage of development, which began with the Spanish conquest and accelerated after independence. The Indian oecumene has been reduced to small, isolated, and infertile areas. Few of the remaining forested lands are suitable for agriculture or stock rearing, although some could be exploited for their timber and mineral resources. Today's farming systems and land use patterns are the culmination of four centuries of predominantly spontaneous, unorganized colonization. Over large parts of the country, man's occupation has been ecologically destructive and economically inefficient. Major changes are now required to achieve more rational exploitation of natural resources, greater productivity, and higher levels of living in the rural areas.

In the census of 1973, 63 percent of the population was classified as rural (DGEC 1974a). This category, however, included suburban residents commuting to urban places of work. Between 40 and 50 percent of the country's inhabitants probably still lived in villages, hamlets, and dispersed settlements and worked in the countryside (Fox and Huguet 1978, 80-82; Zumbado and Raabe 1976). The proportion of the population directly dependent on the land has decreased since the second third of the present century, but, in absolute terms, it continues to rise. Only in the Valle Central does the urban and suburban population outnumber that of the countryside; the rest of the country remains predominantly rural.

Slightly over two-thirds of the country had been converted into farmland by 1973.[1] Agriculture was still by far the most important rural industry. It provided more than a third of the total number of jobs and employed between 70 and 90 percent of the labor force in the countryside. No other primary activity accounted for more than

---

[1]Unless otherwise stated, all statistics quoted in this chapter are taken from DGEC 1953b, 1965, 1974b.

1 percent. Agriculture's contribution to the GNP has declined to about one-fifth, but it still generates three-
quarters of the country's exports.

FARMING SYSTEMS

     Few Costa Ricans now practice the indigenous system
of resource exploitation that combined shifting cultivation with hunting, gathering, and fishing, although the
indirect influence of Indian agriculture is still apparent
in the persistence of many native crops and some cultivation practices. Contemporary farming systems are predominantly Hispanic American. Their roots can be traced to
the colonial period, although they have suffered profound
transformations during the nineteenth and twentieth centuries.
     Farms have several characteristics in common. First,
they involve permanent cultivation; the temporary reversal
to shifting cultivation on sparsely settled frontiers of
colonization is fast disappearing as population pressure
on the land increases. Second, they are concerned almost
exclusively with the production of crops and livestock.
In 1973, woodland occupied 23 percent of the farm area,
but forestry is an incidental activity undertaken primarily to clear the land for crops and pasture. Regular timber production is restricted to a small number of farms
where silviculture is being experimentally integrated with
crop production and stock rearing. Living fences, however,
are widespread, giving a pleasant bocage effect in the
countryside, providing shade and shelter, and producing
considerable quantities of timber (J. Sauer 1979). Third,
all the contemporary farming systems are fundamentally
commercial enterprises. Subsistence production makes a
valuable contribution to the domestic economy of many rural families, but it is no longer the major activity on
most farms. In 1973, more than 97 percent of the total
volume of crops was sold off the farm, although some subsistence products are not included in the census nor are
very small patches of food crops registered. Fourth, in
contrast to many other Latin American countries, there is
a high proportion of owner-occupied farms, reflecting the
ease with which land for farming could be acquired in the
past (Table 4.1).
     Farming systems vary according to the ways in which
inputs of land, labor, capital, and management are combined to produce outputs of foodstuffs, animals, and industrial raw materials. They are extremely difficult to
classify, and no typology can hope to be more than a broad
generalization. Making precise, quantitative definitions
of every characteristic of a farming system is difficult,
and the existing statistical sources, principally the agricultural censuses, contain only a fraction of the information required to implement criteria.

TABLE 4.1
Tenure of farmland, 1973

Type of Tenure	Number of Farms	Percentage	Area in Hectares	Percentage
Owner occupied	69,660	85.40	2,836,059.6	90.82
Rented (payment in cash)	1,474	1.81	24,925.6	0.80
Rented (payment in kind)	359	0.44	3,562.5	0.11
Loaned (no payment)	1,744	2.14	6,793.4	0.23
Others (including mixed tenure systems)	8,325	10.21	251,115.0	8.04
TOTAL	81,562	100.00	3,122,456.1	100.00

Source: DGEC 1974b. The census does not include squatters, who probably numbered several thousand.

Stouse (1971), in a pioneer classification, identified four principal farming systems. These were assigned to specific regions and subdivided into nuclear areas where they were originally developed and into other areas to which they were subsequently diffused. Stouse's first category was the finca comercial de los valles centrales, characterized by intensive land use, dense rural population, the subdivision of land into small holdings, and the predominance of cash crops. Initially developed in the Valle Central, the system later spread to peripheral areas such as Guápiles, San Carlos, Tilarán, the Nicoya peninsula, and the General and Coto Brus valleys. The commodities produced vary from region to region. They include coffee, sugar, tobacco, milk, fruit, flowers, and vegetables. The second system, the hacienda guanacasteca, is devoted to extensive cattle ranching in areas of sparse population and poor communications. In the province of Guanacaste and adjacent parts of Puntarenas, this system dates back to the sixteenth century. It has recently expanded into other areas, such as the mountains to the south of the Valle Central, the northern plains, the Caribbean coastal lowlands, and parts of the General Valley. The third system, the plantación en tierras bajas, has been characterized since the late nineteenth century by intensive production of cash crops, mainly for export, in large holdings where the physical environment has been radically transformed by modern technology. This system has been spatially unstable, oscillating between the Caribbean and Pacific coastal lowlands. The fourth and most

recent system, the finca-jardín limonense, is restricted
to the Caribbean lowlands where Negroes of West Indian descent cultivate a variety of cash and food crops, simulating the heterogeneous tropical forest.

Stouse's scheme has three major limitations. First,
by equating each system with specific regions it overlooks
the coexistence and interrelations between different systems within individual regions. Second, there is no distinction between peasant and nonpeasant farms; both are
included in the categories of finca comercial de los
valles centrales and finca-jardín limonense. Third, the
concept of plantation is used too restrictively, eliminating large, intensively exploited farms beyond the coastal
enclaves.

An alternative classification of the farming systems
not only of Costa Rica but of all of Central America has
been made by the Programa Centroamericana de Ciencias Sociales (CSUCA 1977). Taking as their fundamental criterion the relative importance of capitalist farming involving
wage labor and a market economy, they propose two major
categories: capitalist systems, characterized by extensive
use of large holdings for export production with the employment of wage labor, high levels of mechanization, and
well-developed ancillary services; and usufruct systems,
in which small units of land are directly and intensively
cultivated by their occupants (whether or not they have
legal title to the land) who with family labor and little
mechanization produce for their own consumption and for
sale on the home market. Each major category is subdivided according to its tendency to absorb or repulse labor.
The authors make a tentative regionalization: expansive
capitalist agriculture, capable of absorbing labor, is ex-
emplified by the banana regions of the south Pacific and
Caribbean coastal lowlands, whereas the coffee farms in
the Valle Central are classified as intensive capitalist
systems where no further labor can be employed; overpopulated regions of usufruct agriculture in the mountains to
the south of the Valle Central are contrasted with expanding zones of usufruct agriculture in peripheral regions
such as the General Valley, the northern plains, and the
Nicoya peninsula.

The authors recognize that the applicability of their
scheme to Costa Rica may be more limited than to the rest
of the isthmus because of the country's particular historical and geographical characteristics. Many Costa Rican
farms certainly do not fall squarely into the categories
of capitalist and usufruct farming as defined by the Programa Centroamericana de Ciencias Sociales. Not only do
most small holders produce goods for sale, but many practice a virtual monoculture of export crops. Large farms
supply the home market as well as generating exports, and
by no means are all efficient, modern units of production:
mechanization is restricted by topography and by the nature of many important cash crops, and many large farms

TABLE 4.2
Farms classified by farming systems, 1973

Farming System	Number of Farms	Percentage	Area in Hectares	Percentage
Minifundios (less than 4 has.)	31,677	41.15	43,197.1	1.38
Peasant small holdings (4-19.9 has.)	21,438	27.85	203,436.7	6.51
Medium-sized farms (20-199.9 has.)	21,159	27.47	1,175,365.2	37.65
Large estates (200 or more has.)	2,724	3.53	1,700,456.4	54.46
TOTAL	76,998	100.00	3,122,455.4	100.00

Source: DGEC 1974b.

are occupied mainly by rough pasture. As in Stouse's scheme, an oversimplified regionalization conceals the co-existence and interdependence of different farming systems.

A third classification, also applicable to all of Central America, was made by dependencies of the United Nations (CEPAL et al. 1972, 1973) and is the basis of the typology used in this book. It eschews the delimitation of regions according to farming systems, because different systems not only exist side by side but are functionally interrelated by flows of labor, crops, credit, and technology. Systems are classified according to a variety of factors, including farm size, labor resources and organization, capital investment, patterns of land use, and farm output. Five basic systems can be defined: the minifundio, the peasant small holding, the medium-sized farm, and the large estate, which may be either a plantation or an hacienda. Since there are also transitional types, the systems can best be considered as forming a continuum that ranges from the tiny minifundio to the large estate. As the size of the farm increases, so does the level of capital investment (even though cultivation may be labor intensive), the hierarchical organization of the labor force, the importance of commercial production, the productivity of individual crops (although not of the farm as a whole), and the proportion of pasture and uncultivated land. Conversely, the smaller the farm, the greater its resources of labor in relation to its resources of land, the more important subsistence production, the higher the overall productivity of the farm, and the larger the proportion of land devoted to crops.

The agricultural census contains no comparable classi-

fication of farming systems. The systems will therefore
be defined according to area, plantations and haciendas
being grouped together as large estates (Table 4.2). Cal-
culations made on this basis are only very approximate,
since the area occupied by each type of farm varies from
place to place depending on land capability, technology,
and land use. The census also lacks information about
farm size by cantons and districts. Data is available only for provinces and agricultural regions. The latter are
more homogeneous than the provinces, but they nevertheless
conceal important spatial variations so that, once again,
only general patterns emerge.[1]

The Minifundio

The minifundio is a subfamily farm that combines
scarce resources of land and capital with an excess of labor. Lacking sufficient land to support his family
throughout the year, the minifundista is obliged to seek
additional sources of income. Traditionally, he worked as
a wage laborer on larger farms; today, particularly if
close to the metropolitan area of San José, he may seek
work in the secondary or tertiary sector of the economy.
Except for very intensively cultivated market gardens,
most farms with less than four hectares of land can probably be regarded as minifundios.[2] Two-fifths of the country's farms fall into this category, although together
they occupy little more than 1 percent of the farm area.
Minifundios have proliferated during the nineteenth and
twentieth centuries as a result of the successive subdivision of family farms at each generation among large numbers of sons and daughters. In the densely settled, central regions of the country, they account for more than
half the farms; in the more sparsely populated peripheral
regions, with the exception of the north Pacific colonized
principally during the past hundred years, only one-quarter

---

[1]Census data exists in three forms: (1) tables published in the various volumes of the census; (2) unpublished tables kept in the offices
of the Dirección General de Estadística y Censos in San José; (3) the
original forms filled in by the census enumerators. There are no tables, published or unpublished, of farm size by cantons and districts.
For this reason, it was impossible to perform a factor analysis to
detect in detail the spatial patterns of farming systems.

[2]The Instituto de Tierras y Colonización considers four hectares to
be the minimum area required for a family farm. The Centro Agronómico
Tropical de Investigación y Enseñanza at Turrialba, currently engaged
in research into production systems suitable for small farms, regards
four hectares as the minimum required to support a family with most
types of land use. With exceptionally productive systems, a family
could be maintained on two hectares of land.

TABLE 4.3
Land use, 1973

Land Use Category	Minifundios		Peasant Small Holdings		Medium-Sized Farms		Large Estates	
	Hectares	Percentage	Hectares	Percentage	Hectares	Percentage	Hectares	Percentage
Crops	33,281.3	77.05	83,904.6	41.10	207,770.8	17.65	167,524.3	9.85
Pasture	8,445.2	19.55	85,605.6	42.08	610,090.8	51.92	863,909.4	50.81
Uncultivated	1,470.6	3.40	34,226.5	16.82	357,503.6	30.43	669,022.7	39.34
TOTAL	43,197.1	100.00	203,436.7	100.00	1,175,365.2	100.00	1,700,456.6	100.00

Source: DGEC 1974b.

TABLE 4.4
Subsistence production, 1973

Farming System	Total Volume of Crops '000 kgs.	Volume of Subsistence Crops '000 kgs.	Subsistence Crops As % of Total
Minifundios	169,190	21,920	12.95
Peasant small holdings	481,663	40,577	8.42
Medium-sized farms	1,467,646	27,126	1.84
Large estates	2,353,646	2,949	0.12
TOTAL	3,471,655	92,572	2.66

Source: DGEC 1974b.

to one-third of the farms are minifundios (Figure 4.1).

Because they contain such small areas of land but ample supplies of labor, minifundios are the most intensive farming systems. They are devoted primarily to crop production. Pasture occupies less than one-fifth of their area, and only 3 percent of the land is uncultivated (Table 4.3). Subsistence production is more important than in any other system, but it would be misleading to regard the minifundio as a predominantly subsistence unit (Table 4.4). Only 13 percent of the volume of crops produced are consumed on the farm. Most minifundios combine a variety of cash and subsistence crops. They sow about 12 percent of the cultivated area in three staple foodstuffs: maize, beans, and cassava. One-tenth of the minifundios grow sugar cane and over half cultivate coffee, some as a virtual monoculture in the Valle Central. The technology of minifundios relies on human energy and simple tools such as hoes and machetes, but, because of the need to produce as large an output as possible, a substantial proportion of the major crops are fertilized: over half the coffee and almost one-third the maize, rice, and sugar cane. Minifundios have insufficient land to keep large numbers of livestock. The majority keep chickens and over a quarter raise a few pigs or cattle.

The Peasant Small Holding

In a recent study of Costa Rica, Seligson (1980, 19-20) uses the term peasant to describe all lower-class people employed in agriculture, irrespective of whether they work their own land or are laborers on larger farms. As a farming system, however, the peasant small holding implies

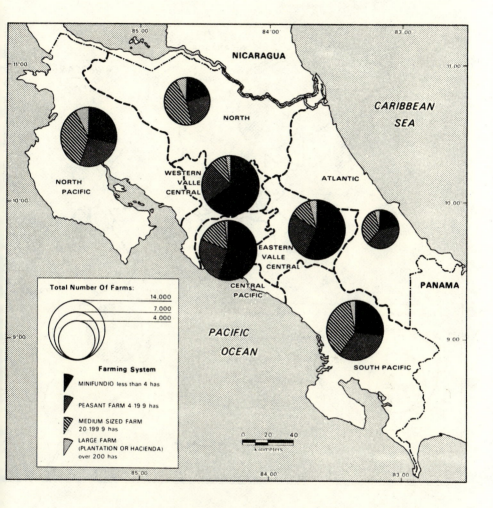

Figure 4.1a   Regional distribution of farming systems:
Number of farms

Source: DGEC 1974b.

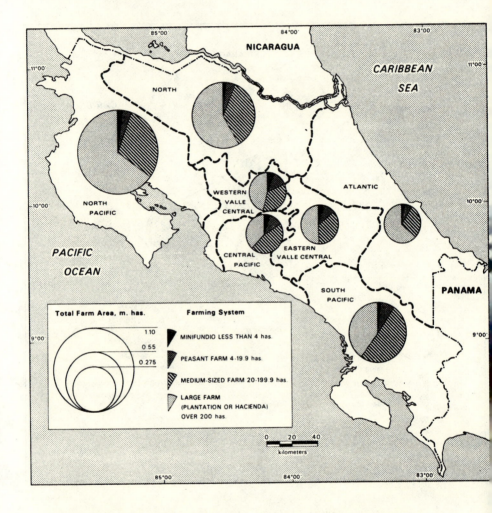

Figure 4.1b Regional distribution of farming systems:
Area

Source: DGEC 1974b.

access to land, whether this be via legal tenure, usufruct rights, or squatting. In contrast to the minifundio, the peasant small holding contains enough land to support a family throughout the year. Whereas the minifundista is obliged to seek additional sources of income, the peasant can make a living from the exploitation of his own farm, although he may work for short periods on larger farms at the peak of the harvest season. The amount of land sufficient to maintain one family but not requiring the labor of additional wage earners ranges from a lower limit of about 4 hectares to an upper limit of about 35.[1] The census categories include farms of less than 20 and more than 50 hectares. Farms of between 4 and 20 hectares will be considered as including the majority of peasant units, although some family farms are thus excluded. Peasants run more than a quarter of Costa Rica's farms, but they cultivate only 6 percent of the farm area. They are fairly evenly distributed throughout the country. Their share of farmland is highest in the same densely populated, central regions where minifundistas are most numerous.

The peasant farm is run as both a business and a household, a unit of production and a unit of consumption (Wolf 1966, 2-13). It has its roots in the colonial chacra, but, today, commercial production exceeds subsistence cultivation in the peasant small holding as it does in the minifundio. Only 8 percent of the volume of crops produced is consumed on the farm. In isolated zones of recent spontaneous colonization the proportion is usually higher, whereas in the principal regions of export agriculture nearly all the peasant's land is devoted to cash crops. With a greater area of land at his disposal than the minifundista, the peasant is able to combine cultivation with stock rearing. Crops and pasture each occupy slightly more than two-fifths of the area of peasant farms. Most holdings are too small for specialized beef or dairy production, but cattle provide subsistence foods and manure as well as a periodic source of income. With a level of technology similar to that employed by minifundistas, peasants produce export crops and foodstuffs for the home market. Their farms contain more than a quarter of the land sown in maize, beans, coffee, and cocoa and nearly one-fifth of the area of sugar cane.

Although the peasant does not work regularly on larger farms, he relies on nearby estates to process many of his crops. Peasants lack the capital to install complex processing plants, and, unless they are affiliated to cooperatives, they sell crops such as coffee and sugar cane to large farmers who operate mills. Estate owners in turn often supply credit to small farmers in the form of advance payments on their harvests.

---

[1]Estimate of the Centro Agronómico Tropical de Investigación y Enseñanza at Turrialba.

TABLE 4.5
Farms administered by managers, 1973

Farming System	Number of Farms Admin- istered by a Manager	Percent of Farms Admin- istered by a Manager
Minifundios	885	2.80
Peasant small holdings	905	4.23
Medium-sized farms	1,848	8.74
Large estates	1,306	47.95

Source: DGEC 1974b.

The Medium-Sized Farm

Whereas the peasant system relies entirely on family labor, the farmer with a medium-sized holding engages non-family wage laborers or peones, some of whom may be minifundistas. On both medium-sized farms and large estates, there are two types of peón: permanent workers engaged at a regular weekly wage throughout the year; and additional laborers, generally working on piece rates, contracted for harvesting and other specific tasks. Medium-sized farms often find it difficult to compete for laborers with large estates, where wages may be higher and fringe benefits greater. The number of workers on a medium-sized farm is not usually sufficient to warrant a complex subdivision of labor, nor the employment of foremen to supervise gangs of workers. In most cases, the farmer runs his own enter-prise and works on the land himself (Table 4.5). Like the peasant small holdings, most medium-sized farms have no mills for processing crops, which are sold to cooperatives or large estates. In the case of medium-sized banana farms, plantation companies not only transport and pack the harvest but also provide technical assistance such as crop spraying.

The lower limit of medium-sized farms lies between 20 and 50 hectares and the upper limit at about 200. Though in some respects transitional between the peasant small holding and the large estate, the medium-sized farm is nevertheless a very important element in Costa Rican ag-riculture. Over the country as a whole, more than a quar-ter of the farms and over a third of the farmland fall in-to this category. In the more sparsely populated and re-cently colonized peripheral regions, medium-sized farms account for more than a third of the total number of farms and contain up to half of the farmland.

Less than 2 percent of the volume of crops produced is consumed on the farm. Land use is less intensive than in minifundios or peasant small holdings: less than one-fifth of the land is devoted to crops, more than half is used for pasture, and a third is uncultivated. The distinction between the intensively cultivated crop farm and the extensively exploited cattle ranch, which reaches its maximum development in the plantation-hacienda dichotomy of the large estates, is already incipient in medium-sized farms although difficult to substantiate from census data. Many medium-sized farms are highly efficient, specializing in the production of export commodities or foodstuffs for the home market. Between 30 and 45 percent of the total area of coffee, sugar cane, and cocoa is located in medium-sized farms. They are the major producers of maize and beans and important suppliers of rice. They also contain half the country's dairy and dual-purpose cattle. At the other extreme, there are many medium-sized farms that contain a high proportion of uncultivated land and are devoted primarily to extensive beef cattle ranching.

The Large Estate

Large estates with over 200 hectares of land account for only 3 percent of Costa Rica's farms but occupy more than half the farm area. The country shares with nearly all the Latin American republics as yet unaffected by major agrarian reforms this heavy concentration of farmland in the hands of a small number of landowners, although in absolute terms Costa Rican estates are quite small. According to census data, there are only eighty farms with more than 2,500 hectares of land, but some farmers and farming companies own more than one estate. These eighty holdings contain 15 percent of the total farm area. Large estates are most numerous and occupy the highest proportion of land in the sparsely populated north Pacific, north, and Atlantic regions, where they contain up to two-thirds of the farm area; by contrast, they occupy less than half the farm area in the more densely populated central regions, where there are many peasant small holdings and minifundios, and in the south Pacific region, where medium-sized farms are the most extensive single group. Nearly half the large estates are administered by a farm manager; landowners running estates rarely undertake manual labor.

Taken as a whole, large estates are the most extensively exploited and least productive farms: only one-tenth of their lands are sown in crops, half are used for pasture, and nearly two-fifths are uncultivated. As in the majority of Latin American countries, however, they can be subdivided into two basic types: plantations and haciendas.

Plantations are intensive, specialized production units that employ large amounts of capital, modern technology, and a large, hierarchically organized labor force. The plantation has been one of the most dynamic farming

systems, and the term will be used here in the widest
sense to take account of recent changes that have occurred
both in Costa Rica and in other parts of the world (Gregor
1965). Previous definitions of plantations in the Central
American context have restricted the term mainly to the
monocultural banana plantations of multinational fruit
companies (Stouse 1971; Wolf and Mintz 1957). A more
flexible definition allows the inclusion of large farms
specializing in other products or combinations of products.
Plantations may be owned by Costa Ricans or foreigners,
and produce may be destined for either home or export markets.

Plantations were poorly developed in Costa Rica during the colonial period, and the cocoa farms of the Caribbean lowlands were very different from modern plantations.
The latter evolved after the consolidation of the agricultural export economy in the nineteenth century. Plantations, however, have never established a monopoly over
cultivation of Costa Rica's principal cash crops. They
exist side by side with other farming systems on which
they often rely for labor and for crops in order to use
their mills to full capacity. Plantations contain approximately four-fifths of the area sown in bananas and almost
half the area in sugar cane. They are less important in
the cocoa and coffee sectors. In contrast to sugar cane,
neither of these crops is suitable for mechanized cultivation; nor, like bananas, do they require heavy investment
in infrastructure. In the past, plantations made little
contribution to the production of food crops for the home
market. Today, they are the major producers of rice and
African oil palm, but their output of other staples, such
as maize and beans, is still very small. Subsistence production is insignificant and limited mainly to by-products
from the major cash crops, such as firewood from coffee
prunings and fruit from shade trees.

With the exceptions of coffee, cocoa, and beans,
yields per hectare of the major crops are higher in plantations than in any other farming system (Table 4.6).
Most plantations are both capital and labor intensive.
Capital is invested in fertilizers and other chemical inputs, the installation of drainage, irrigation, and mechanized transport, and the construction of sophisticated
processing and packing plants, the nuclei around which
many estate villages have developed. Cultivation and harvesting are mechanized on some estates, particularly in
the north Pacific region where the major crops are rice,
maize, sorghum, cotton, and sugar cane. Tree crops such
as coffee, cocoa, bananas, and African oil palm, however,
must be tended and harvested by hand. Ever since the
nineteenth century, Costa Rican estates have faced serious
shortages of labor, a major constraint on the expansion of
the plantation system. While agricultural frontiers remained, landless workers and minifundistas could choose
between wage labor on large estates and pioneer coloniza-

TABLE 4.6
Yields of major crops, 1973

Farming System	Coffee (kilos)	Sugar Cane (tons)	Bananas ('00 kilos)	Cocoa (kilos)	Maize (kilos)	Beans (kilos)	Rice (kilos)
Minifundios	3624	45.99	114	234	1085	419	1051
Peasant small holdings	4117	47.33	126	209	1027	409	1095
Medium-sized farms	4965	50.80	209	249	945	415	1195
Large estates	4708	67.78	366	197	1215	413	2120

Source: DGEC 1974b.

tion on their own land. In spite of the rigors and isolation of frontier life, many preferred this choice to the status of landless peón. In the premontane zone, the labor shortage is particularly acute during the harvest periods of coffee and sugar cane when farmers rely on extra workers from minifundios, peasant small holdings, and nearby towns and villages. In the plantations of the tropical zone, the labor shortage was initially solved by the immigration of West Indian Negroes. Today, wages on the banana and oil palm plantations of the coastal lowlands are among the highest in the whole agricultural sector.

In common usage, the term "hacienda" is often applied in Costa Rica to any farm, regardless of size or productivity. It will be used here to refer to a large, extensively exploited estate where, in contrast to the plantation, capital investment is low, technology is relatively primitive, and the labor force small. The hacienda developed during the colonial period in the tropical dry zone around the Gulf of Nicoya, taking the form of an extensive cattle ranch. As the Hispanic American oecumene expanded after independence similar haciendas were established in all the frontier regions where spontaneous colonization prevailed. The nature of the census data precludes an exact calculation of the present extent of haciendas; they are probably more widespread than plantations throughout the north Pacific and northern regions and in the interior of the Atlantic and south Pacific regions.

On the haciendas in some of the more recently colonized peripheral regions, timber out of the natural forest is still an important farm product. Once the land is cleared, haciendas are devoted primarily to cattle ranching. Crop production is insignificant; even subsistence cultivation by sharecropping tenants or colonos is uncommon. Productivity is low, particularly in haciendas located in mountainous or excessively wet regions ecologically unsuitable for both pastures and cattle. Nearly half the pasture is unimproved natural grassland, and there is little cultivation of fodder crops. The haciendas contain almost half the country's beef herd. In the past, they produced meat, hides, and tallow, mainly for the home market. The recent consolidation of beef as an export commodity has given new life to what is essentially an archaic farming system.

There is already an incipient transformation of haciendas into plantations as technology is modernized and land use intensified. This tendency is most pronounced in the north Pacific, the oldest region of haciendas. Some beef cattle farms are now highly efficient units of production, employing carefully bred stock, selected pastures, and modern rotation systems. Other estate owners have introduced mixed land use, combining intensive beef production with mechanized cultivation of grains, cotton, and sugar cane (Carcanholo 1977). In the newer estates of the humid tropical zones, some farmers produce beef cattle, rice, African oil palm, and bananas. Squatters have also appropriated hacienda lands for crop cultivation. The threat of expropriation by the Instituto de Tierras y Colonización is a major stimulus to hacendados to intensify production and reduce the area of rough pasture and uncultivated lands, the principal target of squatters.

AGRICULTURAL LAND USE

The pattern of land use in Costa Rica's farms still mirrors the past abundance of land and the relative paucity of agricultural labor and capital investment. In 1973, only two-thirds of the farm area was under production, and the majority of this land was used for extensive grazing. Less than one-fifth was sown in crops (Table 4.7). In spite of the country's rapidly growing population and diminishing agricultural frontiers, there has been little intensification of land use in recent years. The proportion of farmland sown in permanent crops has stagnated since 1950. The area in annual crops declined after 1963 not only in relative but also in absolute terms. The area of pastures, on the other hand, more than doubled between 1950 and 1973, and their share of the farm area rose from one-third to one-half. The growth of beef exports stimulated an unprecedented expansion of cattle ranching, the most important single change in land use in recent years. The proportion of uncultivated farmland has gradually declined, but, in absolute terms, this category contained a larger area in 1973 than in 1950.

As in many other developing countries with agro-export economies, a fairly sharp division can still be drawn between the highly productive export sector and the antiquated, inefficient sector that supplies foodstuffs

TABLE 4.7
Major categories of agricultural land use, 1950, 1963, and 1973

Year	Annual Crops '000 has	%	Permanent Crops '000 has	%	Pasture '000 has	%	Forest '000 has	%	Abandoned '000 has	%	Others '000 has	%
1950	220	12	131	7	617	34	570	32	210	12	41	3
1963	382	14	198	8	945	36	808	31	274	10	25	1
1973	283	9	207	7	1558	50	717	23	284	9	74	2

Sources: DGEC 1953b, 1965, 1974b.

for the home market. A threefold classification into export crops, food crops for the home market, and pasture
underlies most of the general maps of land use.

One of the earliest land use maps was that of the
German geographer, Leo Waibel (1948), who visited Costa
Rica in 1938. Limiting his study to the center of the
country, at that time the principal region of settlement,
Waibel observed four concentric, elliptical zones of land
use: coffee monoculture in the center around the capital
city, San José; a zone of coffee and sugar cane beyond
this center; then a belt of mixed arable and pasture land;
and finally an outer forest zone in which there were only
isolated patches of shifting cultivation. Waibel's model
excluded the banana plantations in the coastal enclaves
and the cattle haciendas in the tropical dry zone. His
gradation from intensive export agriculture to more extensive food crop production and pasture has been followed by
all those who have subsequently attempted to define land
use regions and is still a salient feature. Waibel, however, seeing a superficial resemblance, proposed Costa
Rica as an empirical confirmation of von Thünen's (1966)
model of concentric zones of land use, wherein an agro-
export economy oriented via coastal ports to foreign markets is the antithesis of an isolated state focused on an
internal urban market.

The land use maps of León (1948) and of A. W. Peterson and West (1950), produced when much of the north and
south of the country was still in the early stages of colonization, showed a similar distinction between intensively cultivated areas used mainly for export crops and
sparsely settled regions devoted to food crops and pasture.

The most recent land use survey of the whole country,
made by Nuhn (1973a), was based on field work, air photographs, topographical maps, and secondary sources. It
shows the great expansion of the farm area since the middle of the century and a more complex pattern of land use
than the older maps. Nuhn defined four major categories,
each found in several regions (Figure 4.2). Specialized,
intensive export agriculture is restricted to small areas
containing dense populations and makes a vital contribution to the national economy. These areas include the
Valle Central and the plantation enclaves on the coastal
lowlands. In the second category, crops still predominate
over pasture, but land use is more varied and export commodities are combined with food crops. The regions in
this category include the peripheries of the Valle Central,
parts of Guanacaste, and the General-Coto Brus depression.
Cattle farming, combined with small patches of arable
land, constitutes the third category. This type of land
use, associated with sparse settlement, now covers vast
areas of the country, particularly in the northwestern
quarter. The fourth category, which Nuhn called "subsistence agriculture" (although it also contains some commercial farming), is relegated to the most isolated regions

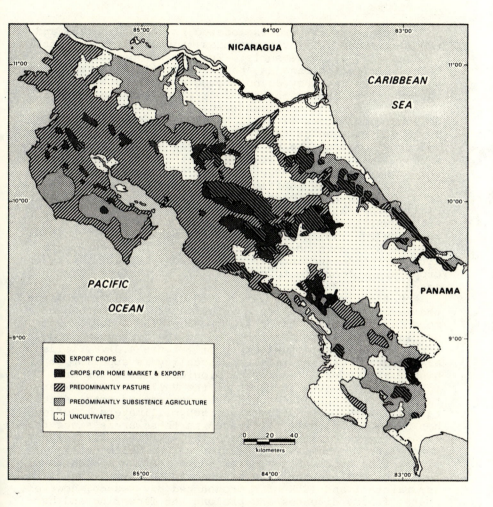

Figure 4.2 Generalized land use, 1971
Source: Adapted from Nuhn 1978b.

of recent Hispanic American colonization and the Indian
reserves.

Export Crops

Export agriculture is located in the premontane and
tropical zones, where it occupies many of the most fertile
volcanic and alluvial soils. The two principal export
crops, coffee and bananas, have quite different ecological
requirements, so they do not compete for land. Coffee is
restricted to the premontane zone where sugar cane is a
second, generally complementary, cash crop. Production
of both commodities is still heavily concentrated in the
Valle Central, which has road and rail outlets to both
coasts. Some sugar cane is also grown in the tropical dry
zone. In the tropical moist and wet zones, bananas are
the principal export crop and have relegated cocoa to an
entirely secondary position. Commercial cultivation of
both crops is restricted to littoral zones connected by
rail to the major ports. Whatever the farming system
within which export crops are grown, there is a marked
tendency towards specialization and monoculture. Cultivation methods have been greatly improved in recent years,
with corresponding increases in yields, but all the export
crops are vulnerable to potentially destructive plant diseases.

Coffee. Coffee, a major item of foreign trade since
the 1840s, still occupies a larger area and is grown on
more farms than any other export crop (Table 4.8). Commercial production is restricted to the premontane zone
where there is no danger of frost (Figure 4.3). Yields
are greater near sea level, but quality is superior at
higher altitudes. The best ecological conditions are
found in the center and west of the Valle Central, where
there are pronounced wet and dry seasons and total annual
rainfall is between 1,500 and 2,500 millimeters. Coffee
has been continuously cultivated in these areas since the
midnineteenth century. On many farms it is a virtual
monoculture. The eastern section of the Valle Central
contains volcanic and alluvial soils that have been sown
in the crop since the late nineteenth century. The heavier rainfall and lack of a pronounced dry season, however,
foster fungus diseases and prolong the flowering and harvest periods. As in the lower areas in western Valle Central, many farms produce sugar cane and pasture as well as
coffee. The Valle Central, most of which had been developed for coffee by about 1930, still contains two-thirds
of the total area sown in the crop.

During the past fifty years, the expansion of the
road network has stimulated the spread of commercial cultivation beyond the Valle Central. In most of the peripheral coffee regions, however, ecological conditions are
inferior, and the crop is grown in mixed land use systems.

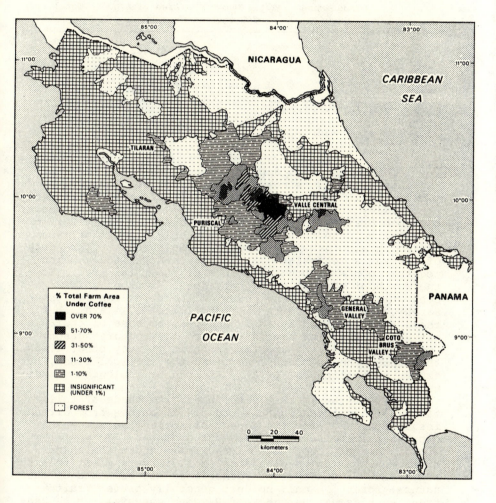

Figure 4.3 Distribution of coffee, 1973

Source: DGEC 1974b.

TABLE 4.8
Cultivation of major export crops, 1973

Crop	Number of Farms Where Grown	Percent of Total Number of Farms	Area Planted (has.)	Percent of Total Crop Area
Coffee	32,350	39.66	83,402.5	22.81
Sugar cane	9,484	11.63	38,762.2	10.60
Bananas	4,255	5.23	36,150.1	9.89
Cocoa	2,856	3.50	20,304.3	5.55

Source: DGEC 1974b.

The General-Coto Brus depression, opened up by the Pan-American Highway, is now the second coffee-producing region, with 16 percent of the total area. Most of the General Valley is covered with relatively infertile latosols; the Coto Brus Valley contains some andosols derived from Chiriqui volcano in Panama but has only a short dry season. Coffee is also grown in three rugged regions to the south of the Valle Central--Dota, Acosta, and Puriscal--which together contain about one-tenth of the total area. To the north of the Valle Central, small areas of coffee have been cultivated for many years in the upper San Carlos and Sarapiquí valleys and in the Cordillera de Tilarán, but these regions are distinctly marginal because of their low elevation, heavy precipitation, and lack of dry season. Coffee for local consumption is grown in many other areas throughout the premontane and even the tropical zones, but export production is strictly limited by ecological conditions.

Most coffee is cultivated under the shade of taller trees. These trees protect the coffee bushes from direct insolation, and from the impact of torrential rains that can knock the ripe berries onto the ground. In wetter areas, however, the humid microclimate under the shade trees fosters fungus diseases. Most farmers plant selected species of shade trees rather than use remnants of the natural forest. Small holders generally prefer fruit trees such as citrus, guavas (Psidium guayava), or bananas and other members of the Musa genus. These trees provide subsistence foods, but the Musa genus extracts large quantities of water and nutrients from the soil and may damage the coffee bushes if blown down by strong winds. On larger farms, where subsistence production is less important, the most common shade trees are legumes such as the Erythrina and Inga genera that restore valuable nitrogen to the soil (Vieillard-Baron 1974, 112-113). The regular pruning of both shade trees and coffee bushes provides large quantities of firewood, a major cooking fuel in rural areas.

Since the premontane regions suitable for commercial coffee production are located away from the coast, all-weather transport to the ports is vitally important. The Valle Central not only has superior ecological conditions for the crop but is also served by the best routes to the coasts. Railways and paved roads connect it with both Puntarenas and Limón. The other coffee regions are farther from the railways and ports. Much of the coffee from the General, San Carlos, and Sarapiquí valleys, as well as from Dota, Acosta, and Puriscal, is taken by lorry to railway stations in the Valle Central and thence by train to the coast. Only coffee from the Coto Brus Valley is exported directly from the local port of Golfito, originally built to serve the banana industry.

Of the four major export crops, coffee is the least important as a plantation commodity and the most widely distributed in minifundios and peasant small holdings (Figure 4.4). Land for the establishment of large coffee estates was plentiful in the past, but labor, particularly at harvest time when many extra workers were needed, was always in short supply. Only in eastern Valle Central has production been concentrated in plantations (Hall 1976a, 53-58). Coffee is well suited to cultivation on small farms; there is little scope for mechanization, and family labor can be used during the peak harvest season. Minifundios not only comprise more than half the farms producing coffee but also contain nearly 17 percent of the area cultivated in the crop--more than the area of coffee on large estates and an extraordinarily high proportion when it is remembered that the minifundios contain little more than 1 percent of the total area of farmland.

Whereas coffee cultivation is widely distributed among thousands of farmers, processing is carried out in 104 beneficios belonging to large landowners or cooperatives. Marketing is controlled by the Oficina del Café, successor to the Instituto de Defensa del Café created by the government in 1932 to safeguard the interests of small growers in their transactions with the beneficiadores. Costa Rica's high-quality coffee is processed by the "wet" method, which includes controlled fermentation of the beans. Coffee pulp, the residue left after the beans have been extracted, either rots on the farm or is thrown into rivers and streams that become heavily contaminated. Experiments have shown that the pulp could be used to produce livestock fodder and fertilizer (CATIE et al. 1974).

For more than a century, while the Hispanic American oecumene was expanding, coffee output was raised mainly by increasing the area sown in the crop. Since the 1950s, the modernization of coffee cultivation has raised productivity per unit area. Many groves have been resown with varieties such as Caturra and Catuai, which give higher yields than the traditional Arabica coffee. The new bushes

162

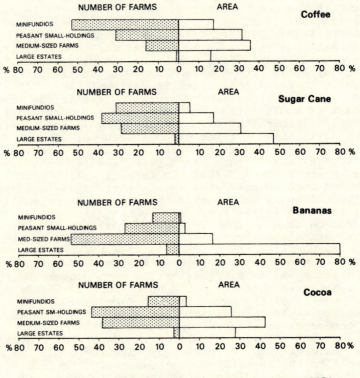

Figure 4.4   Production of major export crops, 1973

Source: DGEC 1974b.

have been planted at three or four times the density of
the old ones (Hall 1976a). Fertilizers are given to 70
percent of the coffee bushes and 14 percent can be irrigated. The record harvests of the 1970s were more than
twice the volume of those registered in the 1950s. Unpre-
cedentedly high export prices after frosts in 1975 destroyed a large part of the coffee crop in Brazil, the
world's leading producer, stimulated planting new groves
and intensifying production. In the longer term, however,
the industry remains vulnerable to both the vicissitudes
of world markets and the damage that would result from the
spread of coffee rust disease, caused by the fungus Hemi-
leia vastatrix, already rampant in neighboring Nicaragua
(Oficina del Café 1978).

　　Sugar Cane. Sugar cane and coffee are cultivated on
many of the same farms in the premontane zone. Sugar cane
has a much longer history than coffee in Costa Rica and
was an important crop in the colonial chacra. Home-produced dulce, or crude brown sugar, and, more recently, refined white sugar have traditionally supplied the whole
internal market, except in occasional years when low
prices made sugar cane unattractive in comparison to coffee. In 1973, the area sown in cane was less than half
that planted in coffee (Table 4.8). Specialized cultivation did not develop in the Valle Central until the late
nineteenth and early twentieth centuries. Most large-
scale production beyond the Valle Central dates back only
two or three decades. Small quantities of sugar were exported sporadically from 1915 onwards, but regular exports
were not consolidated until the 1960s. Between a third
and a half the total production was exported during the
1970s, accounting for about 5 percent of the value of exports. The area under cane doubled and output tripled between 1950 and 1973. The area was subsequently extended
to approximately 50,000 hectares by the late 1970s although less than 39,000 were registered in the agricultural census (Liga Agrícola Industrial de la Caña de Azúcar,
personal communication).

　　The expansion of the sugar industry was due to four
principal factors. First, the closure of the United
States market to Cuban sugar after the 1959 revolution
gave other Latin American countries, including Costa Rica,
an opportunity to increase their quota. Second, coffee
prices, which had been very high during the 1950s, fell
after 1958 to little more than half their previous level.
For many farmers in the premontane zone, sugar cane was an
attractive alternative to the traditional export crop, although it too was subject to wide price fluctuations on
world markets. Third, the government provided credit facilities and technical assistance to the sugar industry as
part of a wider policy of diversifying primary exports to
reduce the country's dependence on coffee and bananas.
Fourth, there was a rapid increase in home consumption.
This increase reflected population growth, the rise in

living standards, and the increasing use of sugar as a raw
material in manufacturing industries, particularly for the
production of sweets, chocolates, and preserves. Since
1979, part of the sugar cane harvest has been converted
into alcohol, which is mixed with imported petroleum to
produce fuel for motor vehicles. If the production of
gasohol continues, sugar cane could become Costa Rica's
most extensively cultivated crop.

Ecologically, sugar cane is a relatively tolerant
plant. It thrives best in areas with annual average temperatures over 19°C, such as the lower part of the premontane zone and the tropical zone where the four principal
cane-growing regions are located: the western Valle Central near the town of Grecia, which contains 31 percent of
the total area cultivated; the eastern Valle Central
around Turrialba, with 24 percent; scattered areas in the
tropical dry zone in Guanacaste and near Puntarenas, which
together account for 18 percent; and the San Carlos Valley,
with 15 percent (Figure 4.5). In the upper part of the
premontane zone, sugar cane was largely replaced by coffee
during the nineteenth and early twentieth centuries, but
it is still grown at higher elevations in some parts of the
Valle Central.

In addition to warm temperatures, sugar cane needs
alternating wet and dry seasons. On the northern and central sections of the Pacific slope, the plant grows during
the rainy season from May to November, matures during the
dry, slightly cooler period from late November to January,
and ideally is harvested during the warm, dry months of
February and March, although labor shortages often force
farmers to cut both immature and overmature canes. Much
of the recent increase in cane cultivation has taken place
on the Pacific slope, in Guanacaste, the central Pacific
lowlands, and the General Valley. There is scope for further expansion in these areas. Very little additional
land could be sown in cane in the more humid Turrialba
Valley, and the northern plains are distinctly marginal
because of their heavy precipitation, lack of dry season,
and poor drainage. A sugar mill was recently dismantled
in San Carlos and relocated in the General Valley.

Sugar cane is extensively cultivated on flood plains
and river terraces, which afford both fertile soils and
flat land. Topography is an important consideration, both
because of the potential for soil erosion after the harvest and because the canes are transported in long, tractor-
drawn carts. Sugar cane is thus complementary to coffee,
which can be grown on steeper slopes without undue erosion
and which is harvested by pickers who collect the grains
in small baskets. The two crops also have different labor
requirements: coffee is picked first, at the end of the
wet season, followed during the dry season by the zafra or
sugar cane harvest. Farmers producing both commodities
can avoid acquiring large numbers of temporary workers for
the short harvest period of a single crop.

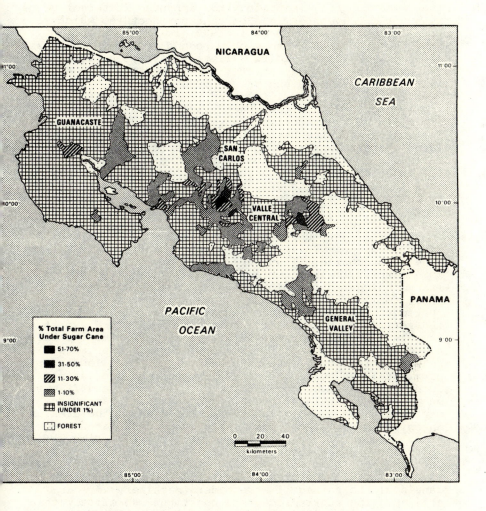

Figure 4.5 Distribution of sugar cane, 1973

Source: DGEC 1974b.

Sugar cane, like coffee, is grown on farms of all sizes, ranging from <u>minifundios</u> to modern estates (Figure 4.4). It is more heavily concentrated in large farms, however, where production can be highly mechanized. As in the coffee sector, technology has improved in recent years although the average yield of cane per hectare, which rose from 32 tons in 1950 to 58 in 1973, is still less than half that obtained in some other countries, such as Hawaii and Peru. Higher-yielding varieties have been introduced, including the B-43-62 variety, which permitted the expansion of cultivation into the tropical dry zone. Sugar cane is now more densely planted in order to raise productivity and to reduce the space available to weeds. Nearly one-fifth of the cane area can be irrigated, two-thirds is fertilized, and the use of herbicides is widespread. Many large estates contain laboratories where production is carefully controlled to ensure the cane is harvested when its sugar content is at a maximum. Like coffee, sugar cane is vulnerable to a number of diseases. Culmiculous smut (<u>Ustilago scitaminea sydow</u>) was discovered in Guanacaste in 1981 and threatens to reduce output on much of the Pacific slope.

In the past, unprocessed sugar cane was an important fodder crop, particularly for oxen. Today, nearly all the cane is processed. <u>Trapiches</u>, which produce <u>dulce</u> for the home market, are located not only in the regions specializing in sugar production but also in many other areas where small patches of cane are grown in mixed land use systems. The twenty-seven <u>ingenios</u>, modern mills producing refined white sugar for home consumption and export, process more than 80 percent of the harvest, and the existence of a nearby <u>ingenio</u> is a prerequisite for large-scale cultivation. Cane is a bulky crop that looses approximately 90 percent of its weight during processing. Once cut, its sugar content rapidly declines, and it must be processed within 48 hours. Mechanized transport has expanded to about 60 kilometers the radius of the area an <u>ingenio</u> can serve, but most large sugar cane farms are still located within 20 kilometers of a mill. Like coffee <u>beneficios</u>, sugar <u>ingenios</u> require heavy capital investment and are found only on large estates. Some still contain antiquated equipment, and yields of sugar per ton of cane could be raised if more modern machinery were installed. The sugar processors constitute an elite within the industry, similar to the <u>beneficiadores</u> in the coffee sector, although a few of the <u>ingenios</u> are now in the hands of cooperatives. The marketing of sugar, like that of coffee, is supervised by a government department, the Liga Agrícola Industrial de la Caña de Azúcar.

Sugar cane yields two important by-products whose industrial potential has not yet been fully realized. Bagasses, cane residue after sugar juice has been extracted, provides fuel for the <u>ingenios</u>. It could also be employed as raw material for the manufacture of fiberboard, coarse

paper, and artificial silk. Molasses, left after the cen-
trifuging process has separated out the sugar crystals,
has long been used as raw material in the national liquor
factory in San José. A variety of chemicals could also be
produced from molasses (BCCR 1972; LAICA 1978; Masefield
1965, 55-58; Ramírez R. 1969, 1974).

Bananas. In 1973, bananas, the principal export crop
in the tropical zone, occupied an area less than half that
sown in coffee (Table 4.8). Export production is concentrated in two regions of monoculture. The most important
area is once again the Caribbean lowlands, redeveloped
since the mid-1950s. In 1973, the region between the Sixaola Valley in the south and Río Frío in the north contained two-thirds the total banana area. Approximately
one-quarter was located in the south Pacific lowlands, in
the Térraba and Coto Colorado valleys (Figure 4.6). Elsewhere, bananas are cultivated only on a small scale in
mixed land use systems. Production for local consumption
extends up into the premontane zone, where bananas are often used as a shade tree for coffee.

The ecological requirements of the crop place fairly
strict limits on the areas suitable for specialized commercial cultivation. On the Caribbean lowlands, rainfall
is sufficiently heavy and continuous for cultivation without irrigation; on the south Pacific lowlands, irrigation
is required during the short dry season at the beginning
of the year. In both zones, bananas are cultivated mainly
on deep, fertile, alluvial soils. Most of the larger
plantations have a complex network of artificial drainage
channels whose installation often constitutes the largest
single capital investment on the farm.

Expansion of banana production in the south Pacific
lowlands, climatically marginal because of the dry season,
seems unlikely. In the Caribbean lowlands, however, it is
estimated that a further 5,000 hectares could be planted
within the present banana region, where there is an adequate infrastructure of transport; many more areas of alluvial soils throughout the northern plains, from Sarapiquí to Upala, could be used for banana production if good
roads or railways were built.

The banana is a sensitive plant, vulnerable to damage
by many natural hazards. Strong winds can produce "blow-
downs," leaving the trees prostrate. Although Costa Rica
lies beyond the paths of Caribbean hurricanes, banana
plants have to be sustained by wooden props, often of
eucalyptus or bamboo grown on the plantation. Floods on
low-lying land are also a serious problem, exacerbated in
recent years by the widespread deforestation in the upper
parts of river basins. Disease remains the greatest
threat. The Giant Cavendish banana, which has now replaced
the Gros Michel variety, is resistant to Panama disease
but vulnerable to Sigatoka, which attacks the leaves of
the plant. Yellow Sigatoka is controlled by aerial sprays
of petroleum-derived fungicides. Black Sigatoka appeared

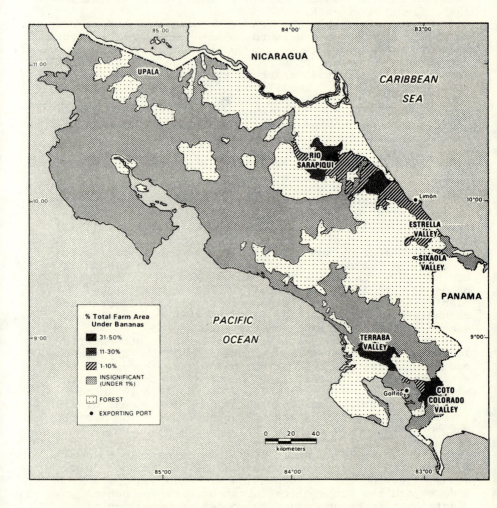

Figure 4.6 Distribution of bananas, 1973
Source: DGEC 1974b.

in Costa Rica during 1980. Control of this easily trans-
mitted variety of the disease is still at an experimental
stage and represents a considerable increase in production
costs.

More than any other export crop, bananas have traditionally been grown on large estates. The risks of heavy
losses from natural disasters and the high costs of land
clearance, drainage, and labor administration make bananas
an unsuitable crop for very small scale production. In
1973, 80 percent of the banana area was located in plantations and a further 16 percent in medium-sized farms (Figure 4.4). Export production was insignificant in peasant
small holdings and minifundios.

The Giant Cavendish banana has a thin skin and is
therefore vulnerable to bruising. Whereas the Gros Michel
variety can be loaded directly onto trains and boats, the
Giant Cavendish must be removed from the stem and packed
into cardboard boxes. A packaging plant requires a minimum of 200 hectares of bananas for efficient operation.
Three multinational companies, United Brands (formerly
United Fruit), Standard Fruit, and Del Monte, which operate under administrative contracts with the Costa Rican
government, pack, transport, and market the crop (La Gaceta, 5 December 1978). United and Standard each handle approximately 40 percent of exports and Del Monte deals with
the remaining 20 percent. All operate in the Caribbean
lowlands, dispatching bananas from Port Limón; United also
exports from its own port installations in Golfito.

The companies are important banana growers, but independent cultivators, financed since 1961 by the nationalized banks, have produced an increasing proportion of the
crop in recent years. In 1978, approximately 14,700 hectares of all banana plantations were owned by the three
exporting companies; assuming the total area sown in the
crop is now somewhat higher than the 36,155 hectares registered in the census of 1973, together these companies
control about one-third of the total area. United grows
bananas in the south Pacific lowlands, Standard and Del
Monte in the Caribbean lowlands. Production costs and
taxes are high in comparison with other countries, labor
unrest is frequent, and United and Standard are no longer
interested in expanding their plantations in Costa Rica.
All the companies rely heavily on the fruit they purchase
under contract with independent growers. They set high
standards for the bananas they receive but, in exchange,
offer technical assistance and credit to local farmers
(Carcanholo 1978; Lara 1970; OEA 1975; Standard Fruit Company 1978; United Brands, Standard Fruit Company, Del
Monte Corporation, and Asociación Bananera Nacional, personal communication).

Recent governments have encouraged continued expansion of the banana industry. Markets have been diversified, and the European Economic Community now purchases
nearly half the harvest (La Nación, 8 January 1979).

Costa Rica is a member of the Organization of Banana Exporting Countries, established in 1974, and hopes to consolidate her position as one of the world's leading producers of high-quality fruit. In spite of the vicissitudes of past production, bananas are regarded a key crop
for future development in view of the favorable ecological
conditions in the Caribbean lowlands and the fact that bananas are at present the most labor-intensive export crop
with the highest wage levels.

Cocoa. Cocoa production has been completely overshadowed by the banana industry, enjoying only a temporary
resurgence as the major export crop of the Caribbean lowlands during the 1940s and early 1950s. After the redevelopment of the banana industry, cocoa was once again
relegated to a minor position, unable to compete for labor
with the region's principal cash crop. In 1973, it occupied a smaller area and was grown on fewer farms than any
other major export crop (Table 4.8).

Cocoa is also the only export crop grown mainly in a
region with adverse ecological conditions. Production is
confined to the tropical zone, but the Caribbean coastal
lowlands, where 85 percent of the cocoa area was located
in 1973 (Figure 4.7), are too wet: rainfall exceeds 2,500
millimeters except in a small part of the Sixaola Valley
and dry spells rarely last for more than two or three
weeks. Heavy rainfall and high humidity foster the propa-
gation of fungus diseases, impede the ripening of the
fruit, and hinder harvesting and processing. Both the
northern lowlands, particularly the district of Upala, and
the tropical moist life zone on the Pacific slope are ecologically superior: total precipitation and the seasonal
rainfall regime approach ideal conditions and there are
fertile alluvial soils similar to those of the Caribbean
lowlands. The expansion of cocoa production in the northern lowlands is limited by lack of transport to the coast;
most of the crop at present produced in Upala finds its
way to Nicaragua. On the Caribbean lowlands, cocoa producers use the infrastructure of railways, roads, and port
installations originally constructed to serve the coffee
and banana industries.

Whereas bananas are produced mainly on large estates,
cocoa is grown on farms of all sizes (Figure 4.4). Cultivation methods are primitive, in spite of the fact that on
many farms there is a virtual monoculture. There has been
little replacement of cocoa trees, many of which are 40 or
50 years old. Most of the crop is grown either on abandoned banana lands or interspersed with remnants of the
natural forest. The majority of groves contain an excess
of shade trees, exacerbating the already high humidity.
Many groves scarcely receive any cultivation, and cocoa
production is relegated virtually to the status of an extractive industry: the pods are picked when world prices
make the harvest worthwhile, but, when prices are low, the
groves are abandoned until the market recovers. It is

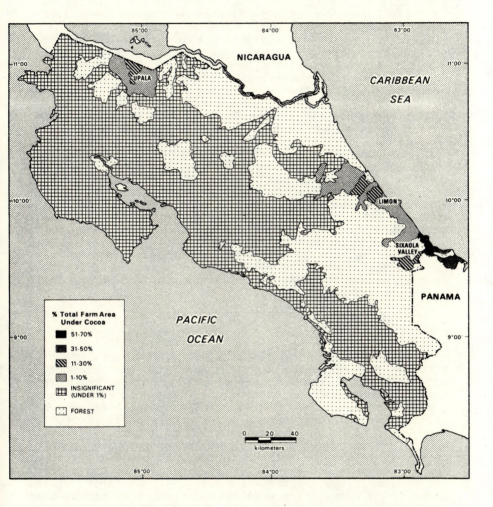

Figure 4.7 Distribution of cocoa, 1973

Source: DGEC 1974b.

hardly surprising that yields are exceptionally low, averaging about 250 kilos of dry cocoa per hectare.

Processing, as primitive as cultivation, is carried out on the farm. In contrast to coffee, which is fermented in modern mills to produce a high-quality bean, cocoa is dried on wooden trays in the sun. Without controlled fermentation only low-grade cocoa is produced. The installation of simple machinery for fermenting and artificially drying the beans would place Costa Rica in a better position to compete with the world's leading producers, Ghana and Nigeria, which export high-quality, classified cocoa processed by the "wet" method. No government department controls the quality or quantity of exports; each farmer makes his own arrangements to sell processed cocoa to independent exporters (Campbell 1962; Keithan 1940; OPSA 1977a).

The outlook for the cocoa industry has been even more bleak since the appearance in 1979 of the fungus disease, Monilia roveri, which has devastated an estimated 80 percent of the groves on the Caribbean lowlands. In view of the region's marginal ecological conditions, neither private nor public investment for redeveloping the industry is likely to be forthcoming unless high world prices make cocoa production particularly attractive. Meanwhile, the Ministerio de Agricultura y Ganadería has recommended the replacement of cocoa by mixed land use, including coconuts, root crops such as cassava and tiquisque, and spices such as pepper and ginger (La Nación, 9 March 1981).

Food Crops

In contrast to the major export commodities, the cultivation of food crops is widely scattered and frequently relegated to regions with suboptimal ecological conditions and a poor economic infrastructure. There is little specialized cultivation and a substantial proportion of subsistence production. Of the three staple foods, rice, maize, and beans, only rice is grown on a large scale with modern technology. On many farms, food crops are grown by primitive methods, resulting in low yields and low incomes for the farmers and expensive, poor-quality products for the consumer (Vieillard-Baron 1974, 236). In spite of the country's adverse balance of trade, recurrent shortages of basic foodstuffs continue to be solved by importing rather than by improving the economic infrastructure to use maximally the country's own ecological potential for agricultural production.

Rice. "Dry" or "upland" rice, today Costa Rica's most important food crop (Table 4.9), is cultivated in mixed land use systems. Production is concentrated in the tropical and lower premontane zones on the Pacific slope where, in some districts, nearly a quarter of the farm area is devoted to the crop (Figure 4.8). Cultivation has

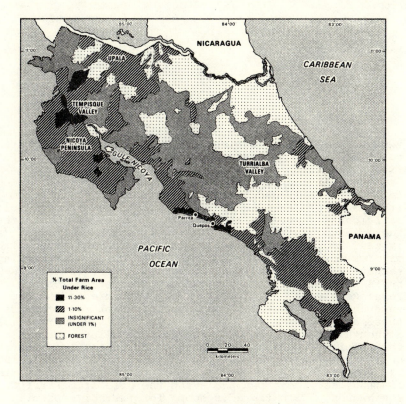

Figure 4.8 Distribution of rice, 1973

Source: DGEC 1974b.

TABLE 4.9
Cultivation of major food crops, 1973

Crop	Number of Farms Where Grown	Percent of Total Number of Farms	Area Planted (has.)	Percent of Total Crop Area
Rice	15,278	18.73	65,458.4	17.90
Maize	30,012	36.80	51,888.3	14.19
Beans	19,149	23.48	26,680.9	7.30

Source: DGEC 1974b.

expanded rapidly as agricultural colonists have migrated to lower elevations: between 1950 and 1973, the area of rice cultivation increased four times.

Much of the crop is grown, however, in areas ecologically not ideal, and harvests fluctuate up to 20 percent from year to year (OPSA 1975). Rainfall is the main climatic constraint. In the Tempisque Valley and along the eastern shore of the Gulf of Nicoya, which contained nearly half the area sown in rice in 1973, the climate is too dry for unirrigated cultivation. The onset of the rainy season is unreliable, and the veranillo frequently disrupts precipitation during the growing period (Coen 1966; Pérez Rosales et al. 1977a). Both bank credit and crop insurance have recently been suspended for rice farmers in these areas (La Nación, 26 May 1978 and 18 January 1979), although, with irrigation, the fertile alluvial soils of the Tempisque Valley could be used for intensive rice production. More than one-third of the area of rice in 1973 was located on the wetter parts of the Pacific slope, including the Nicoya peninsula and the area from Parrita southwards. Here there is scope for further expansion on flat lands with alluvial soils. 7 percent of the harvest was produced in the northern plains, mainly in the Upala district, but most of the Caribbean slope is too wet for "dry" rice. Some areas along the lower courses of the major rivers could be exploited for flooded or paddy rice, but both the initial capital investment and subsequent labor costs would be much higher than for "dry" rice (Econométrica 1970).

Minifundios and peasant small holdings contained 15 percent of the rice area in 1973 (Figure 4.9). On most of these farms cultivation is rudimentary, often carried out on steep slopes with slash and burn techniques. Large-scale production has spread in recent years. By 1973, 40 percent of the rice area was located on medium-sized farms and 45 percent on 549 large estates, many of which (particularly in Guanacaste) were formerly used almost exclu-

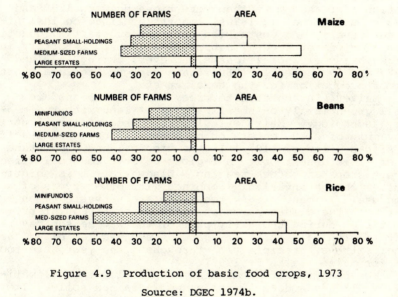

Figure 4.9 Production of basic food crops, 1973

Source: DGEC 1974b.

sively for cattle ranching. Today, rice is rotated with cotton, sorghum, maize, and improved pastures. Cultivation is mechanized on the larger farms. There is widespread use of selected seed, although research is still being carried out to develop varieties resistant to the fungus disease, Pyricularia oryzae (Pérez Rosales et al. 1977a). In 1973, nearly 20 percent of the rice area was irrigated and 63 percent received regular fertilization. Productivity per hectare fell slightly between 1950 and 1963 but doubled between 1963 and 1973, in spite of the climatic limitations of some of the drier regions where the crop is grown.

As a result of the rise in both area and yields, production increased more than five times between 1950 and 1973. During the mid-1970s, imports declined to insignificant levels, and Costa Rica exported substantial quantities of rice for several consecutive years. Exporters incurred heavy financial losses, however, during 1977 and 1978, and by the early 1980s there was once again a shortage of production for the home market.

Maize. In contrast to rice, maize and beans are still grown mainly on small patches of land with rudimentary technology. Maize is cultivated from sea level up to elevations of 2,000 meters on both the Caribbean and Pacific slopes (Figure 4.10). In the tropical and premontane zones it is absent only in regions devoted to specialized export crops and stock rearing. Elsewhere, it is ubiquitous, although invariably combined with other types of land use. In many areas, two crops are harvested each year. In the driest parts of the country irregular precipitation during the early part of the wet season may result in crop failure if irrigation is unavailable; at the other extreme, precipitation throughout the year, are too wet for maize (Salas F. 1969).

The crop is more demanding edaphically than climatically. It needs deep, fertile, well-drained soils. It removes many plant nutrients and therefore requires either rotation with other crops or careful fertilization (Sáenz Maroto 1960). A high proportion of the crop is produced on inferior soils; in the more accessible regions, the majority of the most fertile alluvial and volcanic soils are used for export crops or pastures. There is little maize cultivation in the Valle Central or the flat lands of the tropical dry zone where soils are fertile and production could be mechanized. Most of the crop is grown in areas such as the Nicoya peninsula, Puriscal, and the General Valley on infertile latosols or shallow lithosols (Econométrica 1970). Heavy soil erosion occurs on the steeper slopes where maize is cultivated.

Large-scale, mechanized cultivation is virtually unknown except on a few farms in the tropical dry zone. One-third of the harvest is destined for subsistence consumption. Maize is grown on farms of all sizes (Figure 4.9), but usually on small patches of land averaging less than 2

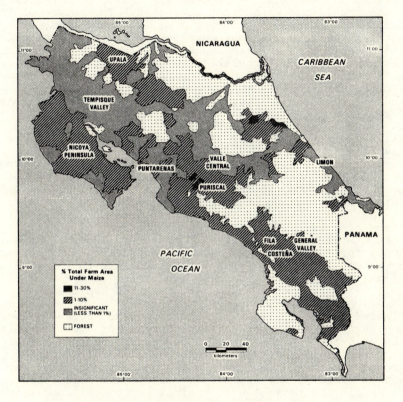

Figure 4.10 Distribution of maize, 1973
Source: DGEC 1974b.

hectares per farm. Cultivation is carried out mainly by
hand, with the aid of simple plows. Only 20 percent of
the maize area was receiving regular fertilization in 1973.

Unsuitable ecological conditions coupled with rudimentary cultivation techniques result in small, poor-
quality harvests. Costa Rica has imported small quantities of maize almost every year since 1883 when official
trade statistics were first published. The volume of imports rose sharply during the late 1960s and early 1970s
until in 1973 they almost equaled that of home production.
The widening gap between supply and demand had two main
causes: first, the population explosion increased the demand for tortillas and other foods made from maize flour;
second, and probably more important, the pig and chicken
industries absorbed over half the maize harvest for animal
feed.

Two solutions have been sought to the deficit in
maize production. Alternative sources of animal fodder
are being developed. The most important is sorghum, particularly valuable as a source of chicken fodder although,
unlike maize, it requires factory processing and cannot be
used directly on the farm (Gómez and Quintana 1977, 40-50).
This draught-resistant crop was introduced into Guanacaste
in the 1950s. By 1973 it was being grown on 3,752 hectares of land, mainly in large, mechanized estates in rotation with rice and cotton (González V. 1969). There is
scope for further expansion, and Costa Rica could soon become self-sufficient. The second response to the shortage
of maize has been to increase production of the grain itself. The area under cultivation, which had declined from
54,247 hectares in 1950 to 51,888 in 1973, rose to an estimated 64,770 by 1975. Yields have also increased in recent years, reflecting the introduction of improved cultivation practices, better seed selection, and greater use
of fertilizers. Output could be further raised if improved technology were more widely adopted on small farms
and if large-scale, mechanized cultivation were established in the regions with optimal ecological conditions
(OPSA 1975).

Beans. The common bean or frijol, the principal
source of protein for most Costa Ricans, is widely cultivated in the tropical and premontane zones (Figure 4.11).
Ecologically, it is more demanding than maize. Beans are
essentially for the wet season in areas of moderate rainfall. Cultivation is heavily concentrated on the Pacific
slope, though in the tropical dry zone irrigation is required to ensure reliable harvests every year. Most of
the Caribbean slope is unsuitable because excessive humidity fosters the development of fungus diseases. Beans
need deep, well-drained soils containing organic material,
phosphorous, potassium, and calcium (Sáenz Maroto 1962).
Most such soils are at present used for export crops or
pasture. Like maize, beans tend to be grown mainly in infertile latosols and lithosols in regions such as the

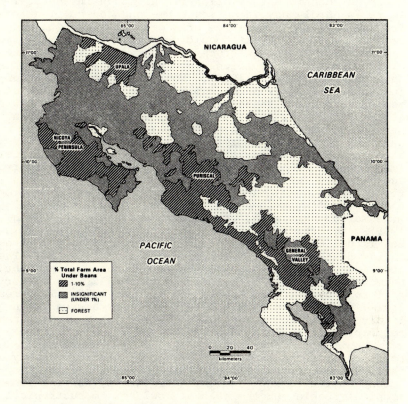

Figure 4.11 Distribution of beans, 1973

Source: DGEC 1974b.

Nicoya peninsula, Puriscal, the upper terraces of the General Valley, and the foothills of the Cordillera de Talamanca and Fila Costeña. Continuous cultivation in these areas, particularly if there are two harvests per year, leads to heavy soil erosion.

Beans are grown on small patches of land in farms of all sizes (Figure 4.9). They are often interplanted with maize, a technique that helps fix nitrogen in the soil. There is hardly any large-scale, mechanized cultivation. Some farmers still practice broadcast sowing of unimproved seed and carry out little cultivation between sowing and harvesting. Most soils receive no artificial fertilizer, although many are deficient in minerals, especially phosphorous (Econométrica 1970). Nor is the application of fungicides widespread, in spite of the vulnerability of beans to fungus diseases. The average yield in 1973 was 413 kilograms per hectare, an improvement of less than 3 percent on the level achieved in 1950.

Few farmers have proper facilities for drying and storing their crop and are obliged to sell their harvest immediately, often at low prices. Some of the best areas ecologically for bean cultivation, such as Upala, lack transportation to potential markets. Over 40 percent of the harvest is consumed on the farm. Bean production, like maize, has lagged behind population growth (Plath 1969). Imports rose sharply to unprecedented levels in the late 1960s and early 1970s. By 1974, more than two-thirds of the country's requirements were imported. The area sown in beans increased by an estimated 33 percent between 1973 and 1975 (Ramírez Bonilla 1975), and imports fell to insignificant levels in 1976 and 1977. They rose again, however, in 1978 and 1979, and Costa Rica is unlikely to achieve permanent self-sufficiency without radical improvements in production methods.

Fruits and Vegetables. Costa Rica's elevational range permits the production of a much greater variety of horticultural crops than otherwise possible in the tropics. Dozens of fruits and vegetables are grown, ranging from tropical species on the coastal lowlands to subtropical and temperate crops in the highlands. The ecological potential for horticulture, however, has never been fully exploited. Only one fruit, the banana, is grown on a large scale for export. Poor transport and lack of marketing facilities hamper commercial cultivation in most regions (González Vega et al. 1970). Specialized fruit and vegetable production is restricted mainly to the center of the country, close to the principal concentration of population. Subsistence horticulture is hindered by petty thieving and by farmers' ignorance of cultivation methods and the nutritional value of fruits and vegetables. Many crops are produced on such a small scale that they fail to warrant inclusion in the agricultural census; most of the data that does appear in the census contains no breakdown by cantons and districts, precluding precise mapping.

The most specialized areas of horticulture are located in the lower montane zone within a 50 kilometer radius of San José. Above the upper elevational limit for the subtropical export crops, coffee and sugar cane, the major activities are dairy farming and horticulture. Larger farms often combine the two; many small holdings specialize in horticulture. The south-facing slopes of Irazú volcano, above the town of Cartago, contain the largest area of fruits and vegetables. A second area of horticulture is located around the town of Zarcero to the west of Poás volcano, and there are scattered patches of fruits and vegetables in the Tarrazú region to the south of the Valle Central. All three areas are located in the drier parts of the lower montane zone, where annual average precipitation is less than 4,000 millimeters. With the exception of Tarrazú, they contain fertile volcanic soils but are generally too steep for large-scale, mechanized cultivation. The main crops are vegetables, including potatoes, carrots, cabbages, cauliflowers, celery, beetroot, and peas. Most are hand grown in small fields. Blackberries, strawberries, and peaches are produced for sale on local markets; other fruits such as apples and pears could also be more widely grown to replace expensive imported supplies. All the horticultural areas in the lower montane zone are linked by paved roads to the urban centers of the Valle Central. Other parts of the same elevational zone are more isolated from the principal home markets and lack the fertile soils and relatively dry climate of the areas near San José.

Horticulture in the premontane zone is usually combined with other types of land use. Ecological conditions are suitable for fruit and vegetable production over large areas, but horticulture is concentrated along the Puntarenas-Limón axis, close to the major urban markets. Vegetables such as onions, garlic, tomatoes, lettuce, green beans, peppers, and squashes are produced in many parts of the Valle Central, particularly in the central and western sections where there is less rainfall. There is some local specialization, such as the concentration of squash cultivation in the Reventazón Valley near Ujarras and of onion and garlic production close to Santa Ana to the southwest of San José. There are few compact orchards in the premontane zone, but a large quantity of fruit is produced from dispersed trees. Coffee is frequently grown under the shade of fruit trees such as oranges, guavas, and plantains.

On the central section of the Pacific slope there is an important region of fruit production in the tropical zone, stretching from Miramar in the north to Orotina in the south. Once again, there is little specialized production, but thousands of fruit trees are scattered in pastures. Among the most important are mangoes, oranges, mandarines, lemons, cashews, avocado pears, and guavas.

Fruit can be rapidly transported on the Pan-American Highway or the Pacific railway to the towns of the Valle Central, but poor marketing facilities restrict commercial
production. Most farmers sell their harvest on the tree
to intermediaries who provide pickers and transport.
Fruit and vegetable production in other parts of the tropical zone is mainly for subsistence consumption or for
sale in local market towns. With the exception of the banana plantations, specialized production is limited to
small areas such as the pineapple farms in the southern
section of the General Valley, the production of cassava,
pineapples, and plantains in the San Carlos Valley, and
the cultivation of melons and papaws in Guanacaste.

    Oil Plants. Costa Rica has little tradition of oil
plant cultivation. The principal oleaginous crop of the
Spaniards, the olive, is ecologically unsuited to the humid tropics. Prior to the 1940s, coastal coconut groves
were virtually the only local source of vegetable oils.
Large quantities of edible oils and fats were imported to
supplement home-produced coconut oil and lard. In recent
decades, a variety of oil plants have been cultivated.
The most important is the African oil palm (Elaesis guin-
eensis), one of the highest yielding of all oil plants,
rich in protein and vitamin A as well as in fats.

    African oil palm flourishes in the south Pacific and
Caribbean lowlands, in a climate similar to that of its
native region in West Africa. Most plantations are located on lands formerly cultivated with bananas, the pioneer
crop in the humid tropical lowlands. African oil palm is
the only food crop produced for internal consumption by a
vertically organized, multinational corporation. In 1978,
the Compañía Bananera was cultivating 11,000 hectares of
oil palm in the hinterland of Quepos and 4,600 hectares in
Coto 47 near the port of Golfito. Crude oil is extracted
on the plantations; margarine, cooking fat, and cooking
oil are manufactured by a subsidiary company in San José.
The Compañía Bananera maintains that profits from oil palm
are poor in comparison with those from bananas because the
government fixes low prices for the home market (Compañía
Bananera, personal communication). The company's standing
in the country, however, was enhanced when it switched to
food production in the Pacific enclaves instead of aban-
doning former banana lands as it had done earlier in the
Caribbean lowlands. In 1979, on lands at El Roble de Coto
Sur recently handed over by the Compañía Bananera to the
Costa Rican government, the Instituto de Tierras y Colonización began planting a further 36,000 hectares of African
oil palm. This project was to be in full production by
1984 when, presumably, Costa Rica would not only become
self-sufficient in edible oils but also produce a surplus
for export (La Nación, 3 June 1979).

    A smaller region of oil palm cultivation is located
in the Sarapiquí Valley. Production began in 1962 in
plantations owned by an old, established firm of vegetable

TABLE 4.10
Expansion of cattle rearing, 1950-1973

Year	Area of Pasture (has.)	Percent of Total Farm Area	Head of Cattle	Number of Farms with Cattle	Percent of Total Number of Farms
1950	617,173.9	34.50	607,857	26,900	32.50
1963	945,306.2	35.90	1,067,819	37,167	32.37
1973	1,558,053.2	49.90	1,693,912	43,699	53.58

Source: DGEC 1953b, 1965, 1974b.

oil and margarine manufacturers in San José. There is
scope for expansion both in the Sarapiquí Valley and in
many other areas on the Caribbean slope (BCCR 1971; OFIPLAN
1976). A detailed survey undertaken by a Dutch consortium
concluded that 5,000 hectares between the Rivers Pacuare
and Matina (including lands planted in bananas in the early twentieth century) contain ideal ecological conditions,
as well as accessibility by paved road and railway (HVA
International 1974). The Sixaola Valley close to the border with Panama could also be developed for oil palm production.

Coconuts are now only a minor source of vegetable oil.
In 1973, the area of compact groves was 1,088 hectares,
less than one-tenth the area sown in African oil palm.
Most groves are located on saline soils behind the Caribbean coast, between Port Limón and Cahuita. Cultivation
techniques are rudimentary, as is the extraction of oil in
small village factories.

Stock Rearing

Stock rearing now occupies three times as much land
as crop production. Cattle rearing, by far the most important branch of the livestock industry, has undergone
enormous expansion in recent years as Costa Rica has
changed from a cattle-importing to a cattle-exporting country. Between 1950 and 1973, both the area of pasture and
the cattle population more than doubled (Table 4.10). New
pastures occupied nearly seven times more area as new crop
lands. Over much of the country, pasture is now the dominant land use (Figure 4.12). The heaviest concentration
is in the center and northwest where, in many districts, a
grassland monoculture occupies over 70 percent of the farm
area. Most of the regions where pasture predominates have
a marked dry season and are among the older areas of colonization. Even in the wetter parts of the country, how-

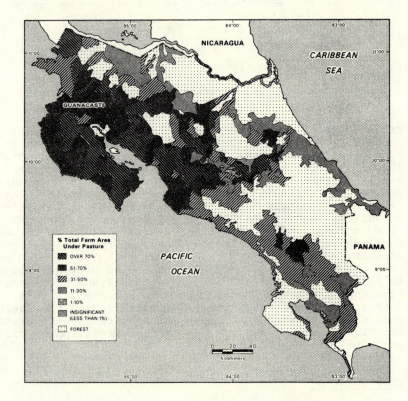

Figure 4.12 Distribution of pasture, 1973
Source: DGEC 1974b.

ever, on the Caribbean and south Pacific slopes where more forest remains, pasture occupies between 10 and 50 percent of the farm area and continues to expand.

In many tropical countries in Africa and Asia, indigenous cattle rearing is a multipurpose enterprise (Webster and Wilson 1966, 369). The Latin American cattle industry, by contrast, is entirely of European origin, and, in Costa Rica as elsewhere in the continent, a clear distinction can be drawn between beef and dairy farming. The majority of cattle are reared principally for meat. More than half the cattle farms produce some milk, but only 8 percent of the herd is used exclusively for dairying. A further 3 percent is composed of dual-purpose beef and dairy breeds.

Beef Cattle. Beef cattle farming has been one of the most dynamic sectors of the economy in recent years. The traditional cattle region in the dry, north Pacific lowlands is still the most important with about half the beef herd, but production is now widespread throughout the tropical and premontane zones (Figure 4.13). The northern plains of San Carlos and Sarapiquí are the second beef cattle region with 17 percent of the herd, followed by the south Pacific region with 10 percent.

Until the early twentieth century, most beef cattle were criollo breeds of Bos taurus, descended from the Spanish longhorns introduced in the colonial period. They adapted to the tropical environment but produced poor-quality meat. Zebu cattle (Bos indicus), more suitable than European breeds for the tropical and premontane zones, were introduced in the 1920s. An estimated 90 percent of the beef herd is now wholly or partly Zebu (OPSA 1979a). Crossbred cattle, such as Santa Gertrudis, are reared to combine the stamina of Bos indicus with the better-quality meat of purebred Bos taurus. European beef breeds, such as Charolais, Angus, and Hereford, have recently been introduced onto some ranches.

Pastures as well as cattle have been improved in recent years. Natural grasses have been replaced by imported Old World plants, including Guinea grass (Panicum maximum), Para grass (Brachiara mutica), and, above all, Jaragua (Hyparrhenia rufa) which quickly encroaches upon natural pastures and tolerates a dry season and poor soils. Jaragua grass permitted both an expansion of the area of pasture and more intensive stocking. More recently, pastures on the more fertile soils of larger farms have been further diversified by the introduction of Pangola grass (Digitaria decumbens) and African star grass (Cynodon plectostachyum).

Most beef cattle are fed only on pasture. In the drier regions, this method creates alternating problems of over- and undergrazing: the carrying capacity of most pastures in the dry season is only one-third to one-half that in the wet season. In Guanacaste, where soils and topography are suitable for cattle farming over large areas,

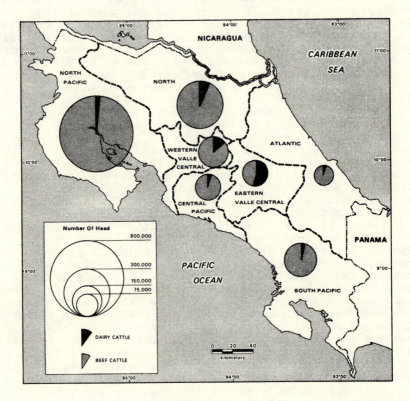

Figure 4.13 Distribution of cattle, 1973

Source: DGEC 1974b.

the dry season is the main constraint on more intensive
land use. Only small patches of poorly drained, low-lying,
bajura pastures along the Gulf of Nicoya and the Tempisque
flood plain remain green throughout the year. In the wetter areas now used for beef cattle ranching, such as the
south Pacific region and the northern plains, pastures are
green throughout the year but are poor in proteins and fibers. Both natural and planted grasses are easily invaded
by unpalatable weeds and secondary bush. Soil leaching
increases when forest is replaced by pasture in hot, wet
climates, and the humid environment provides ideal conditions for the proliferation of plant and animal diseases
(J. J. Parsons 1976; V. Smith 1970).

There is little use of forage crops. The production
of maize, widely used as cattle feed in other countries,
is still insufficient to meet the demand for human consumption. The small area of sorghum grown in the tropical
dry zone is used entirely for fodder, but much is destined
for the dairy farms in the lower montane zone and for the
poultry industry. Cultivation of leguminous fodder crops
is insignificant.

Because of the reliance on pasture feeding, most beef
cattle farms are large, very extensive units of production.
The average rate of stocking is about one head per hectare,
and the recent increase in the beef herd has only been
possible because of the great expansion in the area of
pasture. In many mountainous regions, 2 or 3 hectares of
pasture are required to support a single animal. Less
than 10 percent of the beef herd is reared in minifundios
and peasant small holdings, where stock rearing is usually
combined with crop production (Figure 4.14). With present
levels of technology, specialized beef production requires
a minimum area of 60-70 hectares for breeding and 300 hectares for fattening.

Large-scale exports of live cattle began in 1954.
These exports were quickly replaced by the export of beef
so that by-products, such as hides and offal, could be retained within the country. The major market is the United
States, where Costa Rica receives an annual quota. By
1976, nearly two-thirds the beef herd was destined for
foreign markets; in that year, meat occupied third place
in the export list following coffee and bananas. Beef
consumption per capita on the home market, however, has
decreased over the past twenty years since rising prices
have placed most cuts beyond the reach of the majority of
the population.

The recent increase in beef production has been
hailed as a means of diversifying the primary export economy, and bank credit has been readily available to cattle
farmers. Grave ecological and social problems, however,
have resulted from the growth of the beef industry. Cattle ranching is now widespread in many regions where heavy
rainfall, steep slopes, or a combination of both factors
make ecological conditions totally unsuitable for grazing

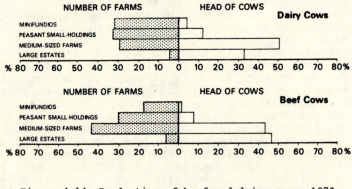

Figure 4.14 Production of beef and dairy cows, 1973

Source: DGEC 1974b.

lands. As forest has given way to pasture, severe erosion
has ruined the soil over wide areas in the hilly western
peninsulas and the cordilleras. Beef ranches occupy large
expanses of land at very low levels of productivity per
hectare. They generate little employment, and there is
substantial emigration from most districts where stock
rearing is the dominant land use (Herrera Soto 1978; Spielman 1972).

Dairy Cattle. Costa Rica's dairy industry, of out-
standingly high quality in comparison with that of the majority of tropical countries, has been developed in the
drier parts of the lower montane and premontane zones
where European breeds of cattle flourish and there is lush
grass during most of the year (Hunter 1959). Topography
is the main ecological constraint. The establishment of
pastures on the steeper slopes of the cordilleras has led
to severe soil erosion, and some areas now used for dairying are more suitable for forestry or permanent tree crops.

Specialized dairy farming developed during the late
nineteenth and early twentieth centuries as colonists penetrated above the coffee regions of the Valle Central.
The dry, south-facing slopes of the Cordillera Central,
with their fertile soils and proximity to major urban markets, still contained approximately 70 percent of the
dairy herd in 1973 (Figure 4.13). Secondary dairy regions
are developing in more recently colonized areas. The most
important is the upper San Carlos Valley, on the north-
facing slopes of the Cordillera Central, which contained
18 percent of the herd in 1973. The remaining dairy cattle are reared mainly in the hills and intermontane depressions of the Pacific slope. In the past, milk production was insignificant in the warmer and wetter parts of
the country, but experiments are now underway to develop
dual-purpose breeds suitable for these areas.

Milk cows are kept on farms of all sizes (Figure 4.14),
but specialized dairying needs a minimum of about 10 hectares of land (Spielman 1972). Much of the milk produced
on minifundios and peasant small holdings is consumed on
the farm. Half the dairy herd is found in medium-sized
farms and one-third on large estates. Most commercial
dairy farmers are members of large cooperatives to which
they sell fresh milk for pasteurization in modern dairies.
The cooperatives supply most of the national market.
Cheese production on the farm, the most important commercial activity prior to the construction of all-weather
roads, is rapidly declining, as is the sale of unpasteurized milk directly from the farm to the consumer.

Most dairy farms employ modern production techniques
and rear Holstein, Jersey, Guernsey, or Ayrshire cattle.
Natural pastures have been largely replaced by planted
grasses that provide better-quality forage. In the lower
montane zone the most widespread is Kikuyu grass (Pennise-
tum clandestinum), particularly suited to cool, tropical
climates. Grass is supplemented by grain fodder on many

farms (MAG 1974).

Capital and production costs of dairying are high,
and the government fixes maximum prices for milk and milk
products. For several years, output has been insufficient
to meet the growing home demand, and Costa Rica has resorted to importing powdered milk. The cooperative dairies
give priority to fresh milk supplies, and there are shortages of other products, particularly butter, even during
the rainy season when pastures provide more fodder. With
the recent growth of meat exports, some farmers have abandoned dairy cattle for beef breeds (Rodríguez Quesada 1974,
27). Although the dairy sector compares very favorably
with the production of other basic foodstuffs in technology and in the quality of its products, the gap between
supply and demand is likely to widen still further unless
the government is prepared to subsidize dairy farmers.

AGRARIAN PROBLEMS AND REFORMS

Costa Rica's agrarian structure poses three complex
and interrelated groups of problems. First, there are
ecological problems stemming from the wide divergence between land capability and land use: in some areas natural
resources are underutilized, over much wider zones the
land is overexploited, leading to the destruction of potentially renewable natural resources. Second, there are
agronomical problems, particularly acute now that output
can no longer be raised primarily by extending the farm
area. It is imperative to increase yields and improve the
quality of many products. A third group of problems, of a
socioeconomic nature, concern the inequitable distribution
of the factors of agricultural production, the infrastructure of processing facilities, transport and marketing,
and the wealth derived from the land. Incipient since the
colonial period, all these problems have been exacerbated
in recent years by the rapid growth of population and the
exhaustion of the frontiers of colonization.

The first step towards the solution of the ecological
problems is to study land capability to determine how the
land can best be used to combine maximum output with the
conservation of renewable natural resources. Most of
Costa Rica's farmland was colonized without any prior scientific investigation of its ecological characteristics;
the foreign fruit companies operating in the plantation
enclaves were among the few entrepreneurs who studied
soils, drainage, topography, and climate before bringing
new lands under cultivation. The first general evaluation
of land capability over the whole country was published by
Plath and van der Sluis (1964) under the auspices of the
Food and Agricultural Organization. This study was part
of a wider survey covering the whole of Central America.
A second general map published by two Costa Rican agronomists, Coto and Torres (1970), showed an almost identical

pattern over wide areas. Nuhn (1973a) published the result of a third survey carried out in collaboration with Pérez Rosales, which contained several major departures from that of Plath and van der Sluis (Figure 4.15). Pérez Rosales et al. (1978b) subsequently prepared a series of regional maps covering the whole country at a scale of 1:200,000. Work is now beginning on a long-term project to map land capability at a scale of 1:50,000 in the areas suitable for farming.

All these surveys used four basic categories: intensive cultivation, extensive cultivation, productive forest, and protective forest. Areas suitable for intensive cultivation are limited to the most fertile soils, mainly andosols in and around the Cordillera de Guanacaste and Cordillera Central and alluvium in river valleys. These small and fragmented areas produce high yields per unit area, even with relatively simple technology. Annual crops, which leave the soil exposed to erosion after harvesting, can be cultivated on flat and gently undulating land; on steeper slopes, a permanent cover of pastures or tree crops is needed to protect the soil. Extensive cultivation, producing lower yields per unit area, can be carried out on poorer-quality soils, including latosols on flat and undulating land and some lithosols in the hills and mountains. A similar subdivision is made on a topographical basis between areas suitable for annual and permanent crops. On still poorer soils in areas of steep slopes or impeded drainage, ecological equilibrium can be maintained only under a permanent forest cover. Large areas of lithosols in the cordilleras and hydromorphic soils in the northern plains are suitable for productive forests, from which selected timbers can be extracted. Rugged watersheds, with only a thin cover of lithosols, require protective forests where no logging is carried out.

Estimates vary of the areas that fall into each of these categories. Plath and van der Sluis calculated that 53 percent of Costa Rica could be used for agriculture and stock rearing; this figure included 23 percent of potentially high-yielding land and 30 percent suitable for extensive cultivation. They recommended that 47 percent of the country be forested, 36 percent with productive forests and 11 percent with protective forests. Tosi (1971) considers only 30 percent of Costa Rica suitable for farming and 47 percent for productive forest; 23 percent should be left under protective forest. Pérez Rosales and his associates calculated that 42 percent of the country is suitable for crops and pasture and 30 percent for productive forestry. They classified the remainder as liable to flood or suitable only for protective forest (Table 4.11).

In spite of these discrepencies, all the evaluations of land capability point to the same overall conclusion. Although Costa Rica has traditionally been an agricultural country with farming providing a major source of employment

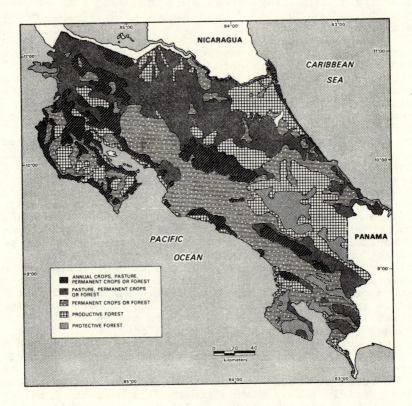

Figure 4.15 Land capability

Source: Nuhn 1978b (Reprinted with the permission
of the Instituto Geográfico Nacional).

TABLE 4.11
Major categories of land capability

Category of Land Use	Capability	
	'000 Hectares	Percent Area of Costa Rica
Annual crops	493.9	9.6
Pasture	1,310.0	25.5
Permanent crops	360.6	7.0
Productive forest	1,542.3	30.0
Protective forest	1,077.3	21.0
Liable to flood	351.8	6.9
TOTAL	5,135.9	100.0

Source: OPSA 1979a.

and the principal exports, her natural resources for agriculture and stock rearing are quite limited. Potential farmland is restricted to the tropical, premontane, and lower montane zones. Above 2,500 meters in the montane and subalpine zones, the climate is too wet and cold for cultivation. The rain forest formations of the lower life zones are also too wet for agriculture (Hunter 1959). Fertile, high-yielding soils, even according to the most optimistic estimates, cover less than a quarter of the country; more than half the potential agricultural land has poor soils capable only of extensive exploitation. On the other hand, enormous areas, variously estimated between one-half and two-thirds of the country, are suitable for forests.

At the moment, there are wide divergences between land use and land capability. Costa Rica is using little more than half her potential for crop cultivation: a further 200,000 hectares could be sown in annual crops and an additional 150,000 hectares in permanent crops. Much of the land suitable for annual crops is currently being used for permanent crops or pasture. Cash crops, such as coffee, African oil palm, and bananas, are unlikely to cede to annual crops unless economic incentives make the latter more attractive. Flat and undulating pasture lands in the tropical dry zone, however, could be profitably used for intensive production of annual crops if they were irrigated. The area of permanent crops could be expanded in hilly areas now occupied by pastures and forest. Pastures exceed the area ecologically suitable for grazing by nearly 250,000 hectares. They occupy vast areas of steep slopes and eroded soils. Ecologists estimate that more than half the present area of pastures should be used only for permanent crops or for forestry (OPSA 1979a).

The Ley de Reforestación, passed in 1977, was the first step opposing the traditional idea of forests as "tierras incultas" (MAG 1978a). This law repealed the tax on uncultivated farmland and established tax incentives, bank credit, and technical assistance for reforestation. So far, however, the few thousand hectares of reforested lands, mostly plantations of single species, are insignificant in relation to the magnitude of the ecological problem they are intended to solve. Between 1 and 2 million hectares require reforestation at the present time. The area will increase if deforestation continues in mountainous regions.

In spite of the legislation now in force, forestry as a specialized, permanent form of land use scarcely exists. It generates between 2 and 3 percent of the GNP and employs less than 1500 people. The present pattern of timber exploitation is a complex mosaic of small-scale cutting in the natural forests. There is little selective extraction of timbers from the forest reserves. Most logging is taking place on privately owned lands that will subsequently be used for crops or pastures. Much of the timber is wasted because of deficient extraction methods and the lack of industries to use the poorer-quality wood. Two-thirds is consumed as fuel. Sawmilling, like logging, is organized in small, inefficient units scattered throughout the country. Few mills receive regular supplies from forests in permanent exploitation, and none is run as part of a vertically integrated industry combining timber production and processing. Most sawn timber is destined for the construction and furniture industries. Shavings and offcuts are thrown away, contaminating rivers and streams (Villasuso et al. 1978).

Because potential farmland is limited in extent, it is essential it be used as efficiently as possible. While there were still frontiers of colonization, there was little incentive to intensify cultivation. Today, the scope for expanding the farm area is extremely limited, but production could be raised by adjusting land use to land capability.

Both drainage and irrigation will be required if Costa Rica is to use her agricultural resources to the fullest. The foreign fruit companies operating in the plantation enclaves pioneered large-scale land drainage. A further 250,000 hectares, located mainly on the Caribbean lowlands, could be drained to expand the farm area, but there are no plans at the moment to undertake this colonization of the country's last major agricultural frontier (OPSA 1979a).

The present irrigated area, developed at the initiative of private landowners, covers approximately 69,000 hectares or 2 percent of the farm area. This total includes about 40,000 hectares of banana plantations, occasionally irrigated during dry spells, as well as coffee and sugar lands on the Pacific slope. Further irrigation

is required mainly in the center and northwest of the
country, where there is a pronounced dry season. The irrigable area of lands with a slope of less than 10 percent
is about 400,000 hectares, equivalent to 13 percent of the
farm area in 1973; including steeper slopes of fertile andosols on the south-facing slopes of the Cordillera Central, the irrigable area might be raised to approximately
600,000 hectares or 19 percent of the farm area. Although
the future expansion of irrigation will continue to depend
in part on the initiative of individual farmers, the government is developing two major schemes. The smaller is
located in the western Valle Central near Itiquis, Alajuela, an area of small and medium-sized farms producing
coffee, sugar cane, vegetables, and cattle. Already 400
hectares are irrigated by local farmers; with government
help, the same volume of water will be used to irrigate a
further 1,100 hectares.

Much larger in scope is the Moracia project, now under construction in Guanacaste. Eventually, 120,000 hectares in the fertile Tempisque Valley will be irrigated in
the dry season. Water will come from two sources: about
30,000 hectares on the right bank of the Tempisque will be
irrigated with river water, and the remainder of the Moracia district will be supplied by water diverted from the
Caribbean to the Pacific slope via the hydroelectric
plants at Arenal, located close to the continental watershed. With irrigation, the Moracia district, at present
used mainly for extensive cattle ranching, could be intensively cultivated to produce rice, maize, beans, soya
beans, improved pastures, and tropical fruits. The major
obstacle to the completion of the project is the structure
of land tenure. In 1975, 134 farms, each with more than
100 hectares of land, occupied 89 percent of the region.
No agreement has yet been reached over a more equitable
distribution of the irrigable lands (MAG 1975; Ing. John
Mannix, personal communication).

Not only are there wide discrepencies between the basic categories of land use and land capability. Some of
the major crops are being grown in ecologically suboptimal
regions, while others could be much more widely cultivated.
Coffee is produced in humid zones at low elevations where
the plant is subject to damage by fungus diseases and the
quality of the bean is poor. Sugar cane is cultivated at
high elevations where the crop requires more than one year
to mature. Cocoa is grown almost entirely in regions that
are too wet. Rice is planted in areas that are marginal
without irrigation. The area sown in bananas and African
oil palm, on the other hand, could be substantially increased. Output of maize and beans could be raised if
they were grown on a larger scale in areas with ideal climatic and edaphic conditions. As a first step towards an
ecologically more rational distribution of the major crops,
the Oficina de Planificación Sectorial Agropecuario, OPSA
(1979b, 54), is undertaking zonification studies to com-

plement the general maps of land capability. These studies will serve as a basis for indirect government control
via restrictions on extension services, credit, and insurance to farmers within the zones designated for each crop.
    For a country so ecologically diverse, the present
range of crops and domestic livestock is very limited.
Four export commodities--coffee, sugar cane, bananas, and
cocoa--and three basic food crops--rice, maize, and beans--
together occupied 88 percent of the crop land in 1973;
pastures, more than three times as extensive as the crop
area, were used almost exclusively for grazing cattle.
Many crops now grown only on a small, or even an experimental, scale, could be more widely cultivated. Wheat,
displaced by coffee in the nineteenth century, is being
resown in the lower montane zone to the north of Cartago,
where it can be rotated with the region's traditional vegetable crops (La Nación, 16 April 1980). Sorghum, peanuts,
sesame, and the highly nutritious soya bean could be extensively grown in the tropical zone. Cotton might be
consolidated as a major crop in mixed land use systems in
the tropical dry zone, replacing imported textiles. Production of the indigenous staple, cassava, is being expanded in the San Carlos Valley. Rubber could be grown in
the Caribbean lowlands to replace imported supplies of
petroleum-derived synthetic rubber. The water buffalo
(Bos bubalis) could be developed as an important source of
meat and milk in the humid tropical regions, where the
climate is unsuitable for other bovine species.
    Many traditionally unimportant crops could constitute
the basis for new agroindustries or agribusinesses, combining the production of raw materials, processing, and
marketing in a single enterprise. The greatest potential
is in the foodstuffs branch, particularly fruits, vegetables, and spices (Castro Vega 1977; del Bello 1979;
Quiroz et al. 1980). The Corporación de Desarrollo Agro-
Industrial, a government authority created in 1979, has
established new export industries producing melons, tomatoes, sweet corn, chillis, and cucumbers in the tropical
dry zone, and pineapples and pejibayes in the northern
plains and the Caribbean lowlands. There is scope for developing many other tropical and subtropical fruit industries, particularly on the Pacific slope. Grown on a
large scale, fruits and vegetables could make a very substantial contribution to export earnings (La Nación, 31
March 1981).
    Ecologists have also pointed out the need to develop
completely new land use systems in the humid tropical and
premontane zones that cover such a large part of the country. Of the plants and animals native to these regions,
very few have yet been domesticated by man. Many wild
plants could be cultivated. Stock rearing could be transformed by domesticating wild fauna and feeding on leguminous trees and bushes instead of grass. By simulating the
heterogeneous structure of the natural vegetation, a mixed

economy of forestry, agriculture, and stock rearing could be developed (Tosi and Voertman 1964). Trees would be a dominant element, providing more organic material than herbaceous plants, protecting the soil from the erosive force of heavy rainfall, repressing competition from weeds, and creating a relatively cool microclimate and thereby reducing the rate of organic decomposition. This type of land use would reduce vulnerability to pests and diseases and diminish the need for fertilization. It would provide employment throughout the year, insurance against crop failure, and a variety of subsistence and commercial products including foodstuffs, fuel, building materials, and industrial raw materials (Holdridge and Tosi 1977).

The domestication of new plants and animals is a long-term goal requiring many years of research in a field neglected by agronomists and ecologists. Holdridge (1959) has indicated the sort of mixed farming system that could be developed on small holdings in the short term, restricted to growing the plants and animals already domesticated in Costa Rica. For a farm of 6 hectares in the tropical moist forest life zone, for example, he suggests an over-story of Laurel (Cordia alliodora) that would produce commercial timber and pejibaye palm, which yields highly nutritious fruit. Beneath these trees could be cultivated an understory of cocoa; the ground crops could include both grains, such as rice and maize, and root crops, such as cassava. A small garden could provide fruit and vegetables. Pigs, chickens, and possibly a milking cow would further diversify the farm economy. The Centro Agronómico Tropical de Investigación y Enseñanza at Turrialba is currently carrying out research and extension work to develop and diffuse land use systems of this type.

The adjustment of land use to land capability is a prerequisite for solving the agronomical problems of low productivity and poor-quality harvests. These problems are particularly severe in the case of annual crops (mainly basic foods) and stock rearing, the two activities most widely distributed in areas with adverse ecological conditions. By contrast, the technology used to produce permanent export crops, especially coffee, sugar cane, and bananas, that on the whole occupy ecologically satisfactory lands has been greatly improved in recent decades.

Farms of all sizes rely heavily on manual cultivation with simple tools such as hoes, machetes, and macanas. Less than 10 percent use machinery (Table 4.12). In tropical, developing countries, however, improvements in farm technology do not necessarily involve mechanization, which may be both ecologically and socially unwise. Much of Costa Rica is too steep for mechanized cultivation, and many of the country's principal crops, particularly permanent tree crops, can only be cultivated and harvested by hand. Scope for mechanization exists mainly on the larger farms, which occupy flat and undulating terrain suitable for grains, legumes, and sugar cane; most small farmers

TABLE 4.12
Use of energy and machinery on farms, 1973

	Number of Farms	Percent of Total Number of Farms
Energy source		
Human	70,256	86.14
Animal	3,482	4.27
Animal and mechanical	5,180	6.35
Mechanical	2,644	3.24
TOTAL	81,562	100.00
Agricultural machinery		
Tractors	6,544	8.02
Tractor-drawn plows	3,266	4.00
Animal-drawn plows	2,847	3.49
Harrows	3,220	3.95
Sowers	1,207	1.48
Harvesters	1,041	1.28

Source: DGEC 1974b.

can mechanize only if they belong to a cooperative. Because of the spread of extensive types of land use, particularly beef cattle ranching, jobs in agriculture have not
kept pace with the expansion of the farm area: the ratio
of farmland per worker increased from 12 hectares per man
in 1950 to 15 in 1973. Raabe (1976) has estimated that
ecologically optimal land use would generate employment
for nearly half the country's labor force, compared with
only one-third employed in farming and forestry in 1973.
The creation of more jobs on the land would be socially
beneficial, because it would help stem the drift of population from the rural areas into the towns where employment opportunities in manufacturing are limited and where
there is widespread underemployment in the tertiary sector.
Costa Rica thus faces the challenge of improving efficiency and raising agricultural output with a predominantly labor-intensive technology (Arias 1979, 59-63).
This result can be achieved in a variety of ways, including the use of modern methods of cultivation and soil preservation, the control of pests and diseases, the application of fertilizers, the use of selected seed and better-
quality livestock, the greater use of fodder crops, and
the judicious combination and rotation of different types
of land use. Agricultural research has already generated
a great deal of knowledge about these techniques. Institutions such as the Ministerio de Agricultura y Ganadería,
the University of Costa Rica, the Instituto Interamericano

de Ciencias Agrícolas, and the Centro Agronómico Tropical de Investigación y Enseñanza have operated experimental farms for many years. The basic problem now is how to disseminate improved technology more widely among farmers. The existing agricultural extension services of the Ministerio de Agricultura y Ganadería are insufficient to meet the growing demand and still tend to concentrate on improving output of the major export crops rather than of products for the home market.

Many agronomical improvements are concomitant upon economic and social change. Agricultural credit is insufficient and unevenly distributed. More credit is available for export production, including beef cattle ranching, than for the cultivation of crops destined for the home market. Politically influential large landowners can obtain loans more easily than can small farmers. The scarcity of long-term loans and of credit for new crops deters farmers from carrying out major changes in land use. The nationalized banks only provide an estimated two-thirds of the credit for agriculture and stock rearing. Farmers also resort to prestamistas or private money lenders, who charge usurious rates of interest. The widespread use of small, short-term credit supplied by friends and relatives reflects a willingness to provide mutual aid that could be more widely canalized via rural savings organizations and cooperatives (Cross and González 1969).

The infrastructure of agricultural marketing and transportation still contains many deficiencies, in spite of a long tradition of government intervention. The most efficient arrangements are found in the major export sectors--coffee, sugar cane, bananas, and beef--and in a small number of industries such as dairying, oil palm, and tobacco, which produce mainly for the home market. The official Consejo Nacional de Producción, with agencies throughout the country, purchases, processes, and distributes rice, maize, beans, and sorghum, but many farmers prefer to sell to private intermediaries offering higher prices. Most other agricultural products consumed on the home market, including chickens, eggs, root crops, fruits, and vegetables, are transported and marketed either by farmers themselves or by private entrepreneurs. There is heavy spoilage of perishable goods due to poor handling, delays, and the damage caused by transport on bad roads. San José, at the hub of the national transport network, is the major center of the wholesale trade in agricultural commodities. Farmers outside the Valle Central lack efficient regional distribution systems. In many peripheral regions, the ecological potential for crop production is unexploited because of the lack of roads and marketing facilities (González Vega et al. 1970).

Land is heavily concentrated in the hands of a small minority of those working in the agricultural sector (Figure 4.16). In 1973, half the farms occupied 2.5 percent of the land while, at the other extreme, 50 percent of the

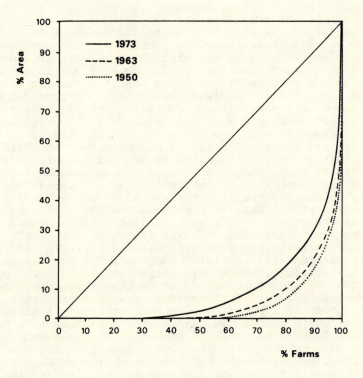

Figure 4.16   Lorenz curves of land tenure, 1950, 1963, and 1973
Sources: DGEC 1953b, 1965, 1974b.

land was concentrated in 3 percent of the farms. The slight improvement between 1950 and 1973 was due to two principal changes: the decline in the number of minifundios from over 50,000 to little more than 30,000, and the decrease in the proportion of land in very large estates of over 1,000 hectares from 35 to 25 percent. In 1973, there were still more than 1 million hectares of uncultivated land within farms; nearly two-thirds was located in large estates and one-third in medium-sized farms. Some of this land is ecologically suitable for crop production, as are some of the 1.5 million hectares of pastures also found mainly in medium and large holdings. Partly because of the heavy concentration of underutilized land in large farms, three-quarters of all those working in agriculture in 1973 had either no land at all or insufficient land to maintain their families. Nearly 60 percent of these individuals were wage laborers and a further 15 percent were minifundistas.

Until 1961, spontaneous colonization of tierras baldías was the principal escape valve for landless laborers and minifundistas. In that year, unorganized colonization was outlawed by the Ley de Tierras y Colonización. The Instituto de Tierras y Colonización, ITCO, set up in 1962, was the first official body entrusted with the solution of agrarian problems. The agrarian reform legislation was in part a response to internal pressures: the population explosion was at its zenith, the frontiers of colonization were approaching exhaustion, squatters were proliferating, and the incipient manufacturing industry being developed in the towns did not provide sufficient jobs to absorb the growing labor force. The legislation also reflected external factors, particularly reaction to the Cuban revolution of 1959 and the United States's insistence that Latin American members of the Alliance for Progress undertake agrarian reforms in order to reduce social tensions (Seligson 1978). Costa Rica's legislation retained the concept of private property, although its social function was recognized. Land was to be more justly distributed in order to eliminate minifundios and squatting, to prevent speculative ownership of underutilized land, and to raise agricultural production. The gradual replacement of uneconomical minifundios and underexploited haciendas by labor-intensive small holdings and medium-sized farms would enlarge the number of landowners; they could achieve economies of scale by forming cooperatives. The law contemplated both further colonization of virgin lands under the auspices of the ITCO and the redistribution of existing farmland with indemnification to previous owners of the full value according to tax returns, payable in cash or government bonds (MAG 1961).

During the early years of its existence, the ITCO's financial resources were exiguous, and it achieved very little. From 1962 to 1966, it adopted the traditional solution to agrarian problems and set up eleven colonies

on virgin lands. The ITCO's estimates put the number of
squatters on state and private lands at this time at approximately 16,500 families; its colonization program benefited only 1,222 families. During the remainder of the
decade, the ITCO was engaged exclusively in granting property titles to squatters. This program was cheaper than
the colonization projects, but, once again, it attacked
the result rather than the cause of agrarian problems. By
1969, it had benefited only 1,700 families, while the number of squatters continued to grow (CEPAL et al. 1972, 99-
130).

The establishment in the 1970s of asentamientos campesinos, peasant settlements where landless agricultural
workers and minifundistas received individual or collective title to lands purchased from private owners, marked
a major change in ITCO policy. The asentamientos campesinos were located in areas that already contained all-
weather roads and access to basic services; the ITCO provided the settlements with a minimum infrastructure of internal roads, housing, credit, and marketing facilities.
Participants were carefully chosen to avoid desertion, and
some of the asentamientos campesinos, like the earlier
colonies, functioned as cooperatives. During the early
1970s, however, the ITCO still lacked the financial resources to undertake large-scale reforms. Conflicts between squatters and landowners outnumbered the establishment of new asentamientos campesinos, and a potentially
explosive sociopolitical situation developed in several
peripheral regions of the country where the problem of
underexploited haciendas was most acute.

In 1975, the ITCO's income was bolstered by indirect
taxes. This financing permitted a rapid increase in the
number of asentamientos campesinos, including the establishment of several large regiones de desarrollo. The
first of these development regions was Coto Sur in the
hinterland of Golfito where 30,000 hectares of land, some
already occupied by squatters, were expropriated from the
Compañía Bananera and other owners. The ITCO set up a
series of self-help programs to install dirt roads,
bridges, and housing. After two years, the region had a
population of nearly 14,000 people settled in twenty villages. The success of the project attracted more landless
laborers to the zone, and in 1978 the ITCO expropriated a
further 3,500 hectares to settle another 400 families. In
subsequent regiones de desarrollo such as Río Frío on the
Caribbean lowlands, uncultivated lands were expropriated
before squatters had moved in.

By late 1979, the ITCO had established over a hundred
asentamientos campesinos, including the regiones de desarrollo; twenty-nine were organized as cooperatives, eighteen had collective land ownership, and eleven maintained
individual tenure. Together, the asentamientos campesinos
contained 5,428 families and occupied 167,134 hectares,
equivalent to 5 percent of the farm area registered in the

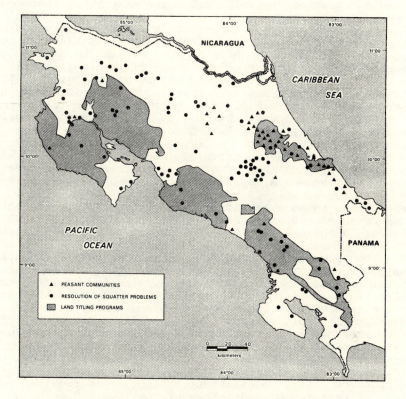

Figure 4.17 Agrarian reform projects
Source: ITCO 1979.

census of 1973. They are widely distributed throughout
the country, except in central and western Valle Central
where there are few underexploited haciendas of the type
that have been expropriated to make way for ITCO programs
(Figure 4.17). Most of the settlements produce foodstuffs
for the home market from land previously uncultivated or
used for grazing; in Coto Sur, a recently established cooperative, bananas are produced for sale to the Compañía
Bananera. The average income of ITCO settlers exceeds
that of the best paid agricultural laborers, although considerable inequalities have emerged within the asentamientos campesinos because of the range of personal initiative.
    Parallel with the asentamientos campesinos, the ITCO
has continued to grant land titles to squatters occupying
state and private lands. This entitlement provides farmers with secure access not only to land but also to agricultural credit, virtually unobtainable without an adequate mortgage. The upper limits of 100 hectares for
arable farms and 300 hectares for cattle farms are designed to prevent the formation of further large estates
that might generate new agrarian problems in the future.
By late 1979, the ITCO had granted 28,079 land titles,
equivalent to more than one-third of the number and nearly
one-fifth of the area of farms registered in 1973 (ITCO
1980a, 1980b; Salazar 1979; Salazar et al. 1977; Seligson
1978).
    The acceleration of ITCO programs since 1975 is grad-
ually transforming the structure of land tenure and the
relative importance of different farming systems. By the
time the next agricultural census is taken, a further decline in haciendas and minifundios and an increase in peasant small holdings and medium-sized farms can be expected.
ITCO reforms, however, are still lagging behind the proliferation of the problems they are intended to solve. A
detailed study carried out in 1978 revealed that more than
10,000 families still needed resettlement in asentamientos
campesinos. This resettlement project would require
165,351 hectares of land, however the ITCO had only 14,703
hectares in reserve (Mesén 1978). Some additional lands
have since been acquired, but there is still a serious
land tenure problem to be solved and squatting has not
been eradicated.

5
The Urban Areas

By the second third of the twentieth century, the rapidly growing population could no longer be accommodated
in the rural areas, where inefficient patterns of land use
and an inequitable structure of land tenure led to the
premature exhaustion of the frontiers of agricultural colonization. The traditional pattern of centrifugal migration gave way to centripetal migration back into the center of the country, where the rural areas absorbed only a
fraction of the incoming population. Most migrants settled in the towns, giving rise to unprecedented urban and
suburban growth.

In 1927, the country's seven towns contained less
than one-fifth of the population; the capital city had
just over 50,000 inhabitants. Today, more than half of
the population lives in urban and suburban areas quite
different in dimensions and quality from the small towns
of fifty years ago. The largest, the metropolitan region
of San José, contains nearly 1 million inhabitants.

Whereas in the developed countries of Europe and
North America, however, urbanization in the nineteenth and
early twentieth centuries was a corollary of the industrial revolution, in Costa Rica, as in most developing
countries, urbanization preceded the establishment of modern manufacturing, and the tertiary rather than the secondary sector generated the bulk of urban employment. Industrialization was delayed until the 1960s and 1970s,
when Costa Rica joined the Central American Common Market
and adopted a policy of desarrollo hacia adentro.

CENTRIPETAL MIGRATION AND THE GROWTH OF URBAN
POPULATION

The reversal in the pattern of internal migration has
probably been the most important single contributary factor in the process of urbanization. There are no detailed
statistics on internal migration for the period prior to
1950. The population censuses taken in 1950, 1963, and

TABLE 5.1
Growth of urban and rural population, 1927-1973

	Urban Population		Rural Population	
Year	Number	Percent of Total	Number	Percent of Total
1927	88,608	19	382,916	81
1950	230,296	29	570,579	71
1963	417,266	31	919,008	69
1973	693,476	37	1,178,304	63
Intercensorial Period	Annual Average Rate of Growth		Annual Average Rate of Growth	
1927-1950	4.24		1.72	
1950-1963	4.68		3.73	
1963-1973	5.21		2.52	

Sources: DGEC 1953a, 1960, 1966a, 1974a.

1973[1] recorded migration between cantons. The only comparable data for these three years are those concerning migration since birth. The censuses of 1963 and 1973 also contain statistics of recent migration, but different criteria were used each year. In 1950, 22 percent of the country's net immigration since birth was registered in San José and in five adjacent cantons; the remaining 78 percent was located mainly in peripheral regions where the frontiers of colonization were still expanding rapidly. By 1963, 44 percent was concentrated in ten cantons centered on San José. A decade later, nearly the whole metropolitan region of San José registered net immigration, and the peripheral cantons in zones of frontier colonization and agricultural redevelopment absorbed only 39 percent (Figure 3.7).

The modern censuses reveal the migration into the metropolitan region of San José, but they conceal immigration into other towns located in cantons of rural emigration. No migration statistics are available for districts, the smallest administrative areas, nor is it possible to distinguish between the urban and rural population when calculating net migration. Indirect evidence, however, leaves little doubt about the importance of internal migration in the urbanization process throughout the country. Natural population growth has been greater in the countryside than in the towns: it is estimated fertility was 60 percent higher in rural than in urban areas in 1950, 67

[1]Unless otherwise stated, all the population statistics quoted in this chapter are derived from four censuses, DGEC 1953a, 1960, 1966a, 1974a.

percent higher in 1963, and 78 percent higher in 1973 (Fernández Arias et al. 1976, 32). The annual average rate of growth of the urban population, however, has exceeded that of the rural population throughout the past half century (Table 5.1). Since foreign immigration has been insignificant, this urban growth can only be attributed to internal migration into the towns.

The centripetal migration now the major process of population redistribution includes movements from rural into urban areas and from smaller to larger towns. A sample survey carried out in San José in 1972 revealed that one-third of the city's population were immigrants. Half had moved into the capital from rural areas and half from other towns. Of these immigrants, 55 percent had undertaken a stepwise pattern of migration during their lives, moving to successively larger places. Three-quarters were under 30 years of age; 75 percent of the men and 50 percent of the women were unmarried (Bermúdez 1973; Ortega 1976).

Migration into the urban areas is a spatial readjustment to economic and social opportunities, operating primarily in response to "push" factors in the countryside and, to a lesser extent, to "pull" factors in the towns (Carvajal et al. 1977a, 76). The fact that most rural areas now register net emigration is not indicative of widespread overpopulation in relation to natural resources; on the contrary, many of the regions from which emigration is taking place are still sparsely populated. The growth of employment in the primary sector, however, has lagged far behind that in the secondary and tertiary sectors; farming now provides only 9 percent of the new jobs available (Liberman 1976; Shaw 1976). Those leaving the countryside cite difficulties in acquiring either land or permanent, well-paid wage employment as major motives for moving into the towns. The agrarian reforms undertaken during the past twenty years have provided only partial solutions to these problems. Rural emigration is particularly heavy from all the cantons where land use is dominated by extensive cattle ranching. It is less pronounced from cantons where plantation agriculture creates relatively well-paid jobs or where there is a fairly high proportion of peasant small holdings and medium-sized farms (Denton 1976). In addition to the basic problems of access to land and employment, deficiencies in the economic infrastructure and social services in rural areas constitute important "push" factors.

Migrants are attracted into the towns by real or perceived opportunities for nonagricultural employment and improved access to social services and cultural activities. Of the immigrants interviewed in the San José survey, 14 percent had moved into the capital city in order to study in institutions of secondary or higher education. Immigrant women taking up employment are heavily concentrated in the tertiary sector, particularly in domestic service.

Men moving into the capital city work in a range of activities similar to that of the native urban population (Bermúdez 1973). Most immigrants believe they have benefited both economically and socially from their move, and the stereotype of rural migrants festering in abysmal shanty towns is only partially true in the case of San José. A survey of migration into the marginal barrios of the metropolitan area showed that only 37 percent were immigrants into the capital city; of these, only two-thirds had come from rural areas. Research carried out in the whole metropolitan area of San José in 1976 revealed that even in upper class barrios nearly 30 percent of the population were immigrants; the proportion in middle and lower class barrios was approximately 50 percent (Bermúdez 1979).

The physical expansion of urban areas and the conversion of villages into towns has also contributed to urban population growth. People have been defined as rural in one census and urban in the next if their neighborhood acquired urban status in the intervening period. Of the urban population growth between 1950 and 1973, 17 percent was the result of transforming villages into towns. The absorption of rural population into the expanding, built-up areas of existing towns must also have been considerable, though it cannot be substantiated from census data.

As a result of the three processes of internal migration, natural population increase, and the physical expansion of towns, the urban population increased from less than 100,000 in 1927 to nearly 700,000 in 1973. The proportion of urban dwellers rose from 19 to 37 percent. By the 1960s, the rate of population growth in the urban areas exceeded 5 percent per year, compared with only 2.5 percent in the rural areas.

Urbanization involved the conversion of former villages into towns, the rapid growth of small towns, and the development of a macrocephalic metropolitan region. The number of towns more than quadrupled between 1927, when there were only seven, and 1973, when there were thirty. Some grew extraordinarily fast during their transformation from rural to urban places: the populations of San Isidro de El General, Siquirres, and Guápiles increased by an average of more than 10 percent per year between 1950 and 1973. Even after urban status has been achieved, the population of many towns continues to grow at well over 5 percent per year. Costa Rica is still, however, a country of predominantly small towns (Figure 5.1). With the exception of the capital, none had more than 35,000 inhabitants in 1973. Approximately one-fifth of the urban population lived in the five towns of Cartago, Alajuela, Heredia, Limón, and Puntarenas, each containing between 20,000 and 35,000 inhabitants. A further fifth lived in twenty-four towns, each with a population between 2,000 and 20,000.

The difference in absolute size between the capital city and the small towns is so great that the rapid growth

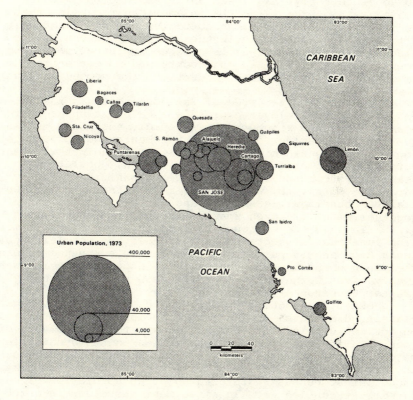

Figure 5.1   Distribution of urban population, 1973
Source: DGEC 1974a.

of the latter is only very gradually diminishing the concentration of urban population in San José. The capital
city had approximately 150,000 inhabitants in 1950 and
just over 400,000 in 1973. It contained 62 percent of all
urban dwellers in 1950 and still housed 59 percent in 1973.
In absolute terms, San José cannot be compared with the
urban areas of the larger Latin American republics that
contain many millions of inhabitants, but its relative position as a primate city in the hierarchy of central
places is similar to that in a large number of developing
countries. In 1973, San José contained more than ten
times as many inhabitants as Cartago, the second largest
town.
        The metropolitan area of San José, defined in 1956 as
an urban zone of eleven cantons with a built-up area of
nearly 40 square kilometers, is rapidly expanding into a
metropolitan region of twenty-seven cantons occupying
about 1,000 square kilometers from Alajuela in the west to
Paraíso in the east. Within this region, population is
being redistributed from the highly urbanized center towards the outskirts, which offer more attractive residential surroundings: less noise and atmospheric pollution
together with more open spaces and cheaper land (Figure
5.2). In 1973 the metropolitan region, with nearly 1 million inhabitants, contained almost half the population of
Costa Rica and 85 percent of the country's urban dwellers.
The urban population in the whole metropolitan region was
twenty times larger than in the second urban nucleus,
Greater Puntarenas (Zumbado 1977).
        Most of the 360,000 people in the metropolitan region
classified as rural in the census no longer rely primarily
on agricultural employment but commute to urban places of
work. This process of suburbanization in the countryside,
which also exists on a smaller scale around other towns,
in large part explains the apparent paradox of a country
whose latest census registered an urban population of only
37 percent coupled with an employment structure in which
63 percent of the labor force was engaged in nonagricultural activities. The urban and suburban populations together probably accounted for between 50 and 60 percent of
the total population in 1973 (Fox and Huguet 1978, 80-82;
Zumbado and Raabe 1976).

URBAN MORPHOLOGY

        The expansion of the urban areas, like the coloniza-
tion of the countryside, has been a largely spontaneous
process. The rapid growth of urban population has provoked two interrelated morphological changes: the transformation of existing urban areas and the expansion of
towns into rural areas. These changes have been most dramatic in San José, transformed in a single generation from
a small, tranquil town into a bustling metropolis, but

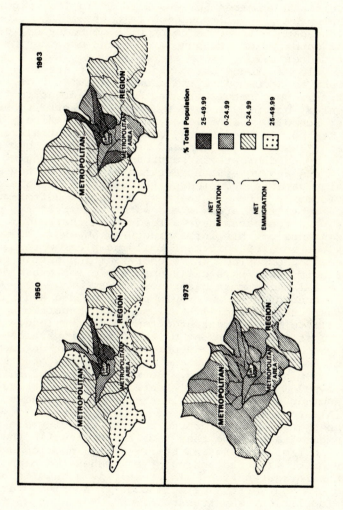

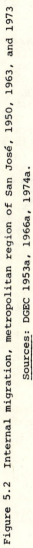

Figure 5.2 Internal migration, metropolitan region of San José, 1950, 1963, and 1973

Sources: DGEC 1953a, 1966a, 1974a.

they are taking place on a lesser scale in nearly all the
other towns.

Most urban expansion outside the metropolitan region
is horizontal. Towns are still composed mainly of single-
story buildings, in spite of the advances of antiseismic
construction techniques. Fast-growing towns such as San
Isidro de El General (Figure 5.4) have extended far beyond
their original gridiron nucleus into a higgledy-piggledy
suburban sprawl, superimposed on remnants of the older,
rural landscape. There is no precise boundary between
town and countryside; ribbon development extends for several kilometers along the main roads.

The blocks around the park and market are no longer
sufficient to accommodate the growing volume of tertiary
activities. Most retail trading is carried out in the
town center, but many services, such as hospitals, health
clinics, schools, and colleges requiring relatively large
sites, are now located on the outskirts. Central residential locations are still prized in small towns, but there
has been a rapid growth in suburban housing, ranging from
shanty towns and government estates to detached houses
with large gardens occupied by the upper and middle classes who formerly lived in the town centers. Better-quality
houses are built in areas where water, electricity, paved
streets, and footpaths have already been installed. The
very existence of this infrastructure, however, pushes up
land values so high that many building plots within the
town remain unoccupied, while poor families settle on the
outskirts in areas physically unsuitable for urban development and lacking most basic amenities.

The concentrated ownership of urban land and buildings constitutes a social problem whose proportions are
comparable to the concentrated tenure of farmland. In San
Isidro, less than 4 percent of the urban properties together contain more than 50 percent of the urban area. A
third of the town's houses and three-quarters of its commercial premises are rented. Between twenty and thirty
people own 75 percent of all rented property, extracting
profits of up to 40 percent in the central business district (Alfaro 1980).

The changes in and around the capital city are still
more complex than those that have taken place in the small
towns. Most of the present built-up area developed without any prior land use zoning or comprehensive planning of
the urban infrastructure. The result is a chaotic pattern
of land use and serious deficiencies in housing, recreational facilities, and transport.

The central districts of San José, in common with
those of big cities throughout the world, are areas of declining population. Their residential function is rapidly
disappearing as houses are first converted to other uses
and then demolished to make way for new buildings. The
reconstruction of the city center has been a piecemeal
process, with no changes in the basic layout of streets.

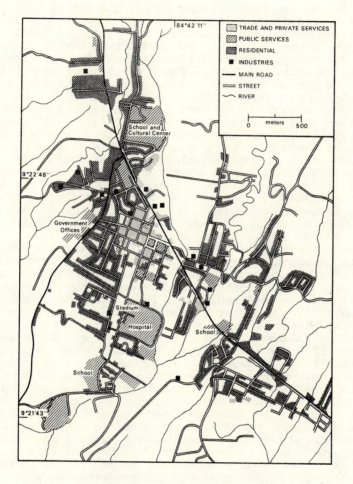

Figure 5.3 Land use in San Isidro de El General
Source: Alfaro 1980.

Single-story buildings of adobes, _bahareque_, and wood have gradually been replaced by skyscrapers constructed of cement blocks and reinforced with iron and concrete girders to provide the antiseismic protection now required by law.

The old core of San José is devoted almost entirely to trade and services (Figure 5.3). Multistory office blocks are located above ground floor shops. Commercial activities extend far beyond the two principal retail markets, the Mercado Central and the Mercado Borbón, and there are marked spatial differences within the central business district (C.B.D.): small shops proffering cheap wares are concentrated around the markets, large department stores are located mainly along Central Avenue, the northeastern quadrant is emerging as a zone of expensive retailers, and artesans are found particularly in the south of the C.B.D. The Parque Nacional on the eastern margin of the C.B.D. has replaced the Parque Central as the main focus of public buildings including the legislative assembly, one of the city's major hospitals, the national library, the national museum, and the law courts. Beyond the C.B.D., old residential districts such as Amón, Escalante, and Paseo Colón are undergoing the first stages of transformation into commercial and service zones (Porras 1979, 50).

At midcentury, San José was still physically separate from the capitals of adjacent cantons and provinces. Since then, vertical expansion in the city center has been accompanied by rapid horizontal expansion into the surrounding countryside (OFIPLAN 1980b, 1) (Figure 5.5). San José is located in the center of a densely settled, intensively cultivated region. Most urban expansion has taken place on prime farmland, sown in coffee since the midnineteenth century. The metropolitan area of San José has uprooted more than 5,000 hectares of coffee groves, which in 1950 produced more than a quarter of the country's coffee and in 1973 less than a tenth (DGEC 1953b, 1974b). High land values and taxes make urbanization more profitable than farming on even the most fertile land. Agricultural output usually declines several years before the actual change in land use, because farmers no longer renovate coffee groves soon to be destroyed. The most suitable area for future urban expansion in the metropolitan region is to the west of the present built-up area, as far as Turrúcares. Located in the lower part of the premontane zone, this area of infertile, stony soils has never been an important producer of coffee, and its potential for other types of agriculture is limited. It contains extensive areas of flat land suitable for building sites. Urban expansion towards the south and southeast is limited by mountains. To the north and east, fertile, permeable soils are underlain by the principal aquifers of the metropolitan region. This area could be preserved for agricultural use if it were designated a green belt where no further urban building would be permitted and where land

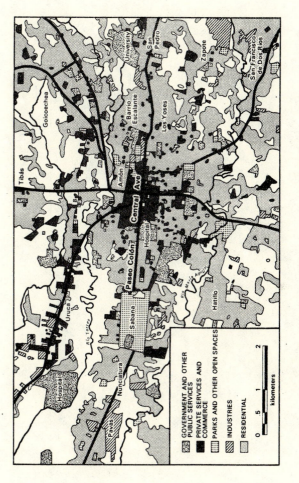

Figure 5.4 Land use in the center of the metropolitan area of San José

Source: INVU 1975.

216

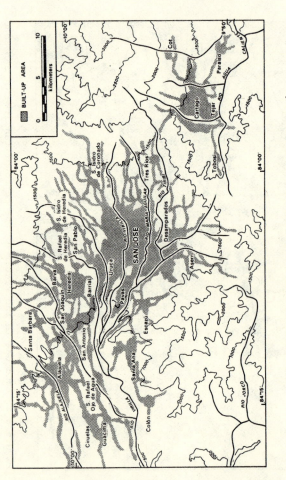

Figure 5.5   The metropolitan region of San José

Source: OFIPLAN 1980b.

taxes were similar to those in other farming regions
(Fournier 1976; OFIPLAN 1980b, 14).

Urban expansion usually takes place first along main
roads; these ribbons of development are subsequently
filled in. Because of uncontrolled property speculation,
plots of land may remain unoccupied for years between the
abandonment of farming and their incorporation into the
built-up urban area. Like capital cities throughout the
world, San José has already engulfed many villages whose
rural character has disappeared. Their conversion into
dormitory suburbs has diminished local community functions;
suburban commuters acquire many goods and services in the
capital city rather than in their own neighborhoods, which
are emptied of population during working hours (OFIPLAN
1980b, 2). The imminent absorption of three of the country's major towns into the metropolitan conurbation is a
more specifically Costa Rican feature, exacerbating the
existing concentration of urban functions in a single
large city and reducing the role of Alajuela, Heredia, and
Cartago as independent provincial capitals.

Most new suburban building is residential. Whereas
offices are increasingly being located in multistory
buildings, apartments are few. Most houses are still
single story. Urban population densities are therefore
relatively low. Many parts of the metropolitan area contain less than 400 inhabitants per square kilometer, and
some suburbs hold less than 100 (INVU 1975). This extensive pattern of urban land use exacerbates the loss of
farmland and raises the cost of installing amenities such
as water, sewerage, electricity, and telephones. Vertical
residential development, however, would depend upon providing an adequate infrastructure of trade and service
centers, parks, recreational facilities, and intraurban
transport to serve a much denser population.

Residential barrios are more sharply segregated by
economic and social status in the capital than in other
towns. The wealthiest suburbs are found mainly to the
east and west of the C.B.D., where there are ample areas
of flat land, and in the hills to the southwest of the
city center, where the inconvenience of sloping sites is
compensated for by spectacular views and a tranquil, semi-
rural environment. In barrios such as Los Yoses, Escal-
ente, Nunciatura, and Belo Horizonte, large, detached
houses stand on their own grounds. Most of the poorest
houses are located to the north and south of the city center, in and around the entrenched valleys that traverse
the metropolitan area. Between these two extremes are
areas of private, middle-class housing, such as Tibas,
Goicoechea, and Zapote, and government estates in Hatillo
and Uruca. Industrial and commercial establishments in-
trude into many residential areas, creating serious problems of noise and pollution.

Shanty towns have not developed on the same scale as
in many other countries of Latin America, but pockets of

tugurios have nevertheless proliferated in recent years. In 1978, they contained an estimated 18,100 houses, equivalent to about 5 percent of the dwellings registered in the housing census of 1973. More than two-thirds are in the metropolitan area, and most of the remainder are found in other towns such as Puntarenas, Cañas, Limón, and San Isidro. Many tugurios are constructed either on very steep slopes or on lands liable to flood. Most of their occupants are squatters on private or municipal property. Their makeshift houses, built of wood, corrugated iron, cardboard, and any other materials on hand, are often erected in a single night. Lacking basic services such as electricity, drinking water, sewerage, and rubbish collection, the tugurios are foci of ill health, environmental contamination, and serious social problems including un- and underemployment, broken families, prostitution, and crime (Perlaza 1977, 1980).

As new residential barrios have proliferated, a series of satellite C.B.D.'s have developed in the suburbs. Some have grown up in former villages that were absorbed into the metropolitan area; others are new shopping precincts, accessible by car but poorly located to act as urban community centers. They contain supermarkets, small specialized shops, branch banks, and post offices. This spontaneous decentralization is converting San José into a polynuclear metropolis, reducing congestion in the city center. Future planning could provide the metropolitan region with a more efficient network of central places functioning not only as commercial centers but also as foci for the development of more closely knit urban communities (OFIPLAN 1980b).

As in the smaller towns, public services are increasingly being relocated in the peripheries of the metropolitan area, where larger building sites are available at lower prices. The transfer of the University of Costa Rica from a city center site to a suburban campus in San Pedro was one of the earliest such change. San José's most modern hospital is located on the outskirts of the city. The presidential offices and the public registry have recently been moved to Zapote, and there are plans to relocate other services, such as the national archives. Modern factories, which also require large, flat, relatively cheap sites, have also been constructed on the margins of the built-up area and even in the open countryside.

There has unfortunately been little concern for the quality of the urban and suburban environment where most Costa Ricans now spend the majority of their lives. Noise and atmospheric pollution have reached alarming proportions, particularly in the capital city. One of the most outstanding defects of all the urban areas is their lack of open spaces. The metropolitan area of San José, whose population is now approaching half a million, contains only 230 hectares of "green areas," one-third of which are inaccessible to the general public (INVU 1975, 17). The

city has few public gardens, and mature trees have been
uprooted to make more room for the asphyxiating traffic.
The parks of the city center, at most occupying two blocks,
are no more than places of shade and repose along the
streets. San José's only large, public open space is the
Sabana, used mainly for organized sports.

Urban growth has been accompanied by aesthetic deterioration as modern buildings of largely indifferent architecture have intruded the attractive Hispanic American
towns of the nineteenth and early twentieth centuries.
With their plethora of advertisements and neon signs, the
main streets of San José resemble the downtown area of a
North American city. Costa Rica's towns contain few
buildings of outstanding architectural merit but many interesting old houses, shops, and offices that are part of
the nation's cultural heritage. Government intervention
to preserve historic buildings dates back to the 1920s,
but only thirty-four had been listed by 1980 (Ministerio
de Cultura 1980; La Nación, 26 April 1981). The opportunity to preserve something of the character of the old town
of San José has already been lost, but the centers of some
of the provincial towns such as Heredia, Alajuela, Liberia,
and Limón could still be saved.

The development of intraurban transport networks has
lagged behind population growth, creating traffic problems
that are most severe in the capital city but by no means
absent in other towns. Because of the unplanned, piecemeal rebuilding in the center of San José, the city's
street network is essentially the same as fifty years ago.
There is no complete ring road, so all vehicles, including
international traffic on the Pan American Highway, must
traverse at least part of the city center. With an average width of only 7 meters, few streets can accommodate
more than two lanes of traffic, and the flow of vehicles
is halted by traffic lights at almost every intersection
in the gridiron pattern of streets. Some streets in the
metropolitan area carry more than 15,000 vehicles per day,
and there is heavy congestion during rush hours (Gomar
1973). The widening of Second Avenue to accommodate five
lanes of traffic has been the first major improvement to
the street network in the city center. An outer ring road,
interconnecting the trunk roads converging on San José, is
under construction, and the main roads between the city
center and the suburbs are being widened. Progress on all
these projects is extremely slow because, by the time they
were initiated, most of the areas they involved had already been built up. Land values have risen sharply and
expropriation costs are high.

By 1977, half a million people were traveling every
day to and from San José, 60 percent using public transport. With the exception of a few, slow-moving trains,
this transport is restricted to buses and microbuses, insufficient to accommodate commuter traffic. Long queues
form during the rush hours. Urban bus routes in the

metropolitan area form a star-shaped pattern (Figure 5.6).
There is only one intersuburban route, so most journeys
from one side of the city to another involve traveling on
two or even three different buses and traversing a stretch
in the city center on foot.

There are several ways to improve transport in the
metropolitan region. The construction of footpaths and
cycle paths would allow more people to move about safely
under their own steam (OFIPLAN 1980b, 23-24). This transport mode would reduce the consumption of expensive, imported petroleum and contribute to public health by diminishing atmospheric pollution and fomenting exercise. The
bus and microbus services could be improved by designing a
more integrated route network and increasing the number of
vehicles in circulation during rush hours. In the longer
term it will probably be necessary to develop other types
of collective transport, such as trolley buses, trams, or
fast trains, that carry a large volume of passengers and
that run on clean, home-produced electricity (Munro 1980).

The need for comprehensive town planning has been apparent for many years. The problems Solow (1948) identified in San José when the city's population scarcely exceeded 100,000 have only been exacerbated by the rapid,
uncontrolled expansion of the past thirty years: urban
growth has buried many of the country's most fertile soils;
diverse and often incompatible types of land use have developed cheek by jowl; tugurios have proliferated; the
lack of parks and other open spaces has become increasingly acute as population has grown; and the narrow streets
are unable to accommodate the flow of modern traffic.
These problems are most severe in the metropolitan region,
but, on a smaller scale, they affect nearly every urban
area in the country.

Solow's recommendation that Costa Rica set up an urban planning authority was implemented with the creation
of the Instituto Nacional de Vivienda y Urbanismo, INVU,
in 1954. The INVU was empowered to draw up a Plan Nacional de Desarrollo Urbano, setting out general policy on the
growth and development of urban areas. In cooperation
with the municipalities, it was also to prepare a Plan Regulador for each town. This policy would regulate virtually every aspect of the physical expansion of urban areas:
land use zoning, the provision of public amenities and
recreational facilities, housing, and the networks of roads,
electricity, telecommunications, drinking water, and sewerage. A separate department, the Oficina de Planeamiento
del Area Metropolitana de San José, was set up to plan the
development of the capital city; the Departamento de Urbanismo was to oversee other towns (INVU 1954, 1961, 1968).

Several urban development plans have been prepared by
foreign consultants, and one by the INVU itself.[1] None

---

[1]These plans could not be located in the public libraries in San José,
nor was it possible to examine them in the INVU's offices.

221

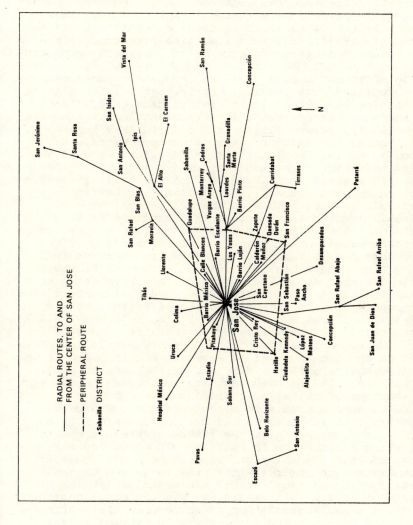

Figure 5.6 Bus routes in the metropolitan area of San José
Source: MOPT, unpublished statistics.

has ever been implemented. Planes Reguladores have at one
time or another been drawn up for most towns, but few have
been kept up-to-date. In the majority of towns, plan and
reality are still very different. In practice, the INVU's
intervention in urban development has been largely restricted to approving or rejecting building proposals made
by private entrepreneurs; even these decisions are not always made in accordance with the Plan Regulador. There
has been little coordination with other central government
departments or with the municipalities also concerned with
urban development (Arq. Zuleyka Salom, personal communication).

In addition to town planning, the INVU also took over
responsibility for government housing projects, replacing
a succession of earlier agencies that between 1939 and
1954 had constructed less than a thousand houses (Chavez
Méndez 1981). Between 1954 and 1979, the INVU built
22,987 houses for sale on low-interest mortgages and
granted loans for the construction of a further 15,156
houses. Of INVU houses, 65 percent are located in the
capital city where the suburb of Hatillo, built in stages
to accommodate more than 6,000 families, is by far the
largest single project. A further 24 percent of INVU
housing is located in the provincial capitals of Alajuela,
Heredia, Cartago, Limón, and Puntarenas, and the remaining
11 percent are in small towns and villages (INVU 1979).
The poorest people cannot afford even the cheapest INVU
housing. Some have been provided with shelter by the Instituto Mixto de Ayuda Social (IMAS), a government agency
created in 1971 to coordinate public and private organizations concerned with the eradication of extreme poverty
(IMAS 1971). Between 1971 and 1979, the IMAS built 5,511
houses located in both urban and rural areas (IMAS 1977-
1981). Government intervention, however, has failed to
solve the chronic shortage of low-cost housing, and it is
estimated that the INVU, IMAS, and private constructors
together are building only half the new houses needed each
year (Montoya et al. 1976, 118-123).

Costa Rica probably requires a program of urban reform that, like its agrarian counterpart, would regulate
not only land use but also the tenure of urban property,
eliminating speculation in building plots and rentals
(Kaplan 1972). The solution to urban problems, however,
is not limited to reforms within the towns and cities.
The roots of Costa Rica's rapid urbanization lie in the
countryside, which fifty years ago was the major destination of internal migrants and is now one of their principal sources. Developing rural areas to provide decent
levels of living for a growing population must be conceived of as an integral part of any solution to the problems now faced in the towns and cities.

TERTIARY URBANIZATION

In common with the majority of developing countries, Costa Rica has experienced a process of tertiary urbanization involving a massive transfer of labor from the primary direct to the tertiary sector of the economy (CEPAL 1976; McGee 1971, 27; Santos 1973, 15). The censuses of 1927 and 1950 contain no breakdown of employment for the urban and rural populations. Those of 1963 and 1973 record the predominance of tertiary over secondary sources of urban employment and the growing importance of jobs in the tertiary sector (Table 5.2). The slow growth of employment in the secondary sector precisely during this period, when the government was encouraging the establishment of modern factories, is indicative of the failure of manufacturing to provide a solid basis of urban employment.
The largest branch of the tertiary sector, services, provides more jobs than the whole secondary sector (Table 5.3). More than half of those occupied in this branch are government employees, working in public administration, defence, and social services such as health and education. Employment in the public sector is currently growing more than three times as fast as in the private sector in the country as a whole, and more than eight times as fast in the metropolitan area of San José (DGEC 1979c). To a certain extent, the burgeoning state bureaucracy is a residual employer, providing a subsidized solution to urban underemployment (Arias 1977a; Liberman 1976). Trade constitutes the second largest branch of urban tertiary activities, occupying roughly half as many people as do the service industries.
The tertiary sector harbors many "primitive" occupations in petty trade and personal services. These require little training or capital investment and absorb large quantities of labor, although they also often conceal substantial underemployment. About 40,000 people registered in the census of 1973 had recognizably "primitive" occupations. Together, these occupations accounted for about 15 percent of employment in the tertiary sector. By far the largest group were domestic servants, who alone comprised 12 percent. In some other "primitive" categories, such as street hawkers and bootblacks, the census data almost certainly underestimates the volume of employment. This inaccuracy is partly because many petty street traders operate illegally. Children under twelve, not registered as part of the labor force, also participate in these activities.
The secondary sector, which generates approximately one-quarter of urban employment, comprises two major branches: manufacturing and construction. Most of those employed in manufacturing now work in modern factories, but there are still several thousand artesans who combine manufacturing with retail trading. Largely because of the rapid expansion of urban areas during recent years, the

TABLE 5.2
Urban employment, 1963 and 1973

| | 1963 | | 1973 | | Annual Average Rate of Growth in the |
Sector	Number of Jobs	Percent	Number of Jobs	Percent	Number of Jobs, 1963-1973 (%)
Primary	11,816	8.08	14,213	5.59	1.86
Secondary	45,381	31.05	67,720	26.64	4.08
Tertiary	88,967	60.87	172,306	67.77	6.83
TOTAL	146,164	100.00	254,239	100.00	5.69

Sources: DGEC 1966a, 1974a.

TABLE 5.3
Composition of urban employment, 1973

Sector	Number of Jobs	Percent
Primary		
Agriculture, forestry, and fishing	13,875	5.46
Mines and quarries	338	0.13
Secondary		
Manufacturing industry	44,967	17.69
Construction	19,154	7.53
Tertiary		
Services	85,628	33.69
Trade	46,889	18.44
Transport and communications	16,656	6.55
Finance	11,451	4.50
Public utilities	3,599	1.42
Others	11,682	4.59
TOTAL	254,239	100.00

Source: DGEC 1974a.

construction industry provides one-third of the employment in the secondary sector and is growing more rapidly than the manufacturing branch.

There are few major departures from the general pattern of urban employment in individual towns (Figure 5.7). No town owes its origin to the development of manufacturing, nor could any at the moment be described as an indus-

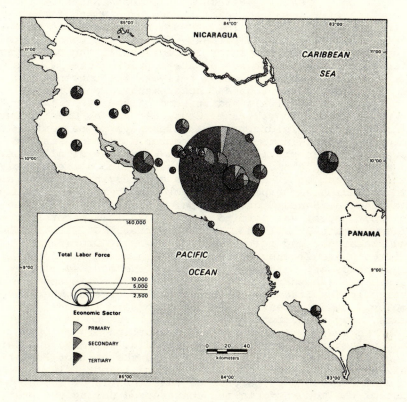

Figure 5.7 Distribution of urban employment, 1973
Source: DGEC, unpublished statistics.

trial town. Modern manufacturing and social services have
gravitated towards the larger urban areas, where they have
taken their place alongside the existing activities of
multifunctional towns. Most urban places are still engaged primarily in supplying goods and services to the local population.

In only one town, Paraíso, does less than half the
labor force work in the tertiary sector. Most of the
towns with a relatively low proportion of tertiary employ-
ment--between 50 and 65 percent--are small places, where
over 15 percent of the labor force is still engaged in agriculture. The importance of the service sector varies
quite widely. This variation reflects the concentration
of major public services and government administration in
the provincial capitals and in some of the other larger
towns, such as Nicoya, Santa Cruz, San Ramón, Grecia, Turrialba, and San Isidro, all of which have 38 percent or
more employment in the service sector. In many smaller
towns, services provide less than 30 percent of all jobs.
In addition to the capital city, several towns relatively
isolated from other urban centers and serving large rural
hinterlands have 20 percent or more employment in trade.
They include Santa Cruz, Quesada, Guápiles, Orotina, San
Isidro, Quepos, and Golfito. Transport is a minor source
of employment except in the three ports of Golfito, Limón,
and Puntarenas and in the railway towns of Orotina and Siquirres where it provides up to one-third of all jobs.
These towns are perhaps economically the most specialized
towns in the country. Financial activities are concentrated in San José and the provincial capitals, where they
employ 4 to 6 percent of the labor force. In smaller
towns, they contribute only 1 to 3 percent to employment.

The towns with the highest proportion of employment
in manufacturing are San José, Alajuela, Heredia, and Cartago, in the metropolitan region, and the port of Puntarenas and nearby town of Esparza, where industrial workers
account for 16 to 21 percent of the urban labor force.
Most of the modern factories constructed during the past
twenty years are located in or near these towns and the
port of Limón. In the remaining urban areas, the highest
level of industrial employment is found where there are
jobs in agricultural processing in or near towns, such as
sugar refining in Grecia and Filadelfia, tobacco processing in Puriscal, and coffee milling in San Ramón, Naranjo,
and Palmares. Most other industrial workers are artesans
or employees of small factories and workshops producing
goods for local markets. The fact that employment in the
construction industry exceeds the national average of 7
percent in half the urban areas (excluding, significantly,
San José) is indicative of the rapid growth of the smaller
towns (DGEC 1973).

MANUFACTURING INDUSTRY

Prior to the 1960s, manufacturing fell into two principal categories. The majority of firms were workshops where artesans transformed raw materials into finished goods and retailed their own products. Carpenters, joiners, shoemakers, tailors, bakers, saddlers, and others were scattered throughout the country in both urban and rural places, supplying small, local markets. With a few exceptions, such as printing works and the production of soap, beverages, and matches, larger-scale manufacturing was restricted to the processing of crops, including export commodities such as coffee and sugar (Ramírez Boza and Solís 1979). This industry was a predominantly rural activity, located in the same areas where crops were grown. Virtually all capital goods and many consumer goods were imported.

In response to the contraction of international trade during the Great Depression and the Second World War, Costa Rica made a premature attempt to develop new manufacturing industries to supply the home market. The Ley de Industrias Nuevas, passed in 1940, offered manufacturers a variety of fiscal incentives, but these were applicable only if 75 percent or more of the raw materials were home produced. This restriction effectively reduced potential industries to those processing agricultural products and timber. Even without this restriction, though, industrial development would still have been hampered by the small internal market: Costa Rica's population in the 1940s was less than 1 million. Only fifty-five firms took advantage of the Ley de Industrias Nuevas during the two decades it was in force (Weisenfeld 1969). The first modern industrial census, taken in 1952, registered over 3,000 firms, but most were workshops rather than factories (Figure 5.8). Their principal products were foodstuffs and wooden articles made from local raw materials and clothing manufactured from imported textiles (DGEC 1954). Between 1952 and 1958, when the second industrial census was taken, the number of firms almost doubled and employment in manufacturing rose by nearly 50 percent. This increase, however, still reflected mainly an increase in labor-intensive workshops rather than in factories (DGEC 1962).

In 1959, the industrial legislation of 1940 was replaced by the Ley de Protección y Desarrollo Industrial (MAI 1959). The aims of the new law were to decrease the country's dependence on the export of primary products, to diversify economic production, to supply the internal market with home-produced manufactured goods, to stimulate national and foreign investment in manufacturing industries, and to create new sources of productive, nonagricultural employment. Once again, fiscal incentives were the principal mechanism by which hopefully to develop modern factories, but, in contrast to the 1940 law, there was

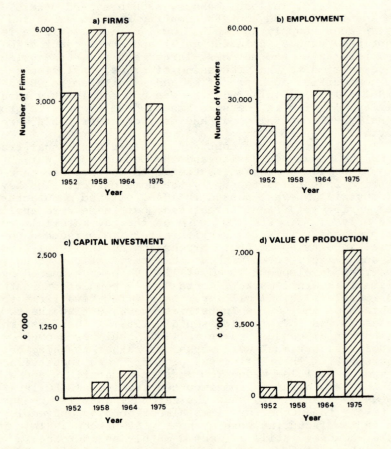

Figure 5.8 Growth of manufacturing industry, 1952-1975
Sources: DGEC 1954, 1962, 1967, 1977-1978.

no stipulation about the use of locally produced raw materials. The new law protected local industries from foreign competition by establishing low tariffs on imported
raw materials, fuel, and capital goods and high tariffs on
finished consumer goods. Industrialists were exempted
from paying land taxes, municipal taxes, capital gains
tax, export tax, and income tax on money reinvested in
workers' housing and factory improvements. The law placed
no restrictions on the type of industry that could benefit
from these incentives. Most of the new firms established
during the 1960s produced consumer goods and relied heavily on imported capital goods and raw materials.

Costa Rica's entry into the Central American Common
Market in 1963 was a further stimulus to industrial development. In addition to free trade between the five member
countries, common external tariffs were established. The
Banco Centroamericano de Integración Económica channeled
investment into manufacturing industries. Costa Ricans
participated in the Instituto Centroamericano de Investigación y Tecnología Industrial. One of the principal aims
of the Common Market was to integrate the region's industrial development and distribute between member countries
basic industries such as oil refining and the production
of iron and steel, aluminium, chemicals, glass, pulp, and
paper (Lizano 1975). In practice, these industries have
been little developed, and many Central American manufacturing industries, like the older agro-export industries,
are competitive rather than complementary (Navarro 1974,
92-93). Internal disorders in the isthmus--of which the
most serious have been the hostilities between El Salvador
and Honduras in 1969, the civil war in Nicaragua during
1978-1979, and the guerrilla uprising in El Salvador since
1980--have periodically disrupted both manufacturing and
trade. Even under normal conditions, transport between
member countries is restricted to a small number of routes.
Costa Rica is disadvantageously located at the southern
end of the market. The Pan-American Highway is her only
overland link with neighboring republics, although regular
Central American shipping lines are now being developed.

In 1969, the fiscal incentives established under the
individual legislation of each member country of the Common Market were replaced by the Convenio Centroamericano
de Incentivos Fiscales de Desarrollo Industrial. Whereas
Costa Rica's 1959 law was applicable to any manufacturing
industry, the Central American agreement divided firms into three groups. Those producing capital or intermediate
goods or consumer goods that used at least 50 percent local raw materials comprised Class A and received fiscal
incentives similar to those of Costa Rica's 1959 law.
Smaller incentives were offered to Class B industries,
which in spite of using a high proportion of imported raw
materials nevertheless produced high added value or foreign exchange savings. Other industries, in Class C, received virtually no incentives (Navarro et al. 1973).

Between 1960 and 1975, more than a thousand firms signed contracts with the government to take advantage of the fiscal incentives available under the 1959 law and the Central American agreement. The process of industrial expansion, incipient by the time of the third census in 1964, was clearly apparent by 1975, the year of the fourth and most recent census (Figure 5.8). During this period, the manufacturing sector underwent major changes both in structure, as modern factories replaced artesans and workshops, and in composition, as completely new industries were developed (Izurieta 1979, 16).

Many manufacturers still operate on a relatively small scale. One-third of the firms included in the census of 1975 were workshops that employed no wage labor; there were probably several thousand more artesans not registered in the census (OSPI 1978a). A further 53 percent were firms with less than thirty employees. Many essential consumer goods, including foodstuffs, clothing, shoes, and furniture, are still produced at this scale. These small units of production are owned mainly by Costa Ricans. Most are labor rather than capital intensive and are an important source of employment. They use many locally produced raw materials and are widely distributed throughout the country. During the early years of protected industrial development, large factories were encouraged at the expense of small workshops. In the 1970s, the government reversed this policy and set up the Consejo Nacional de Pequeñas Industrias y Artesanía. Small industries and artesans are now receiving more bank credit, special training, and technical assistance. Further development of this type of manufacturing would be highly beneficial, since labor is much more abundant than capital (Bolaños 1977).

The proliferation of large, modern factories during the past twenty years has added a new dimension to the manufacturing sector. Only 13 percent of the firms registered in the 1975 census had more than thirty workers, but they employed three-quarters of the industrial labor force and accounted for 87 percent of the total value of production. The eighty-one largest factories, each with more than 150 workers, alone provided 41 percent of industrial employment and produced 46 percent of industrial goods. Many branches are now dominated by monopolies and oligopolies (Izurieta 1979, 20). They use modern, capital-intensive production techniques and imported machinery and tools; many also rely on imported raw materials. They have the advantage over artesans and small factories of scale economies and pose a serious threat to the survival of small producers in many branches of industry.

Much of the capital invested in manufacturing is of foreign origin. In contrast to regions such as Medellín in Colombia (J. J. Parsons 1968, 174-188) and Sao Paulo in Brazil (Morse 1954), Costa Rica's coffee producers have provided little capital for manufacturing. Many opposed

entry into the Central American Common Market on the
grounds that the country's elevated production costs (because of relatively high wages and social benefits) would
make industries uncompetitive and detract foreign investment. Local industrialists, among whom descendents of
Lebanese and Askenak Jews are prominent, tend to come from
artesan or trading families rather than from the farming
sector. They provided roughly half the capital during the
first decade of protected industrial development, invest-
ing mainly in small firms. Costa Rica's political stability attracted foreign companies; their role in the secondary sector surpassed earlier participation in the primary
sector, where direct productive investment was restricted
mainly to the cultivation of bananas and African oil palm.
United States companies have been the principal foreign
investors, contributing about one-third of all industrial
capital mainly through Costa Rican subsidiaries of multinational corporations. Other investors include Japanese,
Mexicans, and exiled Cubans (S. Stone 1973). The government played little direct part in industrial production
until the establishment of the Corporación Costarricense
de Desarrollo (CODESA) in 1972. Operating specifically in
fields unattractive or unfeasible for private investors,
CODESA has experienced great difficulty in consolidating
economically viable industries.

The rapidly growing population has provided an ample
quantity of potential factory labor, including women for
whom, in the urban areas, manufacturing offers one of the
major sources of employment. Women comprise 26 percent of
industrial workers, compared with only 17 percent of the
labor force as a whole. Costa Rica's high rate of literacy together with much innate aptitude for mechanical
tasks have facilitated the training of industrial workers.
The Instituto Nacional de Aprendizaje and the colegios
vocacionales prepare skilled and semiskilled workers for
factory jobs. In the universities, particularly the Instituto Tecnológico in Cartago, teaching and research in
fields such as engineering and the natural sciences have
been increasingly oriented towards industrial requirements.
There is still, however, a shortage of trained industrial
personnel, and factories rely very heavily on technology
acquired under patents issued by foreign companies.

In spite of the abundance of unskilled manpower, most
factories are capital rather than labor intensive. Eighty
percent work at less than full capacity and 38 percent at
less than one-third capacity, operating only 8 hours a day.
The fiscal incentives available since 1959 have made capital artificially cheap. Factories can operate profitably
on a single shift, and many lack sufficient skilled workers to function 24 hours a day. The protection afforded
by the Common Market external tariffs exacerbates these
inefficiencies; many factories would find it very difficult to compete on an open market (Liberman 1976).

Home-produced electricity supplies approximately

three-quarters of the energy used in manufacturing industry; the remainder is derived from imported petroleum.
Oil seeps in Baja Talamanca in the southern part of the
Limón Basin were discovered in the late nineteenth century,
but there has never been any commercial exploitation of
petroleum or natural gas. Exploration is currently underway in this zone. There are no known reserves of good-
quality coal. The dense network of voluminous rivers,
however, has enormous hydroelectric potential, less than
5 percent of which has so far been exploited. The first
small hydroelectric plants were built in the late nineteenth and early twentieth centuries. In 1949, the government created the Instituto Costarricense de Electricidad (ICE) to produce and distribute electric power. Between 1956 and 1979, the ICE constructed four large hydroelectric plants and four thermal stations run on imported
diesel oil (Figure 5.9). The first three hydroelectric
plants--La Garita, Rio Macho, and Cachí--were located in
the Valle Central, close to the major centers of consumption but in a region where the dry season severely reduces
the volume of water in the rivers. For several months
each year hydroelectric production had to be supplemented
by the output of the thermal stations. The rapid rise in
world petroleum prices during the 1970s obliged the ICE to
increase the output of hydroelectricity. The capacity of
the Rio Macho and Cachí plants was more than doubled.
Construction also began on a vast multipurpose project at
Arenal in the province of Guanacaste, where water from the
Caribbean slope was diverted to extend a natural lake into
a reservoir of 84 square kilometers supplying two power
stations, Arenal and Corobicí.
    In 1975, three-fifths of industrial raw materials
were home produced (Table 5.4). They included agricultural products such as sugar, cocoa, palm oil, tobacco, cotton, milk, and meat, as well as fish, timber, leather, and
nonmetallic minerals. Two-fifths of industrial raw materials were imported. Between 1958 and 1975, industry's
share of the total value of imports rose from 18 to 35
percent. Less than 5 percent came from the remaining
countries of the Central American Common Market and neighboring Panama. The principal suppliers were the developed, capitalist countries: the United States, western
Europe, and Japan. Some imported inputs are truly "raw"
materials, which undergo little transformation. They include wheat, rubber, timber, cotton and other fibers, and
nonmetallic minerals such as salt and gypsum, many of
which could be produced in Costa Rica. A high proportion
of imported inputs are intermediate or semimanufactured
goods, such as chemicals, steel, textiles, and paper, or
virtually finished products such as vehicle parts, medicines, and cosmetics that require only assembly or packaging in Costa Rica.
    Virtually all capital goods for the manufacturing in-
dustry, principally machinery and tools, are also imported.

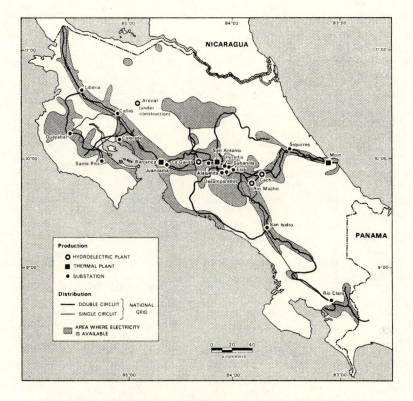

Figure 5.9 Production and distribution of electric power

Source: ICE 1980c.

TABLE 5.4
Origins of industrial raw materials, 1975

Origin	Value ¢'000	Percent
Costa Rica	2,514,073	60.10
United States	807,620	19.31
Central American Common Market	176,765	4.22
Europe	170,677	4.08
Panama	12,121	0.28
Other countries	502,654	12.01
TOTAL	4,182,910	100.00

Source: DGEC 1977-1978.

Fuel, raw materials, and capital goods for industry together account for nearly half the total value of imports--
a clear indication of the failure to achieve real import
substitution via industrialization (Zúñiga 1978).

The composition of the manufacturing sector is the
antithesis of the agricultural sector (Figure 5.10). Primary production, particularly for export, is still characterized by what the Economic Commission for Latin America
has called desarrollo en profundidad: continued investment
in a small number of highly specialized activities. In
manufacturing, by contrast, desarrollo en extensión has
involved the constant development of new activities (CEPAL
1974). Since the principal objective of industrialization
has been the substitution of imports rather than the generation of exports, Costa Rica produces a wide variety of
manufactured goods instead of specializing on activities
for which she has comparative advantages over other countries.

After twenty years of protected industrialization,
nearly three-quarters of the country's factories still
produce consumer goods. Many require only small economies
of scale and can function within the limits of the home
market. In 1975, they accounted for approximately two-
thirds of both employment in the manufacturing sector and
the value of industrial production. Because of the predominance of consumer industries, linkages between firms
are weak; inputs are acquired mainly from Costa Rica's own
primary sector or from imports, and finished goods are
destined for retail trade.

The consumer industries are dominated by two large
branches. The production of food, drink, and tobacco exceeds in value all intermediate and capital goods together.
Many of these industries can trace their origins to the
first half of the twentieth century; most have grown

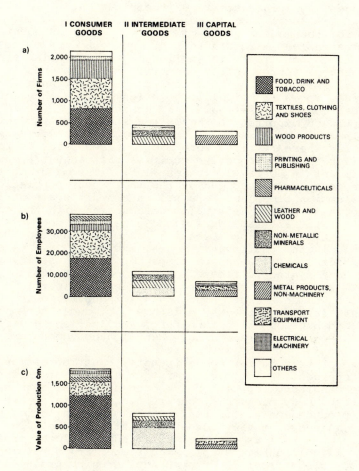

Figure 5.10 Composition of manufacturing industry, 1975
Source: DGEC 1977-1978.

rapidly in the past two decades. Their products include
processed meat, milk, and fish, animal and vegetable fats,
flour, bread, biscuits, fruit and vegetable preserves, refined sugar, chocolate, sweets, alcoholic and nonalcoholic
beverages, and cigarettes. Of their raw materials, 83
percent are locally produced; the principal import is
wheat for the modern flour mill in Alajuela. Production
units range from large factories, many owned by multinational corporations, to small family firms using simple
technology. Approximately one-fifth of the output is exported. This consumer industry is the only branch of
manufacturing where significant sales outside the Central
American Common Market have been achieved. Many food
products are exported to the United States and Europe.

In contrast to some of the larger Latin American
countries where textiles were manufactured prior to the
establishment of protective tariffs, this industry was insignificant in Costa Rica before 1959. The manufacture of
cotton textiles, developed by the indigenous population in
pre-Columbian times and retained on a small scale during
the colonial period, virtually disappeared with the growth
of international trade during the nineteenth century.
Large textile mills and clothing factories have been constructed in the past twenty years, including several owned
by subsidiaries of Japanese companies. Most use imported
cotton and synthetic fibers. Nearly one-third of their
output is exported, mainly to countries within the Central
American Common Market. The leather industry, which uses
raw materials from the whole isthmus, produces not only
shoes and bags but also furniture, saddles, and other ap-
purtenances for horse riding. Many leather goods are
still manufactured by artesans.

No other consumer goods industry contributes more
than 5 percent to employment or to the value of production
in the manufacturing sector. Wooden articles, such as
furniture, souvenirs, and construction materials, are
still produced mainly in small workshops. While Costa
Rica remained a heavily forested country, there were ample
reserves of precious tropical hardwoods for local crafts.
Today, dwindling home supplies of timber are supplemented
by imports, particularly from Honduras which produces
large quantities of pine. Printing and publishing, another old-established industry, owes its long history to
Costa Rica's outstanding achievements in literacy and basic education. There are a few, large, specialized firms
and many small ones that combine printing with the stationery trade. All rely largely on imported pulp and
paper.

The manufacture of pharmaceuticals, cosmetics, and
domestic electrical appliances has been developed since
1959. With a few exceptions, such as the manufacture of
soap, only the final stages of production are carried out
in Costa Rica. Sixty-seven percent of the inputs required
by the pharmaceuticals and cosmetics industries, and 86

percent of those used to produce electrical appliances are
imported from Europe, the United States, and Japan. Subsidiaries of multinational companies dominate all these
industries. This type of manufacturing is typical of the
process dubbed "pseudo-industrialization," which contributes little more than employment and a certain amount of
added value to the developing country where it is located.
Nearly half the pharmaceuticals and cosmetics and over a
quarter of the electrical appliances are exported, mainly
to neighboring Central American republics.

In 1975, factories producing intermediate goods accounted for only 28 percent of the value of production, 20
percent of employment, and 15 percent of the firms in the
manufacturing sector. Costa Rica lacks many of the major
industries producing intermediate goods, including iron
and steel. The preparation of leather and wood for use in
local consumer goods industries is still carried out mainly by small, dispersed units of production. Whereas the
wood industry faces rapid depletion of natural resources,
the output of leather has risen sharply in recent years as
cattle ranching has expanded. Exploitation of local supplies of nonmetallic minerals for the construction industry is another traditional activity, where there are still
many small firms. In addition, large, modern factories
produce bulky items such as cement and glass, which were
previously imported, from local raw materials. The chemical industry has been almost entirely developed during the
past twenty years. Modern factories, some of which are
subsidiaries of multinational corporations, use advanced
technology to manufacture refined petroleum and petroleum
by-products, paints, varnishes, synthetic rubber, plastics,
fertilizers, and other agricultural inputs. Since Costa
Rica produces no petroleum and few basic chemicals, this
group of industries relies on imports for almost half of
its raw materials. Nearly one-fifth of the output is exported, mainly to countries within the Central American
Common Market.

The manufacture of capital goods is weakly developed
and shows no sign of rapid expansion in the near future.
Most of the existing firms in this category are either
small workshops carrying out simple engineering tasks,
such as soldering, or large factories, subsidiaries of
multinational companies, engaged in the assembly of imported parts of vehicles and machinery. Apart from the
absence of basic metal industries, Costa Rica lacks the
technology and internal market for manufacturing capital
goods. Even the Central American Common Market, with a
total population of about 20 million, is a small economic
unit for advanced engineering.

Modern factories are heavily concentrated in the center of the country (Figure 5.11). In 1975, the metropolitan region contained two-thirds of the modern firms, accounted for a similar proportion of the value of industrial production, and generated more than four-fifths of the

Figure 5.11   Distribution of employment in manufacturing
industry, 1975

Source: DGEC 1977-1978.

employment in the manufacturing sector. With a few exceptions, such as the milk consumed by dairies near San José,
the deposits of calcite used for cement production at
Aguacaliente and Patarrá, and the sands to be employed in
the manufacture of glass near Cartago, the industries of
the metropolitan region obtain few of their raw materials
from local sources. For most firms, the region offers
three locational advantages over the rest of the country.
First, its central position in the road and rail networks
facilitates both the transport of raw materials and the
distribution of finished goods. Second, with half the
country's population, the metropolitan region contains a
heavy concentration of the labor force and the domestic
market. These factors are not merely quantitative however:
manpower is more skilled and purchasing power greater in
the central region than anywhere else in the country.
Third, because it contains many urban central places, the
metropolitan region is also well equipped with ancillary
services such as banks, insurance offices, private professional services, social services, telecommunications,
electricity, and water supplies.

There are three major patterns of industrial location
within the metropolitan region. First, artesans and workshops serving local communities are scattered throughout
the urban and suburban area, although they are finding it
increasingly difficult to obtain premises at prices they
can afford. Second, there are dispersed factories located
within the built-up area, particularly in deteriorating
residential districts. Poor transport and lack of expansion space are forcing many of these firms to consider re-
location on the peripheries of the metropolitan region.
Third, and most important, are the industrial zones of the
city, the majority of which are the result of spontaneous
development by private entrepreneurs (Figure 5.12). Since
interindustry linkages are weak, there is little areal
specialization; dissimilar and unrelated factories stand
side by side. The oldest and most consolidated industrial
zones, where there is now little space available for further factory construction, are located close to the center
of San José. In Uruca, Calle Blancos, and the Cementerio
quarter, modern factories are interspersed with older
workshops, commercial activities, and houses; Pavas, on
the other hand, has been developed during the past twenty
years as a private industrial estate occupying part of
what was previously one of the largest coffee plantations
in the metropolitan region. New industrial zones are developing beyond the built-up area, where there is cheaper
land and easy access to the principal roads and railways.
The largest zones are located to the northwest of San José
at Valencia and Ribera-Pitahaya; smaller industrial zones
are emerging to the east at Ochomogo, Ipis, and San Francisco de Dos Ríos. The Oficina de Planeamiento del Area
Metropolitana has delimited a third group of areas suitable for future factory construction. At present, these

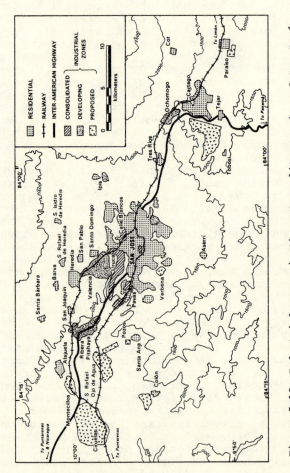

Figure 5.12 Industrial zones in the metropolitan region of San José

Source: OPAM 1979.

areas contain little infrastructure and, with the exception of the industrial park at Paraíso, will be developed
by private entrepreneurs. The future industrial zones
lie within a 25-kilometer radius of the center of San
José, in areas of flat land where there is still little
urban development. All are located to the west of existing built-up areas so that the prevailing northeast winds
minimize atmospheric pollution in the towns and villages
(OPAM 1979; Arq. Garrett Cotter, personal communication).

The heavy concentration of factories close to the
capital city has exacerbated ecological and social problems in Costa Rica's most densely populated region. In a
country where only a small proportion of the land is suitable for intensive cultivation, it is highly questionable
whether the long-term national interest is to bury fertile
soils beneath factories. Many industries are the source
of heavy environmental pollution: the rivers of the metropolitan region are contaminated with industrial waste and
the air with smoke and dust. The spatial concentration of
manufacturing has been a powerful stimulus to internal migration to the center of the country. Since most factories, however, are capital rather than labor intensive and
many migrants are unskilled, would-be industrial workers
are often forced to eke out a living in the "primitive"
tertiary sector. Those who do obtain a factory job frequently fail to find housing close to their place of work;
lower-class housing is concentrated in the southern districts of San José whereas the majority of factories are
located to the north and west of the city center.

Beyond the metropolitan region, there are no large industrial zones. Most manufacturing units are either small
workshops or agricultural processing plants. Artesan-
traders still abound in towns and villages throughout the
country, although their wares are facing increasing competition from factory goods. Primary processing of agricultural products, whether in large, modern units such as the
sugar ingenios or in rudimentary plants like those extracting coconut oil, is carried out mainly in the countryside
close to the sources of bulky and perishable raw materials.
Other types of manufacturing are little developed outside
the metropolitan region. In western Valle Central, a textile factory has been located at Naranjo. The national liquor factory, which at present operates in the heart of San
José, is to be relocated near Grecia in the center of the
largest sugar-producing region. The two principal ports
have a few large factories relying on maritime transport or
resources: fish canning and the production of fertilizers
in Puntarenas, and oil refining in Limón.

Industrialization within the framework of the Central
American Common Market has diversified the economy, created
some new jobs, and stimulated the development of business
management and the diffusion of new technology. It has
failed, however, to reduce the balance of payments deficit;
between 1960 and 1977 the value of imports exceeded that of

exports by at least 20 percent, and in some years by more
than 50 percent (DGEC 1979d). Nor has it generated as
much employment as was initially anticipated; in 1973 the
manufacturing industry employed less than 70,000 people,
only 12 percent of the labor force. Many factories produce high-cost, low-quality goods unable to compete in
world markets, use capital- rather than labor-intensive
technology, and rely heavily on imported raw materials.
Neither of Costa Rica's principal resources for industri-
alization--labor and home-produced raw materials--is fully
utilized (D. Camacho 1978, 89). Government encouragement
of manufacturing at the expense of agriculture has exacerbated inefficiency and low productivity in the primary
sector. The industrial policies of the past 20 years are
now being subjected to serious criticism as Costa Rica
searches for a more efficacious strategy for development
involving all sectors of the economy and all regions of
the country.

6
Regional Structures

The concentration of urban and industrial development
in what was already one of the major zones of export cultivation exacerbated the regional imbalance inherent in
the geography of Costa Rica since the sixteenth century.
Many peripheral regions were still undergoing the initial
stages of Hispanic American colonization when the capital
city expanded into a complex metropolitan region. Inequitable structures of land tenure and inefficient patterns of land use persisted in the countryside, depressing
living standards and fomenting migration into the urban
areas.

The dichotomy of a small, relatively well-developed
central region and a variety of large, less-developed
peripheral regions may be an inevitable part of the socioeconomic development process (Alonso 1968; Williamson
1965). In Costa Rica, the dichotomy can be clearly discerned in the distribution and density of population, the
hierarchy of central places, the transport network, the
spatial distribution of wealth and welfare, and the ana-
chronomic system of administrative areas. The latter's
incipient replacement by a system of planning regions constitutes the first official attempt to spread development
more evenly throughout the country.

The precise delimitation of center and periphery is
more difficult than their definition. Boundaries vary according to individual phenomena: some centers are spatially concentrated in a smaller, others in a larger, central
region. Center and periphery are rarely separated in
practice by a sharp boundary; rather, they merge across
transitional zones. Both are heterogeneous and can be
subdivided according to their spatial organization and
level of socioeconomic development. Figure 6.1 is therefore a model rather than a map.

The more-developed center, containing a dense population, the largest urban areas, an integrated transport
network, the highest levels of wealth and welfare, and the
major centers of political decision making, can be concep-
tualized at different scales, thereby producing three

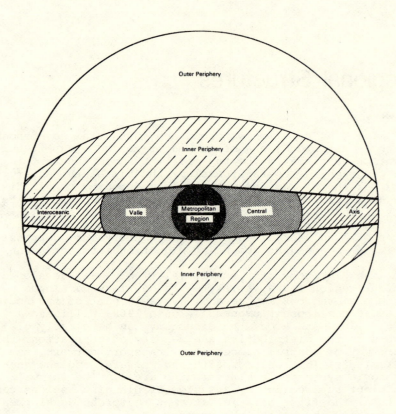

Figure 6.1 Model of central and peripheral regions

concentric regions: the metropolitan region, a predominantly urban and suburban area developed during the second half of the twentieth century; the Valle Central; and the interoceanic zone between the Caribbean Sea and the Pacific Ocean, axis of the agro-export economy since the nineteenth century. At its maximum extent, the center occupies about 10 percent of the area of the country.

The remainder constitutes a less-developed, predominantly rural periphery, bisected by the interoceanic axis. The periphery can be subdivided into inner and outer zones whose real contours are more irregular and fragmented than in the model. The inner peripheral zones have now been almost entirely colonized for farming. They contain small towns and are linked with the interoceanic axis by all-weather, overland transport. Their population is sparse in comparison to the center, but it has access to basic social services. In the outer peripheral zones, farmlands are still interspersed with large tracts of forest. There are no urban central places, paved roads, or railways. The sparse population lives in poverty and extreme isolation, with no regular access to most social services.

The hegemony of the central region is reflected in a basically two-tiered spatial organization: national, and local or municipal. The country lacks a well-developed intermediate or regional level of organization. In the central place hierarchy, there is a huge gap between the primate city and the other towns. Transport and trading systems operate at a national and local scale but are weakly developed at a regional level. Public administration is carried out by a strong, highly centralized national government and by the municipalities, but the provinces play virtually no part in running the country. The population in the periphery is therefore acutely disadvantaged in comparison to the center of the country, which is within easy reach of the metropolitan region of San José.

THE DISTRIBUTION AND DENSITY OF POPULATION

The very irregular distribution of Costa Rica's 2.2 million inhabitants is shown by the Lorenz curve of population plotted against area (Figure 6.2). The average population density for the whole country--approximately 42 persons per square kilometer in 1979 (DGEC 1979b)--has little meaning, except for a general appraisal of the relationship between population and resources. Most of the country is still sparsely settled, but population density varies over very short distances (Figure 6.3).

In the periphery, agriculture remains the principal economic activity, and nine-tenths of the population lives in the countryside, many in isolated hamlets or dispersed settlements. The remainder inhabit small towns, none of whose populations exceeded 11,000 in 1973. Inner and outer peripheral areas can be clearly distinguished on the

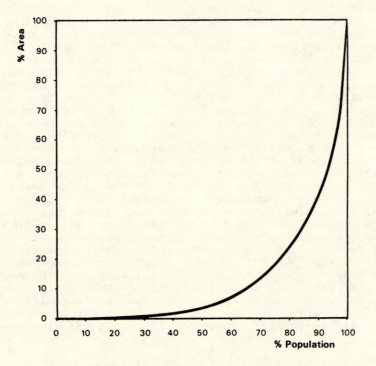

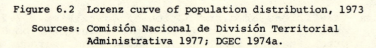

Figure 6.2   Lorenz curve of population distribution, 1973

Sources: Comisión Nacional de División Territorial
Administrativa 1977; DGEC 1974a.

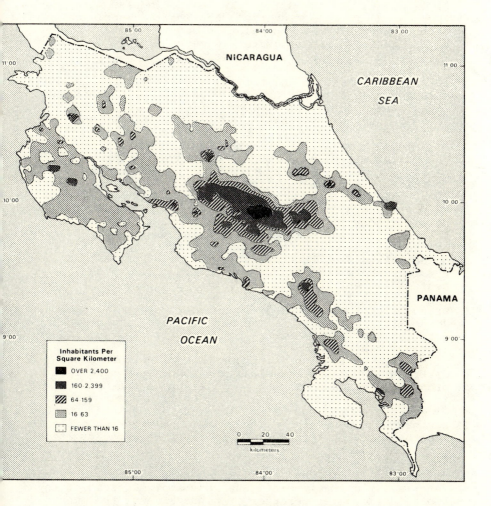

Figure 6.3   Population density, 1973

Source: Nuhn 1978b (reprinted with the permission of the Instituto Geográfico Nacional).

population map. The outer periphery contains less than 16
inhabitants per square kilometer and no towns at all. The
zone extends right across the north of the country and
continues south of the interoceanic axis in the Cordillera
de Talamanca and the Osa and Burica peninsulas. In the
fragmented, inner peripheral areas located mainly on the
Pacific slope, average population density ranges from 16
to 63 individuals per square kilometer. Small areas in
and around the main towns are more densely populated.

In contrast to the periphery, the interoceanic axis
is densely populated and heavily urbanized. In the zone
between Puntarenas and Limón, 70 percent of Costa Rica's
inhabitants occupy only 10 percent of her territory. The
Valle Central alone contains 63 percent and the metropolitan region 49 percent of the country's population. Overall density exceeds 160 per square kilometer in most of
the Valle Central and around Puntarenas and Limón; small
parts of the metropolitan region contain more than 2,400
inhabitants per square kilometer. Rural population densities, which in some central areas exceed 400 per square
kilometer, are among the highest in Latin America, comparable to those in parts of Southeast Asia. In much of the
Valle Central there is almost continuous settlement along
the roads. More than half the population of the interoceanic axis are urban dwellers, and many classified as
rural in the census are suburban commuters. Ninety percent of the entire urban population of Costa Rica is concentrated in this region. It contains most of the country's large towns, including the metropolitan area of San
José with a population of nearly half a million. Secondary and tertiary economic activities are therefore heavily concentrated in this region.

There is no consistent correlation between population
distribution and the physical environment. There is a
pronounced concentration of population on the drier Pacific slope, but both high and low densities occur within a
wide range of life zones and in areas of extremely varied
agricultural potential. The major concentration of population, in the Valle Central, is located in the premontane
zone, but other premontane areas are sparsely settled.
Population density is high in areas of volcanic and alluvial soils in the center of the country but low in some
fertile peripheral areas. The most sparsely settled regions in the outer periphery include some of the most difficult habitats for human occupation: the majority are
either hot, humid, poorly drained lowlands, or rugged,
rain-drenched mountains (Nunley 1960). Their heavy precipitation, dense natural vegetation, and excessively
leached soils make them unsuitable environments for traditional Hispanic American farming systems; most of the surviving Indian communities are now confined to these regions. Although agricultural potential is quite limited
here, other economic activities, such as forestry, mining,
and tourism, could be developed.

The present distribution of population reflects the historical processes outlined in earlier chapters: the concentration of population in the Valle Central since the colonial period; the centrifugal migration of Hispanic American colonists after independence; and the recent centripetal migration into the urban and suburban areas in the center of the country. In the rural areas, population density is closely related to land use and employment opportunities: it is higher in regions of export agriculture than in areas devoted to food crop production and extensive cattle ranching. The uneven distribution of population in turn underlies many of the spatial irregularities in the central place hierarchy, the transport network, and access to economic and social services.

THE HIERARCHY OF CENTRAL PLACES

The hierarchy of central places, which provides the population with goods and services, includes some thirty towns, several hundred villages, and several thousand hamlets. At the moment, it differs substantially from the models expounded in classical geographic literature (Christaller 1966; Lösch 1954). Central functions are concentrated in a primate city, and there are many more high- and medium-order places in the center than in the periphery of the country. The hierarchy, however, is very dynamic. A wide range of basic services and amenities, initially available only in the major towns, were diffused during the 1960s and 1970s, from larger to smaller places and from the center to the periphery of the country. As services and commercial functions proliferate, villages are transformed into towns.

Since tertiary activities predominate in all the central places, it is hardly surprising that their populations and central functions are closely correlated. Ratcliffe (1970) discovered correlation coefficients of 0.98 between population and the number of buildings where central functions are located, 0.96 between population and the number of functional units, and 0.92 between population and the number of different functions. These correlations are in line with findings in other parts of the world, including regions in developed countries such as the United States and Britain (Carter et al. 1970; Stafford 1963). Population data, readily available in censuses, may thus be as useful an indicator of the relative importance of different places as are measures of their functions (Davies 1969). The collection of data about central functions is extremely tedious, and no entirely satisfactory method has yet been devised to weigh functions of varying importance.

Figure 6.4 shows the rank-size relationships of towns and larger villages, measured according to population. The hierarchy is dominated by a primate city, San José,

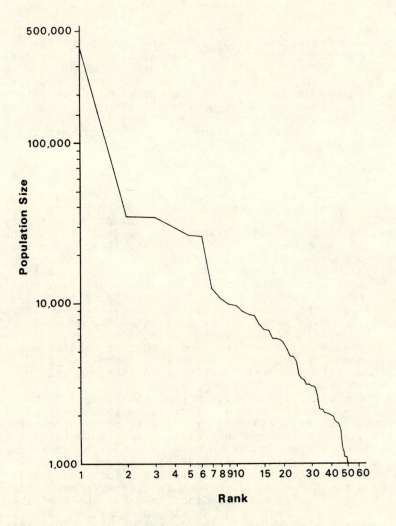

Figure 6.4   Central place hierarchy: rank-size relationships

Source: DGEC 1974a.

approximately ten times larger than any other town. This
pattern is typical of many developing countries, and the
Costa Rican case supports most of the hypotheses put forward to explain primacy: (1) historically, urbanization is
a relatively recent phenomenon, and the central place hierarchy is still in the process of formation; (2) the agro-
export economy precluded the development of industrial
cities and generated relatively low incomes, limiting the
demand for goods and services of the type offered by large
cities; (3) the country's small area, similar to that of a
single state or province in many other countries, is insufficient to warrant the development of several big cities; and (4) population is heavily concentrated in a small
region for which the primate city provides goods and services (Berry 1961; Linsky 1965).
     The corollary of primacy is a dearth of medium-sized
towns. There is a wide gap between the primate city, with
more than 400,000 inhabitants, and the second order places,
none of whose populations exceeded 35,000 in 1973. The
existence of stepped hierarchies as postulated by Christaller has been questioned in recent work on central place
theory (Beavon 1977). The data for Costa Rica certainly
indicates the predominance of a continuum over discretely
separated classes, each with a specific population size
and range and number of functions. This finding does not
necessarily invalidate, however, attempts to classify central places; most data classifications in geography are
concerned with ordering continua. At least seven categories can be distinguished, ranging from hamlets to the
capital city (Figure 6.5).
     The lower and middle order places are predominantly
rural; many of their inhabitants work on the land. Sev-
enth order places, the smallest of all, are hamlets with a
few hundred inhabitants. They usually have only three
functions: a pulpería or general store, a cantina or bar,
and a bus stop. Sixth order places, generally with a population of less than 1,000, may contain, in addition to
these ubiquitous functions, postal and telegraph offices,
a church, a primary school, and a mobile clinic. Some are
district capitals with a police station. The pulperías
carry a wider range of merchandise, including drapery and
hardware. Many fifth order places have a health clinic, a
branch bank, and a café. The largest contain about 3,000
inhabitants. Some are cantonal capitals, with executive,
legislative, and judicial branches of local government.
The population of fourth order places ranges from 500 to
5,000. All are cantonal capitals. Most contain a secondary school, an agricultural extension office, a cinema, a
bus station, and specialized traders and artesans such as
butchers, greengrocers, bakers, mechanics, restauranteurs,
tailors, shoemakers, and saddlers.
     The high and medium order places are urban centers.
Third order places contain 2,000-8,000 inhabitants. Their
commercial functions include markets, hotels, slaughter-

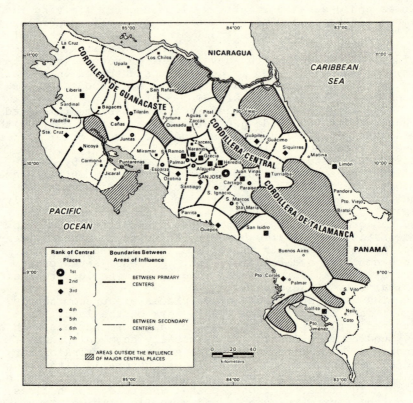

Figure 6.5 Central places and their areas of influence

Source: Nuhn 1978b (reprinted with the permission of the
Instituto Geográfico Nacional).

houses, and specialized shops selling stationery, furniture, and electrical appliances. Many contain local hospitals and a public library. Second order places, with
populations between 6,500 and 35,000, have modern supermarkets, a still wider range of specialized shops, and
large branch banks. Several contain cathedrals and branches of universities. Some are provincial capitals with
courts of justice (Ratcliffe 1970). The primate city, San
José, falls into a class of its own. The seat of a heavily centralized national government, it contains a multi-
tude of functions not found in any other town: the legislative assembly, the supreme court, large hospitals with
specialists in all branches of medicine, the major university, art galleries, museums, theaters, a concert hall,
publishers of books and newspapers, the stock exchange,
and the headquarters of the postal and telecommunications
services, the state insurance monopoly, and the banks.
With several markets, many supermarkets, department stores,
luxury shops, and high-quality hotels and restaurants, the
volume of San José's trade exceeds many times that of any
other town.

With the exception of the central location of San
José, the spatial distribution of towns and villages also
departs from the theoretical schemes outlined by Christaller and Lösch. Eight second order places are located
along the interoceanic axis, only four are in the periphery.[1] In the center of the country, the second order
places are so close together that third and fourth order
places tend to be squeezed out to the margins of the interoceanic axis, for example at Orotina, Santiago de Puriscal, Siquirres, and Guápiles. The distribution of medium and lower order places in the periphery is also irregular: the northern plains have a second order center, Quesada, but no third or fourth order places; the Caribbean
lowlands have no fourth or fifth order places; the hierarchy is fairly evenly distributed in the center of Guanacaste, but there are no third or fourth order places north
of Liberia. In the outer periphery there are only villages, and extensive areas contain no central places at
all.

Nuhn made the first, and so far the only, attempt to
map the hinterlands of the central places (Figure 6.5).
There is no consistent correlation between the relative
importance of the central place and the aerial extent of
its hinterland. In the Valle Central where population
density is high, the hinterlands of places of all sizes

---

[1]Kilgour (1981) identified only Alajuela, Heredia, and Cartago as second order places. The use of the telephone index, however, probably
inflated the relative importance of these three towns, which house
many affluent commuters working in the capital city. Kilgour's second and third order towns coincide with the second order towns identified in Figure 6.5, with the exception of Golfito.

are small, with the partial exception of San José whose hinterland for many functions is the whole country. In the sparsely populated periphery, the hinterlands of nearly all places are much larger; that of a fifth order place such as Upala in the north of the country, for example, is many times greater than that of a second order place such as Grecia or Alajuela in the Valle Central. Although some hinterlands approach the circle or hexagon that classical theory shows to be the most efficient form of spatial packing, many others are elongated up mountain slopes or along intermontane valleys and coastal plains. Some places are fairly centrally located within their spheres of influences, but the majority at all levels in the hierarchy are situated on the edge of the areas they serve. Along the interoceanic axis where many places are located on the principal roads and railways to the ports, hinterland growth to the east and west is restricted by competition from neighboring places; areas of influence therefore tend to extend into the mountains to the north and south, widening towards the periphery to produce triangular hinterlands with the central place located at the apex. Outside the central zone, the eccentric location of many places reflects the processes of colonization. Towns such as Santiago de Puriscal, Quesada, and San Isidro, founded in the areas first settled by migrants from the Valle Central, persisted as the principal urban centers even when colonization had spread far beyond these early nuclei (Sandner 1962).

The regular lattice of Christaller's model was located on an isotropic surface. In Costa Rica, natural environment, population density, and economic activities vary sharply over very small distances. The central place network is still concentrated in the subtropical intermontane depressions and in the dry tropical lowlands; the high, rugged mountains and humid, tropical lowlands contain few towns. Many irregularities in the hierarchy reflect the uneven distribution of population. When plotted in relation to population density rather than area, the distribution of the central places becomes much more regular (Figure 6.6). Nuhn discovered more regularity in the population than in the area of hinterlands: second order places serve between 40,000 and 140,000 people, third order places maintain between 15,000 and 65,000 (Nuhn 1973a, 100). The hierarchy also reflects the patterns of land use and transportation of the agro-export economy. San José and six second order places are located in the major coffee-growing region, where there is a dense network of roads; three other second order places are international ports and railway termini; Limón and Golfito are the major urban centers for the banana-growing regions. In peripheral regions of recent colonization, where cattle ranching and the cultivation of food crops predominate and where the road network is sparse and poorly integrated, the central place hierarchy is rudimentary. In the

255

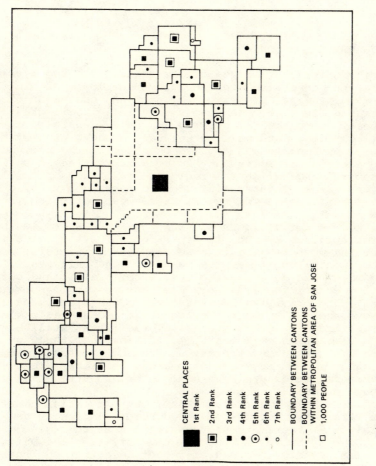

CENTRAL PLACES

◼ 1st Rank
▣ 2nd Rank
■ 3rd Rank
● 4th Rank
⊙ 5th Rank
• 6th Rank
○ 7th Rank

— BOUNDARY BETWEEN CANTONS
--- BOUNDARY BETWEEN CANTONS
     WITHIN METROPOLITAN AREA OF SAN JOSE
□ 1,000 PEOPLE

Figure 6.6 Distribution of central places in population space

Sources: DGEC 1974a; Nuhn 1978b.

northern plains and the General-Coto Brus depression, Quesada and San Isidro are the only large towns. In southwestern Nicoya peninsula, the Herradura region, the Fila Costeña, and the Osa peninsula, there are only rural central places. The first attempt to diversify economic activities--by developing "import-substituting" industries--consolidated the existing pattern of central places since most factories were built in the metropolitan area of San José and in the second order places along the interoceanic axis.

THE TRANSPORT NETWORK

The spatial structure of the transport network, like that of the central place hierarchy, developed within the context of the primary export economy and has undergone relatively few major changes as desarrollo hacia afuera has been accompanied by desarrollo hacia adentro. It is relatively dense and well integrated in the center of the country, but sparse and poorly connected in the periphery (Figure 6.7). It serves the import-export trade and links the central and peripheral regions, but it does not fully meet the needs of internal trade and passenger traffic because it affords few direct links between peripheral regions.

There are five modes of transport--roads, railways, waterways, airways, and pipelines--of which the roads are by far the most important. The 26,086 kilometers of roads exceed twenty-four times the length of the railways. They carry more than 90 percent of passenger traffic and cargo, yet they constitute a network limited in extent, poor in quality, and primitive in structure. On average, there is just over half a kilometer of roads per square kilometer. Many are riddled with potholes. Three-fifths still have only a dirt surface (Table 6.1). These roads throw up clouds of dust during the dry season and are transformed into quagmires during the wet season, when they are impassable for motor vehicles and can only be traversed on foot or horseback.

In the Valle Central, most of the population now lives within easy access of paved roads, and, near the capital city, there are short stretches of four-lane motorway. Beyond the Valle Central, however, only the main roads are paved. In areas of recent colonization (including the plantation enclaves where the railway has been the traditional mode of transport), even gravel and dirt roads are few. Extensive parts of the northern plains, the Caribbean lowlands, and the foothills of the Cordillera de Talamanca, and smaller areas in the Pacific peninsulas and lowlands are still beyond the reach of all modern transport except light aircraft. Lack of all-weather roads continues to be one of the principal obstacles to development in the peripheral rural regions. It deters economic

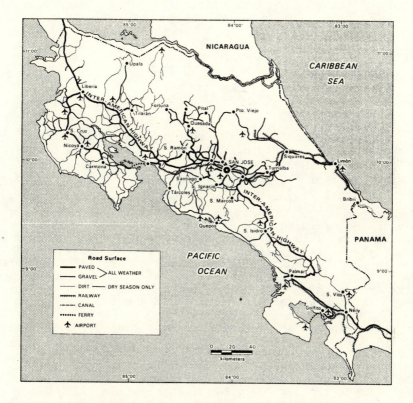

Figure 6.7   The transport network, 1980

Sources: MOPT 1980; Nuhn 1978b.

TABLE 6.1
Road network, 1977

Type of Surface	Kilometers	Percent
Paved (concrete or asphalt)	2,008	7.70
Gravel	8,199	31.43
Dirt	15,879	60.87
TOTAL	26,086	100.00

Source: DGEC 1980.

production because there is often no means of getting merchandise to potential markets. It also condemns the dispersed population to extreme isolation, cutting them off
from regular access to the goods and services available in
towns and villages (IFAM 1974a, 6-12).

Figure 6.8a depicts the national network of trunk
roads reduced to a topological graph from which connectivity can be measured according to quantitative indices.[1]
The Beta index is 1.00, the Gamma index 37 percent, and
the Alpha index 4 percent--values scarcely above the minimum for a network in which there are no isolated subgraphs.
The network as a whole is radial. It is dominated by two
trunk roads, the Pan-American and the interoceanic high-
ways, which converge along the stretch between Barranca
and Cartago. In many peripheral regions, however, there
is only a spinal network with feeders branching off a single main road. Spinal and radial patterns are typical of
poorly integrated networks within which flows between
pairs of vertices are limited to single paths. Only in
the Valle Central does the network of all-weather roads
have higher indices of connectivity: Beta = 1.29, Gamma =
43 percent, and Alpha = 15 percent (Figure 6.8b). In this
region, rectangular and triangular linkages provide alternative routes between many pairs of vertices.

Traffic flows are concentrated on the two principal

---

[1]Following Kansky (1963), the Beta index is the ratio between the number of edges and the number of vertices; it varies from less than 1
to a maximum of 3. The Gamma index is the ratio between the actual
number of edges and the number needed to integrate completely the
given number of vertices; it is expressed either as a value between
0.33 and 1.00 or as a percentage. The Alpha index is the ratio between the actual number of circuits or finite closed paths in the
graph and the number of circuits required to integrate completely the
network; it is expressed as a value between 0 and 1.00 or as a percentage.

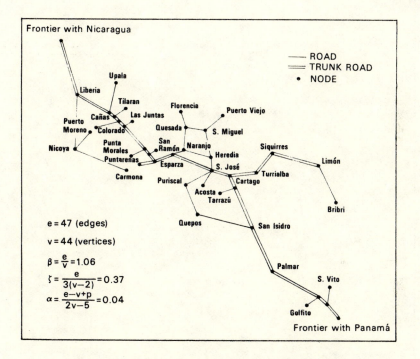

Figure 6.8a   Road networks as topological graphs:
National network of trunk roads

Source: MOPT 1980.

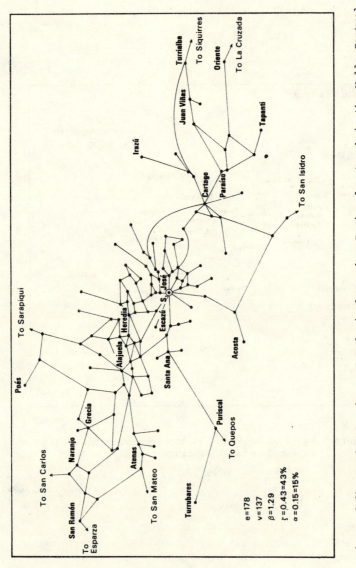

Figure 6.8b Road networks as topological graphs: Regional network in the Valle Central

Source: MOPT 1977a.

trunk roads (Figure 6.9). The flow between Liberia and
Cartago exceeds 2,000 vehicles per day. This stretch of
the Pan-American Highway traverses the most densely populated regions of Costa Rica and is used for overland
transport to and from all the countries to the north. By
contrast, the southern section of the highway carries a
much smaller volume of traffic. It crosses sparsely populated regions of Costa Rica, and international traffic is
limited to vehicles going to and from Panama. The road
east from Cartago is used mainly by local traffic between
the Valle Central and the Caribbean lowlands; no international passenger traffic uses this route, and most import
and export cargoes are carried by train. Traffic flows
decrease rapidly beyond these major axes of the network;
only the roads to Nicoya and Quesada carry more than 500
vehicles per day.

The convergence of the road network and the heavy
concentration of population in the primate city of San
José make this center the hub of freight and passenger
traffic. Regional trading and transport centers are weakly developed. Both internal trade and passenger traffic
display a basically two-tiered pattern composed of long-
distance movements to and from the capital city and shorter journeys between rural areas and nearby central places.

Most freight destined for the home market is moved by
road, in lorries, vans, ox carts, and on horseback. Internal trade and transport involves many thousands of people, both producers and specialized carriers and traders.
Most operate on a very small scale. Farmers and artesans
transport and sell many of their own goods directly to retail merchants and domestic consumers. In many sectors of
the economy there is little wholesaling. Large-scale
freight transport is restricted mainly to factories that
market their own products and to government agencies, such
as the Consejo Nacional de Producción, which distribute
certain foodstuffs.

The municipal markets in the towns and the pulperías
in the villages are engaged mainly in retail trade. They
sell local farm products such as unpasteurized milk, eggs,
fruit, vegetables, grains, and meat, as well as furniture,
leather goods, and clothing made by local artesans. Much
of the merchandise on sale in small towns and villages,
however, has been transported from San José, the principal
industrial region as well as the major center for the redistribution of agricultural products. Most farmers, if
they are unable to sell their products in the nearest
small town or village, send them to San José; conversely,
retailers unable to obtain local goods rely on supplies
from the capital city. No regional market center is large
enough to provide the economies of scale needed to sort,
classify, and pack merchandise for redistribution. Many
opportunities for specialized economic production and in-
terregional trade are lost because the deficient road network fails to integrate the peripheral regions (González

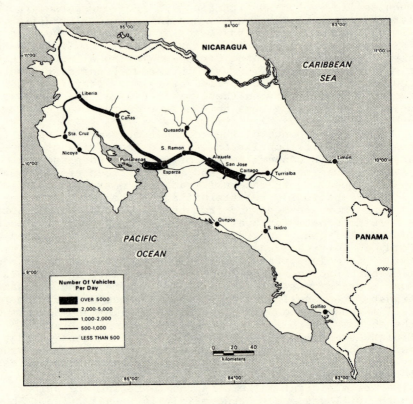

Figure 6.9 Traffic flows on main roads

<u>Source</u>: MOPT 1977b.

Vega et al. 1970).

In spite of the recent increase in the number of automobiles in circulation, there is still on average only one such vehicle per fifty-seven people. Most Costa Ricans rely on public transport for journeys that cannot be made on foot or, in rural areas, on horseback. A dense network of bus services, comprising over 700 routes, serves virtually every town, village, and hamlet tapped by the road network and constitutes the country's principal mode of passenger transport (Figure 6.10). Local services link rural areas to the nearest town or village; long-distance routes connect every town and many villages directly with San José. The radial network that converges on the capital city is repeated at a local scale in almost every canton. There are hardly any cross-country services linking peripheral villages and few direct services between peripheral towns, except where these centers lie on one of the routes to and from San José. On well-maintained, all-weather roads, bus transport is relatively fast and cheap. Traveling times and costs increase up to four times in peripheral regions where poor-quality gravel and dirt roads reduce speed and deteriorate vehicles.

In contrast to the roads, which reach into most of the settled regions of the country and carry the majority of local freight and passenger traffic, the railways are confined to a small number of routes and are used principally for transporting imports and exports (Figure 6.7). The two main railway systems, the former Northern or Atlantic Railway nationalized in 1972 and the Ferrocarril Eléctrico al Pacífico, were united under a single government authority, Ferrocarriles de Costa Rica S.A. (FECOSA), in 1977. Each railway continues to operate from its own station in San José, but unification has facilitated the interchange of rolling stock throughout the interoceanic axis. The only remaining private railway, owned by the Compañía Bananera, is the small Ferrocarril del Sur, which converges on the port of Golfito (Table 6.2).

All the railways, particularly the older Atlantic line, on which the former British owners carried out little maintainance are in urgent need of reconstruction and modernization. They are single track with a narrow gauge of 3 feet 6 inches. They contain curves of up to 35°. In the center of the country, the steepest gradients have a slope of 4.5 percent. Trains are restricted to a maximum speed of about 50 kilometers per hour, and there are often delays at passing places along the lines. The most heavily used section of the railways--a stretch of about 100 kilometers traversing the banana-growing regions between Río Frío and Limón--has recently been electrified and completely rebuilt, with a new track, improved curves and gradients, and an automatic signaling system. In the future, similar reconstruction will be needed on the rest of the Atlantic railway and on the Pacific line (Juan Vargas Soto, personal communication).

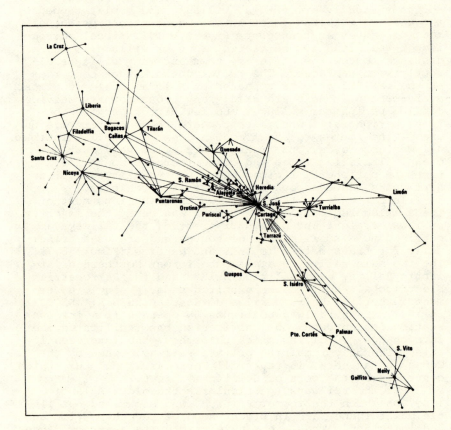

Figure 6.10 Bus routes, 1980

Source: MOPT, unpublished statistics.

TABLE 6.2
Railway network, 1977

| System | Length in Kilometers | | | |
	Main Line	Branch Lines	Station Yards	Total
FECOSA				
Atlantic line	166	275	177	618
Pacific line	116	15	35	166
Ferrocarril del				
Sur	184	48	14	246
TOTAL	466	338	226	1030

Source: DGEC 1980.

TABLE 6.3
Freight carried by Ferrocarriles de Costa Rica S.A. (FECOSA), 1978

	Atlantic Railway (tons)	Pacific Railway (tons)
Exports:		
Bananas	723,074	--
Coffee	42,715	23,316
Fertilizers	--	1,505
Meat	--	794
Others	579	806
Total	766,368	26,421
Imports:		
Grain	3,671	102,432
Iron and steel	40,702	72,805
Agricultural Machinery	19,350	--
Fertilizers	8,204	12,077
Pulp and paper	10,684	6,987
Cement	--	7,041
Others	4,473	26,714
Total	87,084	228,056
Local Freight	305,042	202,666

Source: FECOSA 1978.

The railway network is even more primitive than the road network. It is composed of two isolated subgraphs, both spinal in form. The connectivity indices are very low: Beta = 1.03, Gamma = 37 percent, and Alpha = 6 percent. The railway network is typical of the transport systems built to move primary commodities in underdeveloped countries: its function has simply been to link export-producing areas with ocean ports, not to interconnect regions within the country.

On the Pacific line between San José and Puntarenas, transport of the major export cargo, coffee, is concentrated during the harvest period from November to March. The volume of incoming cargo carried throughout the year is ten times as great as that of outgoing freight (Table 6.3). Imports include wheat, transported to the flour mill in Alajuela, as well as manufactured goods and industrial raw materials destined mainly for the metropolitan area of San José. Export freight on the Atlantic railway is heavily concentrated on the coastal lowlands since bananas, the most profitable of FECOSA's cargoes, comprise more than 90 percent of the volume. Coffee is the principal export commodity carried over the highland stretch of the line. Import cargoes are smaller on the Atlantic railway, but more diverse than exports. They include manufactured goods and raw materials. Bananas are the principal freight of the Ferrocarril del Sur; trains returning inland from Golfito carry only small import cargoes.

Compared to the roads, the railways carry little local freight. This deficit is partly because they serve only two areas of the country and partly because much merchandise is transported in small quantities. Construction materials are the most voluminous local cargoes (BCIE 1977, vol. 4). Railway passenger traffic is only a fraction of that carried on the roads. Travel by train is both slower and more expensive than by bus. The main lines are used by tourists and day trippers traveling between the Valle Central and the coasts. On the Caribbean lowlands, trains are still the principal mode of local passenger transport in some areas, but they are gradually being replaced by buses as the road network is expanded.

The primary export economy has always been dependent on ocean shipping to carry agricultural commodities to developed countries in the temperate zone and to bring foodstuffs, raw materials, and manufactured goods to Costa Rica. The principal ports, Limón and Puntarenas, are located at the termini of the main railways, at either end of the interoceanic axis. The periphery contains only one international port, Golfito, in the southwest of the country.

The rapid growth in the volume of foreign trade--which more than doubled in the decade between 1966 and 1976 alone--has placed increasing strain on the small, antiquated ports. Limón, which contains the largest installations, has three wharves: the Muelle Nacional and Muelle

Metálico, both constructed by the railway companies at the
turn of the century, and the Muelle Setenta, built by the
government during the past decade. Together, they have
only nine berths: six for general import-export cargoes,
one for banana exports, and two for roll-on, roll-off
traffic. Modern port installations are now under construction at Moín, 7 kilometers to the west of Limón. Moín
will deal with imports of crude oil (processed in the
nearby refinery), exports of bananas, and some roll-on,
roll-off traffic. In addition, the port of Limón is to be
expanded. New berths for container traffic will be built
on the breakwater constructed in 1974 at the east end of
the port. Later, the Muelle Metálico and Muelle Nacional
could be eliminated to make way for an artificial harbor
with a larger number of berths.
   The port installations at Puntarenas, completed in
1929, consist of a single wharf with two berths. The present volume of traffic exceeds three times the port's capacity; boats must often anchor for several days in the
Gulf of Nicoya prior to unloading and loading. In 1976
the congestion in Puntarenas led sugar producers to build
their own port for bulk exports at Punta Morales, 18 kilometers to the northwest. Large installations now under
construction at Caldera, 15 kilometers southeast of Puntarenas, will eventually constitute the principal west
coast port for international trade, leaving Puntarenas as
a fishing port. At Caldera, small breakwaters will be
sufficient to form a sheltered harbor, and relatively little dredging will be needed to maintain deep water. There
is also more room for urban expansion than in Puntarenas.
Caldera is closer to the Valle Central, to which it will
be linked by a new paved road and a branch of the Pacific
railway. The first stage of the project will provide five
deep water berths in an artificial harbor, but eventually
the new port could be expanded to contain fifty berths
(BCIE 1977, vol. 5; Ing. José Chacón, personal communication).
   More than four-fifths of the volume of imports and
exports are transported to and from Costa Rica by sea;
most of the remainder are carried overland by road. Over
half of this trade passes through Limón, from whence journeys to and from Europe and eastern North America are
1,000 kilometers shorter than along the alternative route
via Puntarenas and the Panama Canal. Exports from Limón
are dominated by bananas, imports by petroleum. The
freight moved through Puntarenas is more diverse but
smaller in volume. Exports, in addition to agricultural
commodities, include fertilizers manufactured near the
port for sale in Mexico and Central America. The principal imports are wheat and manufactured goods. Golfito's
trade is entirely dominated by the plantation economy in
its hinterland; its major export is bananas and its principal imports, fertilizers and packaging materials (BCIE
1977, vol. 5).

In contrast to ocean shipping, local shipping on rivers, canals, and along the coasts is relatively unimportant and confined to sparsely populated, low-lying, peripheral regions. Since the completion of the Pan-American Highway in the 1960s, shipping along the Pacific coast has been largely limited to the gulfs of Nicoya and Osa. Two vehicle ferries, one between Puntarenas and Playa Naranjo established in 1972 and the other across the mouth of the River Tempisque between Pozas and Puerto Moreno opened in 1974, reduce by more than a hundred kilometers journeys between the Nicoya peninsula and the rest of the country (Figure 6.7). Fluvial navigation is negligible on the Pacific slope.

On the Caribbean slope, even the larger rivers are suitable only for small craft and require regular dredging. The San Juan, which collects most of the navigable rivers of the northern plains, contains dangerous rapids upstream of its confluence with the San Carlos. A series of artificial canals was completed in 1974 to link the natural lagoons behind the Caribbean coast, forming a navigable waterway of 112 kilometers between Moín and Barra de Colorado (BCIE 1977, vol. 6). In contrast to the rough coastal waters, the canal provides a safe route for small craft throughout the year and links navigable rivers that are inaccessible from the sea because of the sand bars across their mouths. It traverses a sparsely populated region, whose swampy terrain impedes the construction of roads. Traffic flows are small, although the canal and rivers together form a network of more than 400 kilometers that could be extended still further by the construction of canals in the district of Upala (Cruz 1973).

Internal air transport, like local shipping, serves mainly the outer peripheral regions. For the past fifty years, the fastest and most modern mode of transport has, paradoxically, carried passengers and small volumes of cargo to and from the most isolated and sparsely populated parts of the country. At the present time, scheduled flights from San José serve four regions: the Caribbean lowlands, the northern plains, the Nicoya peninsula, and the south Pacific (Figure 6.7). The radial network of flights is similar in form to that of the bus services; it includes secondary centers such as Limón, Quesada, and Puntarenas, from which there are short local flights in small aircraft. Internal air transport has always been primarily a social service rather than a profitable business. It is too expensive for carrying bulky cargoes, and passenger fares have been kept artificially low by government subsidies. In 1979 the principal scheduled flights from San José were taken over by Servicio Aereo Nacional S.A., in which Costa Rica's international airline, Lineas Aereas Costarricenses S.A., holds 51 percent of the shares and the Corporación Costarricense de Desarrollo holds 49 percent (La Nación, 4 September 1979). Given the small distances involved, scheduled flights within the country

will probably disappear as the road network is further improved and extended. At present, they carry just under
200,000 passengers a year.
International air transport, by contrast, is continu-
ally expanding. Passenger boats no longer call at Costa
Rican ports, and few people travel by road beyond the Central American isthmus. The bus services operating between
Costa Rica and neighboring republics offer a cheap alternative to air transport, but are subject to long delays at
frontier posts. Although air fares to and from Costa Rica
are high, the volume of passengers moving through San
José's international airport more than doubled between
1970 and 1978, when it exceeded half a million (DGAC 1979;
DGEC 1979a).
The most recently installed mode of transport is the
pipeline, constructed during the last decade to carry petrol, diesel, and paraffin from the oil refinery at Moín
on the Caribbean coast to El Alto, between Cartago and San
José, from whence they are distributed by lorry. The
pipeline is to be continued right across the interoceanic
axis, parallel to the railways it is replacing as the major transporter of petroleum products (RECOPE, personal
communication).
The roads, railways, waterways, airways, and pipeline
constitute a still rudimentary transport system. No single mode serves the entire country. Parts of the outer
periphery are beyond the reach of any form of modern
transportation. The largest inaccessible region is the
Cordillera de Talamanca, where there are still wide tracts
of virtually uninhabited forest. As the transport network
has expanded, other inaccessible regions have gradually
diminished to scattered, isolated pockets. The remainder
of the outer periphery is served by local shipping and internal airlines, which in small areas overlap with all-
weather roads. The inner periphery is accessible throughout the year by road, but lacks other modes of transport
except near the coast and in the south Pacific lowlands.
Across the interoceanic axis, by contrast, roads, railways,
airways, and pipeline occupy parallel routes between Puntarenas, San José, and Limón, the three major nuclei of
the whole transportation system.

SPATIAL DISPARITIES IN WEALTH AND WELFARE

Pronounced spatial disparities in wealth and welfare
are indicative of the extent to which regional imbalance
constitutes a major social problem. In Costa Rica, as in
most capitalist countries of the third world, both income
concentration among the rich and the incidence of abject
poverty are greater than in developed countries. A sample
survey of 3,100 families carried out in 1971 revealed that
the richest fifth received half the total income, the
poorest fifth, only 5 percent (Table 6.4). Costa Rica

TABLE 6.4
Distribution of family income, 1971

Family Income Group	Percentage of National Income	Average Family Income (¢/month)
Lowest 10%	2.1	248
Second 10%	3.3	384
Third 10%	4.2	490
Fourth 10%	5.1	603
Fifth 10%	6.2	730
Sixth 10%	7.5	883
Seventh 10%	9.3	1,085
Eighth 10%	11.7	1,378
Ninth 10%	16.2	1,895
Highest 10%	34.4	4,104
TOTAL	100.0	1,175

confronts the dual problem of raising GNP and sharing it more fairly among the population (Céspedes 1973, 1979). In 1977 an estimated 17 percent of the population existed at a minimum subsistence level (IMAS 1978). Depending on the criteria used, a further 8 to 23 percent lived in poverty. Poor families tend to be large, with a high ratio of dependents to workers. Few live at starvation level, but their consumption of protein foods is low, the incidence of un- and underemployment is three times greater than for the rest of the population, illiteracy rates are higher, and most poor people live in dilapidated, overcrowded houses lacking basic amenities such as drinking water, electricity, and hygenic sewerage (Carvajal et al. 1977b; Céspedes et al. 1977).

Inequalities in income distribution are more pronounced in urban than in rural areas (Céspedes 1973). Most of the very wealthy live in the towns, particularly in the metropolitan region of San José; so, too, do some of the poorest people, who inhabit urban and suburban tugurios. In general, however, levels of living are higher in the towns than in the countryside. Three-quarters of poor families are rural, only one-quarter are urban; between one- and two-thirds of rural families are poor, compared with less than one-third of urban families. The majority of the rural poor are either landless farm laborers or minifundistas. More than a third of the urban poor are unemployed; most of the remainder work in the tertiary sector, especially in "primitive" activities where there is a high incidence of underemployment (Céspedes et al. 1977). The concentration of poverty among the rural popu-

lation reflects inequitable land tenure, inefficient land
use, and the expense of extending the socioeconomic infrastructure into sparsely populated, isolated regions. Low
levels of living in the countryside have been one of the
major causes of migration into the towns.

During the past decade, there have been several studies of regional variations in socioeconomic well-being.
Booth (1974), in a sample survey of twenty districts distributed throughout the country, collected data on income,
employment, agrarian structure, social services, housing
and amenities, migration, and the level of industrialization. These sets of statistics were not mathematically
correlated. In a short analysis, the relatively wealthy
and developed Central Region (subdivided into the Metropolitan Area and the Valle Central) was compared with the
poorer periphery (subdivided into the Atlantic, South Pacific, North Pacific, and Northern regions).

The Instituto de Fomento y Asesoría Municipal, IFAM
(1976b), made a similar but more detailed survey based on
a sample of 860 communities in fifty-six predominantly rural cantons; most of the Valle Central, including the metropolitan region, was excluded. Once again, the communities were classified according to an a priori regionalization. The highest levels of employment, wages, economic
infrastructure, and social services were found in the
Northern and Atlantic regions, where some land is still
available for colonization. The North Pacific region, devoted mainly to extensive cattle ranching, and the old
areas of colonization on the southern margins of the Valle
Central, characterized by eroded, exhausted soils, had the
poorest wages and employment opportunities and the highest
rates of emigration, in spite of their relatively well-
developed economic infrastructure and social services.
Because of well-paid jobs in the banana industry and in
ports, the South Pacific and Atlantic regions were exceptions to the center-periphery dichotomy in income distribution, surpassing the average for the metropolitan area of
San José. The principal socioeconomic problems perceived
by the people interviewed by the IFAM were, in declining
order of importance, the lack of roads, running water,
electricity, health services, education, and recreational
facilities. The IFAM concluded that continued agrarian
reforms and the creation of new sources of employment in
the countryside were prerequisites for improving living
conditions and stemming migration into the towns.

Several recent studies have been concerned specifically with the identification and spatial distribution of
poverty. These aspects of poverty were measured by Céspedes et al. (1977) from 1973 census data of average per
capita incomes, land tenure, housing, and educational at-
tainments. All the methodologies with which the investi-
gators experimented revealed the same basic spatial pattern: the poorest cantons were located in the peripheries
of the country and in the region southwest of the Valle

Central; the lowest incidence of poverty was found in the cantons of the metropolitan region and in the port of Limón. An almost identical analysis by Carvajal et al. (1977b) generated similar results: the proportion of poor families ranged from a minimum of 10 percent in the canton of Tibás in the metropolitan region to a maximum of 49 percent in Turrubares, southwest of the Valle Central. The Oficina de Planificación (OFIPLAN 1981) recognized that income alone was not a sufficient indicator of well-being and attempted to identify poverty in the predominantly rural cantons with data for three social services: education, health, and housing. These data were grouped together to produce a summary index of the satisfaction of basic needs. Once again, the cantons in the periphery of the country and southwest of the Valle Central had the lowest scores.

These pioneer studies reflected growing concern about spatial inequalities in socioeconomic well-being, a problem that had received scant attention before the 1970s. However, the investigations contain certain methodological limitations. All use either a small number of variables or many uncorrelated variables. Three do not cover the whole country. None analyzes spatial units smaller than the cantons, and two classify data by conventional socioeconomic regions.

In order to overcome these limitations, two factor analyses were performed. The first included 31 variables for each of the 80 cantons, the second used 23 variables for each of the 406 districts. For the majority of variables, the most recent data available at the district level was contained in the 1973 censuses; even where there were more up-to-date statistics, the 1973 data was therefore preferred to ensure consistent correlations. The range of variables for which data was available was less than that which has been used in similar studies in developed countries, but sufficient to include the majority of the most significant, "hard" socioeconomic indicators for the third world (Table 6.5). The variables covered five major fields: economic indices, housing and amenities, education, health and social security, and communications and participation in society. There is no data concerning disutilities, such as crime and pollution, or "soft" indicators, such as personal security, congestion, and environmental perception (Coates et al. 1977; D. M. Smith 1977). A sixth set of variables included data on population, distance from the capital city, and land use, which it was thought might be correlated with some of the indices of socioeconomic well-being. (There is no data on land tenure by cantons and districts.) Eight of the variables included in the cantonal analysis had to be eliminated from the district analysis for lack of data.

The correlation matrices produced five factors with an eigenvalue greater than 1 in the cantonal analysis and four factors in the district analysis. F_1 and F_2 together

TABLE 6.5
Variables used in factor analyses of wealth and welfare

Variable	Definition	Source
Economic indices		
Poverty	Percent of poor families	Carvajal et al. 1977
Income	Percent of workers earning more than ¢400.00/month	DGEC 1974a
Employment	Percent of labor force employed	DGEC 1974a
Housing and amenities		
Housing	Percent of houses in good repair	DGEC 1974c
Water	Percent of houses with individual supply of piped water	DGEC 1974c
Sewerage	Percent of houses with mains sewerage or septic tank	DGEC 1974c
Electricity	Percent of houses with electricity	DGEC 1974c
Refrigerator	Percent of houses with refrigerator	DGEC 1974c
Education		
Literacy	Percent of literates in the population of 10 years and over	DGEC 1974a
Primary education	Percent of population 6 years and over who have received primary education	DGEC 1974a
Secondary education	Percent of population 10 years and over who have received secondary education	DGEC 1974a
University education	Percent of population 20 years and over who have received university education	DGEC 1974a
Health and social security		
Social security I	Percent of population insured by CCSS against sickness and maternity	DGEC 1974a
Social security II[1]	Percent of workers insured by CCSS against disablement, old age, and death	DGEC 1974a
Infant mortality[1]	Percent of deaths among infants of less than 1 year	DGEC 1974f
Malnutrition[1]	Percent of malnutrition among children of first grade in primary school	Novygrodt and Diaz 1979
Deaths[1]	Percent of deaths with medical assistance	DGEC 1974f

(continued)

TABLE 6.5 (Continued)

Variable	Definition	Source
Communications and participation in society		
Roads[1]	Road density, kms/sq km	Carvajal et al. 1977
Radio	Percent of houses with radio	DGEC 1974c
Television	Percent of houses with television	DGEC 1974c
Telephone	Percent of houses with telephone	DGEC 1974c
Voters	Percent turnout of voters, presidential elections, 1974	TSE 1974
Others		
Population	Population density, persons/sq km	DGEC 1974a
Urbanization	Percent of urban population	DGEC 1974a
Agricultural employment	Percent of workers employed in agriculture	DGEC 1974a
Distance[1]	Distance in kms between capital of canton and San José	Carvajal et al. 1977
Migration[1]	Rate of net migration since birth	DGEC 1974a
Annual crops	Percent of farm area under annual crops	DGEC 1974b
Permanent crops	Percent of farm area under permanent crops	DGEC 1974b
Pasture	Percent of farm area under pasture	DGEC 1974b
Forest	Percent of farm area under forest and bush	DGEC 1974b

[1]These variables were used only in the cantonal analysis.

account for more than three-fifths of the variance in both analyses. F_1 groups variables reflecting wealth: income; privately purchased amenities such as hygenic sewerage, refrigerators, televisions, and telephones; and secondary and higher education. These variables are positively correlated with population density and the proportion of urban dwellers, and inversely correlated with the proportion of agricultural employment. F_2 groups variables reflecting state investment in basic social services, such as piped water, electricity, primary education, health services, and pensions. These variables are inversely correlated with distance from the capital city (Table 6.6). The factor scores for F_1 contain a greater range of values

TABLE 6.6
Structure of F_1 and F_2 in the analysis of wealth and welfare (varimax rotation)

	Cantons	Districts
F_1 wealth		
Eigenvalue	16.08	11.52
Explained variance	51.9%	50.1%
Highest loadings:		
Telephone	0.94	0.90
University education	0.88	0.74
Urbanization	0.82	0.83
Sewerage	0.79	0.81
Population	0.79	0.81
Refrigerator	0.77	0.84
Television	0.73	0.74
Poverty	-0.71	n.d.
Agricultural employment	-0.69	-0.65
Secondary education	0.64	0.88
Income	0.55	0.60
F_2 welfare		
Eigenvalue	3.60	2.48
Explained variance	11.6%	10.8%
Highest loadings:		
Social security I	0.72	0.52
Social security II	0.63	n.d.
Water	0.62	0.73
Distance	-0.62	n.d.
Deaths	0.54	n.d.
Electricity	0.52	0.56
Literacy	0.48	0.66
Primary education	0.47	0.70

than those for F_2. This finding suggests that, while individual locational decisions still produce a heavy concentration of wealth and amenities in the center of the country, sustained government investment in the diffusion of basic social services has significantly countered this trend.

This interesting differentiation between wealth and welfare did not emerge in any of the previous studies. It underlies the regionalization obtained by plotting the values of F_1 against those of F_2. This regionalization, derived from the data rather than being superimposed upon them (as in the earlier studies), is yet another variation on the model presented in Figure 6.1. It is at this stage in the analysis that the tedium of working with district data is rewarded. The cantonal analysis, though useful

TABLE 6.7
Population and area of wealth and welfare regions

Region	Population		Area	
	Number	Percent	Sq Kms	Percent
I (high wealth; medium-high welfare)	551,236	29.45	185.22	0.36
II (low wealth; medium-high welfare)	894,252	47.77	8,579.72	16.79
III (medium wealth; low welfare)	129,877	6.94	5,434.97	10.64
IV (low wealth; low welfare)	296,415	15.84	36,900.09	72.21
TOTAL	1,871,780	100.00	51,100.00	100.00

Sources: DGEC 1974a; Comisión Nacional de División Territorial Administrativa 1977; factor analyses (see Table 6.5).

because it includes a larger number of variables, yields only a crude map. A much more precise regionalization can be made at the district level.

The districts can be classified into four major categories (Figure 6.11). The first group of districts, with high levels of wealth and medium to high levels of welfare, occupies less than 1 percent of Costa Rican territory but contains nearly a third of the country's population (Table 6.7). All these districts are located in the western section of the interoceanic axis. They include most of the metropolitan area of San José, the nearby provincial capitals of Cartago, Heredia, and Alajuela, the towns of Grecia, Palmares, and San Ramón in the western Valle Central, and the port of Puntarenas. These relatively affluent, developed areas are predominantly urban and suburban. The majority of their population lives well above the poverty line and has access to a complete range of social services. The combination in some districts, however, of a high level of affluence with only a medium level of welfare betrays the existence of tugurios and the concentration of wealth among the middle and upper classes.

Nearly half the population of Costa Rica lives in the districts of group II. The level of wealth is much lower than in the districts of group I, because the population contains a smaller proportion of the very rich and the urban middle class. The level of welfare, however, is as high or even higher, probably because fewer people live in tugurios. The districts of group II cover most of the remainder of the Valle Central, the hinterland of the port of Puntarenas, and the inner peripheral regions such as the upper San Carlos Valley, the General Valley, and the

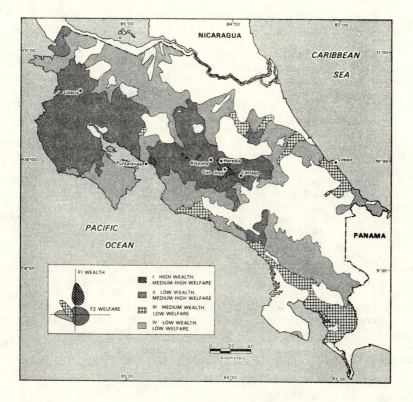

Figure 6.11 Wealth and welfare, 1973
Source: Hall 1984.

central section of the province of Guanacaste. They include the principal areas of colonial settlement and the older regions of postindependence, spontaneous colonization. There are no large urban areas, but the density of population and the central places and transport networks are sufficient to ensure substantial coverage of most basic social services.

The small third category, comprising 7 percent of the population and 11 percent of the area of Costa Rica, emerged only in the district analysis. It groups the plantation enclaves, including the ports of Limón and Golfito, and, interestingly, Monteverde, where the Quaker colony is located. In these peripheral districts, the level of welfare is poor. For many years, the provision of economic infrastructure and basic social services was left to the fruit companies, and government investment lagged behind regions I and II. The level of wealth, however, approaches some of the districts in group I because of the relatively high incomes generated by plantation agriculture and port activities.

The districts in the fourth category have low scores for both wealth and welfare. Located in the outer periphery, they include vast zones of recent Hispanic American colonization and the Indian reserves. They contain nearly three-quarters of Costa Rican territory but only 16 percent of the nation's population. In these isolated regions, the majority of the inhabitants are poor. Their homes lack amenities such as running water, electricity, and hygenic sewage disposal. Because there are no towns and few all-weather roads, many people have no regular access to secondary schools, health clinics, and hospitals. The provision of basic services for the sparse, dispersed population remains an intractable problem, because per capita costs of installation and maintainance are prohibitively high.

ADMINISTRATIVE AREAS

Regional imbalance is perpetuated by the system of administrative areas. Few facets of the country's spatial organization have been so resistant to change as the division into provinces, cantons, and districts (Figure 6.12). Their basic outlines were established more than a hundred years ago. There have been constant subdivisions of territory to create new cantons and districts, but there has never been any comprehensive reform to adapt administrative areas to the country's rapidly changing geography. The existing system evolved empirically when no detailed maps were available and much of the country was unexplored (Barrantes Ferrero 1966). It reflects the expansion of Hispanic American settlement during the nineteenth and twentieth centuries, but it no longer provides an efficient framework for local government and public adminis-

Figure 6.12 Administrative areas

Source: DGEC 1974d.

tration and is an obstacle to regional planning and development. Many of the boundaries between cantons and districts have never been delimited in the field, nor are they shown on topographical maps. The establishment of administrative areas has been based exclusively on population size, irrespective of territorial extent, communications, and financial resources. At a provincial level, this defect has led to serious problems of accessibility for people living in outlying areas; at a cantonal level, it has permitted the proliferation of municipalities that lack the resources to be economically viable (Soto et al. 1980).

There is a four-tier hierarchy of administrative areas: state, provinces, cantons, and districts. In the midtwentieth century when the urban explosion was just beginning, administrative status was still an indicator of central place functions. The provincial capitals were the only major urban areas; most cantonal capitals were villages and district capitals, no more than hamlets (Goldkind 1961). During the past quarter of a century, rapid urban growth and the dissemination of tertiary activities have created a more complex system of central places to which the administrative hierarchy has not yet adapted.

The functions and resources of the provinces and districts are negligible. For most purposes, the country is administered at only two levels: national and cantonal or municipal. Even the role of the municipalities is very limited in comparison with that of the powerful and highly centralized national government. State expenditure exceeds thirty-six times that of all the municipalities together.

The complex structure of national government includes the popularly elected president of the republic and legislative assembly, the judiciary, the supreme election tribunal, the comptroller general, the ministries responsible to the president, and, since 1949, an increasing number of nominally autonomous institutions and public enterprises. The last half century has seen a rapid growth and diversification in the role of the central government, until, today, few aspects of economic and social life are unaffected by state intervention. The functions of the central government include a monopoly of banking, insurance, and the refining and sale of petroleum, as well as participation in the wholesale trade of agricultural commodities and the retail grocery trade--activities which in many democracies are still in the hands of private enterprise. The central government is also responsible for most town planning, public housing schemes, water supplies, and sewage disposal, functions that in many countries are delegated to the municipalities. The ministries and autonomous institutions employ some 130,000 people, nearly one-fifth the labor force (DGEC 1979c). More than 40 percent work in San José (DGEC 1980). Decision making is heavily concentrated in the capital city where all the ministries

and most of the autonomous institutions have their head
offices. The enormous state bureaucracy has been a major
factor in San José's continued primacy in the hierarchy of
central places.

The number and distribution of the regional and local
offices of ministries and autonomous institutions are an-
archic. A survey carried out in 1976 revealed that only
the supreme election tribunal, two ministries, and one
autonomous institution still used the hierarchy of provinces, cantons, and districts. All the remaining government departments had devised their own system of administrative areas. Some operated only at a regional level,
replacing the existing provinces by two to ten regions;
others had also established a local tier of administration
incorporating from less than twenty to over a hundred areas centered on the capitals of selected cantons and districts (Acuña B. 1976). The wide variations between one
system and another impede interinstitutional coordination
at a regional and local scale and cause confusion and inconvenience to the public.

The adoption of alternative hierarchies of administrative areas is indicative of the anachronisms in the
system of provinces, cantons, and districts. The seven
provinces have never operated as effective units of regional administration and development. Their functions
are extremely limited. Each has a court of law, a headquarters of the civil guard, and a governor appointed by
the president of the republic. The governor is responsible to the Ministry of the Interior for the maintainance of law and order, protection of property, and control
of the police. The provinces have no popularly elected
local government, but they are the territorial units for
electing deputies to the national legislative assembly.
Largely for this reason, powerful political interests have
consistently opposed the long overdue reform that would
create an entirely new provincial structure whose aerial
units could be the basis for regional development.

When the republic of Costa Rica was proclaimed in
1848, the four principal towns the Spaniards had founded
in the Valle Central--Cartago, Heredia, San José, and
Alajuela--each became the capital of a province of the
same name. At that time, most of the country was still
forested, and the radius of each town's effective area of
influence was no more than 30 to 40 kilometers. As colonization took place, the provinces incorporated peripheral
areas settled by migrants from their cores. Alajuela came
to include western Valle Central as far as San Ramón and
the San Carlos plains to the north of the Cordillera Central; Heredia expanded northwards into the Sarapiquí Valley; Cartago originally included not only eastern Valle
Central but all the Caribbean coastal lowlands; and San
José's area of influence spread south to the mountainous
regions of Dota, Acosta, and Puriscal and ultimately into
the upper General Valley. Two provinces were established

on the Pacific lowlands. Guanacaste, with its capital in
Liberia, replaced the colonial Alcaldía Mayor or Corregimiento de Nicoya. The province of Puntarenas included the
territories that, prior to the construction of the Pan-
American Highway in the midtwentieth century, were accessible only by coastal shipping: the southern part of the
Nicoya peninsula, a long strip of land along the central
Pacific coast, and the entire southwest of the country including the Térraba, Coto Colorado, Coto Brus, and lower
General valleys. In 1892, after the completion of the Atlantic railway had opened up the Caribbean lowlands for
colonization, this region became a separate province with
its capital in the port of Limón (Meléndez 1979b).

The allocation of land between the seven provinces
was thus completed by the turn of the century. It has remained unaltered to the present day, although there has
always been legal provision for changing the number and
area of the provinces. The Ley de División Territorial
Municipal of 1909 established a minimum population of
40,000 per province; the Ley de División Territorial Administrative de Costa Rica, in force since 1969, stipu-
lates that each province must contain at least 10 percent
of the population of the republic. Any changes in the
number and area of the provinces would require approval in
a plebiscite of the entire population involved.

With the exceptions of Guanacaste and Limón, the
provinces are no longer viable functional regions. The
Valle Central is divided between four provinces, when in
practice it is a single functional unit integrated by modern communications and focused on the metropolitan region,
where the provincial capitals of Cartago, San José, Heredia, and Alajuela are rapidly fusing into a complex conurbation. The regions to the north and south of the Valle
Central, largely colonized during the past hundred years,
are still appended to provinces whose distant capitals are
located along the interoceanic axis: the northern plains
are divided by a geometrical boundary into Alajuela and
Heredia, the south of the country is divided into San José
and Puntarenas. Each of these peripheral regions could
now form a new province. A civic movement in the north of
the country has proposed segregating the cantons of San
Carlos, Los Chiles, Guatuso, and Upala from Alajuela to
form an eighth province (La Nación, 30 April 1979). The
development of an adequate system of administrative areas,
however, will only be achieved by a complete reorganization of the country's provincial structure. Piecemeal
changes, such as that proposed by San Carlos, leaving both
the northern plains and the Valle Central still divided
between several provinces are but partial and unsatisfac-
tory solutions.

The eighty cantons are the only units of autonomous
local government. Their origins can be traced back to the
colonial cabildos and ayuntamientos, although the Crown's
sale of municipal offices impeded the development of demo-

cratic local government. The role of the municipalities was in constant dispute for most of the nineteenth century, and the weakness of the modern system of local government is in part attributable to the failure to consolidate municipalities during the early, formative decades of the republic. Not until 1876 was it finally agreed that there should be one municipality per canton, the system that, with slight modifications, has continued to the present day (Baker et al. 1971, 18-19; Meléndez 1976).

Each canton has a popularly elected municipal council composed of regidores, with the right to vote, and síndicos, each representing one district of the canton with the right to participate in debates but not to vote. Until 1970, the president of the republic appointed for each canton a jefe político who, like the provincial governors, acted as the agent of the national government and also executed municipal business. The power of the jefe político was greatly reduced when the Código Municipal of 1970 created the new post of ejecutivo municipal, a municipal administrator appointed by and responsible to the local council. In other respects, however, the autonomy of the municipalities is still restricted by central government control and exiguous finances. Most municipalities are concerned only with routine administrative business and with the provision of elementary community services such as rubbish collection, street lighting, cemeteries, markets, slaughter houses, and, in some cases, water and electricity. They rarely intervene in major development projects such as housing, land use zoning, or urban planning, all of which are undertaken by ministries and autonomous institutions of the central government. Many cantons have juntas or boards for running schools and maintaining local roads, but these are subordinate to the Ministries of Education and Public Works. The legislative assembly must approve municipal loans, contracts, and taxes. Municipal budgets are scrutinized by the comptroller general. The income the municipalities receive from the land tax, collected by the Ministerio de Hacienda, and from local license fees, taxes, and charges for community services must frequently be supplemented by additional funds from the central government, particularly via the system of partidas específicas, grants made by the legislative assembly on the initiative of deputies representing local interests. Collection of the land tax, potentially the major source of municipal income, is hampered by bureaucratic inefficiency and the incomplete cadastral survey. In 1970, the central government created a new autonomous institution, the Instituto de Fomento y Asesoría Municipal (IFAM). The IFAM has strengthened municipal administration by providing financial and technical assistance, but it nevertheless perpetuates interference by the central government in local affairs (Baker et al. 1971; IFAM 1976a).

In contrast to the provinces, whose number and boundaries have remained unaltered throughout the present century, cantons proliferated as population grew and the Hispanic American oecumene expanded. From a total of forty in 1909, they increased to eighty in 1976. Prior to 1969, the minimum population for the establishment of a new canton was 3,000; since that year, the minimum requirement has been 1 percent of the population of the republic. As colonization took place, new communities aspired first to become districts within existing cantons and then new cantons, created by segregating territory from the old unit. Many new cantons in sparsely populated rural areas, however, lack the funds and personnel to perform even the most basic community services. The haphazard process by which the country has been divided into an ever-increasing number of cantons has created enormous variations in size. The most extensive canton covers 2,828 square kilometers, the smallest consists of 7 square kilometers. Their populations range from less than 6,000 to more than 228,000. There is generally an inverse relationship between population and area: in the densely populated center of the country, many cantons have a small area and large population; in the sparsely settled and more recently colonized periphery, most cantons have a large area but only a small and scattered population.

Most local experts in municipal government agree that there are too many cantons, that their proliferation should be halted, and that any radical reform of municipal functions aimed at creating strong and truly independent municipalities to sustain democratic government and contribute to economic and social development must contemplate a complete spatial reorganization of the country's cantonal structure. This restructuring would include the amalgamation of municipalities whose small populations and incomes preclude efficient administration, as well as the creation of a special institution for governing the metropolitan region, at present administered by twenty-seven municipal councils. The chaotic growth of San José in recent years, like that of many other Latin American cities, reflects the absence of strong municipal government that might have imposed a more orderly and harmonious process of urban expansion (Arauz 1978; Barrantes Ferrero 1966; Soto et al. 1980).

Most cantons are subdivided into districts, of which there were 275 in 1924 and 411 by 1976. Until 1969, a district required a minimum population of 1,000; now, each new district must contain at least 10 percent of the population of the canton in which it is located. The popularly elected síndicos, who represent the districts on the municipal councils, have also presided over district councils since the promulgation of the Código Municipal in 1970. These district councils provide a link between local communities and municipal councils. They report on the efficiency of municipal administration in the district, draw up an annual list of the most urgent public works,

and are empowered to raise money for local development
projects. One of the major anomalies in the present administrative system is the existence of similar institutions at two levels in the hierarchy. As early as 1939,
districts whose major commercial center was located more
than 30 kilometers from the capital of the canton and
whose annual revenue exceeded ¢3,000 could establish a
district council, with functions similar to that of a municipal council. These councils were administered by in-
tendentes, appointed, like the municipal jefes políticos,
by the president of the republic. The special district
councils were replaced in 1970 by "municipal district
councils," which, contrary to the municipal autonomy guar-
anteed by the constitution, are created by presidential
decree (Batalla 1977).

The proliferation of administrative areas created by
the constant subdivision of territory has been common in
countries such as Costa Rica that have recently experienced high rates of population growth and rapid colonization. Once these processes wane, improved transport and
communications and the concentration of population in urban areas favor the amalgamation of small administrative
units to take advantage of scale economies (Coates et al.
1977, 195). Although Costa Rica is now approaching the
transition between these two stages of development and it
is widely recognized that the present system of local government and administrative areas is in urgent need of comprehensive reform, the government only once commissioned
the preparation of an alternative scheme, which was never
put into practice.

In the late 1960s, a United Nations consultant, Arvids
Kalnins (1968-1969, 1971), proposed that the seven provinces be replaced by fourteen departments and that the
number of cantons be reduced to fifty-three. The existing
districts would initially remain unaltered, although they
could subsequently be modified. The new departments and
cantons would be used for all administrative and planning
purposes, providing the basis for a new structure of local
government and replacing the plethora of administrative
areas adopted by the ministries and autonomous institutions of the central government. Effective regional administration would require departments smaller than the
existing provinces to ensure that the whole population had
access to a centrally located capital. A popularly elected metropolitan assembly would govern the whole of Greater
San José. Each of the other thirteen departments would be
administered by a governor or prefect appointed by the
central government and a consultative assembly composed of
popularly elected representatives from each municipality
in the department. The principal criterion for the establishment of cantons would be financial viability, enabling
the municipalities to carry out a wide range of functions.
The reduction in their number would also allow each canton
to be represented by one deputy in the national legislative

assembly. General and local elections would ideally take place at different times so that municipal politics would not be overshadowed by the presidential campaign.

Kalnins's proposals are now over ten years old, and changes would be required if his scheme were to be implanted today. Its basic tenets of effective regional administration and stronger local government, however, are still relevant. The incipient regional planning undertaken by the central government during the 1960s and 1970s has in no way diminished the need for a thorough reform of administrative areas and local government. On the contrary, it has exacerbated the problem by superimposing a scheme of planning regions to be used by the ministries and autonomous institutions on the unchanged structure of the provinces, cantons, and districts.

PLANNING REGIONS

Costa Rica's earliest incursions into regional planning, like in most Latin American countries, were schemes to develop individual problem regions. Between 1963 and 1974, most of the periphery was at one time or another the subject of a regional plan (Figure 6.13). There was no coordinated strategy. Some areas were included in more than one scheme. The plans were drawn up by a variety of institutions, including government departments and international agencies. In most cases, the process stagnated after the initial analyses and resource inventories had been made. The proliferation of plans was a clear recognition of the problem of regional imbalance, but their impact on the country's spatial structure was minimal because of the failure to implement most of their proposals.

The first regional development authority--and the only one still in existence--was the Junta de Administración Portuaria y de Desarrollo Económico de la Vertiente Atlántica (JAPDEVA), an autonomous institution created in 1963 to serve a region traditionally abandoned by the central government because of its enclave economy and large foreign population. The province of Limón contained rich and varied natural resources, but its economy was heavily dependent on the banana and, to a lesser extent, the cocoa industries. Its only links with the rest of the country were by rail and air. There were no modern modes of transport beyond the areas of plantation agriculture. The Negro community was increasingly being incorporated into Hispanic American society, but investment in housing, education, and health services lagged behind other regions (Equipo Cornell-Costa Rica 1973). The JAPDEVA was entrusted with two basic functions: administration of the port installations in Limón and, with the income thus derived, the furtherance of socioeconomic development throughout the Caribbean region (JAPDEVA 1973).

JAPDEVA's major achievement has been the development

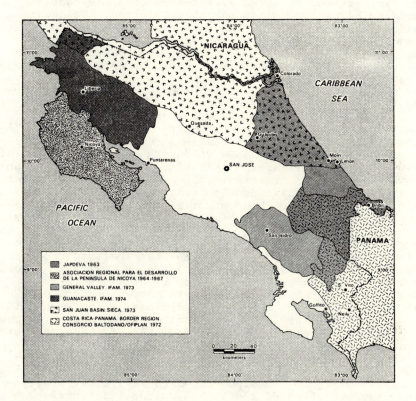

Figure 6.13 Problem regions for which plans have been prepared

of a transport network that in a single decade integrated
the province of Limón with the rest of the country. A
paved road was built across the central part of the province, linking it to the Valle Central. An all-weather
road was constructed south from the port of Limón to the
Sixaola Valley. The Tortuguero Canal, completed in 1974
and administered by JAPDEVA, interconnects the coastal
lowlands between Moín and Barra de Colorado. Following
nationalization in 1972, the Atlantic railway was administered by JAPDEVA until the creation of Ferrocarriles de
Costa Rica S.A. in 1977. The capacity and efficiency of
the port of Limón were enlarged by the construction of a
breakwater and an additional wharf.

For several years, political interference and exiguous finances restricted the JAPDEVA's capacity to undertake other projects, and it deteriorated to little more
than a port administration authority (Nuhn 1972, 23). In
1976, in an attempt to revitalize its participation in regional development, the JAPDEVA published a "Plan Integral
de Desarrollo de la Región Atlántica," which contained ambitious proposals for intervention in almost every aspect
of economic and social development, ranging from agriculture and industry to the control of environmental pollution and crime. In practice, the JAPDEVA's achievements
in recent years have been much more modest. It has set up
several pilot projects to diversify the province's economy.
Tilapia are being bred in cages in the canals to produce
fresh and smoked fish for home and export markets. A herd
of water buffalo was imported from Trinidad in 1975.
Dwarf coconuts, which are easier to harvest and produce
better-quality fruit than the traditional giant coconut,
are being cultivated along the coast and could provide raw
materials for local agroindustries. All of these projects,
however, are at an experimental stage and have yet to be
diffused among the local population. The province's potential for forestry and sea fishing is being studied. In
the field of social development, JAPDEVA's activities include the promotion of sports and cultural activities,
workers' training schemes, and plans to incorporate more
women into the labor force (La Nación, 31 October 1979;
Victor Labarca, personal communication).

The second regional development authority, the Asociación Regional para el Desarrollo de la Península de
Nicoya set up in 1964, had only an ephemeral existence.
The Nicoya peninsula, a peripheral rural region, was selected by the Agency for International Development (AID)
for a pilot project under the auspices of the Alliance for
Progress. The region included a zone of colonial settlement in the north and areas of recent spontaneous colonization in the south and west. Much of the peninsula
lacked all-weather roads, urban centers, and basic services such as water and electricity. Most of the natural
forest had been destroyed, but inefficient land use systems provided only a low standard of living for the major-

ity of the population. The association's major achievement was the preparation of natural resource inventories,
which were to provide the basis for a future development
plan (Budowski 1966; Tirado and Muñoz 1965). It also undertook a series of small, self-help projects including
demonstrations of the use of fertilizers and improved
seeds, the establishment of a cooperative to supply electricity to the rural population, and the construction of
community centers, small bridges, access roads, and latrines. AID withdrew support from the association in 1967,
alleging lack of cooperation from the Costa Rican government, and no further development projects were undertaken.
The failure of the Nicoya peninsula development authority
has been attributed to its poor initial conception, its
complete dependence on an external agency, and lack of local support and leadership (Helwig 1969).

In 1965 the recently created Instituto de Tierras y
Colonización--still concerned with primary colonization
rather than agrarian reform--set up a section for regional
studies. It commissioned two German geographers, Dr. Gerhard Sandner and Dr. Helmut Nuhn, to lead a team to study
the northern plains and the adjacent Caribbean lowlands--
little-known, sparsely populated regions in the humid
tropical zone where there were many frontiers of colonization and little socioeconomic infrastructure. The detailed monographs that were published (Sandner et al. 1966;
Nuhn et al. 1967) would have provided a solid foundation
for future regional development plans, but the project was
abandoned in 1967 for lack of funds.

During the early 1970s, the Instituto de Fomento y
Asesoría Municipal (IFAM) made two regional development
studies. The first was concerned with the General Valley,
which assumed special significance at this time because of
a proposal to exploit local deposits of bauxite. IFAM's
project for the cantons of Pérez Zeledón and Buenos Aires,
however, rather than being a comprehensive plan for regional development was a collection of proposals for municipal public works, particularly in the town of San
Isidro (IFAM 1973). Its more sophisticated study of Guanacaste, including the whole of the Nicoya peninsula, was
subsequently incorporated into the first regional development plan of the Oficina de Planificación (OFIPLAN) in
1975. Agriculture and tourism were identified as potentially the most dynamic sectors of the region's economy,
capable of creating new jobs, stimulating growth in ancillary tertiary activities, and converting Guanacaste from a
region of net emigration to one of net immigration. Most
of the specific projects recommended in the plan--irriga-
tion in the Tempisque Valley, the creation of agroindustries, improvements to the road network in the Nicoya peninsula, and the development of a tourist complex at Bahía
Culebra--are now being undertaken by central government
departments, but no regional development authority has
been established.

Both of Costa Rica's border regions have been the
subject of bilateral development proposals. The border
between Costa Rica and Nicaragua bisects the sparsely populated San Juan basin, selected in the early 1970s by the
Secretaría Permanente del Tratado General de Integración
Económica Centroamericana (SIECA) as a potential international growth pole in the Central American Common Market.
The total area of the basin is nearly 30,000 square kilometers. Slightly more than half is Costa Rican territory
and comprises almost 30 percent of the area of the republic. SIECA's study, begun in 1971 with funds from the International Development Bank, proposed a multipurpose
project, including the development of navigation on 600
kilometers of inland waterways, the construction of all-
weather roads and of a railway between Guápiles and Granada, hydroelectric production, irrigation in the upper
part of the basin close to the Pacific coast, the drainage
of 1,000 square kilometers of swampy land to the south of
Lake Nicaragua, and the development of agriculture, forestry, and associated processing industries in the humid
tropical lowlands that comprise most of the basin (SIECA
1973). None of these projects has been carried out. The
navigation and hydroelectric schemes were abandoned in
1980 after technical studies revealed that thick deposits
of subsurface sands would raise construction costs to uneconomical levels (La Nación, 7 April 1980).

In contrast to the San Juan basin, the heterogeneous
area of some 15,000 square kilometers traversed by the
boundary between Costa Rica and Panama forms neither a natural nor a socioeconomic region. Parts of the Cordillera
de Talamanca are still outside the Hispanic American oecumene. The major areas of settlement, including plantation
enclaves on both coasts, are divided between several functional regions centered on the towns of San Isidro, Golfito, and Limón in Costa Rica, and Almirante, Armuelles,
and David in Panama. A study made by an international
consortium in 1972 proposed that the Pacific frontier post
of Paso Canoas be developed as a binational regional center and industrial growth pole, and that road and electricity networks, forestry, farming, and agroindustries be
planned for the whole border region (Consorcio Baltodano
1972). None of these projects has been implemented.

The limited achievements of this series of projects
for the development of individual problem regions under-
lined the need for a new approach to spatial planning. As
early as 1967, the OFIPLAN expressed its interest in setting up a regional development department to complement
the sectorial planning it had been undertaking since its
creation in 1963. Dr. Helmut Nuhn, who had worked on the
ITCO projects for the northern plains and the Caribbean
lowlands, was once again commissioned to act as consultant
to the Costa Rican government. In 1972 he advocated the
creation of a single authority responsible for comprehensive regional planning throughout the country (Nuhn 1972).

The national development plan for the period 1974-1978 was the first to include specific proposals for regional development, and in 1976 a law was passed setting up the Sistema de Planificación Regional y Urbana (La Gaceta, 26 October 1976).

The existing provinces, lacking in homogeneity and functional coherence, were totally inadequate units for spatial planning. Nuhn's assignment included a technical study to define and delimit a series of planning regions (Nuhn 1973a). Data for a wide range of physical and socio-economic phenomena were collected on a grid of 25 square kilometer squares. A multivariant factor analysis produced six functional regions, each relatively homogeneous in both physical geography and economic development (Figure 6.14a). Some regions, such as the Central and Northwest regions, had been latent in the country's spatial structure since the colonial period; others, such as the North and South regions, were embryonic areas emerging out of recent colonization and settlement. Nuhn recommended that a single regional structure be adopted for all planning and administrative purposes, replacing the existing hierarchy of administrative areas. His scheme was to be conceived as a medium-term proposal, to be modified as the country's geography continued to change.

The Valle Central and adjacent mountains formed the Central Region. This region included the core areas of four of the seven provinces: San José, Heredia, Alajuela, and Cartago. It also contained the metropolitan region, several small towns, and surrounding rural areas. Already housing more than half the country's population, this region was the principal destination of internal migrants and contained a heavy concentration of economic activities and social services. It presented special problems arising out of uncontrolled urban growth. San José was retained as the capital of the Central Region, but it was recommended that future development be concentrated in the subregional capitals.

The West Region comprised the port of Puntarenas and its hinterland around the Gulf of Nicoya. It included the central part of the province of Puntarenas and adjacent cantons in the provinces of Guanacaste and Alajuela. Manufacturing and tourism were identified as the region's two principal growth industries.

The Northwest Region, with its capital in Liberia, comprised the remainder of the province of Guanacaste and the canton of Upala in the province of Alajuela, to which the only access overland was a road from Cañas. Located mainly in the tropical dry life zone, the Northwest Region included a central area, occupied by large cattle haciendas since the colonial period, and surrounding areas of mixed farming, colonized during the nineteenth and twentieth centuries. Its major development priorities were the improvement of transport and communications, the installation of irrigation, the expansion of tourism, and agrarian reform.

The sparsely populated North Region, spanning extensive parts of the provinces of Alajuela and Heredia, occupied humid tropical lowlands and adjacent mountains. Settled mainly as a result of spontaneous colonization in the
late nineteenth and twentieth centuries, its land use was
dominated by subsistence cultivation and cattle ranching.
There was scope for further colonization, although the region's agriculture potential was restricted by heavy precipitation, swamps, and rugged mountains. The area contained only one town, Quesada, and was linked to the rest
of the country by a single paved road. The consolidation
of intermediate central places and a local transport network were prerequisites for regional development.

The geography of the East Region, which included the
province of Limón and adjacent districts in the province
of Heredia, still bore the imprint of an enclave: its
economy was heavily dependent on the production of bananas
and cocoa; linear settlements bordered the railway lines
and gravel roads; and economic infrastructure and social
services were deficient. In spite of the existence of
JAPDEVA, the East was in urgent need of integrated regional development.

The humid South Region, largely settled during the
present century, included parts of the provinces of Puntarenas and San José. It contained banana and oil palm
enclaves on the coastal lowlands and extensive zones of
spontaneous colonization in the General-Coto Brus depression and adjacent mountains. Like the North Region, its
economic and social infrastructure was rudimentary. Its
regional capital, San Isidro, was a dynamic but eccentrically located town, similar to Quesada.

Nuhn's proposals were the basis upon which the OFIPLAN
established the first official planning regions in 1975
(Figure 6.14b). The names of some regions were altered,
and there were changes in boundaries and capitals. The
boundaries were adjusted to fit the existing cantons and
districts, retained as the smallest planning units. The
most substantial changes in the allocation of territory
concerned the central part of the Pacific slope. The
OFIPLAN enlarged the Northwest or North Pacific Region to
include the whole Nicoya peninsula and the central part of
the canton of Abangares; the West or Central Pacific Region was in turn extended southwards along the coast to
include the enclave of Quepos and Parrita. In these two
regions, the capitals selected by the OFIPLAN differed
from those proposed by Nuhn. Cañas, in an area of greater
agricultural potential and more centrally located in the
region's transport network, replaced Liberia as the capital of the North Pacific Region. Esparza, a potential
growth pole in the Central Pacific Region was preferred to
Puntarenas, whose location at the end of a long sand spit
hindered communications and placed severe limits on physical expansion. Only the Central Region was divided into

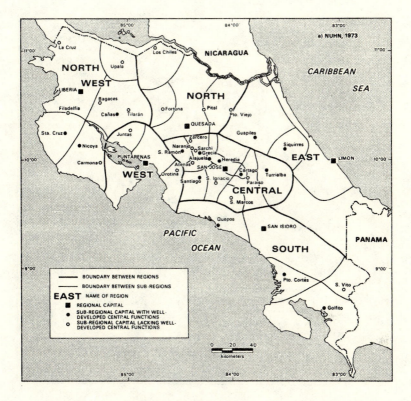

Figure 6.14a Planning regions: Nuhn, 1973

Source: Nuhn 1973a.

294

Figure 6.14b Planning regions: OFIPLAN, 1975

Source: OFIPLAN 1975.

Figure 6.14c Planning regions: OFIPLAN, 1978

Source: OFIPLAN 1978.

subregions. The Metropolitan Area and surrounding Suburban Area would require special planning because of their dense populations and rapid urban growth.

Following the change of government in 1978, the OFIPLAN adopted a new set of planning regions (Figure 6.14c). Nuhn's sophisticated computer analysis was abandoned on the grounds that it reflected only the geography of Costa Rica in the early 1970s without taking into account subsequent changes or future development trends (Lic. Elena Terán de Beck, personal communication). In the definition and delimitation of the new regions, physical geography was relegated to second place. Simple empirical criteria, similar to those used by Kalnins (1968-1969) in his scheme of administrative areas, were employed. Each region was to contain a minimum population of 200,000, a minimum area of 10,000 square kilometers, and a relatively homogeneous structure of economic production. Regional capitals, centrally located in relation to the existing and future transport networks, were to be developed as autonomous service centers with a wide range of specialized central functions. Because of the country's small area and the sparse population in the periphery, the number of regions was limited initially to five. Once the transport network was improved in the periphery, it would be reduced to four. The regions were subdivided into twenty-two subregions, each with its respective capital. The principal criterion in the delimitation of subregions was the access to the subregional capitals afforded by the existing transport network. Except in very sparsely settled areas, the services located in the capital should be within reach of the whole subregion's population.

The West or Central Pacific Region disappeared. The enlarged Central Region included not only the Valle Central and adjacent mountain slopes but also the central Pacific lowlands, which will receive rapid access to and from the Valle Central from roads now under construction. San José was retained as the regional capital. Because of its heavy concentration of population, the Central Region contained many more subregions than did any other region. Major subregions in and around the principal urban areas contained more than 100,000 inhabitants; the population of minor subregions, centered on small market towns, ranged from 20,000 to 40,000. The Chorotega Region was almost identical to the previous North Pacific Region, and Cañas was retained as its capital. The Brunca Region was the same as the former South Pacific Region, but the centrally located village of Buenos Aires, identified as a potential growth pole, replaced the town of San Isidro as the capital. The North and Atlantic regions were eventually to form a single Huetar Region, with its capital in Guápiles. The two areas would continue to be separately planned until improved communications permitted the Huetar Region to function as a single unit. The subregions in the Chorotega, Brunca, and Huetar regions were larger in area than

those of the Central Region. Their populations ranged
from 40,000 to 85,000 (OFIPLAN 1978).

These three sets of planning regions have important
features in common. All include a single central region
comprising the metropolitan region of San José, the rest
of the Valle Central, and adjacent areas. The periphery
is divided into four or five regions. In each region, the
principal areas of settlement are located in the premontane and tropical zones. The sparsely populated cordilleras, traversed by few all-weather roads, form natural
barriers along which boundaries have been delimited (Wood
1977-1978).

Discrepancies have arisen precisely where mountain
barriers are absent. The most problematic area is the
central Pacific lowlands, initially designated as a rather
poorly defined West or Central Pacific Region and subsequently incorporated into the Central Region. A third alternative would be to include the area around Puntarenas
in the North Pacific or Chorotega Region and the Quepos
area in the South Pacific or Brunca Region. Both areas
are functionally distinct from the Valle Central, and
their ecological characteristics and historical development link them with adjacent Pacific regions. The area
around Puntarenas is connected by road and coastal shipping with Guanacaste and forms part of the same tropical
dry region. Its potential for developing agriculture,
tourism, and fishing is similar to the rest of the North
Pacific Region. The completion of the road along the Pacific coast will integrate the Quepos area with the South
Pacific Region, with which it shares a humid tropical environment and a history of recent colonization and settlement. Many of the area's development problems are similar
to those of the other Pacific plantation enclaves in the
Golfito area.

The boundary between the North and Atlantic regions
is also ill defined. They share a humid tropical environment, but their contrasting historical development--the
North a zone of spontaneous agricultural colonization, the
Atlantic a plantation enclave--has bequeathed each region
specific spatial problems. Their fusion would create an
unwieldy, elongated region extending almost 300 kilometers
between Los Chiles and Sixaola. The retention of two regions would provide a more efficacious framework for both
planning and public administration.

If the planning regions are, to a large extent, self-
evident, the choice of regional capitals has been more
polemical. The irregular hierarchy of central places
lacks well-defined regional centers. Second-rank towns
are heavily concentrated in the Central Region. Only San
José has been identified as an undisputed regional capital.
Elsewhere, planners have oscillated between choosing, on
the one hand, large but eccentrically located existing
towns, such as Liberia, Quesada and San Isidro, and, on
the other hand, smaller, more centrally located places

such as Cañas, Guápiles, and Buenos Aires. In the long term, the second alternative might provide better regional capitals, but the cost of developing small towns and villages into major urban centers is much greater than improving the infrastructure of existing large towns.

The definition and delimitation of planning regions and their capitals are open to many interpretations. It would be fallacious to suggest that there is only one scheme that can provide an efficient framework for spatial planning. In the long term, regions and capitals should be flexible, particularly in a developing country such as Costa Rica whose geography is highly dynamic. In the short term, however, it is equally imperative to reach a concensus. Regional planning will never make an effective contribution to socioeconomic development if the planning regions and their capitals continue to be altered every four years with the change of government.

The fundamental goals of regional planning have been clearly identified ever since the establishment of the Sistema de Planificación Regional: to curb the concentration of development in the center of the country, particularly in the metropolitan region; and to promote development in the periphery in order to achieve a balanced spatial structure within which resources are more fully exploited and welfare more equitably distributed. In 1975, the OFIPLAN proposed a "combined spatial strategy." Advantage would be taken of the Central Region's existing external economies, but development would be located in intermediate urban centers rather than in the metropolitan area. In the periphery, concentrated decentralization would eventually give way to dispersed decentralization as development spread from regional centers and growth poles to other areas (Morales 1975, 187-189; OFIPLAN 1975). In 1978, the new government retained the basic policy of concentrated decentralization, but whereas in 1975 this strategy was planned primarily at a regional level, emphasis was now placed on the subregional level. By 1981, development councils had been established in all the subregions as a prelude to the creation of regional development authorities on the lines of JAPDEVA throughout the country (Lic. Elena Terán de Beck, personal communication).

The OFIPLAN is still engaged in the early stages of spatial planning, and the change in the scheme of planning regions and capitals in 1978 was tantamount to starting all over again. Moreover, the OFIPLAN only recommends policy, which must then be implemented by the ministries and autonomous institutions responsible for the allocation of government expenditure in specific fields of economic and social development. Political interests frequently prevail over technical recommendations. Conflicts have arisen between the OFIPLAN and the planning offices of other government departments, many which have yet to adopt the regional system of the OFIPLAN. The planning regions have not superceded the existing hierarchy of administrative areas. Since there is almost unanimous agreement, however, on the inefficiency of the present spatial structure of provinces, cantons, and districts, it would seem logical to fuse the planning regions and administrative areas and to establish a single, local government authority for the whole metropolitan region (Nuhn 1972, 1973a; Wood 1977-1978; Zumbado 1977).

The consolidation of comprehensive regional planning could contribute to the integration of the transport network, the evolution of a more balanced hierarchy of central places, the establishment of industrial growth poles, and the diversification of economic activities in the periphery. The greatest geographical transformation would take place in the periphery, where developmental as opposed to merely adaptive planning is required.

Integration of the transport network is a prerequisite for the establishment of a system of complementary regions and for the diversification of economic activities in the periphery. The trunk roads planned for construction during the 1980s will interconnect all but the South Pacific and Atlantic regions, separated by the Cordillera de Talamanca (Figure 6.15). The roads between Siquirres and San José and between Colón and Caldera will facilitate rapid interoceanic transport via the Valle Central. The road between Guápiles and Cañas will integrate the Northern Region and form part of the first lowland interoceanic route. Preliminary studies have shown that it would also be technically feasible to build a railway across the northern plains between Río Frío and Cuajiniquil (La Nación, 8 March 1981). This railroad would have the advantage over road transport of running on locally produced electricity, but the present flow of traffic is insufficient to warrant the high capital cost. The railway might be economically viable if it were developed as an alternative interoceanic route to the Panama Canal. The Costanera Sur Highway, between Puerto Cortés and Caldera, will replace the interior section of the Pan-American Highway, affording an easy lowland route between the South Pacific and North Pacific regions. Throughout the country, new local roads will improve access to peripheral rural areas (MOPT 1978). The road network will retain its spinal and radial form in outlying regions; complete interconnection between villages is still a long-term goal. The principal zones of settlement, however, will be linked by direct routes, and the national network will approach the final stage of the model of transport expansion depicted in Figure 3.9.

The primacy of San José will probably persist into the next century, but regional planning could narrow the gap in the central place hierarchy between the capital city and the second rank towns. At its current rate of growth, Greater San José will contain more than 2 million inhabitants by the year 2,000; if immigration into the metropolitan region is reduced, its population may reach

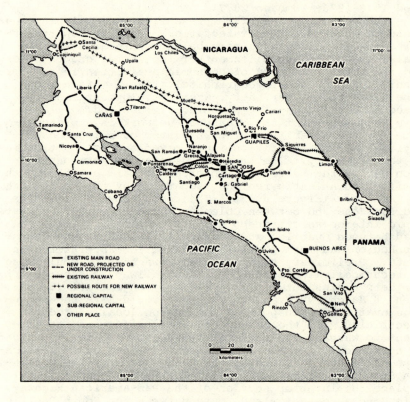

Figure 6.15 New roads, projected and under construction
Source: MOPT 1980.

only 1.7 million (OFIPLAN 1980b, 11). If present trends
continue, no other city would contain more than 100,000
inhabitants by the end of the century; the consolidation
of regional capitals of new provinces could provide the
country with a set of intermediate cities with metropolitan areas containing populations of 150,000 (Fonseca Pereira 1977, 1977-1978).

The principal existing urban areas along the interoceanic axis--Puntarenas, the metropolitan region of San
José, and Limón--have been designated national growth
poles where large industrial parks will be developed. The
metropolitan region of San José already contains so many
locational advantages for manufacturing that it would be
almost impossible to halt completely its industrial development. Rather than factories continuing to be interspersed with other types of land use, however, it is proposed that industries be concentrated in large industrial
parks on the outskirts of the existing built-up area (Figure 5.11). Greater Puntarenas, already the most dynamic
industrial area outside the metropolitan region of San
José, will soon be served by the port of Caldera and the
improved network of trunk roads, permitting rapid transport of industrial raw materials and finished goods. Once
the Costanera Sur Highway is completed, Greater Puntarenas
will be the principal city on the Pan-American Highway between Nicaragua and Panama. The site of the old port is
too restricted for major urban development, but the triangular area between Caldera, Esparza, and El Roble contains
ample room for expansion. New manufacturing industries
would provide jobs both for immigrants from other regions
and for the local population, whose employment opportunities are at present very restricted. Limón's position is
less advantageous for factories supplying internal and
Central American markets, but very favorable for industries processing local farm and forest products for export
to North America and Europe. A thousand-hectare industrial estate is planned at Moín, close to the port installations under construction.

In the periphery, farming is likely to remain a major
industry, but other natural resources could be exploited
to diversify economic production. Forestry, fishing, and
mining could all be developed as vertically integrated industries, producing goods for home and export markets and
creating employment in rural areas currently registering
net emigration.

All the studies of land capability concur that at
least half of Costa Rica should be devoted to forests.
The development of a permanent, efficient forestry industry would require not only the conservation of most the
surviving natural forests but also extensive reforestation,
ideally with heterogeneous forests simulating the natural
vegetation. This reforestation could probably be undertaken only by a government authority, since areas of at
least 50,000-100,000 hectares (many times larger than

existing farms) are needed to make tropical silviculture
economically viable. The initial development would be extremely expensive, and the government lacks the massive
funds required to compensate expropriated landlords. In
the long term, however, such a project would be both ecologically beneficial and economically productive. Forestry could generate the raw materials for three important
groups of manufacturing industries: those producing wooden
articles, such as furniture, souvenirs, and construction
materials; pulp and paper industries; and a wide range of
wood chemistry industries producing plastics, synthetic
fibers, resin, wood oil, and liquid fuels, all of which
substitute petroleum by-products (Tosi 1971; Tosi and
Holdridge 1973).

Fishing, a traditionally unimportant industry employing rudimentary technology, could be modernized and greatly expanded, particularly along the Pacific coast which
contains many natural harbors, three large gulfs, and expanses of shallow waters underlain by the continental
shelf. Costa Rica claims exclusive economic control over
the maritime resources within 200 miles of her coasts (including those of Coco Island)--an area more than ten times
greater than her land surface! It contains a very heterogeneous fauna, including shrimps, lobster, white fish, and
the deep water tuna, most of which could be much more intensively exploited than at present with no danger of depletion. New industries could be established not only to
process and pack fish but also to manufacture by-products
such as fish meal, fish oil, and fertilizers (Ings. Eduardo Bravo Pérez and Eduardo Pizarro, personal communication).

Two metallic minerals are known to exist in sufficient quantities for large-scale exploitation. Porphyry
copper occurs in the Cordillera de Talamanca and bauxite
in the upper terraces of the General Valley. Both could
be extracted by open cast methods, though this extraction
could provoke serious ecological problems particularly in
the forested Cordillera de Talamanca, one of the few regions where remnants of the indigenous ecosystem survive.
The exploitation of copper and bauxite and the development
of industries manufacturing copper and aluminium products
could only be undertaken in the foreseeable future by companies using foreign capital and technology. The conditions under which multinational corporations might be allowed to operate have aroused fierce political controversy,
and, for several years, the Legislative Assembly has been
studying a new Mining Code. Several other minerals occur
in smaller quantities. Gold is once again being extracted
from the mines of Aguacate and Abangares and from the
placer deposits of the Osa and Burica peninsulas. Exploitation of coastal deposits of magnetite and ilmenite sands
and of chromium, nickel, and manganese in Guanacaste could
provide the raw materials for a small iron and steel plant
to supply the home market. Exploration for petroleum and

natural gas is currently in progress in Baja Talamanca on the Caribbean slope (OEA 1978).

Tourism is already an important source of foreign exchange. With an improved infrastructure of transport, hotels, and restaurants, it could be greatly expanded along both coasts and in the mountains. The Instituto Costarricense de Turismo, an autonomous state authority created in 1955, is promoting the first, large-scale tourist complex in Central America on the shores of Bahia Culebra in northern Guanacaste. Tourism, however, can have negative effects, particularly in a developing country: the construction of sophisticated installations to serve wealthy visitors can create cultural discord and social discontent among local populations who have few opportunities for recreation and vacations.

Raabe (1976) has estimated that if present patterns of land use persist until the end of the century, four-fifths of the country's population will live in the Central Region, and there will be an absolute decline of population in the North Pacific Region. Ecologically optimum land use would permit a more even spread of population, and the Central Region would contain less than three-fifths the total. The development on a large scale of agroindustries, forestry, fishing, mining, and tourism might reduce still further the concentration of population in the Central Region.

Comprehensive regional planning will not eliminate the hegemony of the Central Region, an ever-increasing proportion of which will be occupied by the expanding metropolitan region of San José. Nor, in a developing country the size of Costa Rica, would it be wise to attempt to halt all growth in the Central Region and to establish large metropolitan areas throughout the periphery (Brugman and Terán 1975). But spatial planning could produce more orderly growth within the Central Region, consolidate major growth poles along the interoceanic axis, and accelerate development in the periphery, thereby reducing regional disparities in wealth and welfare.

Conclusion

The geography of contemporary Costa Rica is the culmination of spatial structures and processes, some of
which date back many centuries, others only a few decades.
Understanding man's present occupation of the land and the
organization of the oecumene demands an historical perspective.

In the long term, the processes of geographical
change have accelerated over time. The growth of population led to the progressive occupation of territory, increased exploitation of natural resources, and the development of ever more complex cultural landscapes. Within
these general trends, however, distinctive historical periods can be discerned.

The first, and by far the longest, period has the
least direct impact today. During the pre-Columbian era,
indigenous settlement was relatively sparse but fairly
even. Over most of the country the native economy of
hunting, gathering, fishing, and primitive cultivation
caused no permanent disruption to the ecosystem. The Indians developed neither large urban areas nor extensive
political units. Their cultural landscapes were fragile
and ephemeral.

The coming of Europeans was probably the most important turning point in the entire historical evolution of
the geography of Costa Rica. Indeed, it might be argued
that there have been only two major stages of development,
pre-Columbian and post-Columbian. Parts of Costa Rica entered the post-Columbian phase during the sixteenth century, but in many regions there was a prolonged transition
from predominantly indigenous to predominantly Hispanic
American settlement.

Indirectly, the greatest legacy of the pre-Columbian
period was the relative ease with which the Spaniards were
able to lay the foundations of modern Costa Rica, even
though they failed to occupy much of the colonial province.
They imposed new political and economic systems, created a
society racially and culturally distinct from that of the
Indians, instigated processes of radical ecological change,

and concentrated population and economic activities into
small areas. These features have been consolidated and
modified but never profoundly altered to the present day.

The development of a flourishing agro-export economy
during the midnineteenth century marks the beginning of a
third period, which lasted about a hundred years. From
one of the poorest and most isolated provinces of the
Spanish empire, Costa Rica was transformed into a primary
commodity producer and was integrated into the world market. Centrifugal migration, agricultural colonization,
the development of transport, and the foundation of villages and towns led to constant expansion of the Hispanic
American oecumene. The surviving Indian communities were
relegated to remote, peripheral areas.

A fourth period began during the second third of the
twentieth century and continues to the present day. The
population explosion provoked accelerated agricultural
colonization and, within a few decades, the virtual exhaustion of the frontiers of settlement--surely one of the
most momentous changes in the entire process of historical-
geographical evolution, forcing fundamental transformations in land occupation and the pattern of settlement.
The flow of internal migration was reversed, giving rise
to unprecedented urban growth. The adoption of a policy
of desarrollo hacia adentro was the first response to the
need to diversify economic production and provide employment for the burgeoning population of the towns. In many
respects, however, the policy proved less efficacious than
desarrollo hacia afuera, which it purported to replace.

The majority of the population now lives in urban and
suburban areas and is dependent on nonagricultural employment. Traditional primary exports, however, are still the
mainstay of the economy. Farming has yet to adapt to the
new situation of limited land resources. As the population continues to grow, the demand for foodstuffs and industrial raw materials puts increasing strain on antiquated systems of land tenure and inefficient patterns of land
use. In the towns, only a small proportion of the population has found employment in the manufacturing industry.
Most work in the tertiary sector, many in "primitive" activities that provide neither a full-time occupation nor a
regular source of income. In both the urban and rural
areas, the marginal population living in abject poverty
continues to grow in absolute and perhaps even in relative
terms.

World demand for Costa Rica's traditional agricultural exports is relatively inelastic, and there is little
scope for further "import-substituting" industrialization.
During the 1970s, successive reformista governments proposed an alternative model for development. The economy
would be oriented towards a new type of desarrollo hacia
afuera, involving the establishment throughout the country
of vertically integrated industries exploiting diverse local resources to produce manufactured goods for home and

export markets. By creating new jobs, such industries
would help stem the flow of migrants into the center of
the country (OFIPLAN 1973-1974, 1979a).

The need to consolidate a more efficacious strategy
of socioeconomic development became increasingly urgent
towards the end of the decade. The world recession and
the rapid rise in petroleum prices exacerbated the balance
of trade deficit. Costa Rica accumulated the highest foreign debt per capita in the whole world. The neoliberal
policies of the administration of Rodrigo Carazo (1978-
1982) plunged the country into the worst economic and fiscal crisis in half a century. Inflation reached an unprecedented 65 percent in 1981. The colón was devalued by
more than 400 percent against the United States dollar.
Economic growth stagnated, and un- and underemployment
rose. Real wages and levels of living declined sharply in
almost every sector of the population (Fallas 1981).

Costa Ricans of all ideologies questioned the stabil-
ity of the country's political system (Araya et al. 1981;
A. Vargas et al. 1981; Vega 1978; Zelaya et al. 1977).
Would the country succumb either to authoritarian, right-
wing rule as in Chile and Uruguay, once classed with Costa
Rica as model Latin American democracies, or to the revolutionary fervor sweeping through the rest of Central
America? The socioeconomic problems provoking revolutionary movements in neighboring republics were not absent in
Costa Rica. Wealth of all kinds, including farmland, was
concentrated in the hands of a small minority. A large
sector of the population lived at subsistence level and
was the hardest hit by the economic crisis.

The unimpeachable general elections celebrated in
February 1982 gave the new government a clear mandate to
continue the quest for socioeconomic development within
the country's existing institutional framework. In a 79
percent poll, the two principal reformista parties, Liber-
ación Nacional and the coalition Unidad, together received
90 percent of the presidential vote; the Marxist coalition,
Pueblo Unido, obtained slightly over 3 percent. In the
Legislative Assembly, fifty-one seats went to the reformista parties, four to the Marxist coalition, and two to
non-Marxist minority parties (La Nación, 20 February 1982).

How long the present political system will survive,
however, remains uncertain. Solving the economic and fiscal crisis will take years. Success is partly dependent
on changes in the world economy; improved terms of trade
for the third world would constitute a first step towards
transferring wealth from the developed to the developing
countries. Meanwhile, Costa Ricans of all social classes
are likely to suffer stagnation or decline in their level
of living for some time. Some of those who recently voted
for reformismo and parliamentary democracy might in the
future support or tolerate more radical political options.
The growing marginal population constitutes a potentially
explosive force, both in the rural areas where the majority

lack land and in the urban areas where only a small proportion of the labor force is employed in productive sectors of the economy. Costa Rica is located in the vortex
of one of the most unstable geopolitical regions in the
world. The polarization of the ideological struggle in
neighboring countries could overflow into Costa Rica.
Radical political change might transform the country's
geography if new policies were adopted concerning the spatial distribution of the population, access to land and
other resources, the structure and composition of economic
production, the allocation of wealth and welfare, and the
goals of regional planning.

In the long term, the prospects for socioeconomic development give rise to cautious optimism. There is little
likelihood of overpopulation in relation to natural resources. Rosero (1978) has estimated that the country's
farmland could support a population of 11 million on a
diet similar to the average presently consumed in the developed countries and 80-90 million on a minimum subsistence diet (though the latter would probably be unaccept-
able to most Costa Ricans). The major demographic uncer-
tainties include the date the fertility rate will decline
to the replacement level of 2.1 and the size at which the
population will eventually stabalize. Current projections
state the population will reach approximately 3.4 million
by the end of this century and 4.9 million by 2025 (OFIPLAN
1980a, 17). The highest estimate of the population size
at the end of the demographic transition is approximately
14 million, giving an average density of 275 persons per
square kilometer (Rosero 1978, 30-35).

Since the middle of this century, population growth
has exceeded the expansion of both the total farm area and
the area of cultivated land. Agrarian problems formerly
ameliorated by the colonization of virgin lands must now
be solved by further reforms within the existing farm area.
In addition to lands suitable for agriculture, Costa Rica
contains many other resources, including forests, fish,
minerals, and natural resources for tourism, that have
scarcely begun to be explored and exploited. The fundamental problem in the relationship between man and the
land is not a shortage of natural resources, but rather
the failure to exploit these resources in ways combining
efficient economic production, an equitable distribution
of the wealth thus derived, and the conservation of potentially renewable resources for future generations.

Costa Rica contains extraordinary regional diversity.
This variation stems from the wide range of physical environments, distinctive processes of colonization and settlement, and the spatial concentration of cultural minorities such as the Negroes in Limón, the Indians in Talamanca, and even the heritage of historical links with
Mesoamerica and Nicaragua in Guanacaste. At the moment,
there are also pronounced regional inequalities. One of
the major challenges for the future is to take maximum

advantage of the resources of each region in order to combine economic specialization and the preservation of local
cultural identities with acceptable levels of living
throughout the country. This goal will require further
diversification of economic activities, improvements to
the economic infrastructure, and continued diffusion of
basic social services, particularly in peripheral rural
areas.
      Costa Rica is already something of a model in Latin
America. The enormous ecological variety encompassed in
such a small area makes the country a tropical laboratory
for the study of geomorphology, climatology, biogeography,
and land use. Much of the work carried out over the past
thirty years by natural scientists in institutions such as
the Tropical Science Center and the Organization for Tropical Studies in San José and the Centro Agronómico Tropical de Investigación y Enseñanza (formerly the Inter-
American Institute of Agricultural Sciences) in Turrialba
is relevant to tropical ecosystems throughout the world.
      Costa Rica shares with the rest of the continent a
colonial past and problems of underdevelopment, but her
political stability and higher level of living have set
her apart from most of her Central American neighbors.
Social scientists have been studying the country's outstanding parliamentary democracy and welfare state for
many decades. In the convulsive circum-Caribbean region,
Cuba and Costa Rica offer contrasting models for third
world development, the one via socialist revolution, the
other via democracy and reform.
      For the geographer, too, Costa Rica constitutes a
microcosm within which to study the complex problems of
man-land relationships in the humid tropics and the spatial structures generated by socioeconomic underdevelopment. For many years, the little geographical research
completed within the country was undertaken in large part
by foreign visitors. During the past decade, geography
has been established as a separate undergraduate discip-
line in Costa Rican universities, and professional geographers are beginning to participate in public administration and planning. The first Costa Ricans to obtain mas-
ters and doctorate degrees in geography graduated from
foreign universities in the late 1970s and early 1980s.
The country is on the threshold of a new era of intellectual development, not only in this field but in the social
sciences as a whole. Hopefully, the interpretative synthesis attempted in this book will constitute a point of
departure for future research.

References

The following list is not an exhaustive inventory of sources for
the geography of Costa Rica. It includes only those that were found
useful, given the scale and scope of the work in hand. Most sources
are in Spanish, and many are not readily available outside the country.

The topographical and thematic maps produced by the Instituto
Geográfico Nacional are of exceptionally high quality. The censuses
and statistical yearbooks published from 1950 onwards by the Dirección General de Estadística y Censos are comprehensive and generally
reliable; the data in earlier censuses and yearbooks must be used
with caution. A large number of unpublished statistical tables can
be consulted in the offices of the DGEC in San José. These are particularly useful for geographical research because they include a great
deal of data broken down by districts, the smallest administrative
areas. The ministries and autonomous institutions produce many reports containing valuable data for geographical research. Most of
these reports are restricted in circulation but can be consulted without difficulty in government offices in San José. Major data gaps
were filled in by interviews with experts who were invariably helpful
in answering questions and authorizing access to unpublished data.
Their assistance is acknowledged individually in the preface.

Newspaper articles are cited in full in the text. All other
sources are included in a single alphabetical list to facilitate identification of the abbreviated references used in the text. Authors
with Spanish names have been ordered according to their two surnames,
followed by their Christian names. Institutions have been placed according to the acronyms used in the text; their full names are given
in parentheses in the first corresponding entry in the following list.

Acuña B., Olda Maria. 1976. Inventario de esquemas de regionalización
del sector oficial y autónomo de Costa Rica. Heredia: Universidad
Nacional.
Acuña Ortega, Victor Hugo. 1978. Historia económica del tabaco en
Costa Rica. Epoca colonial. Anuario de Estudios Centroamericanos
4:279-392.
Adams, R. N. 1956. Cultural components of Central America. American
Anthropologist 58:881-907.

312

Aguilar Bulgarelli, Oscar. 1973. La esclavitud en Costa Rica durante el período colonial (Hipótesis de trabajo). Estudios Sociales Centroamericanos 5:187-199.
Aguilar Piedra, Carlos H. 1972. Guayabo de Turrialba; arqueología de un sitio indígena. San José: Editorial de Costa Rica.
_____. 1974. Asentamientos indígenas en el área central de Costa Rica. América Indígena 34:311-317.
AID (Agency for International Development). 1965. Costa Rica. Análisis regional de recursos físicos. Washington. (atlas)
Alfaro R., Luis Carlos. 1980. Relaciones entre la renta y el espacio en San Isidro de El General. Thesis, Universidad Nacional, Heredia.
Allen, P. H. 1956. The rain forests of Golfo Dulce. Gainesville: University of Florida Press.
Alonso, William. 1968. Urban and regional imbalances in economic development. Economic Development and Cultural Change 17:1-14.
Altamirano Torres, Angel Roberto. 1978. Aspectos generales del sistema de producción porcina en el Valle Central y del sistema de mercadeo de carne de cerdo en el área de los mercados de San José. Thesis, Universidad de Costa Rica, San José.
Arauz Aguilar, Armando. 1978. El municipio y el desarrollo nacional. San José: Centro de Estudios Democráticos de América Latina.
Araya Pochet, Carlos. 1973. La minería y sus relaciones con la acumulación de capital y la clase dirigente de Costa Rica. 1821-1841. Estudios Sociales Centroamericanos 5:31-64.
_____. 1974. Costa Rica en el contexto iberoamericano. Revista de Costa Rica 5:9-38.
_____. 1977. El segundo ciclo minero de Costa Rica (1890-1930). San José: Consejo Superior Universitario Centroamericano.
_____. 1981. La evolución de la economía tabacalera en Costa Rica bajo el monopolio estatal (1821-1851). San José: Universidad de Costa Rica.
Araya Pochet, Carlos et al. 1981. Crisis en Costa Rica: un debate. San José: Universidad de Costa Rica.
Arias Sanchez, Oscar. 1976. Quién gobierna en Costa Rica? Un estudio de liderazgo formal en Costa Rica. San José: Editorial Universitaria Centroamericana.
_____. 1977a. Futuro socio-económico y político de Costa Rica. In Ministerio de Cultura, La Costa Rica del año 2000. San José, 33-60.
_____. 1977b. Los caminos para el desarrollo de Costa Rica. San José: Centro de Estudios Democráticos de América Latina.
_____. 1979. Nuevos rumbos para el desarrollo costarricense. San José: Editorial Universitaria Centroamericana.
Babarovic, Ivo. 1973. Algunas notas sobre desarrollo regional y la planificación del espacio nacional. In Miguel Morales Alvarez (ed.), Lecturas en problemas urbano-regionales. Santiago: Instituto Latinoamericano de Investigación Social, 73-88.
Baker, Christopher E. et al. 1971. Municipal government in Costa Rica: Its characteristics and functions. San José: Associated Colleges of the Midwest and Universidad de Costa Rica.
Banco Anglo Costarricense. 1941. Informe 1940. San José.
_____. 1961. Informe anual 1960. San José.
_____. 1980. Memoria anual 1979. San José.

Banco de Costa Rica. 1941. Informe 1940. San José.
_____. 1960. Informe anual 1959. San José.
_____. 1978. Memoria del 1877-1977 centenario. San José.
Banco Nacional de Costa Rica. 1942. Memoria anual 1940. San José.
_____. 1960. Memoria anual 1960. San José.
_____. 1980. Memoria anual 1979. San José.
Barahona Riera, Francisco. 1980. Reforma agraria y poder político. El caso de Costa Rica. Transformación estructural. San José: Universidad de Costa Rica.
Barboza V., Carlos. 1980. Relación entre la capacidad y el uso de los suelos de Costa Rica por regiones, sub-regiones y cantones. San José: Oficina de Planificación.
Barrantes Ferrero, Mario. 1965. Las sabanas en el sureste del país. San José: Instituto Geográfico de Costa Rica.
_____. 1966. Apuntes sobre la división territorial administrativa de Costa Rica. San José: Instituto Geográfico Nacional.
_____. 1975a. El Instituto Geográfico Nacional. Breve reseña histórica. San José: Instituto Geográfico Nacional.
_____. 1975b. El catastro rural. San José: Instituto Geográfico Nacional.
Barrantes Herrera, Adrian. 1981. Diagnóstico particular de la avícultura en la república de Costa Rica. San José: Ministerio de Agricultura y Ganadería.
Barrett, E. C. 1970. A contribution to the dynamic climatology of the equatorial eastern Pacific and Central America. Transactions of the Institute of British Geographers 50:25-53.
Batalla Rivera, Elvira. 1977. Consejos de distrito y síndicos. Revista de Ciencias Jurídicas 32:35-71.
Baudez, Claude F. 1963. Cultural development in lower Central America. In Betty J. Meggers and Clifford Evans (eds.), Aboriginal cultural development in Latin America: An interpretative review. Washington, D.C.: Smithsonian Miscellaneous Collections, Vol. 146, No. 1, 45-54.
_____. 1967. Recherches archéologioues dans la vallé du Tempisque, Guanacaste, Costa Rica. Paris: Travaux et Mémoirs de l'Institut des Hautes Etudes de l'Amérique Latine, No. 18.
_____. 1970. Central America. Geneva: Nagel Publishers.
Baudez, Claude F. and Michael D. Coe. 1962. Archaeological sequences in northwestern Costa Rica. Vienna: Akten des 34 Internationalen Amerikanistenkongresses, 366-373.
BCCR (Banco Central de Costa Rica). 1963. Sistema de cuentas nacionales de Costa Rica. 1950-1962. San José.
_____. 1971. Consideraciones sobre el cultivo de la palma africana en Costa Rica. San José.
_____. 1972. Posibilidad de incrementar el cultivo de la caña de azúcar. San José.
_____. 1978. Cifras de cuentas nacionales de Costa Rica. Serie 1957-1976. Estimación 1977. San José.
_____. 1981. Cuentas nacionales de Costa Rica. 1971-1980. San José.
BCCR et al. 1975. Informe sobre algunos aspectos de la producción porcina en Costa Rica y del funcionamiento de la Cooperativa Nacional de Porcicultores. San José.
BCIE (Banco Centroamericano de Integración Económica). 1977. Estudio

314

centroamericano de transporte. 1974-1976. 8 vols. San Salvador.
Beavon, K. S. O. 1977. Central place theory. A re-interpretation.
   London: Longman.
Beck Hemicke, Richard et al. 1979. Plan nacional para el desarrollo
   de las exportaciones. San José: Centro para la Promoción de las
   Exportaciones y de las Inversiones.
Bergmann, J. F. 1969. The distribution of cocoa cultivation in pre-
   Columbian America. Annals of the Association of American Geog-
   raphers 59:85-96.
Bergoeing, Jean Pierre. 1977. Modelado glaciar en la Cordillera de
   Talamanca, Costa Rica. Informe Semestral (Instituto Geográfico
   Nacional) 2:33-44.
_____. 1978. La fotografía aeria y su aplicación a la geomorfo-
   logía de Costa Rica. San José: Instituto Geográfico Nacional.
Bergoeing, Jean Pierre and Luis Guillermo Brenes Quesada. 1978. Mapa
   geomorfológico de Costa Rica (1:1m. with text). San José: Instituto Geográfico Nacional.
Bermúdez M., Vera V. 1973. Migración interna en Costa Rica: el caso
   de la ciudad de San José. Thesis, Universidad de Costa Rica, San
   José.
_____. 1979. Migración y marginalidad en el área metropolitana
   de San José. San José: Séptimo Seminario Nacional de Demografía.
Berry, Brian J. L. 1961. City size distribution and economic development. Economic Development and Cultural Change 9:573-588.
Biesanz, Mavis Hiltunen de, Richard and Karen de Zubris. 1979. Los
   costarricenses. San José: Editorial Universidad Estatal a Distancia.
Bishko, C. J. 1952. The peninsular background of Latin American cattle
   ranching. Hispanic American Historical Review 32:491-515.
Bogan Miller, Marcos W. 1979. La población. In Chester Zelaya (ed.),
   Costa Rica contemporánea. Vol. 2. San José: Editorial de Costa
   Rica, 27-71.
Bogan Miller, Marcos W. and Jessie Orlich Montejo. 1979. Salud y en-
   fermedad. In Chester Zelaya (ed.), Costa Rica contemporánea. Vol.
   2. San José: Editorial de Costa Rica, 73-119.
Bolaños Quesada, Bernal. 1977. El desarrollo de las pequeñas indus-
   trias y artesanías en Costa Rica. Thesis, Universidad de Costa
   Rica, San José.
Bolton, Herbert E. 1917. The mission as a frontier institution in the
   Spanish American colonies. American Historical Review 23:42-61.
Booth, J. 1974. Características sociográficas de las regiones perifér-
   icas de Costa Rica. San José: Instituto de Fomento y Asesoría
   Municipal.
Borah, Woodrow. 1962. América como modelo? El impacto demográfico de
   la expansión europea sobre el mundo no europeo. Cuadernos Ameri-
   canos 125:176-185.
Bosch-Gimpera, Pedro. 1959. La prehistoria del nuevo mundo y Centro
   América. San José: Actas del 33 Congreso Internacional de Ameri-
   canistas, Vol. 1, 137-151.
Bourgeois, W. W. et al. 1972. Geology and soils of comparative ecosys-
   tem study areas, Costa Rica. University of Washington.
Boza, Mario A. 1978. Los parques nacionales de Costa Rica. San José:
   Ministerio de Agricultura y Ganadería.
Bozzoli de Wille, Maria E. 1973. Problemática en torno a proyectos

315

tendientes a prestar ayuda a los indígenas costarricenses. In
Alberto Baeza Flores (ed.), Costa Rica: patrones culturales de
communidades indígenas. San José: Centro de Estudios Democráticos de América Latina.

Bozzoli de Wille, Maria E. 1975. Localidades indígenas costarricenses
(2nd ed.). San José: Editorial Universitaria Centroamericana.

Brenes Castillo, Maria Eugenia. 1978. Matina, bastión del contrabando
en Costa Rica. Anuario de Estudios Centroamericanos 4:393-450.

Brenes Quesada, Luis Guillermo. 1976. Análisis geomorfológico de procesos de remoción en masa de parte de la cuenca del río Reventazón, Costa Rica. Thesis, Universidad de Costa Rica, San José.

Brugman, Barbara and Elena Terán. 1975. La evolución reciente del
crecimiento urbana de Costa Rica como factor de desarrollo nacional. Revista Geográfica de América Central 2:13-27.

Buarque de Hollanda, Teodoro and Carlos Raabe Cercone. 1975. Costa
Rica: migración rural-rural y estructura agraria en el período
1950-1963. Estudios Sociales Centroamericanos 11:9-55.

Budowski, Gerardo. 1966. Inventario de los recursos forestales de la
península de Nicoya. Turrialba: Instituto Interamericano de Ciencias Agrícolas.

Bussing, William A. 1975. Utilidad de los recursos pesqueros nacionales. Revista de la Universidad de Costa Rica 41:17-21.

Camacho, Daniel. 1974. La dominación cultural en el subdesarrollo.
San José: Editorial de Costa Rica.

_____. 1978. Notas introductorias al conocimiento de la sociedad
costarricense y de los efectos de la integración centroamericana.
San José: Universidad de Costa Rica.

Camacho Zamora, Jose A. 1974. El sistema agrícola de los cabécares.
América Indígena 34:469-476.

Campbell Stible, Guillermo. 1962. Estudio agro-económico comparativo
del cacao entre Africa Occidental y Costa Rica. Thesis, Universidad de Costa Rica, San José.

Campos Jimenez, Carlos Maria. 1977. Notas sobre el desarrollo de la
asistencia médica en Costa Rica. Tiempo Actual 2:59-73.

Carcanholo, Reinaldo. 1977. El desarrollo capitalista agropecuario de
Guanacaste. Una interpretación. San José: Consejo Superior Universitario Centroamericano.

_____. 1978. Sobre la evolución de las actividades bananeras en
Costa Rica. Estudios Sociales Centroamericanos 19:143-203.

Cardoso, Ciro F. S. 1973. La formación de la hacienda cafetalera en
Costa Rica (Siglo XIX). Estudios Sociales Centroamericanos 6:22-
50.

_____. 1975. Historia económica del café en Centroamérica (Siglo
XIX): estudio comparativo. Estudios Sociales Centroamericanos
10:9-55.

Cardoso, Ciro F. S. and Hector Pérez Brignoli. 1977. Centro América y
la economía occidental (1520-1930). San José: Editorial Universidad de Costa Rica.

Carranza Picado, Francisco and Adan Chacon Cascante. 1979. Estudios
preliminares sobre la pesca de camarón blanco, café y rosado del
litoral pacífico costarricense. San José: Ministerio de Agricultura y Ganadería.

Carter, H. et al. 1970. Functions of Welsh towns: implications for
central place notions. Economic Geography 46:25-38.

316

Carvajal, Manuel J. et al. 1977a. Políticas de crecimiento urbano. La experiencia de Costa Rica. San José: Dirección General de Estadística y Censos.

_____. 1977b. Pobreza en Costa Rica. San José: Dirección General de Estadística y Censos.

Casey Gaspar, Jeffrey J. 1975. La inmigración china. Revista de Historia (Universidad Nacional, Heredia) 1:145-165.

_____. 1979. Limón 1880-1940. Un estudio de la industria bananera en Costa Rica. San José: Editorial de Costa Rica.

Castro Carazo, Miguel Angel. 1933. Breve reseña del ferrocarril al Pacífico. San José: Imprenta Nacional.

Castro Cartin, Jose Enrique and Hiram Sotela Montagne. 1971. Reseña de la industria turística en Costa Rica. San José.

Castro Vega, Jorge Mario. 1977. Fundamentos para una política agroindustrial. San José.

CATIE (Centro Agronómico Tropical de Investigación y Enseñanza) et al. 1974. Primera reunión internacional sobre la utilización de subproductos del café en la alimentación animal y otras aplicaciones agrícolas e industriales. Informe final. Turrialba.

CCSS (Caja Costarricense de Seguro Social). 1961. Anuario estadístico de 1960. San José.

_____. 1978. Estadísticas patronos, trabajadores y salarios 1978. San José.

_____. 1980. Memoria 1979. San José.

CEPAL (Comisión Económica para América Latina) et al. 1972. Costa Rica: características de uso y distribución de la tierra. San José.

_____. 1973. Tenencia de la tierra y desarrollo rural en Centroamérica. San José: Editorial Universitaria Centroamericana.

_____. 1974. Principales características de la evolución histórica de la industria latinoamericano. In Max Nolff C. (ed.), El desarrollo industrial latinoamericano. México: Fondo de Cultura Económica, 35-108.

_____. 1976. El impacto de la urbanización sobre la sociedad. In Gino Germani (ed.), Urbanización, desarrollo y modernización. Buenos Aires: Paidos, 278-294.

Cerdas Loria, Joaquin B. 1980. Recursos recreativo-turísticos de Costa Rica, por regiones y sub-regiones. San José: Oficina de Planificación.

Céspedes S., Victor Hugo. 1973. Costa Rica: la distribución del ingreso y el consumo de algunos alimentos. San José: Universidad de Costa Rica.

_____. 1979. Evolución de la distribución del ingreso en Costa Rica. San José: Universidad de Costa Rica.

_____. et al. 1977. La pobreza en Costa Rica. Problemas metodológicos para determinar algunas de sus características. San José: La Academia de Centro América.

Chakiel, Juan. 1978. Metropolización y cambio demográfico en Costa Rica. In Miguel Morales Alvarez (ed.), El proceso de metropolización en Costa Rica y América Latina. San José: Universidad de Costa Rica and Instituto Geográfico Nacional, 77-93.

Chacón de Umaña, Luz Alba. 1974. El pueblo de Cía y su transformación en un hato. América Indígena 34:455-468.

Chacon G., Jorge. 1980. La planificación regional y los planes operativos regionales. San José: Oficina de Planificación.

Chapman, Anne M. 1974. Los Nicarao y los Chorotega según las fuentes históricas. San José: Universidad de Costa Rica.

Chaverri, Adelaida et al. 1976. Informe de la gira efectuada al macizo de Chirripó a raíz del fuego occurido en marzo de 1976. Revista de Costa Rica 11:243-279.

Chaves, Ronald and Rodrigo Sáenz. 1970. Efectos de las erupciones recientes del volcan Arenal. Informe Semestral (Instituto Geográfico Nacional) 1:17-24.

Chavez Méndez, Rodolfo. 1981. Ensayo sobre la vivienda en Costa Rica. San José: Instituto de Estudios Políticos.

Christaller, Walter. 1966. Central places in southern Germany. Englewood Cliffs: Prentice Hall.

Coates,B. E. et al. 1977. Geography and inequality. Oxford University Press.

Coe, Michael D. 1962. Costa Rican archaeology and Mesoamerica. Northwestern Journal of Anthropology 18:170-183.

Coen Paris, Elliott. 1953. La meteorología de Costa Rica. In Atlas estadístico de Costa Rica. San José: Dirección General de Estadística y Censos.

_____. 1966. Zonas potenciales del cultivo del arroz y épocas de siembra en Costa Rica. San José: Universidad de Costa Rica.

_____. 1968. Zonas potenciales del cultivo del maíz y épocas de siembra en Costa Rica. San José: Universidad de Costa Rica.

Comisión Nacional de División Territorial Administrativa. 1977. División territorial administrativa de la República de Costa Rica. San José: Imprenta Nacional.

CONAI (Comisión Nacional de Asuntos Indígenas). 1973. Ley de creación de la Comisión Nacional de Asuntos Indígenas. San José.

_____. 1977. Informe de labores. Agosto 1975- agosto 1977. San José.

CONARE (Consejo Nacional de Rectores). 1981. Estadística de la educación superior 1980. San José.

Consorcio Baltodano. 1972. Estudio para el desarrollo integrado de la región fronteriza Costa Rica--Panamá. San José: Oficina de Planificación.

Coto A., Jorge Alberto and Jorge Eduardo Torres H. 1970. Uso potencial de la tierra. Costa Rica. (map, 1:750,000). San José: Ministerio de Agricultura y Ganadería.

Crosby, I. B. 1942. Geology of the Virilla canyon, Meseta Central Occidental, Costa Rica. In Proceedings of the Eighth American Scientific Congress, 1940. Washington, D.C.

Cross Vogel, Robert and Claudio González Vega. 1969. Crédito agrícola en Costa Rica. San José: Associated Colleges of the Midwest.

Cruz Vargas, Armando. 1973. Justificación económica. Proyecto de canalización de la Llanura de Guatusos. Thesis, Universidad de Costa Rica, San José.

CSUCA (Consejo Superior Universitario Centroamericano). 1977. Regiones agrícolas en Centroamérica. Una aproximación socio-económica. Estudios Sociales Centroamericanos 17:95-109.

_____. 1978a. Estructura demográfica y migraciones internas en Centroamérica. San José: Editorial Universitaria Centroamericana.

_____. 1978b. Estructura agraria, dinámica de población y desarrollo capitalista en Centroamérica. San José: Editorial Universi-

318

taria Centroamericana.

DAISA (Corporación para el Desarrollo Agroindustrial Costarricense S.A.). 1981. Análisis y proyecciones sobre la actividad avícola nacional. San José.

Daubenmire, R. 1972. Some ecologic consequences of converting forest to savanna in northwestern Costa Rica. Tropical Ecology 13:31-51.

Davies, Ross L. 1969. A note on centrality and population size. Professional Geographer 11:108-112.

De La O De Ramirez, Julia and Gerardo Hidalgo Cordero. 1978. Breve reseña histórica de la administración pública costarricense; algunos de sus problema (1950-1975). Revista de Ciencias Jurídicas 34:101-122.

del Bello, Juan Carlos. 1979. El sector agro-industrial en Costa Rica. Estudios Sociales Centroamericanos 22:39-69.

Denevan, William M. (ed.). 1976. The native population of the Americas in 1492. Madison: The University of Wisconsin Press.

Dengo, Gabriel. 1962a. Tectonic-igneous sequence in Costa Rica. Buddington Volume, Geological Society of America, 133-161.

_____. 1962b. Estudio geológico de la región de Guanacaste, Costa Rica. San José: Instituto Geográfico.

_____. 1968. Estructura geológica, historia tectónica y morfología de América Central. Mexico: Centro Regional de Ayuda Técnica, Agencia para el Desarrollo Internacional.

Dengo Obregón, Jorge Manuel et al. 1977. Recursos naturales. In La Costa Rica del año 2000. San José: Ministerio de Cultura, 513-638.

Denton, Carlos. 1976. Algunas consideraciones sobre población y políticas de desarrollo en las regiones rurales de Costa Rica. In Sexto Seminario Nacional de Demografía. Informe. Heredia, Vol. 2, 286-313.

DGAC (Dirección General de Aviación Civil). 1979. unpublished statistics.

DGEC (Dirección General de Estadística y Censos). 1885. Censo de población 1883. San José.

_____. 1893. Censo de población 1892. San José.

_____. 1953a. Censo de población de Costa Rica 1950. San José.

_____. 1953b. Censo agropecuario 1950. San José.

_____. 1953c. Anuario estadístico 1950. San José.

_____. 1953d. Atlas estadístico de Costa Rica. San José.

_____. 1954. Censo de comercio e industrias de 1952. San José.

_____. 1960. Censo de población 1927. San José.

_____. 1961. Anuario estadístico de Costa Rica 1960. San José.

_____. 1962. II Censo de industrias en Costa Rica 1958. San José.

_____. 1964a. Anuario estadístico 1963. San José.

_____. 1964b. Comercio exterior de Costa Rica 1963. San José.

_____. 1965. Censo agropecuario 1963. San José.

_____. 1966a. Censo de población 1963. San José.

_____. 1966b. Censo de vivienda 1963. San José.

_____. 1966c. Anuario estadístico 1965. San José.

_____. 1967. III Censo de industrias manufactureras 1964. San José.

_____. 1973. Rama de actividad de la población urbana por cantones 1973 (unpublished). San José.

_____. 1974a. Censo de población 1973. 2 vols. San José.

_____. 1974b. Censo agropecuario 1973. San José.

319

DGEC. 1974c. Censo de vivienda 1973. San José.

_____. 1974d. División territorial administrativa por provincias, cantones y distritos. (map, 1:400,000). San José.

_____. 1974e. Comercio exterior de Costa Rica 1973. San José.

_____. 1974f. Anuario estadístico. Costa Rica. 1973. San José.

_____. 1977-1978. IV Censo de manufactura 1975. 3 vols. San José.

_____. 1978. Comercio exterior. Costa Rica. 1976. San José.

_____. 1979a. Anuario estadístico de Costa Rica 1976. San José.

_____. 1979b. Población de la república de Costa Rica por provincias, cantones y distritos. Estimación al 1 de enero 1979. San José.

_____. 1979c. Encuesta nacional de hogares. Empleo y desempleo. Noviembre 1978. San José.

_____. 1979d. Comercio exterior de Costa Rica 1977. San José.

_____. 1980. Anuario estadístico de Costa Rica 1977. San José.

_____. 1981. Encuesta nacional de hogares. Empleo y desempleo. Marzo 1981. San José.

DGMP (Dirección de Geología Minas y Petroleo). 1968. Mapa geológico de Costa Rica. (1:700,000). San Jose.

_____. 1971a. Mapa de recursos minerales de Costa Rica. (1:750,000). San José.

_____. 1971b. Mapa de localización de aparatos volcánicos y fuentes termales de Costa Rica. San José.

_____. 1977. Mapa metalogenético de Costa Rica. (1:500,000). San José.

Dóndoli B., Cesar. 1943. La región de El General: condiciones geológicos y geo-agronómicos de la zona. Revista del Instituto de Defensa del Café 13:513-528.

Econometrica Ltda. 1970. Granos básicos en Centroamérica. San José.

Ekholm, Gordon F. and Clifford Evans. 1962. The inter-relations of new world cultures: a coordinated research program of the Institute of Andean Research. Vienna: Akten des 34 Internationalen Amerikanistenkongresses, 253-278.

Equipo Cornell-Costa Rica. 1973. El potencial de los recursos naturales para el desarrollo regional de la provincia de Limón. Ithaca: University of Cornell.

Esnaola, Mateo and José Xavier Martini. 1973. Lineamientos de un plan nacional de desarrollo turístico. San José: Organización de Estados Americanos.

Estado del clero de la provincia de Costa Rica, 1972. San José: Imprenta Metropolitana.

Facio, Rodrigo. 1972. Estudio sobre economía costarricense. San José: Editorial de Costa Rica.

Fallas, Helio. 1981. Crisis económica en Costa Rica. Un análisis económico de los últimos 20 años. San José: Editorial Nueva Década.

FECOSA (Ferrocarriles de Costa Rica S.A.). 1978. La fusión de los ferrocarriles. San José.

_____. 1979. Informe anual estadístico. Año 1978. San José.

Fernández Arias, Mario E. et al. 1976. La población de Costa Rica. San José: Editorial Universidad de Costa Rica.

Fernández Guardia, Ricardo. 1968. Reseña histórica de Talamanca. San José: Imprenta Nacional.

Fernández Peralta, Ricardo and José Fabio Gongora. 1940. Mapa de Costa Rica. (1:400,000). Mexico: Instituto Panamericano de Geografía e

Historia.

Ferrero, Luis. 1975. Costa Rica pre-colombina. San José: Editorial de Costa Rica.

_____. 1978. William M. Gabb. Talamanca. El espacio y los hombres. San José: Ministerio de Cultura.

Flores Silva, Eusebio. 1979. Geografía de Costa Rica. 2 vols. San José: Editorial Universidad Estatal a Distancia.

Floyd, Troy S. 1967. The Anglo-Spanish struggle for Mosquitia. Albuquerque: University of New Mexico Press.

Fonseca Corrales, Elizabeth. 1981. Les structures agraires du Costa-Rica a l'époque coloniale. Doctoral thesis, Université de Paris I (Panthéon-Sorbonne).

Fonseca Pereira, Edmur. 1977. La planificación regional en Costa Rica: aspectos geográficos, politico-administrativos e institucionales. Informe Semestral (Instituto Geográfico Nacional) 1:37-69.

_____. 1977-1978. Procesos migratorios y planificación regional en Costa Rica. Revista Geográfica (Instituto Panamericano de Geografía e Historia) 86-87:51-80.

Fournier O., Luis A. 1976. Efecto del urbanismo sobre el future desarrollo agrícola de Costa Rica. Revista de Biología Tropical 24 (suppl. 1):49-55.

Fox, Robert W. and Jerrold W. Huguet. 1978. Tendencias demográficas y de urbanización en América Central y Panamá. Washington: Banco Interamericano de Desarrollo.

Fuentes, Luis G. 1961. Distribución de los grupos sanguineos en indios guatusos de Costa Rica. Revista de Biología Tropical 9:131-140.

Fuertes, José Ramon and Hubert Araya Umaña. 1979. Estudio biológico de las especies de peces costeros del Pacífico de Costa Rica. San José: Ministerio de Agricultura y Ganadería.

Gabb, William M. 1875. On the Indian tribes and languages of Costa Rica. Philadelfia: American Philosophical Society.

Gantz, David. 1969. La aplicación de la ley de protección y desarrollo industrial. Revista de Ciencias Jurídicas 14:113-284.

Germani, Gino. 1971. Sociología de la modernización. Estudios teóricos, metodológicos y aplicados a América Latina. Buenos Aires: Paidos.

Goldkind, Victor. 1961. Socio-cultural contrasts in rural and urban settlement types in Costa Rica. Rural Sociology 26:365-380.

Gomar A., Mario. 1973. Desarrollo de San José y algunos de sus problemas urbanísticos. Revista de Costa Rica 4:139-176.

Gómez B., Miguel and Carlos Quintana R. 1977. Estimaciones del consumo de granos básicos en Costa Rica--1976. San José: Universidad de Costa Rica.

González, Gerardo et al. 1978. Estrategia de desarrollo y transición demográfica. El caso de Costa Rica. Santiago: Centro Latinoamericano de Demografía.

González Flores, Luis Felipe. 1974. El desenvolvimiento histórico del desarrollo del café en Costa Rica, y su influencia en la cultura nacional. Revista de Costa Rica 5:97-112.

_____. 1976. Historia de la influencia extranjera en el desenvolvimiento educacional y científico de Costa Rica. San José: Editorial de Costa Rica.

González Meza, Rodrigo. 1975. Censo de aserraderos realizado durante enero y febrero 1975. Heredia: Universidad Nacional.

321

González V., Rolando. 1969. Situación actual del sorgo para grano en Costa Rica. In Programación de investigación en maíz y sorgo de grano para América Central. Guatemala: Instituto Interamericano de Ciencias Agrícolas, 186-219.

González Vega, Claudio et al. 1970. The marketing of agricultural products in Costa Rica. San José: Associated Colleges of the Midwest and Universidad de Costa Rica.

González Villalobos, Paulino. 1976. Ruta Sarapiquí. Historia socio-política de un camino. San José: Universidad de Costa Rica.

González Víquez, Cleto. 1910. Temblores, terremotos, inundaciones y erupciones volcánicas en Costa Rica, 1608-1910. San José.

_____. 1921. Orígenes de los costarricenses. Revista de Costa Rica.

_____. 1933. El puerto de Puntarenas; algo de su historia. San José: Imprenta Gutenberg.

Gortaire I., Gustavo. 1976. Los recursos forestales y el medio ambiente. Tiempo Actual 1:79-91.

Gregor, Howard F. 1965. The changing plantation. Annals of the Association of American Geographers 55:221-238.

Grigg, D. B. 1974. The agricultural systems of the world. An evolutionary approach. Cambridge University Press.

Gudmundson Kristjanson, Lowell. 1978. Estratificación socio-racial y económica de Costa Rica, 1700-1850. San José: Editorial Universidad Estatal a Distancia.

Haberland, Wolfgang. 1961. Arqueología del valle del río Ceiba, Buenos Aires. Informe Semestral (Instituto Geográfico Nacional) 1:31-62.

_____. 1969. Early phases and their relationship in southern Central America. Stuttgart-München: Verhandlungen des 38 Internationalen Amerikanisten Kongresses 1:229-242.

Hall, Carolyn. 1974. La jerarquía urbana de Costa Rica: una consideración de la aplicación de modelos geográficos. Revista Geográfica de América Central 1:25-48.

_____. 1975. La expansión de los transportes en Costa Rica. Revista Geográfica de América Central 3:9-26.

_____. 1976a. El café y el desarrollo histórico-geográfico de Costa Rica. San José: Editorial de Costa Rica.

_____. 1976b. Los archivos de Keith: algunos aspectos de la geografía histórica de Costa Rica. 1871-1873. Revista de Costa Rica 11:101-127.

_____. 1977-1978. The Tuis archives: cattle ranching on the frontiers of colonization in Costa Rica. 1873-1876. Revista Geográfica (Instituto Panamericano de Geografía e Historia) 86-87:101-117.

_____. 1984. Regional inequalities in well-being in Costa Rica. The Geographical Review 74:48-62.

Halperín Donghi, Tulio. 1970. Historia contemporanea de América Latina. Madrid: Alianza Editorial.

Haring, C. H. 1963. The Spanish empire in America. New York: Harbinger.

Harris, Stuart et al. 1969. Principales zonas de suelos en Costa Rica. Department of Geography, University of Kansas.

Healy, James. 1969. Notas sobre los volcanes de la sierra volcánica de Guanacaste, Costa Rica. Informe Semestral (Instituto Geográfico Nacional) 1:37-47.

Helms, Mary W. 1975. Middle America. A culture history of heartland

and frontier. Englewood Cliffs: Prentice Hall.

Helwig, John Frederick. 1969. Problems of social and economic development in the province of Guanacaste, Costa Rica. Ph.D. thesis, University of Kansas.

Hennessy, Alistair. 1978. The frontier in Latin American history. London: Edward Arnold.

Herrera Acosta, Fernando and Leonardo Garnier Rimolo. 1977. La industria en Costa Rica. Un análisis histórico. Heredia: Universidad Nacional.

Herrera Soto, Danilo. 1978. Exportación de carne de ganado vacuno en Costa Rica. Thesis, Universidad de Costa Rica, San José.

Hill, Carole E. 1973. Convirtiéndose en campesinos: los borucas de Costa Rica. América Indígena 33:447-456.

Holdridge, L. R. 1953. La vegetación de Costa Rica. In Atlas estadístico de Costa Rica. San José: Dirección General de Estadística y Censos.

_____. 1959. Ecological indications for the need for a new approach to tropical land use. Economic Botany 13:271-280.

_____. 1967. Life zone ecology. San José: Tropical Science Center.

Holdridge, L. R. and J. A. Tosi. 1977. Report on the ecological adaptability of selected economic plants for small farm production in six regions of Costa Rica. San José: Tropical Science Center.

Holdridge, L. R. et al. 1971. Forest environments in tropical life zones. A pilot study. Oxford: Pergamon Press.

Hunter, J. Robert. 1959. A new guide to land use planning in tropical areas. Ceiba 8:44-70.

_____. 1969. The lack of acceptance of the pejibaye palm and a relative comparison of its productivity to that of maize. Economic Botany 23:237-244.

_____. 1976. The forest resources of Costa Rica. The biological approach. San José: Associated Colleges of the Midwest.

HVA International. 1974. Feasibility study on oil palm project in Costa Rica. Amsterdam.

ICAA (Instituto Costarricense de Acueductos y Alcantarillados). 1979. Anuario estadístico 1979. San José.

ICE (Instituto Costarricense de Electricidad). 1953. Apuntes sobre el desarrollo de la industria eléctrica de Costa Rica. San José: Trejos.

_____. 1962. Proyecto nacional de telecomunicaciones. Estudio de factibilidad. Primera etapa 1965. San José.

_____. 1973. La generación de energía eléctrica en Costa Rica. San José.

_____. 1977. Inventario de las principales cuencas de Costa Rica. San José.

_____. 1979. Fuentes de energía no convencionales. San José.

_____. 1980a. Desarrollo hidroeléctrico del Río Arenal. San José.

_____. 1980b. Proyecto geotérmico de Miravalles. Antecedentes y situación actual. San José.

_____. 1980c. Realizaciones del Instituto Costarricense de Electricidad en el desarrollo de la industria eléctrica de Costa Rica. San José.

_____. 1980d. Guía telefónica. Costa Rica. 1981. San José.

IFAM (Instituto de Fomento y Asesoria Municipal). 1973. Proyecto de desarrollo del Valle de El General. San José.

IFAM. 1974a. Estudio de caminos vecinales en 25 cantones. San José.
_____. 1974b. Guanacaste. Estudio de desarrollo regional. 4 vols. and atlas. San José.
_____. 1976a. Información básica sobre el sistema municipal. San José.
_____. 1976b. El desarrollo rural en Costa Rica. San José.
IGN (Instituto Geográfico Nacional). 1961. Mapa de Costa Rica. (1: 500,000). San José.
_____. 1967. Cobertura de bosques de Costa Rica. (map, 1:1m.). San José.
_____. 1972. Mapa histórico-geográfico. Costa Rica. (1:700,000). San José.
_____. 1973. Costa Rica. Comunidades indígenas. (map, no scale). San José.
_____. 1977. Mapa físico-político. Costa Rica. (1:500,000). San José.
_____. 1978. Carta aeronautica de Costa Rica. (1:500,000). San José.
IICE (Instituto de Investigaciones en Ciencias Económicas, Universidad de Costa Rica). 1978. Estructura y costos de la educación en Costa Rica. San José: Universidad de Costa Rica.
_____. 1980. El sistema bancario costarricense. San José: Universidad de Costa Rica.
IMAS (Instituto Mixto de Ayuda Social). 1971. Ley de creación y otras disposiciones conexas. San José.
_____. 1977. Memoria 1971-1975. San José.
_____. 1977-1981. Informes anuales de labores, 1976-1980. San José.
_____. 1978. Estimación de la población marginada de Costa Rica por oficinas sectoriales y delegaciones regionales del IMAS. San José.
INS (Instituto Nacional de Seguros). 1981. Algunos datos acerca del Instituto Nacional de Seguros. San José.
INVU (Instituto Nacional de Vivienda y Urbanismo). 1954. Ley orgánica Instituto Nacional de Vivienda y Urbanismo, no. 1788 del 24 de agosto de 1954. San José.
_____. 1961. Ley de erradicación de tugurios y defensa de sus arrendatarios, no. 2760 de 21 de junio de 1961. San José.
_____. 1968. Ley de planificación urbana, no. 4240 del 15 de noviembre de 1968. San José.
_____. 1975. Algunos aspectos de la investigación del Area Metropolitana. San José.
_____. 1976. Memoria 1976. San José.
_____. 1979. Veinte cinco años en cifras. San José.
IPGH (Instituto Panamericano de Geografía e Historia). 1976. Atlas climatológico e hidrológico del istmo centroamericano. Guatemala.
ITCO (Instituto de Tierras y Colonización). 1978. Algunos datos sobre la tenencia y uso de la tierra en Costa Rica. San José.
_____. 1979. Mapa de regionalización y ubicación de proyectos del ITCO. (1:500,000). San José.
_____. 1980a. Informe de la Dirección de Planificación, Departamento de Proyectos. San José.
_____. 1980b. Cooperativas activas establecidas en los diferentes asentamientos del ITCO a febrero de 1980. San José.

Izurieta S., Carlos A. 1979. La concentración industrial en Costa Rica (1964-1975) y las actuales formas de mercado dominantes. San José: Universidad de Costa Rica.

James, P. E. 1941. Expanding frontiers of settlement in Latin America-- a project for future study. Hispanic American Historical Review 20:183-195.

JAPDEVA (Junta de Administración Portuaria y de Desarrollo Económico de la Vertiente Atlántica). 1973. Ley orgánica de la Junta de Administración Portuaria y de Desarrollo Económico de la Vertiente Atlántic, 27 de agosto de 1973. San José.

_____. 1976. Plan integral de desarrollo de la región atlántica 1974-1978. San José.

Jiménez Castro, Wilburg. 1956. Migraciones internas en Costa Rica. Washington: Unión Panamericana.

Jiménez Oreamuno, Ricardo. 1931. Origen y evolución de nuestra ganadería. In Francisco María Núñez (ed.), Costa Rica agrícola, industrial y cultural. Tomo primero. Segunda exposición nacional de ganadería. San José: Alsina, 37-46.

Jones, Chester Lloyd. 1935. Costa Rica and civilization in the Caribbean. University of Wisconsin Studies in the Social Sciences and History, no. 23.

Jones, Clarence F. and Paul C. Morrison. 1952. Evolution of the banana industry in Costa Rica. Economic Geography 28:1-19.

Joyce, Armond T. 1969. A methodology for forest resource and forest industry planning in developing countries in tropical areas: With a case study in Costa Rica. Ph.D. thesis, Syracuse University, Syracuse.

Kalnins, Arvids. 1968-1969. Reorganización administrativa y financiera del régimen municipal de Costa Rica. 3 vols. San José: Oficina de Planificación.

_____. 1971. Proyecto de creación del distrito metropolitano. San José: Ministerio de la Presidencia.

Kansky, K. J. 1963. Structure of transportation networks. University of Chicago, Department of Geography Research Paper No. 84.

Kaplan, Marcos. 1972. La reforma urbana en América Latina. Comercio Exterior (Mexico) 22:534-540 and 635-642.

Keithan, Elizabeth F. 1940. Cocoa in Costa Rica. Economic Geography 16:79-86.

Kennedy, William Jerald. 1968. Archaeological investigation in the Reventazón river drainage area, Costa Rica. Ph.D. thesis, University of Tulane.

Kepner, Charles David and Jay Henry Soothill. 1949. El imperio del banano. Mexico: Ediciones del Caribe.

Kilgour, Mary Cameron. 1981. The telephone in the organization of space for development. Ph.D. thesis, Harvard University.

Kirchoff, Paul. 1966. Mesoamerica. In John A. Graham (ed.), Ancient Mesoamerica, selected readings. California: Peak Publications, 1-14.

Kumm, Henry W. and Horacio Ruiz Soto. 1940. Investigación sobre malaria y zancudos en Costa Rica. San José: Imprenta Nacional.

LAICA (Liga Agrícola Industrial de la Caña de Azúcar). 1978. Situación de la agricultura e industria de la caña de azúcar en Costa Rica. San José.

Lambert, Jacques. 1969. Latin America. Social structures and political

325

institutions. Berkeley: University of California Press.

Lange, Frederick W. 1971a. Northwestern Costa Rica: Pre-Columbian circum-Caribbean affiliations. _Folk_ 13:43-64.

_____. 1971b. _Culture history of the Sapoa River Valley, Costa Rica_. Logan Museum of Anthropology, Beloit College, Wisconsin, Occasional Papers in Anthropology, No. 4.

_____. 1976. Bahías y valles de la costa de Guanacaste. _Vínculos_ 2:45-66.

_____. 1977. Estudios arqueológicos en el valle de Nosara, Guanacaste, Costa Rica. _Vínculos_ 3:27-36.

Lara, Franz. 1970. _Problemas y procedimientos bananeros en la zona Atlántica de Costa Rica_. San José: Trejos.

Lasserre, Guy. 1976. _América Media_. Barcelona: Ariel.

Laurencich Minelli, Laura. 1976. Mesoamerican influences among Talamanca and western Guaymí Indians. In Mary W. Helms and Franklin O. Loveland (eds.), _Frontier adaptations in Lower Central America_. Philadelphia: Institute for the Study of Human Issues, 55-65.

León, Jorge. 1943a. _Nueva geografía de Costa Rica_. San José: Soley y Valverde.

_____. 1943b. La agricultura y colonización en Sarapiquí. _Revista del Instituto de Defensa del Café_ 13:445-452.

_____. 1948. Land utilization in Costa Rica. _Geographical Review_ 38:444-456.

Liberman G., Luis. 1976. Crecimiento económico y absorción de trabajo en Costa Rica. In _Informe del Sexto Seminario Nacional de Demografía_. Heredia: Universidad Nacional, 307-329.

Linsky, Arnold S. 1965. Some generalizations concerning primate cities. _Annals of the Association of American Geographers_ 55:506-513.

Lizano, Eduardo. 1975. El proceso de integración económica. In Edelberto Torres Rivas et al. (eds.), _Centro América hoy_. México: Siglo XXI, 160-235.

Lloyd, J. J. 1963. Historia tectónica del orógeno sur centroamericano. _Informe Semestral_ (Instituto Geográfico Nacional) 1:67-96.

López Leal, Carlos Roberto. 1973. _Una rebelión indígena en Talamanca. Pablo Presbere y el alzamiento general de 1709_. Guatemala: Universidad de San Carlos.

López de Piza, Eugenia. 1974. Xirinachs de Zent. Una comunidad cabécar de Costa Rica. _América Indígena_ 34:439-454.

Losch, A. 1954. _The economics of location_. Yale University Press.

Lothrop, Samuel Kirkland. 1963. _Archaeology of the Diquis delta_. Peabody Museum Papers, Harvard University.

Macleod, Murdo J. 1973. _Spanish Central America. A socio-economic history. 1520-1720_. Berkeley: University of California Press.

Madrigal A., Eduardo et al. 1979. _Estudio preliminar de la situación actual de los manglares del Golfo de Nicoya_. San José: Ministerio de Agricultura y Ganadería.

Madrigal G., Rodolfo. 1961. _Apuntes sobre los recursos minerales y de materias primas industrializables de Costa Rica_. San José: Universidad de Costa Rica.

MAG (Ministerio de Agricultura y Ganadería). 1961. _Ley de tierras y colonización. Decreto no. 2825, 14 de octubre de 1961_. San José: Imprenta Nacional.

_____. 1970. _Precipitación promedio anual en Costa Rica_. (map, 1:1 m.). San José: Instituto Geográfico Nacional.

326

MAG. 1974. Programa nacional de desarrollo forrajero. 1974-1983. San
José.
_____. 1975. Datos básicos del programa de desarrollo integral
de la cuenca del Río Tempisque. San José.
_____. 1977a. Ley forestal, no. 4465, 25 de noviembre de 1969.
San José.
_____. 1977b. Mapa de cobertura de bosques de Costa Rica. (1:1
m.). San José.
_____. 1978a. Ley de reforestación nacional, no. 6184, 29 de
noviembre de 1977. San José.
_____. 1978b. Estadísticas económicas de la pesca y caza marítima.
San José.
MAI (Ministerio de Agricultura e Industrias). 1959. Ley de protección
y desarrollo industrial, no. 2426, 3 de setiembre de 1959. San
José: Imprenta Nacional.
Malavassi V., Enrique and Rodolfo Madrigal G. 1967. Reseña geológica
del área metropolitana. San José: Ministerio de Industria y
Comercio.
Malfait, B. T. and M. G. Dinkelman. 1972. Circum-Caribbean tectonic
and igneous activity and the evolution of the Caribbean plate.
Geological Society of America Bulletin 83:251-272.
Masefield, G. B. 1965. A handbook of tropical agriculture. Oxford:
Clarendon Press.
Masing, Ulv. 1964. Foreign agricultural colonies in Costa Rica. Ph.D.
thesis, University of Florida.
Matarrita Ruiz, Mario. 1980a. Elementos para un interpretación de la
dominación española en Nicoya. In Quinto Centenario de Gonzalo
Fernández de Oviedo. Memoria del Congreso sobre el Mundo Centro-
americano de su Tiempo, 323-330.
_____. 1980b. La hacienda ganadera colonial en el corregimiento
de Nicoya. Siglo XVIII. Thesis, Universidad de Costa Rica.
Matson, G. Albin and Jane Swanson. 1965. Distribution of hereditary
blood antigens among Indians in Middle America. VII. In Costa
Rica. American Journal of Physical Anthropology 23:107-121.
May, Stacy et al. 1952. Costa Rica: A study in economic development.
New York: Twentieth Century Fund.
McGee, T. G. 1971. The urbanization process in the third world. Ex-
plorations in search of a theory. London: Bell.
MEIC (Ministerio de Economía, Industrias y Comercio). 1972. Ley de la
Corporación Costarricense de Desarrollo, no. 5122, 16 de noviem-
bre de 1972. San José.
Meggers, Betty J. 1971. Amazonia. Man and culture in a counterfeit
paradise. Chicago: Aldine Publishing Company.
Meléndez Chaverri, Carlos. 1953. Costa Rica: evolución histórica de
sus problemas más destacados. San José: Imprenta Atenea.
_____. 1957. Legislación indigenista de Costa Rica. México: In-
stituto Indigenista Interamericano.
_____. 1967. Los orígenes de los esclavos africanos en Costa
Rica. Anales de la Academia de Geografía e Historia de Costa
Rica, 99-103.
_____. 1968. Dr. José María Montealegre. Contribución al estudio
de un hombre y una época poco conocida de nuestra historia. San
José: Academia de Geografía e Historia.
_____. 1970. La ilustración en el antiguo Reino de Guatemala.

San José: Editorial Universitaria Centroamericana.

Meléndez Chaverri, Carlos. 1971. Rasgos fundamentales de la geopolíti-
ca centroamericana en la independencia. Revista de la Universidad
de Costa Rica 31:7-25.

_____. 1975. Formas en la tenencia de la tierra en Costa Rica
durante el régimen colonial. Revista de Historia 1:104-144.

_____. 1976. Trayectoria histórica del municipio costarricense.
In Instituto de Fomento y Asesoría Municipal Información básica
sobre el sistema municipal, 55-72.

_____. 1977a. Costa Rica: tierra y poblamiento en la colonia.
San José: Editorial de Costa Rica.

_____. 1977b. Ciudades fundadas en la América Central en el siglo
XVI. (Sinopsis alfabética). Anuario de Estudios Centroamericanos
3:57-79.

_____. 1979a. Historia de Costa Rica. San José: Editorial Univer-
sidad Estatal a Distancia.

_____. 1979b. El medio geográfico. In Chester Zelaya (ed.), Costa
Rica contemporánea, Vol. 1. San José: Editorial de Costa Rica,
39-73.

Meléndez Chaverri, Carlos and Quince Duncan. 1972. El negro en Costa
Rica. San José: Editorial de Costa Rica.

MEP (Ministerio de Educación Pública). 1941. Memoria 1940. San José.

_____. 1961. Estadísticas de educación, 1960. San José.

_____. 1980. Centros educativos de Costa Rica 1980. San José.

Mesén Mora, Rodrigo A. et al. 1978. Algunos aspectos cuantificados del
problema agrario en Costa Rica. San José: Instituto de Tierras y
Colonización.

Ministerio de Cultura, Juventud y Deportes. 1980. Lista de bienes in-
muebles que han sido declarados. San José.

Ministerio de Fomento. 1941. Memoria anual 1940. San José.

Ministerio de Transportes. 1967. Reseña histórica de los transportes
en Costa Rica. San José.

Miyamura, Setumi. 1976. Aspectos importantes de la sismicidad en Costa
Rica. San José: Universidad de Costa Rica.

Monge Alfaro, Carlos. 1942. Geografía social y humana de Costa Rica.
San José: Imprenta y Librería Universal.

_____. 1974a. Historia de Costa Rica. San José: Librería Trejos.

_____. 1974b. Nuestra historia y los seguros. San José: Editorial
de Costa Rica.

_____. 1979. La educación. In Chester Zelaya (ed.), Costa Rica
contemporánea, Vol. 2. San José: Editorial de Costa Rica, 193-249.

Monge Alfaro, Carlos and Francisco Rivas Rios. 1980. La educación:
fragua de una democracia. San José: Editorial Universidad de Costa Rica.

Montoya Montoya, Alfredo et al. 1976. El problema de la vivienda y el
urbanismo en Costa Rica. Thesis, Universidad de Costa Rica.

MOPT (Ministerio de Obras Públicas y Transportes). 1976. Cuadros esta-
dísticos sobre el sector transporte 1975. San José.

_____. 1977a. Mapa de carreteras nacionales y regionales. San
José.

_____. 1977b. Diagrama de flujos de tránsito. San José.

_____. 1978. Inversión realizada y programada en el sector trans-
porte. Período 1974-1985. San José.

_____. 1980. Carreteras nacionales y regionales y caminos vecin-

328

ales. (map). San José.
Morales Alvarez, Miguel. 1975. Estrategías espaciales y desarrollo
    regional en América Latina: el caso de Costa Rica. San José: In-
    stituto Geográfico Nacional.
_____. 1977-1978. Perspectivas de la planificación urbano-
    regional en Costa Rica. Revista Geográfica (Instituto Panameri-
    cano de Geografía e Historia) 86-87:29-49.
_____, ed. 1978. El proceso de metropolización en Costa Rica y
    América Latina. San José: Instituto Geográfico Nacional.
Mörner, Magnus. 1969. La mezcla de razas en la historia de América
    Latina. Buenos Aires: Paidos.
Morse, R. M. 1954. Sao Paulo in the twentieth century: Social and
    economic aspects. Inter-American Economic Affairs 8:3-60.
Mortgat, Christian P. et al. 1977. A study of seismic risk for Costa
    Rica. The John A. Blume Earthquake Engineering Center, Department
    of Civil Engineering, Stanford University.
MS (Ministerio de Salud). 1977. Memoria del cincuentenario del Minis-
    terio de Salud y de la Salud Pública en Costa Rica. San José.
_____. 1981. Memoria 1980. San José.
MSP (Ministerio de Salubridad Pública). 1941. Memoria 1940. San José.
_____. 1960. Memoria 1959. San José.
_____. 1977. Memoria del cincuentenario del Ministerio de Salud
    y de la Salud Pública en Costa Rica. San José.
Munro, John. 1980. Consideraciones en torno a una política de trans-
    porte metropolitano y propuesta de un sistema de tranvía rápido.
    San José: Oficina de Planificación.
Murata, K. J. et al. 1966. The 1963-65 eruption of Irazú volcano,
    Costa Rica. Bulletin Volcanologique 29:765-796.
Navarro Melendez, Rigoberto. 1974. La contribución del sector indus-
    trial al desarrollo económico de Costa Rica. Thesis, Universidad
    de Costa Rica.
_____ et al. 1973. El desarrollo industrial de Costa Rica y sus
    principales problemas. San José: Banco Central de Costa Rica.
Nolff C., Max, ed. 1974. El desarrollo industrial latinoamericano.
    México: Fondo de Cultura Económico.
Norweb, Albert H. 1968. The archaeology of the Greater Nicoya Subarea.
    Department of Anthropology, Harvard University.
Novygrodt V., Rosa M. and Carlos Diaz Amador. 1979. Situación del
    estado nutricional en Costa Rica 1978-79. In Ministerio de Salud
    Vigilancia epidemiológica, nutricional y alimenticia: Costa Rica.
    San José.
Nuhn, Helmut. 1972. Estado actual, organización y problemas de la
    planificación en Costa Rica y consideraciones para un reorgani-
    zación, incluyendo la planificación regional. San José.
_____. 1973a. Regionalización de Costa Rica para la planificación
    del desarrollo y la administración. San José: Oficina de Planifi-
    cación.
_____. 1973b. Geografía y planificación del desarrollo. San José:
    Instituto de Fomento y Asesoría Municipal.
_____. 1978a. Regionalisierung und Entwicklungsplanung in Costa
    Rica. Hamburg.
_____. 1978b. Atlas preliminar de Costa Rica. San José: Instituto
    Geográfico Nacional.
_____ et al. 1967. Estudio geográfico regional. Zona atlántico

norte de Costa Rica. San José: Instituto de Tierras y Colonización.

Nuñez, Francisco Maria. 1924. Iniciación y desarrollo de las vías de communicación y empresas de transporte en Costa Rica. San José.

Nunley, R. E. 1960. The distribution of population in Costa Rica. Washington: National Academy of Science.

OEA (Organización de Estados Americanos). 1975. Estudio sectorial sobre empresas transnacionales en América Latina. La industria bananera. Washington, D.C.

_____. 1978. Diagnóstico del sector minero. San José.

Oficina del Café. 1978. Informe sobre la actividad cafetalera de Costa Rica. San José.

OFIPLAN (Oficina de Planificación). 1963. Ley de planificación no. 3087, 31 de enero de 1963. San José: Imprenta Nacional.

_____. 1964. Consecuencias económicas y sociales de la actividad del Volcán Irazú. San José.

_____. 1966. Plan de desarrollo económico y social de Costa Rica. San José.

_____. 1970. Previsiones del desarrollo económico y social 1969-1972 y planes del sector público. 2 vols. San José.

_____. 1973-1974. Plan nacional de desarrollo. 4 vols. San José.

_____. 1975. Plan operativo 1975. IV. Estrategia de desarrollo regional. San José.

_____. 1976. Programa nacional de oleaginosas 1976-1981. San José.

_____. 1978. Regionalización de Costa Rica. San José.

_____. 1979a. Plan nacional de desarrollo 1979-1982 Gregorio José Ramírez. San José.

_____. 1979b. Plan nacional de desarrollo forestal. 1979-1982. San José.

_____. 1979c. Recomendaciones generales acerca de la ubicación espacial de la industria. San José.

_____. 1979d. La pobreza en Costa Rica. Análisis del sector urbano. San José.

_____. 1980a. Enfoque y decisiones del gobierno de la república en relación a la política de población. San José.

_____. 1980b. Unidades integrales de servicios. Propuesta para iniciar la re-estructuración de San José. San José.

_____. 1980c. Indicadores socioeconómicos para la planificación regional. San José.

_____. 1981. La dimensión de la pobreza: estudio de la pobreza rural en Costa Rica. San José.

OPAM (Oficina de Planeamiento del Area Metropolitana). 1979. Estudio de zonas industriales en la Región Metropolitana. San José.

OPSA (Oficina de Planificación Sectorial Agropecuaria). 1975. Programa nacional de granos básicos. 1975-1978. San José.

_____. 1977a. Proyecto de fomento de la actividad cacaotera. San José.

_____. 1977b. Información básica del sector agropecuario de Costa Rica. San José.

_____. 1979a. Diagnóstico del sector agropecuario de Costa Rica. 1962-1976. San José.

_____. 1979b. Programa agropecuario, recursos naturales y agroindustriales. Período 1979-1982. San José.

Ornes, Mayobanex. 1980. Los caminos del indigenismo. San José: Editorial de Costa Rica.

Ortega G., Antonio. 1976. Situación demográfica actual de Costa Rica y perspectivas futuras. In Sexto Seminario Nacional de Demografía. Informe. Vol. 1. Heredia, 19-70.

OSPI (Oficina Sectorial de Planificación Industrial). 1978a. Una nueva política industrial de desarrollo. 1978-1982. 2 vols. San José.

_____. 1978b. Características del proceso de industrialización, estado actual y potencial de desarrollo en Costa Rica. San José.

Padilla P., Manuel. 1981. Algunas características de la producción porcina en Costa Rica. San José: Ministerio de Agricultura y Ganadería.

Palmer, Paula. 1977. "What happen": A folk history of Costa Rica's Talamanca coast. San José: Ecodesarrollos.

Parsons, F. S. (n.d.). Informe sobre los factores que determinan la buena producción de algodón en Costa Rica. San José: Ministerio de Agricultura y Ganadería.

Parsons, James J. 1964. Cotton and cattle in the Pacific Lowlands of Central America. Journal of Inter-American Studies 7:149-159.

_____. 1968. Antioqueño colonization in western Colombia. Berkeley: University of California Press.

_____. 1976. Forest to pasture: development or destruction? Revista de Biología Tropical 24 (suppl. 1):121-138.

Peralta, Manuel Maria. 1896. Les aborigines de Costa Rica: essai de distribution géographique. Journal de la Société des Américanistes de Paris.

Pérez Brignoli, Hector. 1978. Las variables demográficas en las economías de exportación: el ejemplo del Valle Central de Costa Rica (1800-1950). San José: Universidad de Costa Rica.

_____. 1979. Notas sobre el descenso de la mortalidad en Costa Rica (1866-1973). San José: Séptimo Seminario Nacional de Demografía.

_____. 1981a. Deux siecles d'illegitimité au Costa Rica. 1770-1974. In J. Dupaquier et al. (eds.), Marriage and remarriage in populations of the past. London: Academic Press, 481-493.

_____. 1981b. Economía política del café en Costa Rica. 1850-1950. Algunas notas preliminares. San José: Universidad de Costa Rica.

Pérez Rosales, Samuel et al. 1977a. Determinación de áreas críticas para la siembra de arroz por factores climáticos en la vertiente del Pacífico. San José: Oficina de Planificación Sectorial Agropecuaria.

_____. 1977b. Zonificación para el cultivo del algodón. San José: Oficina de Planificación Sectorial Agropecuaria.

_____. 1978a. Mapa de asociaciones de sub-grupos de suelos de Costa Rica. (1:200,000) 9 sheets. San José: Oficina de Planificación, Sectorial Agropecuaria.

_____. 1978b. Mapa de capacidad de uso del suelo, Costa Rica. (1:200,000) 9 sheets. San José: Oficina de Planificación, Sectorial Agropecuaria.

_____. 1979. Manual descriptivo del mapa de asociaciones de sub-grupos de suelos de Costa Rica (escala 1:200,000). San José: Oficina de Planificación, Sectorial Agropecuaria.

Pérez Rosales, Samuel and F. Protti. 1978. Comportamiento del sector forestal durante el período 1950-1977. San José: Oficina de

Planificación Sectorial Agropecuaria.
Perlaza Guevara, Edgar. 1977. Análisis geográfica de los tugurios en el Area Metropolitana de San José: su repercusión en la morfología urbana. Thesis, Universidad de Costa Rica.
_____. 1980. Un estudio geográfico-social de los asentamientos tuguriosos en Costa Rica: tipología, distribución espacial e infraestructura. San José: Instituto Mixto de Ayuda Social.
Peterson, A. W. and Quentin M. West. 1950. Agricultural regions of Costa Rica. Thesis, Instituto Interamericano de Ciencias Agrícolas, Turrialba.
Peterson, Lyall E. 1947. Agricultural development prospects in Costa Rica. Washington, D.C.: Inter-American Development Commission.
Pittier, Henri. 1908. Ensayo sobre las plantas usuales de Costa Rica. Washington, D.C.
Plath, C. V. 1969. Algunas preguntas que deben ser tomadas en consideración con respecto a los factores económicos de la producción de frijol en América Central. In Reunión técnica sobre programación de investigación y extensión en frijol. Turrialba: Instituto Interamericano de Ciencias Agrícolas, 35-38.
Plath, C. V. and A. van der Sluis. 1964. Uso potencial de la tierra de Costa Rica. Food and Agriculture Organization.
Porras Thames, Ana. 1979. Migraciones internas y proceso de urbanización en Costa Rica (1950-1973). Thesis, Centro de Estudios Urbanos y Regionales, Instituto Torcuato di Tella, Buenos Aires.
Portig, W. H. 1959. Air masses in Central America. Bulletin of the American Meteorological Society 49:301-304.
Prado, Eladio. 1925. La órden franciscana en Costa Rica. Cartago: Imprenta El Heraldo.
Quiros Amador, Tulia. 1954. Geografía de Costa Rica. San José: Instituto Geográfico de Costa Rica.
Quiros Vargas, Claudia. 1976. Aspectos socio-económicos de la ciudad de Espíritu Santo de Esparza y su jurisdicción (1574-1848). Thesis, Universidad de Costa Rica.
Quiroz M., Teresa et al. 1980. Algunos datos de la situación de la agroindustrial en Costa Rica. San José: Universidad de Costa Rica.
Raabe C., Carlos. 1976. Opciones para la distribución espacial de la población de Costa Rica en el año 2000. In Sexto Seminario Nacional de Demografía. Informe. Vol. 1. Heredia, 262-306.
Raccichini, Sergio. 1977-1978. Criterios para la zonificación de Costa Rica en base al riesgo volcánico potencial. Revista Geográfica (Instituto Panamericano de Geografía e Historia) 86-87:147-160.
Ramírez Bonilla, Jose Alfonso. 1975. Análisis de la producción y del consumo de granos básicos en Costa Rica. Thesis, Universidad de Costa Rica.
Ramírez Boza, Mario A. and Solís Avendaño, Manuel A. 1979. El desarrollo capitalista en la industria costarricense (1850-1930). 2 vols. Thesis, Universidad de Costa Rica.
Ramírez R., Carlos A. 1969. Cultivo de la caña de azúcar en Costa Rica. San José: Ministerio de Agricultura y Ganadería.
_____. 1974. El crecimiento de la industria azucera. San José: Ministerio de Agricultura y Ganadería.
Ratcliffe, Jane Elizabeth. 1970. An examination of the population-economic activities relationship and hierarchy of central places:

The Costa Rican example. Ph.D. thesis, University of Indiana.

Redfield, Arthus H. 1923. The petroleum possibilities of Costa Rica. Economic Geology 18:354-381.

Ribeiro, Darcy. 1971. Fronteras indígenas de la civilización. México: Siglo XXI.

Rivas Rios, Francisco. 1979. La conquista de Costa Rica. Primera fase (1502-1560). Thesis, Universidad de Costa Rica.

Roberts, Peggy Orme. 1978. The composition of the Costa Rican population: Some evidence from history, genetics and morphology. Ph.D. thesis, University of Colorado.

Roberts, Ralph. 1944. Manganese deposits in Costa Rica. Washington, D.C.: United States Geological Survey Bulletin No. 935-H.

Roberts, R. J. and E. M. Irving. 1957. Mineral deposits of Central America. Washington, D.C.: United States Geological Survey Bulletin No. 1034.

Rodríguez Quesada, Olman. 1974. La actividad del ganado de carne en Costa Rica. Thesis, Universidad de Costa Rica.

Rodríguez Vega, Eugenio. 1977. Apuntes para una sociología costarricense. San José: Editorial Universidad Estatal a Distancia.

Rosenberg, Mark. 1980. Las luchas por el seguro social en Costa Rica. San José: Editorial de Costa Rica.

Rosero Bixby, Luis. 1978. Dinámica demográfica, planificación familiar y política de población en Costa Rica. San José: Comité Nacional de Población.

Rosés Alvarado, Carlos. 1975. El cacao en la economía colonial de Costa Rica. Thesis, Universidad de Costa Rica.

Sáenz Maroto, Alberto. 1960. Curso técnico sinóptico de algunos cultivos de Costa Rica. El maíz. San José: Universidad de Costa Rica.
_____. 1962. Curso técnico sinóptico de algunos cultivos de Costa Rica. El frijol común. San José: Universidad de Costa Rica.

Sáenz Pacheco, Carlos Joaquin. 1969. Population growth, economic progress and opportunities on the land: The case of Costa Rica. Ph.D. thesis, University of Wisconsin.

Sáenz Pacheco, Carlos Joaquin and C. Foster Knight. 1971. Tenure security, land titling and agricultural development in Costa Rica. San José: Universidad de Costa Rica.

Salas F., Carlos Alberto. 1969. Situación actual del maíz en Costa Rica. In Programación de investigación en maíz y sorgo de grano para América Central. Guatemala: Instituto Interamericano de Ciencias Agrícolas, 8-71.

Salas Marrero, Oscar A. and Rodrigo Barahona Israel. 1973. Derecho agrario. San José: Editorial Universidad de Costa Rica.

Salas Víquez, José Antonio. 1979. Santa Bárbara de Heredia 1852-1927. Una contribución a la historia de los pueblos. Thesis, Universidad Nacional, Heredia.

Salazar Mora, Jorge Mario. 1981. Política y reforma en Costa Rica 1914-1958. San José: Editorial Porvenir.

Salazar Navarrete, José Manuel. 1961. Tierras y colonización de Costa Rica. Thesis, Universidad de Costa Rica.
_____. 1979. Política agraria. In Chester Zelaya (ed.), Costa Rica contemporánea. Vol. 1. San José: Editorial de Costa Rica, 211-232.
_____. et al. 1977. Una política agraria innovadora: el caso de Costa Rica. San José: Instituto de Tierras y Colonización.

Samper K., Mario. 1979. Evolución de la estructura socio-ocupacional costarricense: labradores, artesanos y jornaleros. 1864-1935. Thesis, Universidad de Costa Rica.

Sanabria Martinez, Victor. 1977. Geneologías de Cartago hasta 1850. In Luis Demetrio Tinoco (ed.), Población de Costa Rica y orígenes de los costarricenses. San José: Editorial de Costa Rica, 155-214.

Sánchez-Albornoz, Nicolas. 1974. The population of Latin America. A history. Berkeley: University of California Press.

Sanders, W. T. and J. Marino. 1970. New world pre-history. Englewood Cliffs: Prentice Hall.

Sanders, W. T. and B. J. Price. 1968. Mesoamerica: The evolution of a civilization. New York: Random House.

Sandner, Gerhard. 1959a. La colonización interna, o expansión agrícola en Costa Rica. Progreso o retroceso? Informe Semestral (Instituto Geográfico de Costa Rica) 1:25-33.

_____. 1959b. Investigaciones geográficas en Costa Rica. 1. Sección oriental de la península de Nicoya. Informe Semestral (Instituto Geográfico de Costa Rica) 2:29-41.

_____. 1960. Turrubares. Estudio de geografía regional. Problemas sociales y económicos de la expansión agrícola en Costa Rica. San José: Instituto Geográfico de Costa Rica.

_____. 1961. Aspectos geográficos de la colonización agrícola en el valle del General. San José: Instituto Geográfico de Costa Rica.

_____. 1962. El concepto espacial y los sistemas funcionales en la colonización espontánea costarricense. Informe Semestral (Instituto Geográfico de Costa Rica) 2:57-107.

_____. 1962 and 1964. La colonización agrícola de Costa Rica. 2 vols. San José: Instituto Geográfico de Costa Rica.

_____. 1966. El problema de la definición de "ciudad" y "población urbana" en sus aspectos generales y consecuencias para Costa Rica. Informe Semestral (Instituto Geográfico Nacional) 2:27-41.

_____ et al. 1966. Estudio geográfico regional de la zona norte de Costa Rica. San José: Instituto de Tierras y Colonización.

Santos, Milton. 1973. Geografía y economía urbanas en los países subdesarrollado. Barcelona: Oikos Tau.

Sauer, Carl O. 1959. Age and area of American cultivated plants. San José: Actas del 33 Congreso Internacional de Americanistas, vol. 1:215-229.

Sauer, Jonathan D. 1979. Living fences in Costa Rican agriculture. Turrialba 29:255-261.

Sauter, Franz. 1980. Riesgo sísmico en Costa Rica. In La Nación, 31 August, 6C-7C.

Sawyer, J. O. and A. A. Lindsey. 1971. Vegetation of the life zones in Costa Rica. Indianapolis: Indiana Academy of Science.

Schifter Sikora, Jacobo et al. 1979. El judío en Costa Rica. San José: Editoria Universidad Estatal a Distancia.

Schmidt, Annabelle. 1979. Los extranjeros en Costa Rica. San José: Séptimo Seminario Nacional de Demografía.

Scott, N. J. 1966. Ecologically important aspects of the climates of Costa Rica. San José: Organization for Tropical Studies.

Seligson, Mitchell A. 1977. La tesis de la "sociedad dual": una reexaminación del caso de Costa Rica. Revista de Ciencias Sociales (Universidad de Costa Rica) 10:33-47.

334

Seligson, Mitchell A. 1978. Agrarian reform in Costa Rica, 1942-1976. The evolution of a programme. Land Tenure Center, University of Wisconsin.
_____. 1980. El campesino y el capitalismo agrario de Costa Rica. San José: Editorial de Costa Rica.
Selwyn, Percy, ed. 1975. Development policy in small countries. London: Croom Helm.
Service, Elman R. 1955. Indian-European relations in colonial Latin America. American Anthropologist 57:411-425.
Sharpe, E. Stuart. 1972. Estudio turístico de Costa Rica. San José: Instituto Costarricense de Turismo and Organización de Estados Americanos.
Shaw, R. Paul. 1976. Land tenure and the rural exodus in Chile, Colombia, Costa Rica and Peru. Gainseville: University of Florida Press.
Sherman, William. 1979. Forced native labour in sixteenth century Central America. Lincoln: University of Nebraska Press.
Sibaja Chacon, Luis Fernando. 1968. El límite sureste de Costa Rica. Reseña histórica desde el laudo Loubet hasta su fijación definitiva. Thesis, Universidad de Costa Rica.
_____. 1973. El Sarapiquí como vía de comunicación internacional durante el siglo XIX. Revista de Costa Rica 3:55-70.
_____. 1974. Nuestro límite con Nicaragua. San José: Comisión Nacional de Conmemoraciones Históricas.
SIECA (Secretaría Permanente del Tratado General de Integración Económica Centroamericano). 1973. Diagnóstico y posibilidades de desarrollo en tres cuencas multinacionales en Centro América. Guatemala.
Skutch, Alexander F. 1971. A naturalist in Costa Rica. Gainseville: University of Florida Press.
Smith, David M. 1977. Patterns in human geography. Harmondsworth: Penguin.
Smith, Vernon Arthur. 1970. Beef cattle production and marketing in Guanacaste, Costa Rica. Ph.D. thesis, University of Florida.
SNAA (Servicio Nacional de Acueductos y Alcantarillados). 1963. Informe junio de 1961 a diciembre de 1962. San José.
Snarskis, Michael J. 1975. Excavaciones estratigráficas en la Vertiente Atlántica de Costa Rica. Vínculos 1:2-17.
_____. 1976. La Vertiente Atlántica de Costa Rica. Vínculos 2: 101-104.
_____. 1977. Turrialba (9-FG-T), un sitio paleoindio en el este de Costa Rica. Vínculos 3:13-25.
_____. 1981. The archaeology of Costa Rica. In Suzanne Abel-Vidor et al. (eds.), Between continents. Between seas. Pre-Columbian art of Costa Rica. New York: Harry N. Abrams Inc., 15-84.
Solow, Anatole A. 1948. A planning program for the capital of Costa Rica. Washington, D.C.: Pan-American Union.
Sorre, Max. 1928. Mexique, Amérique Centrale. Paris: Armand Colin.
Soto Guevara, Carlos Manuel et al. 1980. Estudio sobre la división territorial administrativa de la república de Costa Rica. San José: Universidad de Costa Rica and Instituto de Fomento y Asesoría Municipal.
Spielman, Hans O. 1972. La expansión ganadera en Costa Rica. Informe Semestral (Instituto Geográfico Nacional) 2:33-57.

335

Stafford, Howard A. 1963. The functional bases of small towns. Econom-
ic Geography 39:165-175.
Standard Fruit Company. 1978. Standard Fruit Company on Costa Rica.
San José.
Standley, P. C. 1937-1938. Flora of Costa Rica. 4 vols. Chicago: Field
Museum of Natural History.
Stanger, Francis Merriman. 1932. National origins in Central America.
Hispanic American Historical Review 12:18-45.
Stewart, Watt. 1967. Keith y Costa Rica. San José: Editorial de Costa
Rica.
Stone, Doris. 1949. Los grupos mexicanos en la América Central y su
importancia. Antropología e Historia de Guatemala 1:43-47.
_____. 1956. Breve esbozo etnológico de los pueblos indígenas
costarricenses. In Estudios antropológicos publicados en homenaje
al Doctor Manuel Gamio. Mexico, 503-511.
_____. 1968. Fases culturales y su significado en la arqueología
de Costa Rica. Boletín del Museo Nacional (San José) 35:1-8.
_____. 1972. Pre-Columbian man finds Central America. Harvard:
Peabody Museum Press.
_____. 1977. Pre-Columbian man in Costa Rica. Harvard: Peabody
Museum Press.
Stone, Samuel. 1973. Inversiones industriales en Costa Rica. Revista
de Ciencias Sociales (Universidad de Costa Rica) 7:67-89.
_____. 1975. La dinastía de los conquistadores. San José: Editor-
ial Universitaria Centroamericana.
Stouse, Pierre A. D. 1965. Agricultural settlement in former Costa Rican banana regions. Ph.D. thesis, University of Wisconsin.
_____. 1967. Effective agricultural development of former banana
lands: The west coast of Costa Rica. Revista Geográfica (Instituto Panamericano de Geografía e Historia) 66:153-161.
_____. 1970. Instability of tropical agriculture: The Atlantic
lowlands of Costa Rica. Economic Geography 46:78-97.
_____. 1971. La cultura y el ambiente: cuatro Costa Ricas. In-
forme Semestral (Instituto Geográfico Nacional) 2:89-106.
Strahler, Arthur N. and H. Alan. 1978. Modern physical geography. New
York: Wiley.
Sunkel, Osvaldo and Pedro Paz. 1973. El subdesarrollo latinoamericano
y la teoría del desarrollo. México: Siglo XXI.
Swauger, J. L. and W. J. Mayer-Oakes. 1952. A fluted point from Costa
Rica. American Antiquity 17:264-265.
Taaffe, Edward J. et al. 1963. Transport expansion in underdeveloped
countries: A comparative analysis. Geographical Review 53:503-529.
Tax, Sol. 1953. Penny capitalism: A Guatemalan Indian economy. New
York: Octagon Books.
Thiel, Bernardo A. 1896. Viajes a varias partes de la república de
Costa Rica. San José.
_____. 1902. Monografía de la población de Costa Rica en el siglo
XIX. San José.
_____. 1940. Distribución de tierras y encomiendas entre los pri-
meros conquistadores de Costa Rica. In José Francisco Trejos
(ed.), Los conquistadores. San José: Lehmann, 189-197.
Tirado Sulsona, Pedro and Miguel A. Muñoz. 1965. Inventario de los recursos naturales de la península de Nicoya. Asociación Regional
para el Desarrollo de la Península de Nicoya and Agencia para el

Desarrollo Internacional.

Tjarks, German O. E. et al. 1976. La epidemia del cólera de 1856 en el Valle Central: análisis y consecuencias demográficas. Revista de Historia (Universidad Nacional, Heredia) 3:81-129.

Tosi, Joseph A. 1967a. Un estudio de reconocimiento de los recursos naturales y potenciales de las tierras de la reserva indígena de Salitre, el Valle del General, Costa Rica. San José: Food and Agriculture Organization and Instituto de Tierras y Colonización.

_____. 1967b. Capacidad de uso de la tierra determinada por las condiciones de clima, fisiografía y suelos en la parte noreste de la provincia de Guanacaste, Costa Rica. San José.

_____. 1969. República de Costa Rica. Mapa ecológico. (1:750,000). San José: Instituto Geográfico Nacional.

_____. 1971. El recurso forestal como base potencial para el desarrollo industrial de Costa Rica. San José: Tropical Science Center.

_____. 1974. Los recursos forestales de Costa Rica. San José: Tropical Science Center.

Tosi, Joseph A. and L. R. Holdridge. 1973. Potencial para la ordenación técnica del bosque natural en Costa Rica. San José: Tropical Science Center.

Tosi, Joseph A. and Robert Voertman. 1964. Environmental factors in economic development of the tropics. Economic Geography 40:189-205.

Trewartha, G. T. 1961. The earth's problem climates. Madison: University of Wisconsin Press.

TSE (Tribunal Supremo de Elecciones). 1974. Computo de votos y declaratorias de elección. Elecciones del 3 de febrero de 1974. San José.

_____. 1979. Elecciones en cifras. 1953-1978. San José.

UN (United Nations). 1975. Investigaciones de aguas subterraneas en zonas seleccionadas. Costa Rica. New York.

_____. 1979. Yearbook of national accounts statistics 1978. Vol. II. International tables. New York.

Urquidi, Victor L. 1975. The underdeveloped city. In Jorge E. Hardoy (ed.), Urbanization in Latin America. Approaches and issues. New York: Anchor Books, 339-366.

Varese, Stefano. 1973. Au sujet du colonialism écologique. Les Temps Moderns 29:1815-1826.

Vargas, Armando et al. 1981. La crisis de la democracia en Costa Rica. San José: Editorial Universidad Estatal a Distancia.

Vargas Ulate, Gilberto. 1978. Diagnóstico y recomendaciones para el manejo y ordenamiento de los recursos naturales de la cuenca del Río San Lorenzo, Alajuela, Costa Rica. Thesis, Universidad de Costa Rica.

Vega Carballo, Jose Luis. 1978. La crisis de los partidos políticos tradicionales de Costa Rica. San José: Ediciones Academia Costarricense de Bibliografía.

_____. 1980a. Hacia una interpretación del desarrollo costarricense: ensayo sociológico. San José: Editorial Porvenir.

_____. 1980b. San José: antecedentes coloniales y formación del estado nacional. San José: Consejo Superior Universitario Centroamericano.

_____. 1981a. San José en la transformación social del espacio regional: siglo XIX. San José: Consejo Superior Universitario Centroamericano.

Vega Carballo, José Luis. 1981b. Decadencia política y crisis económica en Costa Rica. In Carlos Araya Pochet et al. (eds.), Crisis en Costa Rica: un debate. San José: Universidad de Costa Rica, 38-54.

Vieillard-Baron, Alain. 1974. La production agricole et la vie rurale au Costa Rica. Mexico: Institut Francaise de l'Amérique Latine.

Villasuso E., Juan Manuel et al. 1978. El sector forestal y maderero en Costa Rica. San José: Associated Colleges of the Midwest.

Vives Fernandez, Luis Angel and Abigail Chacon Zuñiga. 1972. Análisis de épocas de siembra del maíz. San José: Universidad de Costa Rica.

Vogt, William. 1946. The population of Costa Rica and its natural resources. Washington, D.C.: Pan-American Union.

von Thünen, Johann Heinrich. 1966. Der isolierte Staat in Beziehung auf Landwirtschaft und Nationalökonomie. Stuttgart: Gustav Fischer Verlag.

Wagner, P. H. 1958. Nicoya. A cultural geography. University of California Publications in Geography 12:195-250.

Waibel, Leo. 1939. White settlement in Costa Rica. Geographical Review 29:529-560.

_____. 1948. A teoria de von Thünen sobre a influencia da distancia do mercado relativamente a utilizacao da terra. Sua aplicacao a Costa Rica. Revista Brasileira de Geografia 10:3-33.

Weber, Hans. 1959. Los páramos de Costa Rica. San José: Instituto Geográfico Nacional.

Webster, C. C. and P. N. Wilson. 1966. Agriculture in the tropics. London: Longman.

Weisenfeld, Lorin. 1969. La ley de protección y desarrollo industrial de 1959. El proceso de su creación. Revista de Ciencias Jurídicas (Universidad de Costa Rica) 14:1-111.

Wercklé, Carlos. 1909. La subregión fitogeográfica costarricense. San José.

West, Robert C. and John P. Augelli. 1966. Middle America. Its lands and peoples. Englewood Cliffs: Prentice Hall.

Weyl, Richard. 1955. Vestigios de una glaciación del pleistoceno en la Cordillera de Talamanca, Costa Rica. Informe Trimestral (Instituto Geográfico de Costa Rica) 2:9-32.

_____. 1971. La clasificación morfotectónica de Costa Rica. Informe Semestral (Instituto Geográfico Nacional) 2:107-125.

Willey, Gordon R. 1959. The "intermediate area" of nuclear America: Its prehistoric relationships to Middle America and Peru. San José: Actas del 33 Congreso Internacional de Americanistas, Vol. 1, 184-194.

_____. 1966. An introduction to American archaeology. Vol. I. North and Middle America. Englewood Cliffs: Prentice Hall.

_____. 1971. An introduction to American archaeology, Vol. II. South America. Englewood Cliffs: Prentice Hall.

Willey, Gordon R. and Philip Phillips. 1958. Method and theory in American archaeology. University of Chicago Press.

Williamson, J. G. 1965. Regional inequality and the process of national development: A description of the patterns. Economic Development and Cultural Change 13:3-84.

338

Wolf, Eric. 1966. Peasants. Englewood Cliffs: Prentice Hall.

Wolf, Eric and Sydney Mintz. 1957. Haciendas and plantations in Middle America and the Antilles. Social and Economic Studies 6:380-412.

Wood, Harold A. 1977-1978. Regionalización nacional para la planificación regional integrada: el caso de Costa Rica. Revista Geográfica (Instituto Panamericano de Geografía e Historia) 86-87:13-27.

Zárate Hernandez, Eladio. 1977. Principales sistemas de vientos que afectan a Costa Rica y sus relaciones con la precipitación. Thesis, Universidad de Costa Rica.

Zelaya, Chester et al. 1977. Democracia en Costa Rica? Cinco opiniones polémicas. San José: Editorial Universidad Estatal a Distancia.

Zelinsky, W. 1971. The hypothesis of the mobility transition. Geographical Review 61:219-249.

Zumbado Jimenez, Fernando. 1977. Perspectivas del desarrollo regional y urbano. In La Costa Rica del año 2000. San José: Ministerio de Cultura, 149-185.

Zumbado Jimenez, Fernando and Carlos Raabe Cercone. 1976. Evolución de la distribución geográfica de la población de Costa Rica. San José: Instituto Geográfico Nacional.

Zúñiga Cortes, Rafael Angel. 1978. La importación de bienes de capital en Costa Rica. Thesis, Universidad de Costa Rica.

Index

Acculturation, 40-42
Acosta, 105, 112, 114, 130, 160-161, 281
Administrative areas, 243, 278-286, 291, 296, 298-299
African oil palm, 119, 182, 192-193, 232, 292
    cultivation of, 88, 118, 152, 154, 182-183, 193, 231
    ecological conditions for, 29, 182-183, 195
Agrarian reform, 111, 121, 151, 201-204, 207, 271, 289, 291-292, 308
Agriculture, 48-50, 85-86, 154-199
    and credit, 199, 204
    See also Horticulture
Agro-industries, 288-290, 303
Air transport, 45, 130, 256, 268-269, 286
Alajuela (province), 281-282, 291-292
Alajuela (town), 97, 210, 217, 219, 253n, 276, 281-282
    employment in, 226
    hinterland of, 254
    housing in, 222
    population of, 65(map), 132, 208
    transport to and from, 116, 125, 136
Alliance for Progress, 201, 288
Apartheid, 42, 63
Archaeological record, 32-40
Asociación Costarricense para la Conservación de la Naturaleza (ASCONA), 89

Atlantic region, 151, 153, 271, 294-295(map), 296-297, 299
    See also Caribbean lowlands; East region

Bahareque, 137, 214
Bananas, 74-77, 85, 138, 167-170, 286, 292
    cultivation of, 27, 75, 77, 86 (table), 110, 115-119, 142, 150, 152, 154, 160(table), 162(graph), 168(map), 182, 193, 204
    ecological conditions for, 29, 158, 167, 170, 195
    exports of, 75, 76(graph), 78, 80(graph), 81, 117, 134, 265, 267
    irrigation of, 194
    transportation of, 128-129, 161, 266
Banco Centroamericano de Integración Económica (BCIE), 229
Beans, 172, 178-180
    cultivation of, 37, 45, 48, 49 (table), 77, 85, 97, 110, 113, 146, 149, 151, 175(graph), 178, 179(map), 180, 195
    ecological conditions for, 178-179, 195
    imports of, 77, 180
    yields of, 152, 180
Beef, 77, 80(graph), 114, 154, 185, 187
Beneficios, 161, 166
Birth control, 101-102
Birth rate, 99, 100(graph), 101-102, 206-207, 308

Borders (political), 56-59, 115
  with Colombia, 56, 58-59
  with Nicaragua, 27, 37, 56, 290
  with Panamá, 56, 58-59, 120,
    130, 290
Boruca peninsula, 3, 8(map), 10,
  59, 248, 302
Brunca region, 295(map), 296-297
Buenos Aires (Costa Rica), 296,
  298
Building materials, 34-35, 39,
  45, 67, 84, 112, 137, 197,
  218
  See also Bahareque; Timber
Buses, 219-220, 221(map), 263,
  264(graph), 269

Cabotaje, 128-129, 134, 268, 282
Caldera, 93(map), 96, 132, 267,
  301
Canals, 268, 288
Cañas, 65(map), 93(map), 97, 136,
  218, 291-292, 296, 298
Cañas-Jerez Treaty, 58
Cantons, 135, 251, 278, 280-286,
  292, 299
Caribbean lowlands, 11, 32, 253,
  289
  administrative areas in, 281-
    282
  agriculture in, 73, 75, 77-78,
    115-118, 141-142, 167, 169-
    170, 196
  British influence in, 92, 98
  population of, 67-68, 105
  settlement of, 39, 98, 121-122,
    134, 194
  transportation to and from,
    128-129, 256, 266, 268
Cartago (province), 281, 291
Cartago (town), 53(map), 54, 56,
  96, 97, 132, 217, 253n, 276,
  281, 282
  earthquakes in, 6, 137
  employment in, 225
  housing in, 222
  manufacturing industry in, 239
  population of, 64-65(map), 66,
    208
  transportation to and from, 125,
    130
Cassava, 48, 85, 172
  cultivation of, 35, 38-39, 44,
    49(table), 67, 117, 146, 182,

196-197
  ecological conditions for, 29
Cattle, 151, 183
  beef, 185-190
  dairy, 189-190
  introduction of, 86-87, 185
  production of, 112-113, 146,
    149, 154
Cattle ranching. See Stock rearing
Cement industry, 237, 239
Central America, 56, 59
  geology of, 3, 4(map), 5-6
  geopolitical organization of,
    51-52, 53(map)
  position of, 1, 2(map)
Central American Common Market,
  60, 79, 81, 131, 205, 229, 231-
  232, 234, 236-237, 241, 290
Central Pacific region, 292, 294
  (map), 296-297
Central place hierarchy, 91, 112,
  123, 131-138, 208, 210, 218,
  243, 245, 249-256, 278, 280,
  292, 297-299
Central region, 271, 291-292, 293-
  295(maps), 296-298, 303
  See also Valle Central
Centro Agronómico Tropical de In-
  vestigación y Enseñanza
  (CATIE), 197, 199, 309
Cerros de Abangares, 8(map), 72,
  77, 108, 302
Cerros de Aguacate, 74, 77, 105,
  108, 302
Cerros de la Carpintera, 10, 123
Chacra, 84, 97, 110, 113, 149,
  163
Cheese, 98, 114, 120, 189
Chickens, 45, 86, 113, 146, 197
Chiefdoms, 34-35, 39-40, 51-52
Chinese, 68, 71, 99
Chorotega region, 295(map), 296-
  297
Citrus, 29, 85, 117, 160
Climate, 7, 12-30, 190
Climatic classification, 22-30
Coasts, 11, 129, 134, 302
Cocoa, 37-38, 170-172, 232, 286,
  292
  cultivation of, 44, 48, 49(table),
    73, 88, 98, 117-118, 149, 151-
    152, 158, 160(table), 162
    (graph), 170, 171(map), 197
  ecological conditions for, 29,

170, 195
trade in, 39, 73, 77, 80, 170, 172
Coconut, 29, 86, 117, 172, 182-183, 241, 288
Coffee, 74-77, 85-86, 138, 158-163, 230
  cultivation of, 74, 77-78, 86 (table), 88, 110-116, 120-121, 141-142, 146, 149, 151, 156, 159(map), 160(table), 161, 162(graph), 163-164, 181, 193
  ecological conditions for, 29, 158, 195
  elimination of, 214, 239
  export of, 75, 76(graph), 80 (graph), 81, 158, 265
  irrigation of, 194-195
  processing of, 161, 225, 227
  transportation of, 58, 74, 130, 132, 134, 158-159, 161, 266
  See also Beneficios
Coffee rust disease, 163
Colombia, 58-59
Colonies, 110, 119-122, 135, 201-202
Colonization, 7, 45-46, 56, 74, 78, 85, 91-139, 149, 152-153, 156, 158, 190, 201, 210, 254, 271, 278, 281, 284-285, 289, 291-292, 297, 306, 308
Compañía Bananera, 118, 129, 134, 182, 202, 204, 263
Construction industry, 223-224
Convenio Centroamericano de Incentivos Fiscales al Desarrollo Industrial, 229
Cooperatives, 149-150, 161, 166, 189, 201-202, 204, 289
Cordillera Central, 6-9, 21, 28, 31-32
  land use in, 189
Cordillera de Guanacaste, 6-9, 28, 31-32
  colonization of, 112
Cordillera de Talamanca, 6, 10, 21-22, 28-29, 32, 299, 302
  cultivation of, 180
  settlement of, 42, 69, 248, 290
  transport to and from, 130, 256, 269
Cordillera de Tilarán, 6, 9, 72, 160
  colonization of, 112, 120

Cortés-Chittenden contract, 118, 134
Costa Rica
  nation-state of, 51-60, 280-281, 283
  position of, 1, 2(map), 12, 18, 26, 59, 229
  studying geography in, 309
Coto Brus (valley), 8(map), 10, 15, 19, 31
  administrative areas in, 282
  agriculture in, 141, 156, 161
  settlement of, 40, 105, 120
  transport to and from, 114
Coto Colorado Valley, 8(map), 11
  administrative areas in, 282
  agriculture in, 115, 118, 167
  colonization of, 115, 118
  transport to and from, 129
Coto Sur, 202, 204
Cotton, 232
  cultivation of, 49(table), 152, 154, 176, 178
  ecological conditions for, 29, 196
  imports of, 234, 236
Culmiculous smut, 166

Dairy farming, 29, 181, 189-190
Death rate. See Mortality
Deforestation, 11, 19, 22, 27, 32, 49, 84-85, 88, 112-113, 167, 194
Del Monte Corporation, 169
Demographic transition, 101-102
Dirección General Forestal (DGF), 121-122
Disease, 42, 75, 87-88, 95-96, 99, 101, 115-116, 118, 120, 158, 160, 167, 178, 180, 187, 195
Districts, 135, 251, 278, 280-281, 283-286, 292, 299
Dota, 105, 112, 114, 160-161, 281
Drainage, 110, 115-116, 118, 122, 152, 164, 167, 169, 190, 194, 290
Dulce Gulf, 8(map), 11, 18, 59, 129, 134

Earthquakes. See Seismic activity
East region, 292, 293(map)
  See also Atlantic region; Caribbean lowlands
Ecological change, 49-50, 83-89

Economic crises, 78, 307
Education, 46, 60, 102, 207, 236, 271-272, 274-275, 286
Electricity, 212, 217, 220, 231, 233(map), 270-271, 274-275, 278, 283, 289-290, 299
See also Hydroelectricity
El Salvador (agricultural colony), 120-121
Employment, 207-208, 270-271, 307
urban, 223-226
Encomienda, 41, 94, 96, 98
Erosion, 9-12, 19, 31, 38, 49, 81, 85, 87-88, 113, 164, 176, 180, 189, 191
Esparza, 97, 226, 292, 301
Estates, 96, 110, 112, 143(graph), 144, 145-146(tables), 147-148 (maps), 149-154, 162(graph), 166, 169, 174, 175(graph), 201, 204
See also Haciendas; Plantations
Ethnohistory, 32, 37-38, 40
Exports, 74, 78, 84, 88, 97-98, 132, 140, 227, 242, 263
of bananas, 75, 76(graph), 117-118
of beef, 77, 154, 187
of cocoa, 77
of coffee, 75, 76(graph), 78
of fruit, 196
of gold, 77
of manufactured goods, 79, 236
of sugar, 77, 163, 166
of timber, 112
of vegetables, 196

Farm area, 87, 122(table), 139, 144-154, 156, 194, 308
Farming systems, 84-85, 139-154, 197, 204, 248
See also Chacra; Estates; Haciendas; Minifundios; Peasant farms; Plantations
Fauna, 34, 85, 302
Fertility, 99, 101-102, 206-207, 308
Fertilizers, 116, 146, 152, 161, 163, 166, 176, 178, 180, 198, 237, 241, 265, 267, 289, 302
Fila Costeña, 8(map), 10-11, 180, 256
Fishing, 33-35, 37, 39, 44, 81, 85, 108, 140, 267, 288, 297,

301-303, 305
Floods, 40, 85, 88, 118, 167
Flora. See Natural vegetation
Fodder crops, 154, 166, 178, 187, 189, 198
Foreigners, 68-69, 116, 134
Forest reserves, 103, 121-122
Forestry, 30, 114, 121-122, 140, 189, 193-194, 197, 248, 288, 290, 301-303
See also Forests; Timber
Forests, 11, 22, 27-29, 81, 301, 308
conservation of, 121-122, 191, 193, 301
economic exploitation of, 112, 153, 191, 193
extent of, 88, 91, 156, 269
Hispanic American perception of, 51, 108, 194
indigenous exploitation of, 40, 49, 83
in farms, 140, 155(table)
See also Forestry; Timber
Frontiers (of colonization and settlement), 41, 52, 85, 91-92, 102-105, 108-122, 139-140, 152-154, 190, 194, 201, 205-206, 306
Fuel, 112, 128, 161, 164, 166, 194, 197, 229, 234
See also Petroleum

Gabb, William, 44
General (valley), 15, 19, 22, 31, 41, 256, 302
administrative areas in, 281-282
land use in, 141-142, 156, 160-161, 164, 176, 180, 182
levels of living in, 276
regional study of, 289
settlement of, 40, 105, 108, 112, 136
transportation in, 114, 130
Geology, 3-7, 31
Gold, 34, 39-40, 52, 72, 74-75, 77, 108, 302
Golfito, 59, 105, 118, 129, 134-135, 161, 169, 225, 253n, 263, 266-267, 278, 290
Golfo Dulce Lands Company, 118
Government
and the economy, 161, 166, 196,

199, 230, 231, 261, 268
and health and family planning,
101, 102
and hydroelectricity, 232
and indigenous population, 46-
48
and tourism, 303
and urban and regional planning,
220-222, 239, 283, 288-289,
291, 298
See also Dirección General Forestal; Instituto de Tierras y
Colonización; Junta de Administración Portuaria y de Desarrollo Económico de la Vertiente Atlántica; Oficina de
Planificación
Grecia, 125, 136, 164, 225, 241,
254, 276
Growth poles, 299, 301
Guanacaste, 253, 282, 291, 297,
308
emigration from, 108, 118, 289
land use in, 108, 141, 156, 164,
166, 174, 176, 178, 182, 185,
187, 195
levels of living in, 278
mining in, 302
regional study of, 289
settlement of, 105, 136
tourism in, 303
transportation to and from, 128-
130
Guápiles, 121, 128, 141, 208, 225,
253, 296, 298
Guatemala (audiencia), 53(map),
54, 56, 73, 92, 94

Haciendas, 84, 98, 113-114, 121,
141, 143-144, 151-154, 156,
201-202, 204, 291
Health, 46, 101-102, 218, 220,
271-272, 274, 286
Heredia (province), 281-282, 291-
292
Heredia (town), 65(map), 93(map),
97, 132, 208, 217, 219, 222,
225, 253n, 276, 281-282
Herradura, 3, 5(map), 8(map), 10,
256
Hides, 98, 114, 154
Horses, 86-87, 96, 129, 256, 261,
263
Horticulture, 29, 97, 117, 144,

180-182, 196
Housing, 222, 229, 270, 272, 280,
283, 286
Huetar region, 295(map), 296
Hunting and gathering, 33-35, 37,
39, 44, 81, 85, 108, 140, 305
Hydroelectricity, 195, 232, 233
(map), 290
See also Electricity

Immigration, 51, 54, 61-71, 74,
92, 99, 101, 110, 118-120, 207
Imports, 74, 77, 79, 125, 132,
227, 229, 234, 241, 263
of basic foods, 172, 182
of industrial raw materials, 232
of manufactured goods, 227
Income distribution, 269-272, 274-
275
Indian communities, 40-50, 71,
74, 86, 248, 306
Indian reserves, 46-48, 84, 99,
103, 158, 278
Indians, 32-50, 51-52, 62-66, 69-
70, 91-92, 96, 98-99, 108,
305, 308
Industrialization, 60, 78-79,
205, 227-242, 256
See also Manufacturing
Industrial location, 218, 225,
237-241, 301
Ingenios, 166, 241
Instituto Centroamericano de Investigación y Tecnología Industrial, 229
Instituto de Tierras y Colonización (ITCO), 46, 110, 121,
154, 182, 201-204, 289
Inter-American Institute of Agricultural Sciences, 309
Irrigation, 18, 38, 152, 163, 166-
167, 174, 176, 178, 193-195,
289-291

Jews, 61, 68, 70-71, 231
Junta de Administración Portuaria
y de Desarrollo Económico de
la Vertiente Atlántica
(JAPDEVA), 286-288, 292, 298

Kalnins, Arvids, 285-286, 296
Keith, Minor Cooper, 116

La Mansión, 120, 135

Land capability, 46, 88, 144, 190-
197, 301
Land clearance, 84, 110, 114-115,
119, 153, 169
Landforms, 3-12
Land tenure, 46, 48, 51, 66, 83-
84, 94, 96, 110-111, 113,
140-154, 195, 199-205, 212,
222, 271, 306
Latifundios. See Estates
Latin America, 51, 91, 102-103,
131, 151, 210, 217, 236, 248,
284, 286, 309
Leaching, 30, 87, 187
Lebanese, 68, 71, 99, 231
Legislation, 46, 108, 111, 121-
122, 194, 201, 227, 282, 302
Levels of living, 269-278, 307,
309
Liberia, 56, 65(map), 93(map),
97, 130, 136, 219, 282, 291-
292, 297
Life zones, 23-30
Limón (port), 118, 134, 219, 241,
290, 301
    administration of, 282, 286
    housing in, 218, 222
    levels of living in, 272, 278
    population of, 208
    port installations in, 266-267,
    288
    transportation to and from,
    125, 128-131, 268-269, 288
Limón (province), 67-69, 71, 116-
117, 282, 286, 288, 292, 308
    See also Junta de Administración
    Portuaria y de Desarrollo Eco-
    nómico de la Vertiente Atlán-
    tica

Maize, 38, 172, 176-178
    cultivation of, 35, 37-38, 44,
    48, 49(table), 77, 85, 97,
    110, 113, 146, 149, 151-152,
    175(graph), 176, 177(map),
    178, 180, 195, 197
    ecological conditions for, 29,
    87, 176, 178, 195
    forage from, 187
    trade in, 73, 77, 178, 196
    yields of, 178
Manila hemp, 29, 77, 117
Manufacturing, 38, 78, 119, 131,
163, 166, 201, 223-225, 227-

242, 291, 301-302, 306
    See also Industrialization
Matina, 55(map), 93(map), 94, 96,
98
Mercedes, 83, 96
Meso-America, 34-35, 37-38, 40,
52, 308
Migration. See Population, migra-
tion
Minerals, 72, 74, 77, 139, 289,
302-303, 308
Minifundios, 84, 110-111, 143-153,
161-162, 166, 169, 174-175,
187- 189, 201-202, 204, 270
Mining, 74, 77, 108, 131, 248,
301, 303
Miscegenation, 40, 42, 48, 61-71
Missionaries, 41-42, 44, 98-99
Moín, 267-269, 288, 301
Monilia roveri, 172
Monoculture, 88, 110, 115-116,
142, 146, 152, 156, 158, 167,
170, 183
Monteverde, 120, 135, 278
Moracia project, 195
Mortality, 40, 42, 92, 99-102
Mosquitia, 59, 92
Mules, 73, 84, 87, 96, 114, 122
Municipalities, 136, 220, 222,
245, 280, 283-286

National parks, 121-122
Natural resource inventories, 88,
289
Natural resources, 1, 33, 59, 85,
88-89, 108, 139, 190, 301,
305, 308
Natural vegetation, 12, 21-30,
85, 88, 94, 120
Negroes, 41, 48, 61, 63, 66-71,
98, 116-118, 142, 153, 286,
308
Nicaragua
    republic of, 44, 56, 58-59, 118,
    290, 308
    Spanish province of, 41, 52, 54,
    73, 92, 96-97
Nicoya (Alcaldía Mayor or Corregi-
    miento), 54, 96, 282
Nicoya (gulf), 8(map), 11, 129,
132, 267-268
Nicoya (peninsula), 3, 10-11, 31,
52
    administrative areas in, 282

agriculture in, 141-142, 174,
176, 180
incorporation into Costa Rica
of, 56, 58-59
mining in, 77
population of, 41, 108
regional study of, 288-289, 292
settlement of, 42, 92, 97-98,
105, 112, 120, 137, 256
transportation to and from, 114,
268
Nicoya (town), 64-66, 93-94, 105,
130, 136, 261
Northern plains, 42, 44, 92, 105,
141-142, 167, 253, 256, 268,
282, 289
North Pacific region, 144, 151,
153-154, 185, 271, 292, 294
(map), 296-297, 299, 303
North region, 151, 153, 271, 291-
297, 299
See also Northern plains
Northwest region, 291-293
Nuhn, Helmut, 156, 289-293, 296

Oficina de Planificación (OFIPLAN),
289-290, 292, 296, 298
Oil refining, 229, 241, 269, 280
See also Petroleum
Organization for Tropical Studies
(OTS), 309
Organization of Banana Exporting
Countries, 170
Osa peninsula, 3, 5(map), 8(map),
10, 59, 248, 256, 302
Ox carts, 74, 114, 125, 129, 261
Oxen, 87, 110, 166

Pacific lowlands, 10, 31-32, 296-
297
administrative areas in, 282
agriculture in, 75, 115, 118,
141-142, 164, 167, 169
settlement of, 97, 108, 118, 134
transportation to and from, 129-
130, 256
Panamá, 41, 52, 54, 58, 73, 92,
118, 125, 290
Panamá Canal, 59, 115, 123, 125,
130, 267, 299
Panamá disease, 75, 117-118, 167
Parishes, 132, 135
Parrita, 8(map), 11, 115, 118,
129

Pastures, 12, 22, 83
ecological conditions for, 87,
193
establishment of, 86-88, 112-
114, 118, 194
expansion and improvement of,
154, 155(table), 183(table),
185
extent of, 145(table), 156,
184(map), 193, 201
production of, 110, 143, 149,
151, 158, 176, 185, 187, 193,
195
soil erosion associated with,
31, 87
See also Stock rearing
Peasant farms, 84, 112-113, 121,
142-151, 153, 161-162, 169,
174-175, 187-189, 207
Peasants, 84, 110-111, 113-114,
146-149
Pejibaye, 29, 38-39, 44, 48, 85,
196-197
Peones, 110, 150, 153
Petroleum, 81, 164, 220, 232,
237, 267, 302, 307
See also Oil refining
Pigs, 45, 86, 113, 146, 197
Pirris Farm and Trading Company,
118
Plantains, 44, 86, 113, 117, 181-
182
Plantation enclaves, 110, 115-
120, 128, 135, 142, 156, 194,
256, 278, 290, 297
Plantations, 84, 98, 113, 115-
119, 141-144, 151-154, 156,
161, 169, 182, 207, 286
Plate tectonics, 3, 6-7
Political independence, 54, 56
Political system, 60, 307
Pollution, 88, 217-218, 220, 241,
288
Population, 89, 308
decline of, 41-42, 92, 99
density of, 34-35, 40, 88, 92,
114, 136, 156, 207, 217, 243,
245-249, 274, 278, 308
distribution of, 7, 28, 94-95,
99-108, 131, 243, 245-249,
254-255, 303, 308
growth of, 35, 37, 39, 63, 78-
79, 91-92, 99-102, 110-111,
113, 118, 121, 131, 154, 190,

201, 205-210, 285, 305-306, 308
migration of, 28, 37, 71, 91, 103-108, 112, 116-118, 131, 189, 205-208, 241, 249, 271, 306-307
racial composition of, 33, 40, 45, 48, 61-72
rural, 131, 139, 206
size of, 35, 37, 92, 99-102, 308
urban, 131, 139, 205-210, 274
See also Birth rate; Disease; Immigration; Mortality
Ports, 58, 74, 96, 110, 114-115, 118-119, 123, 125, 129, 131-135, 138, 156, 158, 161, 266-267, 271
Poverty, 269-272, 275, 306
Precipitation, 12, 15-19, 23, 26-31
Primacy, 131, 245, 249, 251, 253, 281, 299
See also Central place hierarchy
Provinces, 245, 253, 278, 280-286, 291, 299
Pueblas, 63
Pueblo Unido, 307
Punta Morales, 267
Puntarenas (port), 132, 134, 266-267, 292, 301
employment in, 225
housing in, 218, 222
levels of living in, 276
manufacturing industry in, 241
population of, 208, 210
as a port, 118, 161, 267
transportation to and from, 112, 125, 128-131, 268-269
Puntarenas (province), 68, 141, 282, 291-292
Puriscal, 105, 112, 114, 130, 160-161, 176, 180, 226, 281

Quepos, 105, 115, 118, 129, 134-135, 226
Quesada, 130, 136, 226, 253-254, 256, 268, 292, 297

Race. See Population, racial composition of
Racial segregation. See Apartheid
Railways, 58, 111, 112, 116, 122-131, 138, 161, 256, 263, 265-

266, 269, 282, 286, 288, 290, 299
Reducciones, 41-42, 63, 97
Reforestation, 85, 194, 301
Reformismo, 60, 306-307
Regional planning, 243, 280, 286-303, 308
Reventazón (valley), 39, 96, 98, 128, 136, 181
Rice, 85, 172-176
cultivation of, 44-45, 86(table), 87, 113, 146, 151-152, 154, 172-174, 178, 195, 197
ecological conditions for, 29, 195
trade in, 77, 176
Rio Frío, 117, 167, 202, 263
Rivers, 10, 11, 85
navigation of, 11, 58, 123, 125, 128-129, 268
Roads, 45, 78, 96-98, 122-131, 138, 199, 256-263, 269, 271, 289-290, 292, 299, 300(map), 301
Pan-American Highway, 45, 120, 130-131, 160, 182, 219, 229, 258, 261, 268, 282, 299, 301
Rubber, 29, 44, 77, 117, 196, 232

Salt, 34, 37, 45, 81, 232
San Carlos (valley), 8(map), 108, 136, 276
administrative areas in, 281
agriculture in, 141, 160-161, 164, 182, 196
colonization of, 105, 112, 114, 120
stock rearing in, 185, 189
transportation to and from, 130
Sandner, Gerhard, 289
San Isidro del General, 130, 136, 208, 212, 213(map), 218, 225, 254, 256, 289-290, 292, 296-297
San José (city), 54, 56, 97, 254, 281-282, 291, 296-297, 303
administrative areas in, 284-285
as primate city, 210, 249, 253, 281, 299
concentration of wealth in, 270, 276
employment in, 223, 225, 280
manufacturing industry in, 167,

239-241
migration to, 105, 108, 206-208
morphology of, 137, 210, 212,
214-222, 239, 241
population of, 65, 131-132, 205,
210, 212, 248, 299, 301
town planning of, 220
transportation to and from, 125,
128-131, 134, 261, 263, 268-
269
San José (province), 281-282, 291-
292
San Juan (basin), 290
Santa Elena peninsula, 3, 5(map),
8(map), 10
San Vito de Java, 120, 135
Sapoa Valley, 37
Sarapiquí (valley), 130, 185, 281
agriculture in, 160-161, 167,
182
colonization of, 105, 112-114,
117-118
Savannas, 22, 81, 87
Sawmills, 112, 119, 194
Seismic activity, 3, 6-7, 137
Settlement, 7, 21, 27-28, 306
Hispanic American, 41, 43, 61,
83, 91-99, 278
indigenous, 33-35, 37, 39-40
See also Colonization
Shanty towns, 208, 217-218, 270,
276
Sheep, 86
Shifting cultivation, 32-35, 40,
81, 83, 108, 113-114, 140,
156
Shipping, 11, 58, 74, 123, 125,
128-129, 132-135, 266-268
See also Cabotaje; Ports
Sigatoka, 75, 77, 117, 167, 169
Sixaola (valley), 8(map), 92, 115-
116, 167, 183, 288
Slaves, 58, 66, 74, 84
Indian, 41, 44, 96-97
mulatto, 63
Negro, 41, 61, 63, 70-71, 92,
98
Social classes, 38, 63, 66, 72,
78, 99, 102, 217, 307
Social security, 272, 275
Sociedad Económica Itineraria, 125
Soils, 7, 30-32, 190, 191
alluvial, 9, 31-32, 118, 158,
167, 170, 174, 191, 248

andosols, 31-32, 158, 160, 181,
191, 195, 248
latosols, 30-32, 34, 160, 176,
178, 191
lithosols, 31-32, 87, 176, 178,
191
Sorghum, 29, 86-87, 152, 176, 178,
187, 196
South Pacific region, 151, 153,
185, 271, 294(map), 296-297,
299
South region, 291-292, 293(map)
Squatting, 111, 116, 121, 149,
154, 201-202, 204
Standard Fruit Company, 117, 169
Stock rearing, 29, 77, 83, 86-87,
98, 108, 113-114, 136, 138-
139, 141, 149, 153-154, 156,
183-191, 195-197, 207, 237,
249, 271, 292
See also Beef; Cattle; Dairy
farming; Pastures
Stouse, Pierre A. D., 141-142
Sugar cane, 85, 163-167, 232
by-products of, 166-167
cultivation of, 44, 86(table),
88, 97, 110, 112-114, 136,
141, 146, 149, 151-152, 154,
156, 158, 160(table), 162
(graph), 163-167
ecological conditions for, 29,
164, 195
export of, 77, 80(graph), 163,
267
processing of, 166, 225, 227
yields of, 166

Talamanca, 42, 93(map), 96, 98,
232, 303, 308
Temperatures, 12, 18-21, 23, 26,
27-30
Tempisque (valley), 8, 11, 19,
37, 174, 187, 195, 289
Térraba (valley), 8(map), 11
administrative areas in, 282
agriculture in, 167
settlement of, 40-42, 66, 94,
96, 98, 115, 118
transportation to and from, 129-
130
Textile industry, 235-236
Thiel, B. A., 44
Tierras baldías, 83-84, 111, 116-
117, 121, 201

Timber, 84-85, 112, 122, 137, 139-140, 153, 194, 197, 214, 232, 236
See also Forestry; Forests
Tiquisque, 35, 38, 172
Tobacco, 29, 48-49, 56, 73, 75, 97, 114, 141, 225, 232
Topographical maps, 88, 280
Tourism, 248, 266, 289, 291, 297, 303, 308
Town planning, 220, 222, 280, 283
Towns, 63, 91, 94, 96-99, 103, 108, 131-138, 153, 205-226, 245, 248-249, 306
See also Central place hierarchy; Urbanization
Trade, 34, 37, 39, 45, 54, 59-60, 71, 73-82, 136, 227, 229, 241-242, 245, 256, 261, 266, 307
See also Exports; Imports
Traffic flows, 258, 261, 262 (map), 265-269
Transportation, 7, 19, 74, 91, 112-131, 229, 245, 254, 256-269, 285, 291, 303, 306
See also Air transport; Buses; Cabotaje; Canals; Mules; Ox carts; Railways; Roads; Shipping
Transport network, 123-131, 243, 249, 256-269, 278, 288, 292, 296, 299
Trapiches, 87, 119, 166
Tropical Science Center, 309
Turrialba (valley), 136, 164

Underdevelopment, 51, 72-81, 89, 309
United Brands, 169
United Fruit Company (UFCO), 75, 116-118, 134, 169
United States, 58, 69, 75, 130, 163, 187, 201, 231-232, 234, 236-237
Upala, 105, 136, 167, 170, 174, 180, 254, 268, 282, 291
Urbanization, 102, 205-210, 251, 275, 306
See also Central place hierarchy; Towns
Urban morphology, 210-222
Urban reform, 222

Valle Central, 5(map), 6, 8, 10, 15, 18, 28, 132, 244-245, 296, 297
administrative areas in, 281-282
central places of, 253-254
core area of Costa Rican state, 54, 96, 103, 130
emigration from, 105, 112, 118
Hispanic American settlement of, 52, 54, 92, 94-97, 103-104, 110-112, 137
indigenous settlement of, 39, 42-43, 66
land use in, 73, 85, 141-142, 156-167, 181
planning regions in, 291
population of, 99, 139
transportation in, to, and from, 96, 125-131, 161, 256, 258, 260(graph), 299
See also Central region
Villages, 131-139, 208, 217, 249, 306
Volcanoes, 3, 4(map), 6-7, 9, 31
von Thünen, J. H., 156

Waibel, Leo, 156
Walker, William, 58, 99
Water supply, 85, 212, 217, 270-271, 274-275, 278, 280, 283
West region, 291-293, 296-297
See also Central Pacific region
Wheat, 77, 85, 87, 97, 110, 196, 232, 236, 266
Winds, 9, 12, 15, 18-19, 85, 167, 241

Zambos Mosquitos, 41

Dellplain Latin American Studies
Published by Westview Press

No. 8   *Studies in Spanish American Population History*, edited by
         David J. Robinson

No. 9   *The People of the Colca Valley: A Population Study*, Noble
         David Cook

No. 10   *Tierra Adentro: Settlement and Society in Colonial Durango*,
         Michael M. Swann

No. 11   *Andean Reflections: Letters from Carl O. Sauer While on a
         South American Trip Under a Grant from the Rockefeller
         Foundation, 1942*, edited by Robert C. West

No. 12   *Credit and Socioeconomic Change in Colonial Mexico: Loans
         and Mortgages in Guadalajara, 1720-1820*, Linda Greenow

No. 13   *Once Beneath the Forest: Prehistoric Terracing in the Río
         Bec Region of the Maya Lowlands*, B. L. Turner, II

No. 14   *Marriage and Fertility in Chile: Demographic Turning
         Points in the Petorca Valley, 1840-1976*, Robert McCaa

No. 15   *The Spatial Organization of New Land Settlement in Latin
         America*, Jacob O. Maos

No. 16   *The Anglo-Argentine Connection, 1900-1939*, Roger Gravil

No. 17   *Costa Rica: A Geographical Interpretation in Historical
         Perspective*, Carolyn Hall

Previous Dellplain Studies
Available from University Microfilms International

No. 1   *Social Fabric and Spatial Structure in Colonial Latin
         America*, edited by David J. Robinson

No. 2   *New Towns for Colonial Brazil: Spatial and Social Planning
         of the Eighteenth Century*, Roberta Marx Delson

No. 3   *Carl Sauer's Fieldwork in Latin America*, Robert C. West

No. 4   *Studying Latin America: Essays in Honor of Preston E.
         James*, edited by David J. Robinson

No. 5   *First Among Equals: Great Britain and Venezuela, 1810-1910*,
         George E. Carl

No. 6   *Amazon Economics: The Simplicity of Shipobo Indian Wealth*,
         Roland W. Bergman

No. 7   *The Mining Society of Potosí, 1776-1810*, Rose Marie Buechler